In early modern England, boys and girls learned to be masculine or feminine as they learned to read and write. This book explores how gender differences, instilled through specific methods of instruction in literacy, were scrutinized in the English public theatre. Close readings of plays, from Shakespeare's *Love's Labour's Lost* to Thomas Dekker's *Whore of Babylon*, and of poems, didactic treatises, and autobiographical writings from the same period, offer a richly textured analysis of the interaction between didactic precepts, literary models, and historical men and women. At the cross-roads between literary studies and social and cultural history, Eve Sanders' research offers new insights into poems, plays, and first-person narratives (including works by women writers, such as Mary Sidney and Anne Clifford) and into the social conflicts that shaped individuals as the writers and readers of such texts.

Cambridge Studies in Renaissance Literature and Culture 28

GENDER AND LITERACY ON STAGE IN EARLY MODERN ENGLAND

Cambridge Studies in Renaissance Literature and Culture

General editor
STEPHEN ORGEL
Jack Eli Reynolds Professor of Humanities, Stanford University

Editorial board
Anne Barton, *University of Cambridge*
Jonathan Dollimore, *University of York*
Marjorie Garber, *Harvard University*
Jonathan Goldberg, *Duke University*
Nancy Vickers, *Bryn Mawr College*

Since the 1970s there has been a broad and vital reinterpretation of the nature of literary texts, a move away from formalism to a sense of literature as an aspect of social, economic, political, and cultural history. While the earliest New Historicist work was criticized for a narrow and anecdotal view of history, it also served as an important stimulus for post-structuralist, feminist, Marxist, and psychoanalytical work, which in turn has increasingly informed and redirected it. Recent writing on the nature of representation, the historical construction of gender and of the concept of identity itself, on theatre as a political and economic phenomenon and on the ideologies of art generally, reveals the breadth of the field. Cambridge Studies in Renaissance Literature and Culture is designed to offer historically oriented studies of Renaissance literature and theatre which make use of the insights afforded by theoretical perspectives. The view of history envisioned is above all a view of our own history, a reading of the Renaissance for and from our own time.

Recent titles include

Discovering the Subject in Renaissance England
ELIZABETH HANSON, Queen's University, Kingston, Ontario

Foreign bodies and the body politic: discourses of social pathology in early modern England
JONATHAN GIL HARRIS, Ithaca College

Writing, gender and state in early modern England: identity formation and the female subject
MEGAN MATCHINSKE, University of North Carolina, Chapel Hill

The romance of the New World: gender and the literary formations of English colonialism
JOAN PONG LINTON, Indiana University

A complete list of books in the series is given at the end of the volume.

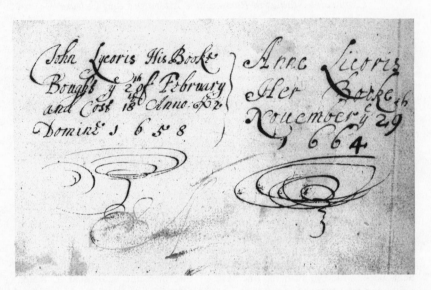

Frontispiece. Inscriptions by two seventeenth-century book owners found in a copy of a writing manual by Edward Cocker. *Art's Glory. Or the Pen-Man's Treasurie* (London, 1657).

Gender and Literacy on Stage in Early Modern England

Eve Rachele Sanders

University of California, Los Angeles

CAMBRIDGE
UNIVERSITY PRESS

PUBLISHED BY THE PRESS SYNDICATE OF THE UNIVERSITY OF CAMBRIDGE
The Pitt Building, Trumpington Street, Cambridge CB2 1RP, United Kingdom

CAMBRIDGE UNIVERSITY PRESS
The Edinburgh Building, Cambridge CB2 2RU, United Kingdom
40 West 20th Street, New York, NY 10011–4211, USA
10 Stamford Road, Oakleigh, Melbourne 3166, Australia

First published 1998

Printed in the United Kingdom at the University Press, Cambridge

Typeset in Times 10/12 pt. [CE]

A catalogue record for this book is available from the British Library

ISBN 0 521 58234 2 hardback

For my mother, Marilyn Sanders

Contents

Illustrations

Preface

The spread of literacy in early modern England was accompanied by a redefinition of identities. New practices of reading and writing, unequally distributed between the sexes, helped to shape the contrasting models of male and female selves promoted in conduct manuals such as Richard Brathwait's *The English Gentleman* and *The English Gentlewoman*. In the public theatre, this reconfiguration of identities through literate practices was taken up as a topic by contemporary playwrights. While the first chapter surveys works ranging from medieval devotional texts to Spenser's *Faerie Queene*, it concludes with a reading of Shakespeare's *Love's Labour's Lost*. This dramatization of social conflicts triggered by the creation of an exclusively masculine academy introduces the primary theme of this book: the place of the theatre in debate over sex-specific modes and means for acquiring learning. Chapter two turns to Shakespeare's *Hamlet* to explore the problematic consequences of humanist pedagogy, in particular the predicament of the male reader, constrained in his actions by the principle of imitation, the imperative to emulate examples uncritically. Correspondingly, chapter three investigates dilemmas specific to the woman reader by analyzing Mary Sidney's *Antonius*, a translation of a French play about Cleopatra, in the light of rereadings of her text by male writers: Samuel Daniel's *The Tragedy of Cleopatra*, Samuel Brandon's *The Tragicomedy of the Virtuous Octavia*, and Shakespeare's *Antony and Cleopatra*. With the next chapters, the focus shifts from reading to writing. Chapter four traces the passage of a cultural paradigm, the male subject as writer, through the play *Richard III*. The fifth and final chapter contrasts the scribal practices of two actual women, Grace Mildmay and Anne Clifford, with representations of female writing by monstrous pen-women in Thomas Dekker's *Whore of Babylon*.

In preparing this book for publication, I have tried to convey a sense of what Margreta de Grazia and Peter Stallybrass term the "materiality of the text." In particular, the original, idiosyncratic spellings of the stage directions (indicating acts of reading and writing) that appear as epigrams recall the actual books, marked by early modern typefaces, design conventions, and spellings, that circulated, along with quill pens, paper, and ink, as tangible stage props in the plays discussed here. In addition, I have kept intact the original spellings of middle English texts, when the edition chosen did so, as well as the deliberately anachronous spellings of Spenser's *Faerie Queene*. However, I have not taken a strictly antiquarian approach which would have required reproducing not only the original spellings but also, in some cases, black letter type and various manuscript hands. For the rest of the early modern printed texts cited, therefore, contractions using tildes or superscript ("y^e" for "the") have been silently expanded, italics elided, commas substituted for slashes, and "i," "u," and long "s" replaced with modern "j," "v," and "s." Set beside these last texts, the works of Shakespeare and other writers cited in modern editions, will still appear strikingly current. In the spirit of the books discussed here, in which interpretive glosses were common, the reader is asked to take the variation between editions for what it is, an effect of different conventions, an engagement on our part, as readers and writers, with the complexities of the textual traces of our past.

Acknowledgments

Stephen Greenblatt and Janet Adelman guided this project from the outset and offered suggestions and inspiration throughout. Heartfelt thanks to them and to Margaret Ferguson for her encouragement and for our ongoing conversation about literacy.

This book was written on the road between Berkeley, Paris, Washington, Chicago, Montreal, and Florence. For what I've learned, I'm grateful to Michael J. B. Allen, whose Renaissance courses started me on that journey. I also wish to thank those who offered much appreciated assistance along the way: Leslie Thomson for giving me access, with great generosity and patience, to her exhaustive compilation of stage directions for all of the plays written for the English public theatre; Randolph Starn for providing a historian's perspective on the project; Margaret Hannay for answering queries about Mary Sidney and reading chapter three; Roger Chartier for allowing me to participate in his seminar at the Ecole des hautes études en sciences sociales; Laetitia Yeandle and Georgianna Ziegler at the Folger Shakespeare Library and Paul Gehl at the Newberry Library for sharing their expert knowledge; Michaelyn Burnett for helping with bibliographic searches; Alan Young for enabling me to consult from a distance his database of Shakespeare illustrations owned by the Folger; Teresa Faherty for sharing her observations on the first chapters; the Shakespeare in the Theatre Research Group at McGill University for extending their hospitality during revision of the manuscript; Laurie Valestuk for lending heroic editorial assistance; Linda Woodward for her meticulous copy-editing; and all of the many colleagues who contributed comments and questions at different stages in the process. From first to last, I have been indebted to Mary Ann Koory, whose friendship and readerly insight made the writing a pleasure. Finally, I owe particular thanks to Raphaël Fischler. His architect's sense of structure and, when it mattered most, of unerring perspective helped me bring this book to completion.

Research for the project was made possible by the Woodrow Wilson Fellowship Foundation, the Soroptimist Foundation, Phi Beta Kappa, the Folger Shakespeare Library, the Newberry Library, and the National Endowment for the Humanities.

1   On his breast writ

> *Enter an Anticke habited in Parchment Indentures, Bills, Bonds, Waxe*
> *Seales, and Pen, and Inkhornes, on his breast writ*, I am a Scrivener.
> *Dances a straine, and stands right before him.*
> *Enter dauncing another streine, on written o're his breast*, I am a Knave.
> *Stands as the other.*
> *Enter a third with this word*, I am a Prodigall.
> *Enter a fourth with this*, I am a Beggar.
> *Enter a fifth with this*, I am a Puritan.
> *Enter a sixt with this*, I am a Whore.
> *Enter a seventh with money Bagges, and this Motto*, I am an Usurer.
> *Enter an eighth with this*, I am a Divell.[1]

Following the Reformation, men and women were taught to learn and communicate in ways that fostered new differences between them. This book investigates how the acquisition of literacy contributed to the formation of gender identities in early modern England and how the public theatre intervened in that process. In the wake of humanist and religious reform, literacy spread through defined channels in ways that reinforced social distinctions.[2] Knowledge of reading and writing was not distributed uniformly between any groups in the population at large. In every country, literacy rates varied between cities and rural districts, between Protestants and Catholics, between native speakers of the dominant language and speakers of regional languages or dialects, between different social classes, between different occupations, between different ethnic groups, and between different regions. But the most "glaring" inequality was between men and women: "everywhere the male literacy rate is higher than the female, with a gap between the two as high as 25 or 30 percent."[3]

Not only did men and women acquire literacy at different rates during this period; the specific practices of expression and interpretation in which each was instructed were designed to form them as male and female subjects: "The purpose of education was to train men and women to be appropriately different from one another."[4] Acts of reading and

1

writing became sexualized, expressions of a woman's virtue (or shame-lessness) and of a man's virility (or effeminacy), and they became sex-specific, indicators of the relative status of men and women, with different levels and forms of literacy assigned to each. Richard Mulcaster, headmaster of the Merchant Taylors' School, writes in *The Training up of Children* (1581) that separate programs of instruction were justified by differences in men's and women's roles: "Our owne traine is without restraint for either matter or maner, bycause our employment is so generall in all thinges: theirs is within limit, and so must their traine be."[5] Like Shakespeare's Hamlet and Ophelia, both men and women in early modern England were literate; however, the languages and scripts they learned, the kinds of books to which they had access, and the reading habits they cultivated helped to engender new and profoundly different forms of subjectivity. It was not practical skills alone that were being taught. Sex-specific methods of reading and writing, humanists believed, would bring subjects to pattern themselves after humanist models of the gendered self. For Jacques Du Bosq, the explicit aim of his *Complete Woman* (1639) is to mold female readers into the perfect subject implied by the title of his treatise: "To enkindle within their hearts a longing to become like so goodly an Image, and by this meanes insensibly to oblige them to a change of life, and to reforme themselves according to this modell."[6] The assumption was that individuals could be brought to internalize paradigms of exemplary masculinity or femininity by reading a book or copying an aphorism.[7]

The desire to imprint subjects through education with the models and values of humanist culture, to reform society by shaping the individual's inner being, led sixteenth-century pedagogues to develop techniques of self-formation that twentieth-century social theorists would later redis-cover and highlight in formulations of the structural underpinnings of modern subjectivity. In his work on early modern court society, Norbert Elias describes the history of the modern subject as a process of interaction between the individual and society through which both are formed; the evolution of the individual involves autonomous action as well as social patterning. "What is shaped by society," Elias comments, "also shapes in its turn . . . . [T]he individual is both coin and die at the same time."[8] Echoing Elias as well as Anthony Giddens and Pierre Bourdieu, Louis Montrose asserts that subjects exist in dynamic relation to the societies in which they live, that both structure and agency are critical to an understanding of the subject: "The possibilities for action are always socially and historically situated, always limited and limiting. Nevertheless, collective structures may enable as well as constrain individual agency; and they may be potentially enabling precisely when they are experienced by the subject as multiple, heterogeneous, and even contradictory in their imperatives."[9]

To say that subjectivity is socially situated as Montrose does is not to say that it is conceived and imposed from above. It is to say that paradigms, practices, and forms of interiority evolve in societies, enmeshed in divisions between asymmetrically positioned groups, in short, through conflict and confrontation.[10] The possibilities for action available to individuals, to differing degrees depending on their gender, class, ethnicity, and circumstances, include appropriating self-fashioning techniques for ends for which they were not originally intended. "The tactics of consumption," Michel de Certeau observes, "the ingenious ways in which the weak make use of the strong, thus lend a political dimension to everyday practices."[11] Reading and writing, two such everyday practices, could be used both for reinforcing conformity and for improvising disruption. The teaching of specific modes of expression and interpretation helped to create systematic differences between men and women but also created openings for inventive contestation.

The conceptual shift that I posit, this new linkage of gender and literacy, does not signal the end or beginning of a golden age. It does not fit neatly into any of the three accounts of the transition between medieval and early modern times that have dominated discussions of women's relative status in the two periods: darkness to light (Jacob Burckhardt), light to darkness (Joan Kelly-Gadol), or uninterrupted darkness (Sandra Gilbert and Susan Gubar).[12] For my purposes, a more precise formulation of what changed in the sixteenth century is that offered by Margaret Ferguson: "If women did not have a Renaissance, they did at least have a Reformation."[13] In contrast to "Renaissance," a term with broad celebratory connotations, the term "Reformation" (like its analogue "Counter-Reformation") calls to mind specific cultural and institutional changes, implemented differently depending on the country and region, and affecting both sexes and all classes; the term also leaves room for a critical consideration of the impact, positive and negative, uneven and contradictory, of those changes on groups and individuals. Differences between medieval and early modern society, as Tessa Watt cautions, resist simplification, for "the culture could absorb new beliefs while retaining old ones, could modify doctrines, could accommodate words and icons, ambiguities and contradictions."[14] Broad-based social transformation, in sixteenth-century England as in other places, occurred subtly and over time, through conflicts over resources and positions, countless localized skirmishes whose outcomes were uncertain and variable.

Didactic texts from this period, sermons, conduct manuals, and educational treatises, show how humanist efforts to institute dual programs of

Fig. 1. The English Gentleman. Richard Brathwait, *The English Gentleman* (1630; rpt. London, 1633).

Fig. 2. The English Gentlewoman. Richard Brathwait, *The English Gentlewoman* (London, 1631).

literacy instruction fit within a larger project of social regulation based upon partitioning all activities and domains according to sex. Like Thomas Hoby's translation of *The Courtier* (1561), which included two separate appendices at the back of the book, the first an exhaustive list of "the chiefe conditions and qualities in a courtier" and the second a somewhat shorter list of the "chief conditions and qualityes in a wayting gentylwoman," Richard Brathwait's companion volumes *The English Gentleman* (1630) and *The English Gentlewoman* (1631) put in relief the discrepancy between male and female subjects. [15] *The English Gentleman* begins with a page of eight tableau-like pictures (captioned in Latin) of the prototypical English gentleman, *The English Gentlewoman* with eight comparable images (captioned in English) of the English gentlewoman (figs. 1 and 2). Half of the small pictures of her show a female figure sitting in a chair alone in a windowless room; the others, except for a view of heaven, and a garden, also depict indoor scenes. Her surroundings are characterized largely by the drapes and tapestries that hang from the walls and ceiling. By contrast, the pictures of her male cohort include images of mountains, trees, sky, houses, digging implements, a ship, a horse, and a bird in flight. The use of these eight small pictures at the beginning of each book, complemented by similarities in their organization, sets up a parallel between the male and female subject in order to make disparities between them more conspicuously visible. While none of the illustrations of various masculine activities in *The English Gentleman* incorporate contemplation of a devotional text, the central panel of the title page to *The English Gentlewoman* depicts a woman standing with a small book in one hand and the message "Grace my guide, Glory my goale" coming from her mouth. A woman's grace and glory, the image indicates, proceed from her private meditational reading.[16]

Conduct manuals such as these present only one side of the story. They relay rules for expression and behavior, many of which helped to institutionalize female subordination as religious principle and state policy, that were codified by humanists and enforced by teachers, preachers, and other authorities. Acceptance of such dicta, however, was by no means automatic. One minister who would have given husbands complete mastery over their wives, denying women all property rights upon marriage, met with opposition from parishioners. In his edition of marriage sermons, *Of Domestical Duties*, William Gouge recalled that "when these Domesticall Duties were first uttered out of the pulpit, much exception was taken against the application of a wives subjection to the restraining of her from disposing the common goods of the family without, or against her husband's consent."[17] While the sermon collection does, in that passage, record an instance of disagreement, tensions raised in the aside are quickly neutralized in service of the overarching orthodox message of its minister-author.

For critical analysis of how humanist prescriptions might have provoked resistance as well as compliance, we need to turn from didactic treatises to a more familiar set of texts: the surviving body of plays written for performance in the English public theatre. As Valerie Wayne observes, Desdemona pointedly contradicts conduct manual directives when she advises Emilia to disregard her husband's truisms about women's proper place.[18] The social friction written into dramatic texts is partly a matter of genre. Crossing uncrossable boundaries is a requisite skill in a playwright. It is what accounts for the intensity of that moment in *M. Butterfly* when Song Liling, the beautiful opera singer, stands undressed, buttocks to the audience, and forces René Gallimard to see her maleness. Tudor-Stuart dramatists revelled in enacting their own manipulations of gender for theatrical effect. The finale of Ben Jonson's *Epicoene* in which the title character, the so-called silent woman, lifts off her wig to reveal the man underneath has a similar shock value. Performed in a theatre in which actors were by definition male, the play does not trick the audience about the sex of the actor, only about that of the character. However, Jonson's rough unmasking of theatrical convention to make a misogynist joke (a silent woman is a man in drag) is also a vivid demonstration of the artificiality of gender. For an early modern audience, unsettling set paradigms about men's and women's relation to literacy could be equally daring. A play such as George Chapman's *Bussy D'Ambois* overturns the received notion of writing as a male prerogative by staging the spectacle of a woman using a pen. In *Richard III*, the dissonance between the humanist teaching of writing to cultivate exemplary masculinity and a character's use of the skill to destroy and deceive likewise heightens the drama.

This book explores how the diffusion of literacy, fueled by economic and political as well as evangelical imperatives, affected the self-conceptions and social relations of both sexes. It is an inquiry, set largely within the parameters of the English public theatre, into the pressures that humanism brought to bear on men and women as literate subjects and into the resistances that they offered in return. By portraying readers and writers of both sexes on stage, the theatre engaged the complex social implications of humanist pedagogy in plays ranging from Shakespeare's *Hamlet* to Thomas Dekker's *The Whore of Babylon*. Paradigms lifted from the pages of humanist-inspired treatises were presented to large audiences. They were also analyzed, their contradictions exposed and their social consequences enacted. What Jean Howard has said of

Thomas Heywood's *Wise Woman of Hogsdon*, a play which ends with the resolution of gender and class conflict, is true of the theatre as an institution: "It has recorded traces of that struggle."[19] By staging the construction of gender identities through dissimilar literacies, the theatre provided an arena in which the inscription of male and female selves could be publicly scrutinized.

A Mad World, My Masters by Thomas Middleton is a case in point of a contemporary play that opened to analysis conduct manual truisms about gender and literacy. The view that women's reading needed to be restricted to devotional works was reiterated by authors ranging chronologically from the 1530s to the 1630s, from Juan Luis Vives to Richard Brathwait. In *The Mirror of Modesty* (1579), Thomas Salter repeats the dictum:

I would not have a Maiden altogether forbidden, or restrained from reading, for so muche as the same is not onely profitable to wise and vertuous women, but also a riche and precious Jewell, but I would have her if she reade, to reade no other bookes but suche as bee written by godlie Fathers, to our instruction and soules healthe, and not suche lascivious Songes, filthie Ballades, and undecent bookes as be moste commonly now a daies sette to sale.[20]

The message is not that women should be restricted from print culture wholesale; rather, it is that their access to different books should be supervised in order to shield them from potentially corrupting influences. In *A Mad World, My Masters*, Middleton enacts a husband's attempt to limit his wife's reading on precisely those terms. Unwittingly, however, Master Harebrain looks to a prostitute (disguised as a sober maid) for help in securing his wife's chastity. He tells her to read Mistress Harebrain a religious tract, *A Book of Christian Exercise Appertaining to Resolution*, procured for that purpose:

I have convey'd away all her wanton pamphlets, as *Hero and Leander*, *Venus and Adonis*; oh, two luscious mary-bone pies for a young married wife! Here, here, prithee take the *Resolution*, and read to her a little . . . Terrify her, terrify her; go, read to her the horrible punishments for itching wantonness, the pains allotted for adultery; tell her her thoughts, her very dreams are answerable.[21]

That a husband could mold his wife's character by regulating her reading is an unquestioned commonplace in contemporary conduct manuals. In the context of that discourse, the idea that "her very dreams are answerable" is far from extreme. Yet in Middleton's play, such precepts are the stuff of comedy. The limitations inherent in the humanist program for shaping selves through literate practices are only too apparent in this spectacle of a husband instructing a prostitute to read *A Book of Christian Exercise* to his wife with the admonition, "terrify her, terrify her."

I

In 1508, a new schoolhouse was under construction in London. This was St. Paul's school, the model academy that came to symbolize the aspirations of English humanists for secondary instruction. John Colet was its founder, William Lily its headmaster, and Erasmus the author of its primary textbooks. Like the royal and aristocratic benefactors of higher education that Virginia Woolf imagined pouring huge sacks of gold into the earth, Colet spent thousands of pounds, nearly his entire patrimony, on establishing the grammar school. His money, however, was not the largesse of a prince or noble but the earnings of a prosperous London merchant; Colet's father had been a member of the leading city company, the Mercers. Colet took measures to annul the rights of the cathedral chapter, which had operated the school for centuries, and placed St. Paul's instead under the jurisdiction of the Mercers' Company. He also chose the textbooks and designed the curriculum. At Erasmus' direction, a picture of God the Father was displayed in the schoolroom with the dictate, "Hear ye Him." Colet himself also hung a picture of Christ teaching over the master's chair.

Colet's choice of pictures, as Joan Simon comments, amounted to "a manifesto."[22] On a doctrinal level, placing Christ at the center of the classroom signified a rejection of the cult of the saints, customarily affiliated with community institutions such as schools, in favor of the worship of a single omnipotent God. But that shift in iconography had a crucial gender dimension as well. The promotion of Christ as teacher was unmistakably a demotion of Anne and Mary from that same role. During the late Middle Ages, a time of increased book ownership on the part of laywomen, images of women learning and teaching became common features of Christian art. In some cases, Mary's reading appears to abstract her from the domestic sphere: she reads while midwives prepare for her delivery (East Germany or Bohemia, 1406); she reads after giving birth while Joseph cradles the baby in his arms (Northern France, early fifteenth century); she reads perched atop a donkey as Joseph carries the baby during their flight into Egypt (Netherlands, c. 1475).[23] In addition to scenes of private reading, images proliferated of Anne teaching Mary to read, Mary teaching Jesus, and, in some instances, Anne teaching Jesus.[24] An English manuscript dating from about 1300 depicts Anne sheltering the child Mary, who holds an alphabet psalter, within an ermine lined cloak (fig. 3). A second English manuscript from the fourteenth century shows Anne, her head resting on her daughter's, teaching the child to read; Anne encircles Mary with one arm and with the other points to a text of Psalm 24 (fig. 4). Such images

Fig. 3. Saint Anne teaching Mary to read. MS. Douce 231, fol. 3r. (England, *c.* 1300). From a psalter that belonged to the Countess of Leicester.

Fig. 4. Saint Anne teaching Mary to read. MS. FR 400, fol. 38v. (England, fourteenth century).

were not confined to the provenance of well-to-do laity who could afford illuminated books. The education of the Virgin was also part of the narrative of Christian history built into the physical construction of parish churches. The same scene of Anne teaching Mary to read was pictured in a fifteenth-century window in All Saint's Church in York.

In England at the time of the dissolution, many other such images, in stone and glass, were smashed in the rush to empty churches of the trappings of the old religious order. Along with the icons themselves and their particular doctrinal meanings, what was being cleared away were the subject positions from which women could give instruction and girl children receive attentive focus on their spiritual development. While the pre-Reformation church barely tolerated female participation in intellectual life, at times brutally suppressing it, its battle against insurgent heresies forced it to accommodate demand from women for access to ideas and texts being spread by the *devotio moderna*. This late-medieval movement of lay piety, with strains of female mysticism from the Continent among its many influences, created a niche in otherwise hostile surroundings in which women could seek out book-learning within orthodox limits. The contemplative method taught by the influential *Meditations on the Life of Christ*, a text popularized in England through mystical writings in the vernacular, called upon readers to project themselves imaginatively into scenes from the New Testament. For Margery Kempe, a laywoman versed in works such as Richard Rolle's *Meditations on the Passion*, immersion in the events of Christ's life turns ordinary moments into occasions for godly reflection. In her eyes, the sight of a poor woman nursing becomes that of Mary suckling the infant Jesus; a man beating a child or horse in the street transformed into a pageant of the abuse that Christ suffered as a man. Kempe steps into the narrative of the Passion as a literal participant; in her reenactment of events, she waits upon the grief-stricken Mary, bringing a drink of hot gruel and spiced wine to her bedside to comfort her, she mourns with Mary Magdalene at Christ's grave, and she chides the apostles when they object to her loud weeping.

Scenes of education featuring Anne and Mary multiplied in number during the same period that the *devotio moderna* increased in popularity. For royal figures, the personal identification with saints practiced by ordinary parishioners could take on political significance; this was the case for Anne of Brittany, the powerful queen of Louis XI and ruler in her own right of an important duchy, who enhanced her image by appealing to the cult of the matron saint of the same name. As a gift for her daughter Claude, Anne commissioned an illuminated primer, a book of prayers in Latin and French used to teach elementary reading, that depicts Anne instructing her daughters. The image establishes a parallel between the queen and Mary's saintly mother; at the same time, it legitimates the intervention of other women in the education of their children. In the last miniature in the primer, Claude kneels, an open book before her, to adore St. Anne (her mother, Anne of Brittany) who is teaching Mary (Claude's younger sister Renée) how to read.[25] All attention is on the triad of female readers, while the only male figure in the scene, the older daughter's patron saint, keeps to the background. The active role that Anne played in her daughter's education, including her gift of the beautiful primer, was a duty that the queen shared with mothers of all classes. When the church renewed its commitment to instructing the lower clergy and laity following the fourth Lateran Council in 1215, parents of both sexes were prevailed upon to accept the task of instructing their children as one of their primary obligations as Christians. The fifteenth-century *Dives and Pauper* stipulates that "Father, mother, godfathers and godmothers be bound to teach their children God's Law or else do them to be taught."[26] In the words of another book from that century titled *A Myrour to Lewde Men and Wymmen*, responsibility for teaching the untaught was owed not only by clergy to laity and by masters to students, but also by "fadres & modres to her children, & also euery man & womman to other." Parents who failed to provide proper instruction at home would answer to God for the sins committed by their children.[27] However, while both parents were accountable for imparting basic doctrine, instruction in reading came to be seen as the special province of women. By 1300, according to Nicholas Orme, "it was possible to make the general statement that 'woman teacheth child on book'."[28]

Many mothers must have simply trained their children in works of orthodox piety. Christine de Pisan, writing in 1405, describes this as one of a woman's primary duties: "When her daughter is of the age of learning to read, and after she knows her 'hours' and her 'office,' one should bring her books of devotion and contemplation and those speaking of morality."[29] Yet women's roles in teaching reading and in promoting vernacular literature also put them in peril of finding themselves on the wrong side of the contested and shifting line dividing orthodox from unauthorized forms of piety. Some women such as Alice Rowley of Coventry breached that frontier in no uncertain terms. In her heresy trial, Rowley confessed to having read publicly before other Lollards; a witness at the trial, Thomas Flesshour, concurred that he had heard Rowley lecture from the Book of Commandments in the house of one Roger Landesdale. She must have been a persuasive reader; two men attributed their conversions to her.[30] In a later case, a baker from

Colchester testified that he had received Lollard texts, including the epistles in English, from his mother Agnes.[31] Other women managed to become versed in vernacular works without arousing ecclesiastical wrath. When Anne of Bohemia married Richard II in 1382, she brought with her Czech and German translations of the gospel, a potentially dangerous act given the campaign against Lollard translations of the Bible then underway in England. Only a year later John Wycliffe, who was formally charged as a heretic, cited the example of Anne to justify his controversial translation of the Bible into English: "It is lawful for the noble queen of England [Anne] the sister of the Emperor, to have the gospel written in three languages, that is in Czech and in German and in Latin; and it would savor of the pride of Lucifer to call her a heretic for such a reason as this! And since the Germans wish in this matter reasonably to defend their own tongue, so ought the English to defend theirs." Ironically, Anne was praised at her funeral by Archbishop Arundel himself, Wycliffe's foe, before an assembly of hundreds of mourners, because she was "so great a lady, and also an alien, and would so lowlily study in virtuous books."[32]

It is within the context of traditions that recognized women as readers and teachers, positions honored in images of Mary and Anne in the same roles, that humanist hostility to female members of the holy family needs to be considered. In the early phases of the Reformation, women played a critical role in supporting imperiled Protestant activists. When Thomas Becon set out on a journey across England in 1543, he met with a hundred sympathizers who had studied his works and those of William Tyndale and John Frith, including "both men and women of the nobility which greatly delight in reading the holy scriptures."[33] However, even as Protestantism gained momentum with the backing of spiritually inclined laywomen, its leaders sought to domesticate unruly female religiosity, much as Catholic churchmen had tried to do before them. The assertion of masculine control in church institutions was accompanied by a similar effort in the school. An image of a Northern humanist classroom, taken from a mid-sixteenth-century writing handbook, reflects this preoccupation with male pedagogical authority (fig. 5). It depicts the schoolmaster as a magisterial presence who imparts his learning from a massive chair that dominates the room.[34]

Humanism supplied both practical procedures and rhetorical skills for securing the field of education as a masculine sphere. Juan Luis Vives, for instance, redeployed the Pauline prescription against women speaking in public, a text frequently cited in the Middle Ages to prevent women from preaching, as an argument against female teachers. Though Catherine of Aragon had learned Latin from a Spanish woman and herself taught her

Fig. 5. Northern humanist classroom from a mid-sixteenth-century writing manual. Urban Wyss, *Libellus valde doctus . . . multa et varia scribendum litterarum genera complectens* (Zurich, 1549). The Latin inscription, "Nulla dies abeat quin linea ducta supersit," can be translated as, "Let not a day go by without a line [of text]."

daughter Mary to write Latin, Vives argued against employing women teachers on the grounds that it "becomes not a woman to rule a school"; only if an appropriate man, "either well-aged or else very good and virtuous, which hath a wife whom he loveth well," could not be found would he agree to hire a "holy and well-learned woman" as teacher.[35] Not coincidentally, the job description that Vives, Princess Mary's tutor, presented to his employer fit his own qualifications. Colet, like Vives, had a particular interest in displacing images of Mary and Anne teaching with a rival image of Christ instructing his followers. At St. Paul's, the authority of the schoolmaster, the distinguished humanist scholar William Lily, flowed from the figure on the wall representing Christ as teacher directly down to the male pedagogue seated just below.

The drive to marginalize mothers and schoolmistresses alike, can be traced in contemporary representations of the holy family. Unlike previous images in which Anne is often at the center of a scene of learning, early sixteenth-century versions begin to minimize Anne's role as teacher. "Not only do fathers move into the central space," observes Pamela Sheingorn, "but they also take over some of the responsibilities formerly reserved for mothers, particularly that of education." A woodcut (c. 1510) by Lucas Cranach the Elder offers evidence of this substitution of roles. In that picture, Anne does read to Jesus, but the baby's gaze is directed toward Joseph, his father, and away from his grandmother. Alpheus stands as a figure of pedagogic authority, his schoolmaster's rod firmly in hand, as he teaches his children to read. Another father, Zebedee, sees his son off to school. While the women in the picture devote themselves to childcare, here distinguished from instruction, the men claim education as their exclusive domain.[36] Though Cranach's woodcut speaks to the problem of primary instruction in Germany, a similar repositioning of men and women, with literacy as the line of demarcation between them, was also underway in early sixteenth-century England. The agenda of educational reform aimed not only at imparting new knowledge but also at effecting a redistribution of education and skills along gender lines.

Changes to contemporary legislation contributed to that end. The contrast between two English laws, one from the early fifteenth century and the other from the mid-sixteenth century, illustrates a trend of intensified bifurcation of the sexes. In 1406, the Statute of Artificers mandated that "every Man or Woman, of what Estate or Condition that he be, shall be free to set their Son or Daughter to take learning at any manner School that pleaseth them within the Realm."[37] The 1406 Statute overturned previous laws intended to keep tenants on the estates of their lords by preventing them from learning to read. The conspicuously inclusive language of the law – the stipulation that "every Man or Woman" may educate "their Son or Daughter" – promised to ensure that the new access to learning would extend to female laborers as well as to their male counterparts. By contrast, the 1543 Act for the Advancement of True Religion turned gender into a category for excluding women specifically. The law ordered that "no woomen nor artificers prentises journeymen serving men of the degrees of yeomen or undre, husbandemen nor laborers shall reade within this Realme or in any other the Kings Domynions, the Byble or Newe Testament in Englishe, to himselfe or any other pryvatelie or openlie." The law made an exception for noblewomen and gentlewomen who were permitted to read the Bible and New Testament "to themselves alone and not to others"; the same proviso applied to merchants. Only noblemen and gentlemen were authorized to read scripture to their families.[38] The special attention given to preventing women from reading aloud to others parallels the downgrading of women from teaching roles that we have traced in contemporary iconography. While the act was later repealed, the tenet behind it became institutionalized in sixteenth-century England. For the authors of the 1543 legislation, the principle that literacy needed to be regulated on the basis of gender was so critical that they were willing to override considerations of class to enforce it, to place a noblewoman under the same restrictions that applied to a tradesman.

Other laws that followed this same course were those regulating appeals for benefit of clergy. Under English law, defendants convicted of capital crimes could avoid execution by demonstrating their ability to read. The defendant would be given a book, usually a Psalter, from which to read aloud. The judge would ask the Bishop's commissary, *"legit ut clericus?"* If the answer was *"legit,"* the judge would direct the defendant to have his hand branded "T" for "thief" or "M" for "mansleer." If the answer was *"non legit,"* the judge would pronounce the death sentence.[39] Prior to the Reformation, the law already applied unequally to men and women. While any literate man could claim the privilege, the only women who could do so were professed nuns; other women were excluded because they were considered ineligible for ordination.[40] After the Reformation, with the closure of the convents, women were excluded as a class from claiming the privilege. Moreover, at the very time that benefit of clergy was being denied categorically to all women, learned and unlearned alike, it was being extended to illiterate men of noble rank. Edward VI's first parliament allowed peers to plead benefit of clergy in regard to criminal offenses even if they could not read, and protected them, if convicted, from the penalty of being branded.[41] More than half a century would pass before women became eligible to plead benefit of clergy in 1622. Even then, for women the privilege was restricted to limited instances, the few cases that involved the larceny of goods worth between one and ten shillings. It was not until 1692, during the reign of William and Mary, that they were given the right to claim benefit of clergy on an equal basis with men.[42]

Just as men and women were covered differently by laws concerning literacy, so too institutional changes brought by the Reformation affected their opportunities for education in contrasting ways. Schools for girls had been far fewer in the late Middle Ages and less prestigious than those for boys; yet permanent facilities for instructing girls had existed in significant numbers. Possibly two thirds of convents accepted children for instruction; some operated schools, including coeducational ones, catering to the upper classes.[43] Nuns in these institutions included recognized schoolmistresses. In 1501, Agnes Cox was Senior Teacher (*dogmatista*) while the novices were taught by Margaret Legh. Alice Whytingstale was Mistress of the School at Romsey in 1502. Sister Elizabeth Cresner, Prioress of Dartford Nunnery, was granted permission in 1527 to receive young ladies and give them a suitable training "according to the mode heretofore pursued"; she had already been prioress for seven years at the time that a concession allowing Latin lessons to be given in the convent was granted.[44] Illustrious clergy and nobility entrusted the instruction of their children, boys as well as girls, to nuns and abbesses. In 1527, upon deciding to enter a monastery, John Stanley drew up a will specifying that his son and heir was to be brought up until the age of twelve by the Abbess of Barking after which he was to pass to the care of the Abbot of Westminster. Bishop Hugh placed five-year old Robert de Noyon in the convent at Elstow "to be taught his letters." Even Cromwell sent his son Gregory and a companion to be supervised, though not taught, by Margaret Vernon, Prioress of Little Marlow.[45]

The dissolution had a particularly negative impact on female education because the closures of convent schools, with few exceptions, were permanent, whereas a much greater number of schools that had been operated by monasteries were later reestablished; in addition, many alternative schools with lay affiliations were available to take in boys.[46] Though clerical recruitment declined in the first two decades after the dissolution, the organization needed to oversee the dismantling of ecclesiastical institutions and to extend state power in other directions helped to stimulate demand for male education: A new cohort of "augmentations men" overseeing monastic and chantry properties joined an increasing number of lay administrators. Important officials, no longer only the king's personal servants, began to supervise the growing bureaucracy and the demand for legal training increased.[47]

The elimination by reformers of another social institution, the confraternity, likewise impinged on the educational equilibrium between men and women. Confraternities, sometimes referred to as religious gilds, established active centers of spiritual experience open to both men and women, organized by members of every social stratum, and controlled by laypeople. An association of laypeople under the patronage of a saint, the Virgin, the Trinity, or the Corpus Christi, the confraternity provided funerals and masses for its members. It also provided the opportunity, unparalleled in post-Reformation England, for laypeople to hire clergy.[48] Confraternities, whose membership included men and women, wives as well as single women, encouraged all members to be educated. The Rule of the Gild of Saint Katherine at Norwich required "at the Dirige euery brother and sister that is letterede shul seyn for the soule of the dede, placebo and dirige, in the place wher he shul comen togeder; and euery brother and sister that bene nought letterede, shul seyn for the soule of the dede xx sythes the pater noster with Aue maria."[49] According to Lucy Toulmin Smith, "even where the affairs were managed by a company of priests, women were admitted as lay members; and they had many of the same duties and claims upon the Gild as the men."[50] Following the Reformation, no comparable institution encouraged men and women to achieve the same educational attainments for the same practical purpose.

In addition to breaking down frameworks for coeducation, the dissolution also disrupted networks, operating through religious foundations, which had preserved and transmitted texts written by or for women. The Briggitine double-monastery of Sion, built on the opposite bank of the river Thames from the Carthusian house of Sheen, was at the center of a religious and literary circle whose associates included Lady Margaret Beaufort, Bishop John Fisher, and, at a later date, Thomas More and Catherine of Aragon. It was common for texts to circulate between the Carthusian and Briggitine houses; one example is that of Joanna Sewell and James Grenehalgh who communicated through annotations inscribed in the margins of books.[51] Moreover, Sion maintained an association with All Souls College, Oxford, by which the abbess and nuns were admitted to services held at the men's college; "Syon [sic] Abbey was the nearest approach to a learned institution for women that existed in England."[52] Among the works diffused by the Briggitines were translations of continental women writers: the *Revelations of Bridget of Sweden*, which appeared in no less than seven distinct English versions, the *Dialogues* of St. Catherine of Siena (published in English as the

Orcherd of Syon in the early-sixteenth century), and the *Meditations* of Elizabeth Schönau. An English version of *The Booke of Gostlye Grace* by Mechtild of Hackeborn also may have been translated for the nuns of Sion.[53] In addition, monks at the neighboring Carthusian monastery of Sheen translated the French original of Marguerite Porete's *Mirror of Simple Souls* into both English and Latin. Works by native English-women, though less widely circulated, were also meticulously copied and conserved by monastic communities. The single surviving copy of Margery Kempe's autobiographical *Book* belonged to another Carthusian monastery, Mount Grace Priory, in Yorkshire; annotations added by readers in the community compared Kempe's experiences with those of Richard Methley, the celebrated English mystic from Mount Grace.[54] A shorter version of the *Showings* by the English anchoress Julian of Norwich can be traced to the Sheen Charterhouse, where it passed through the hands of James Grenehalgh, while a longer version owes its survival to a community of English Benedictine nuns who established themselves at Cambray after the Reformation.[55]

What the loss of that collective memory of women writers, along with the mechanisms needed to conserve their texts, may have meant for English literary history registers in some chance connections between medieval and early modern women writers established via convents on the Continent. It was at La Madeleine, a center for the reformist spirituality she championed, that Marguerite de Navarre probably discovered a manuscript of the mystical allegory written in French by Marguerite Porete around the turn of the fourteenth century. In her poem "Prisons," de Navarre describes having found, among many other religious tomes, a book "By a woman, / Written a hundred years ago"; the text, as she describes it, is clearly Porete's.[56] The convent's copy of the *Mirouer des Simples Ames*, transcribed between 1450 and 1530, at least a century and a half after its author's death, and consulted by the queen in the sixteenth century, testifies to continuities between medieval and early modern female writers and readers in France. The manuscript was itself a mother's legacy to a daughter; at the bottom of the first page, Jehanne Bontemps inscribed her wish that the book pass, after her death, into the keeping of her daughter, Claudine Bontemps, a nun at La Madeleine.[57]

In France, unlike England where English and Latin translations of *Le Mirouer* had also circulated in the Middle Ages, some memory of the author remained connected with the text. While de Navarre places its composition in the wrong century, suggesting that she was unaware of Porete's name and heresy conviction, she repeatedly calls attention to the author's gender. Praising the book over those of learned clerics, she exclaims, "How intent was this woman / To receive the love that burned / Her heart and the hearts of those she addressed!"[58] Similar possibilities for the transmission of writings by Englishwomen, if not foreclosed, were at least diminished by the eradication of convents in Protestant England. One such community, reestablished in France, served as the repository both for the most complete text of Julian of Norwich's *Showings*, as just mentioned, and also for the *Life* of Elizabeth Cary, author of *The Tragedy of Mariam* (1613). To this day, that important biography of the first woman to publish an original play in England remains in the archives of the Département du Nord in Lille. Four of Cary's daughters were nuns at the Benedictine convent in Cambray where one of them, possibly Anne or Lucy, wrote the story of her mother's life.[59] And the rare manuscript of Julian's *Showings* is written in the hand of that same daughter.

While institutional changes brought by the Reformation had the effect of deepening the divide between male and female learning, this development was by no means straightforward or universally accepted. The closure of convent schools, in certain cases, incited active protest. In 1536, one school, Saint Mary's, Winchester, was briefly exempted from the execution of the decree ordering the dissolution in that year. A sympathetic county commission report stated that there were twenty-six daughters of "lords, knights and gentlemen brought up in the same monastery" and listed their names.[60] In 1537, Henry VIII's commissioners petitioned Cromwell on behalf of Polesworth Nunnery where at one time some thirty to forty gentlemen's children were "right vertuously brought up."[61] With help from the Goodere family, the school was kept running from 1539 until the family bestowed a landed endowment on it in 1573.[62] At Godstow, witnesses reported that "most of the gentlewomen of the county were sent there to be bred, so that the gentry of the country desired the King would spare the house."[63] In Yorkshire, Robert Aske included among the benefits that the monastic houses had conferred upon the gentry, the "bringing up in virtue" of their daughters.[64] Disagreements sparked by closure of the convent schools show that the humanist educational agenda excluding formal schooling for girls was not a conventional expression of age-old misogyny.[65] Rather, it was a purposeful intervention, spurred by diverse incentives, that sometimes overruled community preferences in the interest of asserting the greater authority of the state over local custom.

Statutes of sixteenth- and seventeenth-century grammar schools that expressly forbid the admission of girls suggest that the debate over female schooling remained alive, though underground, over the hundred years that passed between the Reformation and the English Civil War.

Thomas Becon, the early reformer exiled for his religious views, had lamented the disappearance of convent schools that in former times ensured that young maids were "godly brought up," and he had called for the construction of public schools for girls.[66] A century later, Thomas Fuller and John Aubrey still remembered convent schools with nostalgia, "good Shee-schools" as Fuller termed them, and attributed the defects of contemporary women to their lack of education.[67] The notion that woman was created in the image of God and therefore entitled to the same benefits of formal schooling as man was neither unthinkable nor unsayable in the early seventeenth century. William Austin, a barrister of Lincoln's Inn whose name was included in a list of members for a proposed Royal Academy of Literature, cited Scripture to argue for the equality of the sexes in his *Haec Homo, wherein the Excellency of the Creation of Women is Described*, published posthumously by his widow in 1637 and reprinted the following year. He expressed his position on women's equality in unambiguous terms: "In the sexe, is all the difference; which is but onely in the body. For, she hath the same reasonable soule; and, in that, there is neither hees, nor shees; neither excellencie, nor superiority: she hath the same soule; the same mind; the same understanding."[68] Writing in the same decade, Comenius, a Moravian educator well-known in England, contended in his *Magna Didactica* that both sexes should attend established schools "whether in Latin or in their mother tongue" because women as well as men are "formed in the image of God."[69]

For prohibitions against female admission to have been necessary, some parents had to have wanted to send their daughters to grammar school.[70] Those individuals could have found an enabling rationale in the ideal of universal literacy espoused by early Protestants, eager to widen their base of support by exposing a maximum number of potential converts to their ideas. The contradiction between that objective of the first reformers, driven by the political exigencies of the moment, and broader theories of education advanced by humanist scholars created opportunities for limited dissension, for an occasional exception to be made to the grammar school statutes, for some female teachers put out of work at the dissolution to continue offering instruction, for Protestant women escaping persecution on the Continent to set up a few schools, for some women to express themselves as writers through the translation of devotional texts, in short, for a certain residual untidiness to clutter up the carefully drawn schemes developed to establish sex-specific instruction.

II

The structural changes surveyed here paralleled changes in the specific methods of learning that institutions taught. The influence of reading and writing in this period can be grasped only if they are understood as historically contingent practices. Early modern literacies developed through an ongoing reconfiguration of existing practices and beliefs, with classical and continental influences grafted on, that both informed and adapted to technological, institutional, and cultural innovations. Not only do the size and makeup of the pool of potential readers and writers differ at given moments; the specific mental and practical procedures involved in reading and writing also change over time and between cultures.[71] Neither practice entails an encounter between a transcendent subject and transparent thought. Both necessitate the construction of meaning through culturally specific methods of expression and interpretation. Roger Chartier describes reading as a concrete act "at the crossroads between readers endowed with specific competences, identified by their positions and their dispositions . . . and texts whose meaning is always dependent on their particular discursive and formal mechanisms."[72] Acts of reading differ according to whether one is reading aloud or to oneself, in a private or in a communal setting, fluidly or with hardship, in many languages or in one only, with an intensive focus on a single book or for brief experiences with multitudes of books. They also differ depending upon the cultural frames of reference and upon the social purposes with which readers approach the text.

In early modern England, the imperative to construct subjects according to humanist schemata informed the approaches of contemporary readers and writers. Sixteenth-century literate practices, however, did not emerge *ex nihilo*. As David Aers points out, they were based largely upon Augustinian traditions that already emphasized inwardness and self-scrutiny. These and other classical and medieval traditions were appropriated, not invented, by humanists.[73] The innovation in this period was the reorganization of earlier practices and beliefs with the aim of shaping subjects to serve the emergent Tudor state. The new political order and incipient Protestant ideology, Stephen Greenblatt concludes, provided the impetus for "a heightened consciousness of identity, an increased attention to its expression, and an intensified effort to shape and control it. The fashioning of the self is raised to the status of a problem or a program."[74] Humanist reformers drew on previous pedagogic approaches in order to develop and institutionalize more systematic techniques for shaping selves and society. What most distinguished the reading practices they promoted from those of Augustine was a changed vision of the model subject. In the Middle Ages, the aim of hermeneutics had been to produce an orthodox Christian; in the sixteenth century, it was intended "to fashion a gentleman."

The technique developed by Augustine teaches readers to accept established interpretations of texts, even when those interpretations contradict the words on the page, and, in doing so, to internalize an awareness of their subordinate position in relation to the greater authority of the Church. The emphasis of the method, what Lee Patterson has termed a "preemptive hermeneutic," is on the reader rather than the text. "The Christian reader," Patterson explains, "comes to the text (Scripture) already possessed of its message . . . and his task is to understand not its meaning but its way of signifying that meaning."[75] Since ecclesiastical commentators assume that only readers, never authorized texts, can express errors or contradictions, readers either have to confirm the official interpretation assigned to a given text or to acknowledge the blasphemous inclinations which keep them from doing so. The process of reconciling a received interpretation with the text which the reader has at hand becomes one of self-evaluation and self-alteration. Saint Ignatius succinctly defines the tenet behind this practice in the spiritual exercises that he devised in the aftermath of the Counter-Reformation. "If we wish to be sure that we are right in all things," Ignatius advises the exercent, "we should always be ready to accept this principle: I will believe that the white that I see is black, if the hierarchical Church so defines it."[76]

This mode of interpretation also guides the English translator of Marguerite Porete's *Mirouer des simples ames* (*Mirror of Simple Souls*). His glosses reveal how it was possible for a reader trained in ecclesiastical hermeneutics to turn potentially heretical propositions into expressions of orthodox belief. M. N., a Carthusian monk identified only by his initials, does not reject the text as heretical; rather, he assumes the task of reconciling its meaning with Catholic dogma. In a gloss which explicates the Soul's decision to take leave of the Virtues, M. N. compares the process by which the Soul acquires spiritual intuition to that of cracking open a nut with one's teeth: "So longe oon may bite on þe bitter bark of þe note, þat at þe laste he schal come to þe swete kernel."[77] M. N.'s pleas that readers interpret his translation "in þe same hooli wise as it is deuoutli yment" (355) and take time both to taste and see the text (248) suggest that a conception of divine truth as something hidden and difficult to recover guides his reading of the text. His belief that Love leaves the kernel of meaning within its unbroken shell allows M. N. to crack open the words of the text as though they were grains or nuts in order to give readers access to the words' essential (orthodox) meaning.

This assumption that the text is sacred means that only the reader's orthodoxy, not that of the text, can ever be in question; to locate errors in *Þe Mirour of Simple Soules* (the title given to the Middle English translation) is to betray the fallen nature of one's own imperfect understanding. In explaining the statement that the Soul gives to Nature all that Nature asks (without regard for church teachings), M. N. casts aspersions on the morality of any reader who might interpret this incorrectly. "God forbeede þat eny be so fleischli to þenke," M. N. writes, "þat it schulde mene to ȝiue to nature eny lust þat drawiþ to fleischli synne" (259). The implication is that only a carnal or spiritually blind reader will fail to see the true, benign meaning of seemingly dangerous propositions. According to the Augustinian hermeneutic, a divergent reading of the text is unspeakable; to suggest that the text, not the reader, may be blasphemous would itself constitute blasphemy. The conversion a reader undergoes before arriving at M. N.'s interpretation becomes a process of spiritual enlightenment:

Riȝt þus alle suche wordis moste be declared wiþinne hemsilf þat reden þis boke. For þese derke wordis and hiȝe maters derkli spoken in þis writynge, it is don for to make þe soules of þe rederis þat ben disposid to goostli felinges to circuie and enserche bi sotilte of wit to come to þese diuine vnderstandinges, bi þe whiche þei may be þe more able to receyue and folewe þese heuenli usages of Goddes werk. (304–5)

Difficult or potentially dangerous words must be processed internally, to undergo some kind of alchemical change within the individual reader. Ideally, one trained in the Augustinian method of interpretation could "bi sotilte of wit to come to . . . diuine vndirstandinges" of any text. St. Jerome advised a mother named Laeta to give her daughter a thorough grounding in Scripture and the early Fathers so that eventually she would be able to read even the Song of Songs without peril.[78] For M. N., reading entails a comparable kind of self-modification. "Dark" words, those that seem false or obscure, can be glossed and understood inside oneself with an ecclesiastical glossator to guide readers, as he puts it, "to brynge ȝou in þe weie" (314). The discipline of repeatedly reading the text, with God's grace, will permit readers to see it in an acceptable spiritual light.

The techniques of reading illustrated in M. N.'s glosses, inspired by Augustine and taught in monastic communities, were largely the same for men and for women. Two treatises on reading practices also from the Middle Ages, William of St. Thierry's *Letter to the Brothers of Mont-Dieu* and Bonaventure's *On the Perfection of Life, Addressed to Sisters*, contain similar instructions. Each author tells his audience, male clergy in the first instance and female clergy in the second, to use the same techniques of meditational reading on the life of Christ in order to attain spiritual transformation.[79] Initiates of this form of contemplation, as we have seen in the later example of Margery Kempe, aspired to an imitation of Christ that was both outward, the practical emulation of his compassion through acts of charity and self-sacrifice, and inward, a psychic reenactment of his suffering that would bring the believer to an experience of personal intimacy. The stigmata famously conferred on St. Francis are the sign of that radical identification, the moment at which the believer, inwardly at one with the pain of his crucified God, receives the outward marks of the crucifixion in confirmation.

It is an important aspect of this broad spiritual reawakening of thirteenth-century Europe that the yearnings it aroused were shared by women as well as men. The first stigmata were reported not by Francis of Assisi but by laywomen who never became saints. Marie d'Oignies made herself a literal example of holy imitation by inflicting Christ's wounds upon her own body; other women such as Ida of Louvain were said to have received the stigmata as a sign of divine blessing.[80] Like their male counterparts, devout women drew followers from far and wide and acquired important allies within the Church. However, wherever male ecclesiastical privilege seemed threatened by female spiritual activism, the ecclesiastical hierarchy drew the line. While St. Francis was allowed to minister to the poor and sick in imitation of Christ and the apostles, St. Clare was ordered to submit to enclosure.[81] Harsher measures were adopted against the Beguines who followed a religious life outside of approved orders. To punish those women, who were accused of translating the Bible into the vernacular and of preaching in public squares, authorities staged the show trial and execution of Marguerite Porete in Paris as a prelude to the violent persecution of whole communities of Beguines across Western and Central Europe.[82]

The gender-neutral instructions for reading that we find in the works of contemplatives from the twelfth century onward coexisted with attitudes in the Church that established gender bias as official policy, backed up at times, as in the case of the Beguines, by programs of grim coercion. As Anne Bartlett points out, a devotional text that offered impartial guidelines for interpretation also could contain statements of virulent misogyny. The author of the late-fourteenth-century *Book to a Mother* tells his female reader that she may learn to understand scripture better than any clerk, better than any master of divinity, by virtue of the depth of her love for God. Illogically, that same author, a priest, then goes on to attack women, in the venomous terms of anti-feminist diatribes. He is certain, he tells the female reader, that women "stink worse before God and the angels than any stinking carrion or dung or any stench, except sin."[83]

While such attitudes inspired measures that limited female authority and learning, they did not, in this period, translate into sex-specific techniques for understanding texts. Three fifteenth-century English books, all concerned with exemplarity and correspondingly titled "Mirrors," reflect the prevalence of gender-neutral practices of reading in the period. Though different in audience and scope, all three works regard the obligation to model one's self after Christ and the saints through the habitual study of texts as a task that applies to all Christians regardless of sex. Dating from the beginning of the century, *The Mirror of the Blessed Life of Jesus Christ* was a translation by Nicholas Love, prior of Mount Grace Charterhouse, of the influential work that had long, though erroneously, been ascribed to Bonaventure. Love tells his reader that he has translated the text, originally written for a nun in Latin, so that it will be available not only to Latin-speaking clerks but also to unlearned men and women. According to Love, the technique of contemplative imitation holds the promise of salvation for any reader, regardless of gender or class, who meditates on Christ who "ʒaff himself to vs in to ensaumple of gode leuyng. Wherfore nowe boþe men & women & euery Age & euery dignite of this worlde is stirid to hope of euery lastyng lyfe."[84] Love looks to Christ as an "example" for both men and women to follow. This was also how medieval Christians saw Mary. In his *Life of Saint Bridget*, Thomas Gascoigne, the Chancellor of Oxford, cites an angel's revelation that Mary is a model for all Christians, including male clergy: "she taught to confessours the very true lessons of helth & they by hir doctrine & example perfytly lernyd to ordre the tymes of the day & of the nyght wysely to the laude & glory of almyght god."[85] The process of internal transformation accomplished through reading, through beholding the model "inwardly" and then shaping one's self appropriately, will enable any believer to keep from straying and to arrive at salvation. Both models and readers, it was assumed, could be of either sex.

The *Myrour to Lewde Men and Wymmen*, which we have seen addressed the task of education to fathers and mothers alike, defines its readership as broadly as its title would suggest. Invoking the same pilgrimage topos as Love, the author explains that we are all wanderers and exiles, pilgrims far from our native countries, en route either to Jerusalem or Babylon, to endless bliss or endless pain, heaven or hell. Following Augustine, the author teaches that meditation will enable the reader to stay on the right path and avoid the wrong one. The reader could be either male or female, for the author explicitly addresses both sexes in his audience: "þis writyng is made for lewed and menliche lettred men and wymmen in suche tonge as þei can best vnderstonde, and may be cleped a myrour to lewde men and wymmen in whiche they may see God þorgh stedfast byleue and hemself þorgh mekenes, and what is vertu and what is synne."[86] The choice facing the reader is stark, virtue or sin, but, as with the educational level of its "menliche lettred" readers, it is the same for women as for men.

Even *The Myroure of oure Ladye*, which unlike *A Myrour to Lewde Men and Wymmen* is addressed to women alone, specifically to the members of the convent of Sion for whom it was written, proposes that both sexes adopt the same techniques of reading. In a section titled "how ye shall be gouerned in redyng of this Boke and of all other bokes," the author defines the reading method that he has outlined, one derived from Augustine, as the same approach that Cato taught his son. Like Cato's son, the nun has a share in the salvation promised by ecclesiastical hermeneutics and receives equivalent mental training to that end. The author directs her to avoid worldly books, to dispose her mind to reverence and devout attention, and to work to understand what she reads. He tells her that her responsibility as a reader is "pryncypally to enforme your selfe." Her self-formation depends upon a set of mental procedures: "yf ye fele & se in youre selfe. that ye lacke suche verteows gouernaunce as ye rede of . . . Ye ought to abyde thervpon. & inwardly sorow for the defaulte & lacke that ye se in yourselfe. & besely to kepe in mynde that lesson that so sheweth you to youre selfe."[87] For the nun, no less than for Augustine, the reading process is far from a passive exercise. It involves laboring over meanings, diagnosing one's faults, stirring one's emotions, concentrating one's mind, transforming one's being. The promise that the author makes the nun is illumination through disciplined reading: a moment in which the text becomes mirror, when the lesson "so sheweth you to youre selfe."

These "Mirror" books and the *devotio moderna* tradition to which they belong still defined popular beliefs in England at the time that Dean Colet asked Erasmus to provide a text for his newly opened grammar school in London. That volume, which became one of the most influential of the humanist classroom, was *De Copia*.[88] Published in 1512 with a dedication to Colet and his school, the book taught students how to embellish their writing style by means of rhetorical devices. Chief among these was the example. Students were told to choose examples, gleaned from their reading of classical texts, and to imitate them. This technique for self-fashioning did not, in itself, represent a break with the past. The imitation of examples, as we have seen, was a basic method for forming subjects in late medieval piety. What was new, in the English context, was the humanist reenvisioning of these models and techniques through the lens of gender. In the trajectory that can be traced from the anonymous fifteenth-century *Myrour to Lewde Men and Wymmen* to Richard Brathwait's seventeenth-century *English Gentleman* and *English*

Gentlewoman, De Copia stands at a critical juncture. When culling examples from one's reading, Erasmus explains, one must sort them according to date, national origin, and subject matter as well as the age, rank, position, and gender of the person described. In fact, Erasmus concludes, "each class of person prefers what is his own, or else something that makes him feel superior, such as anecdotes about women, children, slaves, and barbarians."[89]

Erasmus signals the importance of gender in male self-fashioning in his explanation of how to persuade a man to control himself after the loss of a son. In such a situation, he proposes citing the example of a "barbarian" woman who bore the death of several sons with fortitude:

After telling the story, the speaker will proceed to compare the two: Can you, a Roman and a man, not evince the qualities that a weak barbarian woman could? She was ignorant of learning and yet she could scorn something that shatters you in spite of your education and your great profession of philosophy.

Later in the treatise, Erasmus refers to the same woman to point out that the persuasiveness of the example could be further enriched by the addition of *sententiae*:

After the first contrast – 'Can you, a grown man, not bear what a feeble woman could?' – one could introduce striking sayings such as 'Nature made a distinction in sex; do you make no distinction in mind?'; 'A woman is not expected by anyone to win praise for courage, but if a man is not courageous he is not even classed as a man'; 'The name man indicates both the stronger sex and strength of mind; it is shameful to sport a beard and be surpassed by a woman in firmness of heart.'[90]

These instructions, like those offered in Nicholas Love's *Mirror of the Blessed Life of Jesus Christ*, indicate how one should fashion one's self in response to examples found in a text. In explaining how to counsel the bereaved father, Erasmus also is telling the schoolboy how he should react as a reader. Yet unlike Love, who stressed that God's son had "bothe men & women" in mind when he "ʒaff himself to vs in to ensaumple," Erasmus assumes that a male reader's response to a given example will be conditioned fundamentally by his sex and by the sex of the person serving as an example. A male example, an Alexander or Caesar, would be invoked to inspire a male reader to equal heroism; the example of a woman in order to shame the reader into greater fortitude.

This parcelling out of models according to sex made the kinds of gender-inclusive communities of readers that formed under the auspices of the *devotio moderna* untenable. It also changed the purposes that readers brought to texts. For the reader of M. N.'s controversial *Mirrour of Simple Soules*, the task was to arrive at the correct doctrinal interpretation. In a gloss attached to a Latin translation of the text, Richard

Methley, a monk in the same order as M. N., warns the reader of the *Mirror* to "beware, lest you believe" that the approved text is heretical "for to feel or to say this is not of grace but of blasphemy."[91] Any act of reading governed by ecclesiastical hermeneutics presented an implicit danger; one was always, to some degree, at risk of dropping out of the category of orthodox Christian, of falling from grace into blasphemy. In the sixteenth century, under the influence of educational reform, this criterion for evaluating the reader changed. Effeminacy was the new heresy in humanist hermeneutics. The task set the reader of *De Copia* is to exhibit the correct social comportment; if he does not surmount his female counterpart in every way, from his educational attainments to his emotional responses, "he is not even classed as a man."

III

The shift from Nicholas Love's text to Erasmus' is not a movement from freedom to repression or from gender neutrality to gender bias in society at large; rather it is the transplantation of common themes of female inferiority from other fields of social regulation to that of reading practices. Humanists were able to harness the power of an already vigorous intellectual tradition, whose destabilizing potential was unmistakably apparent in the actions of townswomen such as Margery Kempe, in order to monopolize the benefits of the new learning and to sustain existing inequities more effectively. This purpose is behind the rationale that Spenser attaches to *The Faerie Queene*: "the generall end therefore of all the booke is to fashion a gentleman."[92] In his epic, sex-specific practices of reading produce compartmentalized subjects. The male reader becomes a gentleman by learning to demarcate truth from falsehood and himself from social inferiors. The female reader forms her identity by disassociating herself from evil and epitomizing truth. Yet there are also moments, as in Guyon's sea passage to the Bower of Bliss, when that diagrammatic formula seems to break down and internal tensions in the humanist program itself threaten to send the poem off its scheduled course. At those times, the author, like Guyon's pilgrim escort, keeps a particularly watchful eye. For Spenser, the category of gender continues to inform, at every turn, his obligation as an author to guide his male and female reader on separate paths toward truth and self-understanding.

Pilgrimage as a metaphor for hermeneutic inquiry, a pervasive theme in the earlier devotional literature that we have surveyed, also structures the narrative of Book 1 of *The Faerie Queene*. Redcross Knight undergoes a series of ordeals in which suspense centers on whether the knight will be able to distinguish between hidden verities and deceptive appearances, between faith and fakery, the Anglican church and the Catholic one, between Truth and Falsehood, Una and Duessa, Fidelia and Fidessa. Spenser explicitly offers the poem to his audience as an exercise in interpretation. He describes it as a "darke conceit" similar to the book owned by Faith "wherein darke things were writ, hard to be vnderstood" (1.10.13). In his letter to Raleigh, Spenser explicates the text, "for your better light in reading thereof," and specifically terms its underlying aim that of teaching "doctrine by ensample." By invoking other examples of male heroism, Homer's Ulysses, Ariosto's Orlando, Virgil's Aeneas, he frames the assignment that he is giving his gentleman reader, the imitation of Spenser's Arthur, in the familiar terms of a pedagogic exercise. The work is similar to the medieval texts discussed earlier in this chapter, not only because of its structure as a spiritual pilgrimage, but also because of its use of the mirror as a metaphor for the inspirational example, for instance that of Queen Elizabeth, whose mind Spenser compares to "a mirrour sheene" (6.proem.6). Yet Spenserian allegory is unmistakably a product of contemporary humanist culture. In *The Faerie Queene*, putting one's self in peril of damnation, swerving from the true path, has a strictly gendered meaning: to stray is to turn womanish, to abandon one's masculine role, to lay by one's armor to recline in the shade.

Arthur's observation, "Full hard it is . . . to read aright" (1.9.6), governs the narrative of Book 1 in which repeated hermeneutic errors land Redcross in trouble. It is through the process of learning to differentiate between allegorical representations of Truth and Falsehood that Redcross emerges at the end of the book as an exemplary reader and gentleman. Being fooled by Duessa, the "great maistresse" of the art of deception is part of his education. In his interactions with her, Redcross repeatedly fails to perform the single analytic procedure required of him: "to descry the crafty cunning traine, / By which deceipt doth maske in visour faire . . . / To seeme like Truth, whose shape she well can faine" (1.7.1). It is for this reason that Redcross' denunciation of Fidessa/ Duessa at the end of Book 1 is not anti-climactic. Earlier Una forced Duessa to perform a kind of semiotic striptease; in that scene in Canto 8, she exposed Fidessa's "true" identity by revealing the discrepancy between signifier and signified, between Fidessa's youthful exterior and the hidden wrinkles and sagging breasts that identify her as Duessa: she that does seem not she. It is not until Canto 12, however, that Redcross himself demonstrates the critical acumen to distinguish Truth from Seeming Truth. The language of strength and weakness employed by Redcross suggests that his failure to descry Duessa's cunning was emasculating. It allowed his "weaker sight" to be overcome by her "strong" arts (1.12.32). Redcross' inability to interpret signs accurately brought him to the subservient position Una laments when she sees him pale and gaunt in Orgoglio's dungeon; what evil star, she asks, has "berobbed" him of his "selfe" and given him the sickly hew which mars his "manly looks" (1.8.42). It is only when Redcross demonstrates that he no longer confuses Deception with Faith that he is equipped to identify Fidessa as "this false woman," "the falsest Dame on ground," and "most false Duessa" (1.12.32).

The process by which Redcross comes into his own, both as a reader and as a man, reproduces what was supposed to be the normative development of a schoolboy under humanist tutelage. In his "first aduenture," as Una refers to it (1.1.27), in which Error wraps him in her train, and in other moments, Redcross survives only with Una's help; he would have killed himself with the knife that Despair handed him if Una had not knocked it from his hand. However, through those experiences, Redcross matures; he acquires the self-sufficiency that humanists spoke of cultivating in students. Erasmus explains that if you put students through a rigorous set of exercises seven or eight times, "then they will begin 'to swim without cork,' to quote Horace, and it will be sufficient to supply the bare subject of the exercise, and no longer necessary, as with infants, to be constantly putting predigested food into their mouths."[93] In the final combat, the encounter toward which all of Book 1 moves, Redcross shows that he has learned self-sufficient bravery, the hallmark of a heroic man, in the jubilant moment in which he stands alone to slay the dragon that had spread fear over the land. Spenser stresses that Redcross does not backslide again. At the beginning of Book 2, the same traps that Archimago had laid for Redcross before now fail to deceive him; "so wise and warie was the knight / By triall of his former harmes and cares, / That he describe, and shonned still his slight" (2.1.4). Spenser's use of "describe" to praise Redcross' new acumen, the same word that he used earlier to indicate his lack of discernment, confirms this view of Redcross as the praiseworthy pupil who grows into wisdom through repeated effort and trial and acquires strength from his ability as a reader of signs.

While he does not mention her in his letter to Raleigh, Spenser is concerned also with fashioning the gentlewoman reader, whom he addresses directly in Books 3 and 6. Her task is set forth in the story of Serena, Calepine's companion in Book 6, who acquires the standing of a virtuous gentlewoman as she figuratively learns to read. The interpretive technique she exemplifies originated in works such as Juan Luis Vives' *The Instruction of a Christian Woman*. This conduct manual, translated into English by Richard Hyrde with editorial oversight from Thomas More, defines what and how women should read. Vives recommends reading, along with sewing and spinning, as a positive alternative to playing cards, thinking lustful thoughts, or talking with one's gossips: "womans thought is swyfte, and for the most parte unstable, walkyng and wandrynge out from home . . . Therfore redyng were the best, and therunto I gyve them counsaile specially."[94] The form of reading recommended here, devised specifically for women, does not involve the complex hermeneutical operations laid out by M. N. in his translation of Marguerite Porete's *Mirouer*. Its function is not to teach readers, regardless of gender, to convert blasphemous thoughts to benign ones but rather to quarantine female readers from all impurity from the start.

Spenser adopts the stance of a conduct manual author in apostrophes addressed to his gentlewomen readers. In Book 6, he warns them to distance themselves from the example set by Mirabella. Speaking directly to "ye gentle Ladies," he admonishes them, "Ensample take of *Mirabellaes* case, / Who from the high degree of happy state, / Fell into wretched woes, which she repented late" (6.8.2). "Taking ensample," as Vives defines the procedure for women, is very different from the hermeneutic procedure of "descrying cunning." While both men and women were supposed to learn from examples, Spenser's female reader is enjoined to refrain from the bad conduct of Mirabella and to adopt the passive obedience of Pastorella. Imitating in actual deeds, not merely in thought and attitude, is a task for the male reader alone. He is challenged to enact the willful heroism of Arthur. Humanist emphasis on the demeanor of women, rather than their actions, extended to the task of interpretation as well. The female reader was supposed to focus attention on cultivating mental attitudes, not on making critical evaluations. Vives expressly tells women not to attempt to distinguish between Truth and Seeming Truth: "The woman ought nat to folowe her owne jugement, lest whan she hath but a lyght entryng in lernyng, she shuld take false for true, hurtful in stede of holsome, folishe and pevyshe for sad and wyse."[95] Instead of learning to differentiate between Truth and Seeming Truth, the virtuous female reader is taught to *be* Truth herself. In Vives' words, a young woman should "be in dede as she sheweth demure . . . bothe let her seme so and be so."[96] A century later, Richard Brathwait admonished the female readers of *The English Gentlewoman* in a similar fashion: "You are to be really, what you appeare outwardly."[97]

In *The Faerie Queene*, Spenser teaches his gentlewoman reader the supposed virtues of her sex by coding Pastorella as commendable and Mirabella as blameworthy. Pastorella is that catalogue of adjectives listed in Vives' book: "demure, humble, sobre, shamfast, chaste, honeste and vertuous."[98] The Angel in the House, she obeys her father, herds sheep, makes dinner, clears the table, spurns lower-class suitors and chooses knightly Calidore instead. Mirabella, on the other hand, is the Duessa to this Una. If Pastorella's "virtue" is submission, Mirabella's "vice" is defiance. Her name, a play on "rebellious," marks Mirabella as "damned to endure this direfull smart, / For penaunce of [her] proud and hard rebellious hart" (6.8.19).

Serena learns to despise and dispraise unvirtuous female models only after a bad encounter with the Blatant Beast. In Canto 3, she anticipates Milton's Eve by getting in trouble after she leaves the company of her mate to "wander" alone:

> The faire *Serena* . . .
> Allur'd with myldnesse of the gentle wether,
> And plesaunce of the place, the which was dight
> With diuers flowres distinct with rare delight;
> Wandred about the fields, as liking led
> Her wauering lust after her wandring sight,
> To make a garland to adorne her hed,
> Without suspect of ill or daungers hidden dred.
>
> All sodainely out of the forrest nere
> The *Blatant Beast* forth rushing vnaware,
> Caught her thus loosely wandring here and there,
> And in his wide great mouth away her bare.   (6.3.23–4)

Vives' charge that "Womans thought is . . . unstable, walkyng and wandrynge out from home" is enacted literally in this scene: Serena strays physically and mentally from the way prescribed. Spenser emphasizes the illicit nature of Serena's perambulation by referring to it three times as an act of "wandering" and by giving her nature-walk sexual associations. Serena can't admire the flowers without Spenser characterizing her as being "allur'd with mildness . . . and plesaunce" and "led" by "wauering lust." If Redcross' mistake is having made wrong choices in the world, Serena's is having ventured out into the world at all.

From the wanderer of Canto 3 whose sexually suspect behavior is linked with subsequent suffering, Serena develops into an exemplary gentlewoman reader in Canto 8. The anxiety that she displays upon encountering Mirabella offers insight into the kind of reader-response that Spenser demands of his female reader:

> faire *Serena* . . . fled fast away, afeard
> Of villany to be to her inferd:
> So fresh the image of her former dread,
> Yet dwelling in her eye, to her appeard,

That euery foote did tremble, which did tread,
And euery body two, and two she foure did read.   (6.8.31)

Spenser does not explain why the sight of Mirabella being beaten up by
Scorn and Disdain should cause Serena to fear that she, too, will be
accused of "villainy." Timias was also wounded by the Blatant Beast,
and yet he responds by trying to save Mirabella, not by running away.
Serena's flight from Mirabella provides a pictorial representation of the
interpretive technique recommended to female readers: "Ensample take
of Mirabellaes case." For the gentlewoman reader, "taking ensample"
involves inferring that the blame or virtue assigned to the female model
before her is transferable; she cannot afford to make the mistakes which,
for Redcross, are part of learning. Her task is not to differentiate
between Mirabella and Pastorella but to shun Mirabella and to be
Pastorella. Like Serena, she is supposed to match "the image of her
former dread" with the image of Mirabella before her, to juxtapose
herself with the figure of a bad woman and to fear that she may be
tainted by association. Ironically, Serena's misreading, the double-vision
which distorts her view, proves that she is reading correctly. Her terror
leads her to interpret the appearance of Mirabella, Scorn, and Disdain as
more dangerous than it actually is: "That every foote did tremble, which
did tread, / And every body two, and two she foure did read." Serena
"reads" every figure before her as two figures and every two figures as
four. Magnifying threats to a disproportionate extent, fearing social
stigma as a casually transmittable disease, and withdrawing into seclusion in consequence, Serena proves herself as a gentlewoman and as a
reader.

The dichotomy established between Spenser's gentleman and gentlewoman reader is meant to be as immutable as the two parts, one
triangular and the other round, of the foundation of the House of
Temperance, "The one imperfect, mortall, foeminine; / Th'other immortal, perfect, masculine" (2.9.22). Gender applies to the reader as it
does to Truth and Time. Nonetheless, the poem acknowledges that there
is a cost to maintaining sexual division in all realms, to modelling selves
on the basis of bifurcating the universe. This is an implicit theme of Book
2. If Book 1 is a triumphant panegyric to the pedagogic value of
humanist self-fashioning, then Book 2 is a sobering commentary on its
side-effects. It exposes a fundamental inconsistency in humanist doctrine
that marks the limits of its instructional claims. Humanism proffers the
gentleman full autonomy predicated on absolute difference. His superior
status, his right to rule over inferiors, derives from his incontrovertible
distinction from them. A gentleman who subjects himself to others is less

than a gentleman. Yet, paradoxically, he can achieve mastery only by being mastered himself. Guyon's failure to exhibit self-reliant agency, his inadequacy and curious passivity, suggests that the celebrated autonomy of Renaissance man lay not in freedom of action, as theorists claimed, but in social superiority.

Jacopo Sadoleto, the reform cardinal and accomplished Latin scholar, inadvertently exposes this tension between humanist promises and methods when he discusses the importance of students' motivation. In *De Pueris Recte Instituendis* ("On the Proper Instruction of Boys"), Sadoleto draws a distinction between two forms of habit, "disciplined training," the kind of habit imposed by others, on the one hand, and, on the other hand, the habit that is "our own personal choice, virtue." The nephew in the dialogue comprehends, correctly according to Sadoleto, that what separates the two is that discipline is constraining while virtue is liberating: "Now I think I see the difference between these two kinds of habit, the one imposed from without and bearing the impress of another's will, without initiative, almost lifeless, the phantom of a real habit, a mere picture pencilled on a tablet that is outside oneself: the other the true offspring and very product of reason itself, acting designedly, conscious of its own function and duty, and capable of maintaining its existence as the former type of habit never is."[99] Almost lifeless, without initiative, a mere picture pencilled on a tablet: this is Sir Guyon himself. And yet, the difference between Guyon and a figure such as Arthur, Spenser's preeminent example of manhood, is not the source of constraint, which is imposed from without, in both cases by types of humanist pedagogues, the Palmer and Merlin. As Arthur remembers from his youth, his teacher, like Guyon's, "had charge my discipline to frame, / And Tutours nouriture to ouersee" (1.9.5). The difference is that where Arthur assimilates his instruction comfortably, Sir Guyon stumbles and chafes. Sprezzatura in Arthur looks like "personal choice," obdurance in Guyon like lack of initiative. The fiction in Sadoleto's argument is that humanist training grants the male initiate a power of rational decision-making without making him subject to the will of another, that one under the "impress of another's will" is really "acting designedly," that dictated discipline is inner "Virtue," constraint really freedom. Sadoleto excludes coercion from his picture of true humanist education because to do otherwise would be to negate his definition of the educated man as a free subject.

Rather than gloss over the importance of discipline to the formation of masculine *virtù*, Spenser invokes those very terms to describe his poem in pedagogic terms as an exercise in "vertuous and gentle discipline." His insistence on the ambiguity of the gentleman's position is a response to the complicating factor of having a queen as head of state. Like the Elizabethan courtier, elevated in rank but driven to face-saving acts of chivalry before his female ruler, the Spenserian gentleman is at once master and subject. Sir Guyon, the hero of Book 2, rights the gender inversion implicit in the poem's elaborate tribute to Elizabeth by distancing himself from the feminine and by vanquishing the Bower's seductive queen; however, he does so only by making himself subordinate to his humanist teacher.

The image of horse and rider introduced in Canto 4 highlights this predicament of Spenser's gentleman:

> But he the rightfull owner of that steed,
>   Who well could menage and subdew his pride,
>   The whiles on foot was forced for to yeed,
>   With that blacke Palmer, his most trusty guide;
>   Who suffred not his wandring feet to slide.
>   But when strong passion, or weake fleshlinesse
>   Would from the right way seeke to draw him wide,
>   He would through temperance and steadfastnesse,
> Teach him the weak to strengthen, & the strong suppresse.   (2.4.2)

Commonly, the metaphor of breaking a horse was used to describe the gaining of control over social inferiors. In William Whately's marriage sermon, the horse metaphor defines the position of wife: "It is laudable, commendable, a note of a vertuous woman, a dutifull wife, when shee submits her-selfe with quietnesse, cheerefully, even as a wel-broken horse turnes at the least turning, stands at the least check of the riders bridle, readily going and standing as he wishes that sits upon his backe."[100] Shakespeare's Antony draws on the same cliché imagery found in the sermon to comment ironically on the impracticality of requiring husbands to enforce absolute female subordination: "As for my wife, / I would you had her spirit in such another. / The third o'th' world is yours, which with a snaffle, / You may pace easy, but not such a wife."[101] Achieving mastery over himself, as he has proven capable of doing over his horse, depends upon Guyon accepting constraints on himself, the "snaffle" or bridle invoked by Antony, that a gentleman only should be able to imagine imposing on others. Spenser's description of Guyon's inner self slides from Guyon mastering his horse to the Palmer mastering Guyon, directing his steps and reining in his animal desires. The pedagogue does not confer unfettered freedom upon his charge; he teaches him self-control and control over others. Sir Guyon is a gentleman not because he is an independent agent but because he is a superior subject. This is the lesson he must learn, both intellectually and viscerally.

Like Redcross, Guyon encounters a series of signs over the course of his journey and is rated according to his ability to read them correctly. At the outset, he even meets up with Redcross' old adversary, Duessa, and similarly falls prey to her ruses. In the passage that brings Guyon to the Bower of Bliss, the Palmer explicitly turns the sea voyage into a reading lesson; the broken remains of ships on the Rock of Reproach, their ribs stuck through with human cadavers, are so many signs for Guyon to interpret:

> The Palmer seeing them in safetie past,
>   Thus said; behold th'ensamples in our sights,
>   Of lustfull luxurie and thriftlesse wast:
>   What now is left of miserable wights,
>   Which spent their looser daies in lewd delights,
>   But shame and sad reproch, here to be red,
>   By these rent reliques, speaking their ill plights? (2.12.9)

The "ensamples" singled out by the Palmer to be "red" (read) indicate the peril of the journey which takes them through the Gulf of Greediness, the Rock of Reproach, the Wandering Islands, the Quicksand of Unthriftiness, and the Whirlpool of Decay. Along the way, they also encounter sea monsters, mermaids, swarms of birds, and herds of wild beasts. However, unlike the interpretive puzzles in Book 1, which are about dissimulation, a phony Una cloned from liquid air, in Book 2, the signs placed in Guyon's path are characterized more by allure than fakery. His obstacle course is more psychological and emotive than hermeneutic.

The risk to Guyon is not that he will be tricked by women but that he will be moved by them. He must learn to harden his emotions rather than to spy out duplicity. Self-control founded on impassivity is what Guyon will need in order to gain the upper hand over Acrasia and accomplish his mission. His power to resist must be greater than hers to entice him. This capacity enables him to master a technique of interpretation that is antithetical to an intuitive apprehension of the text. The humanist method of reading, like its Augustinian antecedent, was a trained and structured approach to the text; it was intended to position the male subject correctly in relation to inferiors and superiors by inculcating a systematized procedure along with the values and interests it encoded. The vaunted self-mastery that Guyon acquires in this book is not personal volition controlled by individual reason but rather the suppression of autonomous judgment in deference to the greater authority of the Palmer. Guyon's training in masculine reader-response techniques aligns him with the humanist enterprise and prepares him to take his eventual place within the hierarchy ordered by it.

While the muscular strength of the boatman and mental acuity of the Palmer get the three men beyond physical barriers, Guyon's ability to check his immediate responses is required to take them safely past traps designed to appeal to their emotions and senses. In an earlier scene, the Palmer tells Guyon, who is "moued" by the plight of a pagan fighter he has just defeated, "thy causeless ruth represse, / Ne let thy stout hart melt in pitty vayne" (2.5.24). During the voyage and in the Bower of Bliss, the figures that threaten to arouse Guyon, emotionally or sexually, are female. Phoedria, who tried to seduce him earlier, returns in her magic gondola to tease him with "vaine allurements," a beautiful damsel calls out in distress, and the mermaids sing to him; once in the Bower, he is beset by visions of naked women wrestling in their bath and by the sight of Acrasia embracing a new lover. Repeatedly, the Palmer intervenes, as Spenser specifies, to "represse" Guyon's responses. When Guyon wants to help the maiden, the Palmer tells him that her cries for help are only intended to sway his feelings, his "stubborne hart t'affect with fraile infirmity" (2.12.28). When Guyon asks to hear the mermaids, the Palmer "from that vanity, / With temperate aduice discounselled, / That they it past" (2.12.34). And when Guyon reveals his rising passion in the Bower, the Palmer "much rebukt those wandring eyes of his" (2.12.69). The threat to Guyon is loss of masculine potency and privilege. A pagan knight with less self-control, waylaid first by a flock of maidens and then by Phoedria, did "To weake wench . . . yeeld his martiall might" (2.6.8), an experience that leaves him a "womanish weake knight" (2.5.36). Artegall suffers a similar fate in Book 5; after conquering an Amazon in battle, he sees her beauty revealed for the first time, throws down his sword, and allows himself to be led away, weaponless, emasculated, a woman's thrall. To fall for a woman is to fall to her level, to be weakened, to lose authority and standing.

From this danger arises the need to cultivate impassivity in the male subject. And yet, even as Spenser impresses this upon us as a necessity, he also acknowledges damage done in the process. Guyon lacks, if one can say this about an allegorical figure, the human qualities of Redcross, his uncertainty, openness, ardor. Guyon always seems to have the Palmer's hand on his shoulder. We get a fleeting glimpse of personality when he first enters into the Bower of Bliss:

> Much wondred *Guyon* at the faire aspect
> Of that sweet place, yet suffred no delight
> To sincke into his sence, nor mind affect,
> But passed forth, and lookt still forward right,
> Bridling his will, and maistering his might.   (2.12.53)

Spenser is less than forthcoming in this description of the hero's reaction, impulsive and then "bridled." Guyon can experience wonder only if his mind and senses have been affected, yet Spenser argues that he "suffred no delight." From the passage itself, it seems not that Guyon is unmoved but rather that, like a good horseman or a good horse, however one chooses to read the image in the light of its ambivalent earlier use, he is emotionally either in or under control.

Spenser implies, however, that that remoteness masks a sensibility open to esthetic pleasure. We see this in the single moment in Book 2 in which Guyon takes initiative in setting their course and asks the boatman to row more slowly so that he can hear the sirens' song meld with the wind:

> The whiles sweet *Zephirus* lowd whisteled
> His treble, a straunge kinde of harmony;
> Which *Guyons* senses softly tickeled,
> That he the boateman bad row easily,
> And let him heare some part of their rare melody.   (2.12.33)

The Palmer, of course, overrules Guyon at this point, as he will continue to do even when they are standing in Acrasia's Bower. We will never see Guyon emerge out from under that tutelage. By Erasmian standards, his formation as a male subject remains incomplete. He will not learn to swim without cork or to eat without being spoonfed; even as late in the narrative as Book 3, Guyon will turn to the Palmer when the Amazon heroine Britomart knocks him off his horse. Spenser's knights react violently when others resist the imposition of reformatory discipline; in Book 2, when a pagan knight, defeated and disarmed, refuses to renounce his "miscreaunce," Arthur angrily cuts the man's head off (2.8.51–2). But it seems that it is not only recalcitrant subjects – women, rebels, conquered peoples – that struggle against being fashioned. In that moment in the boat when we see Guyon straining to hear a song not quite audible over the sea, we find resistance within the conquerer himself. Guyon is not the automaton he seems; his senses can be tickled. It appears that only the Palmer's hovering presence, not any inner virtue, keeps Guyon's capacity for wonder from overruling the capacity for non-response on which his safety, his identity, depends.

The appeal for help from a doleful maid on an island, one of the events in the voyage, bears out this notion. Unlike the mermaids, said to kill weak travelers, or Phoedria, whose provocative "dalliance" Guyon disparages (2.6.21), the anonymous lady on the island is not described in a negative light. She appears to be simply a damsel in distress, much like the lady whose sad story at the beginning of Book 2 strengthens Guyon's resolve to destroy Acrasia. In spite of his responsibility as a knight to respond to such pleas, Guyon leaves the island lady behind not because he has any evidence for distrusting her but only because the Palmer tells him she is dangerous. The sheer gratuitousness of this incident underscores the point that unfeeling, over and above any knightly code, is essential in a gentleman whose responsibilities in serving the state might well contradict chivalric ideals. In his account of his own experiences as a colonial administrator in Ireland, Spenser laments the charge made against Lord Grey to Queen Elizabeth, "that he was a bloodye man: and regarded not the lyfe of her subjectes, noe more then dogges," on the grounds that "the necessitie of that present state of thinges enforced him to that violence, and almost changed his verie naturall disposition."[102] In effect, the self-transformation described by Spenser in *A View of the Present State of Ireland* as an after-effect of repressive action is portrayed in *The Faerie Queene* as its necessary precondition.

It has been observed that the culminating violence enacted in Guyon's destruction of the Bower of Bliss is one of the "great cruxes" of Renaissance literature. For Stephen Greenblatt, the episode raises the question of why, in this fictional instance as in historical campaigns to eradicate Native American culture in the New World, Gaelic language and customs in Ireland, and the Catholic religion in England, esthetic pleasure elicits brutality as a response. He argues that "the Bower of Bliss must be destroyed not because its gratifications are unreal but because they threaten 'civility' – civilization – which for Spenser is achieved only through renunciation and the constant exercise of power."[103] The reading of *The Faerie Queene* offered here focuses on the ways in which mastery over self and others, inflected and justified by an insistence on gender difference, was inculcated through pedagogical practices of reading and writing that humanists made part of a national grammar school education. "Doctrine by ensample," the technique that Spenser draws on to fashion his reader, served to instill in the male pupil aptitudes and preferences befitting a gentleman and to initiate him into a network of loyalties and obligations from which he derived his position as one.

That training, Keith Wrightson concludes, fostered "the development of a greater degree of cultural cohesion among the English ruling class."[104] Mulcaster defined his aim in writing *The Training up of Children* as precisely that of helping to implement "some one good and profitable uniformitie" in the country's educational system.[105] Standardization, imposed by the state and facilitated by the new technology of printing, insured that the schooling from which women were excluded was both more widespread and more uniform than was the case in the fifteenth century. It made the impact of excluding women and lower-class men from the institutions responsible for producing that cohesion even more significant.[106] In *The Faerie Queene*, this goal of a monopoly on education animates the Palmer's mission against Acrasia. What is at stake in the duel between Guyon's stern pedagogue and the Circean witch in their battle to form and transform the world is who will have license to fashion the minds of men. The vividness of the narrative recounted by Amavia in the opening canto of Book 2 obscures the role that the Palmer played in initiating the quest against Acrasia. Misleadingly, Spenser makes Amavia's tale of the murder of her husband appear to have motivated the campaign to destroy the Bower of Bliss. This is the impression that one gets from the gruesome ritual performed at the gravesite of Amavia and her husband in which Guyon cuts locks of hair from their bodies, daubs the hair with blood and earth, throws the mixture back to the grave, and swears an angry oath to revenge their deaths. It is only afterward at Medina's castle, almost in passing, that Guyon relates that the Palmer had on an earlier occasion, before Guyon had started on his journey, lodged a complaint against Acrasia at the court of the Fairy Queen:

> There this old Palmer shewed himselfe that day,
> And to that mighty Princesse did complaine
> Of grieuous mischiefes, which a wicked Fay
> Had wrought, and many whelmd in deadly paine,
> Whereof he crau'd redresse.   (2.2.43)

The nature of the Palmer's grievance is left calculatedly vague; however, the description of her actions in Book 2 places Acrasia in direct competition with the Palmer as a shaper of minds. Spenser's emphasis on the near pubescence of her lover, whose "tender lips the downy heare / Did now but freshly spring" (2.12.79), foregrounds a concern central to the epic as a whole: who will instruct the youth of the nation?

The Palmer's grudge against Acrasia was rehearsed in more prosaic terms in cases of complaints against unlicensed schoolmistresses in early modern England. William Watts, for example, a licensed schoolmaster at St. Nicholas-at-Wade on the Isle of Thanet, protested to the Archdeacon that a Mistress Foster of Chislet, "doth teach school, namely to write and read, to the prejudice of me and my license, in regard that all or most of her scholars are of the parish of St. Nicholas; wherefore I humbly desire that she may be inhibited from teaching."[107] The attempt of a schoolmaster to protect his license, a local and personal affair, stands for a larger effort, supported by the Tudor State and Church, to install a specific category of male teacher, distinguished by his erudition in classical learning, as master and sole authority of the early modern grammar school. Though male pedagogues tolerated or even advocated allowing women to care for the "petties" or youngest children, they were zealous in their drive to reserve prestigious positions in the profession for themselves and their protégés. As we have already seen, this sidelining of women, including those who had been employed as teachers in convents prior to the dissolution, was both aided and legitimated by the replacement of the image of Anne or Mary as teacher by the image of Jesus in that role. The gender dimensions of the conflict over pedagogic authority, domestic and petty as they appear in contemporary court cases, shape Spenser's account of the Bower as much as the exotic imagery of his classical sources.

Acrasia vies with the Palmer over competing pedagogical projects. She is dangerous because she seeks to undo the Palmer's civilizing function. "These seeming beasts," Acrasia's victims, "are men indeed, / Whom this Enchauntresse hath *transformed* thus" (2.12.85) [italics added]. The Palmer reverses that process and turns them back into men. In Spenser's lexicon, such acts are coded according to the prefix attached to the root word; "misshape," "transform," "deface," and "deform" connote destructive (female) transformation while the term "reform" refers to its constructive (masculine) corollary. Acrasia calls the spirits out of men whom then "she does *transforme* to monstrous hewes, / And horribly *misshapes* with vgly sightes" (2.5.27). "Great pittie was to see," Spenser says of Acrasia's young lover, "Him his nobilitie so foule *deface*" (2.12.79). Like the mob of peasants that attacks the House of Temperance, "Vile caytiue wretches, ragged, rude, *deformd*," (2.9.13) the sea creatures that Acrasia sends across the ocean during Guyon's voyage are "dreadfull pourtraicts of *deformitee*" (2.12.23) and "*deformed* Monsters" (2.12.25) "with visages *deforme*" (2.12.24). Alternatively, Spenser tags the devastation initiated by Artegall in Book 5, an allegorization of England's repression of the Irish, as a constructive act:

> His studie was true Iustice how to deale . . .
> How to *reforme* that ragged common-weale . . .
> To search out those, that vsd to rob and steale,
> Or did rebell gainst lawfull gouernment;
> On whom he did inflict most grieuous punishment.   (5.12.26)

In his *View of the Present State of Ireland*, Spenser uses the same term when he argues on behalf of waging a remorseless, all-out military campaign against the Irish: "Yt must be foreseene and assured that after once entring into this course of *reformacion*, there bee afterwardes noe remorse or drawinge backe, for the sight of any such ruefull object as must thereupon follow nor for Compassion of theire Calamities."[108]

The term "reformation," which had a disciplinary as well as sectarian connotation, was used to describe actions ranging from the correction of a text to the suppression of rebellion, from the institution of justice to the razing of a church, from molding a wife to instructing a student.[109] In *The Institution of a Young Noble Man* (1607), a work which describes the tutors of young noblemen as "fathers of the minde," James Cleland says that these instructors should show "great diligence 1. in Forming. 2. *Reforming*" the boys in their tutelage.[110] The Palmer draws on all the powers contained in that single term, the reestablishment of good government, the transmission of proper education, and the chastening of the recalcitrant, in his effort to undo the transformation done by Acrasia: "Streight way he with his vertuous staffe them strooke, / And streight of beasts they comely men became" (2.12.86). Only the Palmer, a male pedagogue, a father of the mind, can reform what a malign female teacher has deformed.

The efficacy of the Palmer's instruction is tested in the final episode of the book. Based on our reading of Book 1, we expect at the end of Book 2 for Guyon to demonstrate what he has learned by facing his adversary in a climactic battle, to challenge Acrasia just as Redcross took on the dragon. Instead, it is the Palmer who weaves the net used to trap Acrasia; it is cast with his help and is magically fool-proof. Guyon himself faces only one test alone: not the conquest of the Bower but its vandalization. In the end, he slays no dragons. He chops down trees, demolishes buildings, sets grand halls on fire. He displays, in short, all the courage of a wrecking crew. But he does establish through that act of destruction that his reformation is complete, that he "changed his verie naturall disposition," as did Lord Grey, in order to fulfill his manly duty.

Greenblatt observes that the reader, taken up with the esthetic emotion of Spenser's lush imagery, can share in the experience of renunciation embodied in Guyon's act of razing the place to the ground.[111] Spenser the poet invites us to consider where we stand in relation to Guyon's sensual experience of the Bower and to his violent repudiation of that pleasure. But Spenser the pedagogue assigns us another, more specific challenge. Like the translator M. N., who presented his reader with a seemingly insoluble crux, a clearly heretical passage to be interpreted as true doctrine, as a test of the reader's orthodoxy, Spenser challenges his gentleman reader to prove his masculinity by not responding to a passage crafted to make him respond. In his choice of words in the passage, Spenser has coded the destruction as negative while at the same time declaring it to be positive:

> But all those pleasant bowres and Pallace braue,
> Guyon broke downe, with rigour pitilesse;

Ne ought their goodly workmanship might saue
Them from the tempest of his wrathfulnesse,
But that their blisse he turn'd to *balefulnesse*:
Their groues he feld, their gardins did *deface*,
Their arbers spoyle, their Cabinets suppresse,
Their banket houses burne, their buildings race,
And of the fairest late, now made the *fowlest* place.   (2.12.83)

The words attached to Guyon's act of destruction do not recall the Palmer's restorative powers but rather the harmful ones associated with sinister women and black magic. The "balefulnesse" of the ruins created by Guyon brings to mind Archimago's "baleful" books, Guyon's move to "deface" the gardens how Acrasia did "deface" her young lover, and the razed Bower, "now made the fowlest place," the "fowle" appearance of Duessa "with dong all fowly dight" (1.2.2, 2.12.79, 1.2.41, 1.8.48–9).

If we react negatively to the destruction of the Bower, it is not only because the richness of Spenser's description of it brings us to regret its loss; nor only because we have come to see in such a moment a vision of the actual terror being visited on colonized peoples in Ireland and the Americas; nor even because we know that Spenser, as Lord Grey's secretary, was among the English functionaries who oversaw the violence and legitimated it in verse. We react negatively also because Spenser himself, by linking Guyon's actions with Archimago, Acrasia, and Duessa, has inclined us to read the passage that way even as he tells us, paradoxically, to see the destruction as a good thing. We are not expected to reach that judgment based on our experience of the text. Rather, we are challenged to override our own understanding because Spenser, our Palmer, tells us to do so. If we have read the text correctly, we will be ready to renounce our immediate response to the destruction and accept it as what Spenser tells us it is: a critical component of the program of reformation, both of selves and institutions, based upon humanist principles that made possible the emergence of a modern society and empire. Fulfilling his initial promise to Raleigh, Spenser calls upon current theories of self-fashioning through disciplined reading in order to create the reliable, authoritative, and masculine subject needed to administer that new world.

IV

Enter D. Shaw pensiuely reading on his booke.[112]
He writes in his tables sometimes scratching his head, as pumping his Muse.[113]
Enter Ingen reading a letter, sits downe in a Chaire and stampes with his foote.[114]

She reads the letter, frownes and stamps.[115]
Hee dilivers her that letter which he found in the villaines pocket, to murder him, written by her brother. Shee starts in the reading.[116]
All the Lords peruse the Papers. They shew various countenances: Some seem to applaud the King, some pity Eulalia.[117]
Shews the paper to the States, they seem sorry.[118]
Rreades to her selfe. starts as yf afrighted, shakes wth feare. & speakes.[119]
Flower smiles reading the Letter, they snatch the Letter from each other.[120]

The playgoer, no less than the reader, was the object of extravagant fantasies about the power of texts to shape selves. In defense of the theatre, Thomas Heywood argues that it had been, from earliest antiquity, an instrument for the same civilizing process invoked by Spenser. Heywood attributes the greatness of classical antiquity to its public performance of plays and reminds us that the Greeks themselves found "no neerer or directer course to plant humanity and manners in the hearts of the multitude then to instruct them by moralized mysteries, what vices to avoyd, what vertues to embrace . . . which borne out as well by the wisedome of the Poet, as supported by the worth of the Actors, wrought such impression in the hearts of the plebe, that in such short space they excelled in civility and governement."[121] Like Spenser, Heywood advertises the benefits of his art in stock phrases from educational treatises. The difference is that the playwright, whose audience was far removed from Spenser's courtly circles, claims that his end is to fashion a plebian in virtuous and obedient discipline. In Heywood's account, the playwright stands in for Spenser's Palmer and the actor for his Arthur. For Stephen Gosson, by contrast, these same theatre professionals are more like mermaids singing men to their deaths. A former playwright turned sectarian critic, Gosson contends that plays bring audiences strange melodies to invade their ears, effeminate gestures to ravish their senses, and wanton speech to whet inordinate desire: "These by the privie entries of the eare, slip downe into the hart, & with gunshotte of affection gaule the minde, where reason and vertue should rule the roste."[122] The theatre, for Heywood a font of peace, order, and good government, was for Gosson a den of Acrasian debauchery.

Not surprisingly, the two men offer very different views of the role of the theatre in fashioning gender. Heywood envisions the theatre as an extension of the university for male playgoers, teaching them rhetoric and inspiring them to brave deeds, and as a kind of revival meeting for female playgoers, driving seemingly virtuous matrons to collapse in the aisles with confessions of hidden lurid crimes. To this end, he tells the story of a play performed at Lynn in Norfolk by the Earl of Sussex's

Men. The production of *The History of Friar Francis*, about a woman whose husband was murdered by her lover and who was subsequently haunted by his ghost, provoked a hysterical response from a female playgoer: "A townes-woman (till then of good estimation and report) finding her conscience (at this presentment) extremely troubled, suddenly skritched and cryd out Oh my husband, my husband! I see the ghost of my husband fiercely threatning and menacing me." The woman then confessed to having fallen in love with a young man and to having poisoned her husband. In a second case in Amsterdam, a travelling company of English comedians was performing a scene in which laborers kill a rival by driving a nail through his skull: "As the Actors handled this, the audience might on a sodaine understand an out-cry, and loud shrike in a remote gallery, and pressing about the place, they might perceive a woman of great gravity, strangely amazed, who with a distracted & troubled braine oft sighed out these words: Oh my husband, my husband!" After the play, when a church warden announced that he had discovered a skull pierced by a nail, the woman confessed that the skull was that of the husband she had murdered twelve years earlier. She was arraigned, condemned, and burned.[123]

For Gosson, the theatre has less in common with a university, church, or court of law than with a brothel. It weakens men by drawing them from warlike pursuits to pursue frivolous pastimes and assignations with prostitutes. Gosson portrays his own mistake of having written plays as that of succumbing to female temptation and apostrophizes the theatre as a mermaid. "Sith I have in my voyage suffred wrack with Ulisses," he writes, "and scrambled with life to the shore, stand from me Nausicaä with all thy traine, till I wipe the blot from my forhead, and with sweet springs wash away the salt froth that cleaves too my soule."[124] Rather than punish female lust, Gosson contends that the theatre incites it by representing "privie meetinges of bachelours and maidens on the stage" and by providing playgoers of both sexes with a common meeting place: "in our assemblies at playes in London, you shall see suche heaving, and shooving, suche ytching and shouldring, too sitte by women . . . [E]very wanton and his Paramour, every man and his Mistresse, every John and his Joan, every knave and his queane, are there first acquainted."[125]

Anxieties about female interest in plays were expressed even by those who did not have an anti-theatrical ax to grind. John Johnson, author of *The Academy of Love* (1641), claims to have heard from Cupid that Shakespeare himself "creepes into the womens closets about bed time." If, he concludes, "it were not for some of the old out-of-date Grandames (who are set over the rest as their tutoresses) the young Sparkish Girles would read in Shakespeere day and night."[126] In *The English Gentleman*, Richard Brathwait cites the story of a young gentlewoman who flouted convention as she lay on her deathbed. An avid playgoer, the woman refused to call upon God and addressed her last words instead to a character in Thomas Kyd's play *The Spanish Tragedy*. Brathwait warns male readers that they may suffer the same fate if they attend the theatre too frequently:

So as I much feare mee, when they shall be struck with sicknesse, and lie on their death-bed, it will fare with them as it fared with a young Gentlewoman within these few yeeres; who being accustomed in her health every day to see one Play or other, was at last strucke with a grievous sicknesse even unto death: during which time of her sicknesse, being exhorted by such Divines as were there present, to call upon God, that hee would in mercy looke upon her, as one deafe to their exhortation, continued ever crying, Oh Hieronimo, Hieronimo, methinks I see thee brave Hieronimo! Neither could shee be drawne from this with all their perswasions; but fixing her eyes intentively, as if she had seen Hieronimo acted, sending out a deepe sigh, she suddenly died.[127]

According to Brathwait, the gentlewoman's experience of playgoing enables her to resist the clergymen's efforts to dictate her last words. With her deathbed cry of "Oh Hieronimo, Hieronimo," she enacts a scene from a secular play in place of the scripted *ars moriendi* ritual which the divines urge her to perform.

There is some historical truth to both Heywood's and Gosson's arguments about the impact of the theatre on the construction of gender. The theatre, like the humanist classroom, was a site for identity formation and nationalist acculturation. Prince Hal's "reformation" in *1 Henry IV*, accomplished through his participation in subduing the rebellious Welsh, enacts the same process of masculine self-civilization that Sir Guyon undergoes in *The Faerie Queene*. The theatre celebrated many of the ideas about gender that passed for dogma in educational treatises and conduct manuals, and it helped to diffuse such views more widely. Yet, as Gosson feared, it also presented male and female characters behaving on stage in ways that directly contradicted humanist prescriptions. In addition to the romantic heroes and heroines singled out by Puritans, plays depicted alternative models of men and women as readers and writers and alternative models of identity for them to emulate than those found in didactic treatises. Plays opened the masculine monopoly on erudite learning up to scrutiny, explored how women's exclusion from full literacy was being contested, and staged the appropriation of humanist practices for unanticipated ends.

Shakespeare exploits this potential for creative contestation in his early comedy, *Love's Labour's Lost*. In that play, the principle encoded in

Spenser's separate addresses to his male and female readers, the appor-
tioning of literacy along gender lines, generates the "civil war of wits"
waged between Navarre and his men and the Princess and her women
(2.1.225). Unequal access to reading, in all its gradated forms, ranging
from an ability to decipher printed black letter texts to the ability to read
Latin and Greek in several penned scripts, worked to regulate the
distribution of social positions. This inequity is behind "the liberal
opposition" of their spirits that the Princess and her ladies voice in
response to Berowne's metaphor of women as books (5.2.715). Male and
female characters in Navarre struggle over who will occupy the subject
positions of interpreter and of sign. While the men exercise a monopoly
on the learning that authorizes one to assign values and to construct
categories, in short, to interpret and order the world, the women resist
being made into signs for their male counterparts to evaluate and classify.
They answer the men's attempts at imposing meaning with their own
virtuoso textual interpretations. The play reveals that what was at issue
in the early modern debate over who could read which texts and in what
manner was no less than the structure of society and the construction of
the self.

Reading is explicitly thematized in *Love's Labour's Lost*, both the
specific act, "painfully to pore upon a book," and hermeneutics more
generally, questions about signifiers and signifieds raised through jokes
such as Costard's gleeful discovery that the word "remuneration" is the
Latin word for three farthings and that "guerdon" means one shilling
(1.1.74, 3.1.134, 3.1.156). The play also inquires into the ways in which
unequal access to books and schools is linked with social differences. The
two lower social groups represented in the play – the village schoolmaster
and curate, and the plain countryfolk – derive their place in the world
from their relation to the erudite humanism flaunted by Navarre and his
entourage. All the play's male characters lose or gain status according to
their perceived standing in the new learning: the King and courtiers who
break into sonnets upon a whim, Holofernes and Nathaniel who speak in
the canned phrases of grammar school textbooks, Dull who is put down
by the schoolmaster and curate for lacking the faulty Latin grammar of
which they are so proud. At one point, the village schoolmaster
challenges the reputation of a courtier by disputing the quality of his
sonnets: "I will prove those verses to be very unlearned, neither
savouring of poetry, wit, nor invention" (4.2.145–6). In the same scene,
the curate vaunts his supposed knowledge by disparaging the ignorance
of his inferior, a constable: "For as it would ill become me to be vain,
indiscreet, or a fool, / So were there a patch set on learning, to see *him* in
a school" (4.2.27–8).

However, as much as male characters contend with one another along class lines, the play centers upon the competition between men and women. The written oath to which the King and his courtiers put their signatures in the opening scene establishes Navarre as an intellectual center and bars women from entrance to it (upon penalty of having their tongues cut out). That piece of paper which defines study as a male domain drives the comedy from its opening scene to its anti-comic Jack-Hath-Not-Jill conclusion. The men are comfortably lodged in their "little academe" (1.1.13); yet the King, as Boyet observes to the Princess, "means to lodge you in the field" (2.1.85). Throughout the play, this spatial segregation of Navarre's academy, women outside and men inside, rankles the female visitors. The Princess, in the final act, redefines the boundary drawn by the King to ban her from his court as the line that divides him from her love: "This field shall hold me, and so hold your vow" (5.2.345). The problem posed by the creation of Navarre's academy, as the Princess serves notice, is not merely academic. Whether the issue is sovereignty over Aquitaine or lack of hospitality, the resolution of disputes depends in large measure upon who is allowed to assign meanings to signs, to "prove" the veracity of a contention, and thereby to affect the outcome of events. Rather than acceding to their marginalization on the periphery of Navarre's court, the Princess and her friends successfully argue on behalf of their own contrary reading of the men's oath and send them into exile beyond the "forbidden gates" formerly barred against the women (2.1.26). Both in their initial oath and in their later reinterpretation of it, the King and his "bookmen" elevate themselves, at the expense of women, by making scholarly reading an exclusively male perquisite (4.2.31); in staging their Mock-for-Mock anti-masque, the women, in turn, reject the subject position of text assigned to them and assert instead the prerogative accorded to male readers to interpret texts and to claim authority for the meanings they construct.

The contractual oath signed by the King, Berowne, Longaville, and Dumaine in the opening scene consists of the following "statutes": "Not to see ladies, study, fast, not sleep" (1.1.48). While not seeing ladies is presented as part of a general ascetic routine that includes fasting and depriving themselves of sleep, the rest of the scene shows that what motivates the men to study is a desire not for self-denial but for social distinction. The purpose of reading books is to know "things hid and barred . . . from common sense." That, says the King, "is study's god-like recompense" (1.1.57–8). As Pierre Bourdieu argues, cultural distinctions between highbrow and lowbrow, the noble and the vulgar, are means of reinforcing social stratification. These distinctions, which do not so much create as solidify and codify differences, institutionalize class and gender differences by legitimating official classifications and the distribution of positions within social structures.[128] In classifying common sense as common and study as god-like, the King classifies himself, too, as a member of the cultural elite that defines and justifies its exclusivity on the basis of cultural preferences. In categorizing women as inimical to study, he implies that god-like distinction accrues to himself and his male "fellow scholars" alone (1.1.17).

"No woman," the King proclaims, "shall come within a mile of my court . . . on pain of losing her tongue" (1.1.119–20, 122). The rest of the scene is taken up with the chastisement of Costard for having violated the newly instituted law by seeing Jaquenetta. Though class is an important dimension of the courtiers' bid for distinction, the punishment proposed for female violators of the law (a shrew joke contributed by Longaville), the mile-wide corridor stipulated by the King, and the focus on rebuking Costard put the emphasis on the problem of maintaining masculine privilege. The new interpretation of the oath that Berowne offers in act 4 reinforces, rather than dissolves, distinctions between men and women based on unequal access to learning. After the King and courtiers have all confessed to being in love, Berowne tries to absolve them of the crime of breaking their pledge by arguing that its terms were impossible to fulfill. After reiterating the text they signed, he manages to reduce its provisions from four promises to two: to study and not to see women. He then collapses those clauses into one; seeing women, it turns out, is a form of study:

> From women's eyes this doctrine I derive.
> They sparkle still the right Promethean fire.
> They are the books, the arts, the academes,
> That show, contain, and nourish all the world.   (4.3.324–7)

The sonnets which the four men addressed to their loves provide the grounds for Berowne's comparison of women with books. His reasoning draws on the humanist notion that facility in composition depends upon having an adequate supply of quotations stored up from one's reading. Berowne concludes that women are like books in the sense that they induce fits of sonneteering in the men who desire them: "Never durst poet touch a pen to write / Until his ink were tempered with love's sighs" (4.3.320–1). Armado, like the king and his courtiers, styles himself as a writer when he falls in love: "Devise wit, write pen, for I am for whole volumes, in folio" (1.2.163–4). After observing that the Princess and her ladies inspire more "fiery" verses than books and are therefore *like* books, he proceeds to argue that women *are* books.[129]

The women-as-books metaphor does not signal a reversal of the men's exclusionary policy. The purpose of the oath had been to declare learned reading off-limits to women. Though Berowne's interpretive sleight of hand has nullified Navarre's edict, it has not broken the links between men, learned reading, and social distinction established in the document. No more than a commonplace out of a commonplace book, like the epithet overheard in conversation that Nathaniel copies into his "table-book" (5.1.14), his "women = books" formula leaves intact the asymmetry instituted by establishment of Navarre's academy. Women are the objects of inscription and interpretation; only men are "authors" (4.3.333). From the first, the contract was less about the Latin tomes being stockpiled in Navarre than it was about the subject positions from which it is possible to use texts to construct the social world and distinguish oneself in it. The point of the comparison between women and books is that it enables Berowne to argue that the contract he and his companions signed was inherently impossible to carry out: "we have made a vow to study, lords, / And in that vow we have forsworn our books" (4.3.292–3). If women are books, it is a contradiction in terms for men to consecrate themselves to books and abjure women.

Berowne's interpretation, however, is at odds with that of the Princess and her ladies. In assuming the roles of readers and in successfully imposing their explication of the oath on its male signatories, they make good on the warning that the Princess initially issued to the King: "We arrest your word" (2.1.158). Self-deputized, the women recapture the original meaning which the men first assigned to the text, to the detriment of the women, and which they altered only when their wishes changed. One of the layered ironies of the men's monopoly on study is that the women are acute readers, in some cases more so than the men. When the Princess reads Armado's letter, she critiques the modish language that had so charmed the King and courtiers: "What plume of feathers is he that indited this letter? / What vane? What weathercock? Did you ever hear better?" (4.1.90–1). Similarly, Rosaline demonstrates that she has the critical sensibility to judge a poem's prosody and the aptness of its imagery. She praises the meter of Berowne's verse (the "numbers," she says, are "true") but faults the exaggerated imagery he uses to depict her: "I am compared to twenty thousand fairs. / O, he hath drawn my picture in his letter" (5.2.35, 37–8). Rosaline's appraisal, as Berowne concurs, fits a metaphor that the King employs in his sonnet to the Princess: "No drop but as a coach doth carry thee, / So ridest thou triumphing in my woe" (4.3.30–1). To refute the King's protestation that he is not in love, Berowne jokingly refers to that awkward image of the Princess riding a coach in a teardrop: "Your eyes do make no coaches. In your tears / There is no certain princess that appears" (4.3.151–2). This convergence of male and female readings, the sensitivity to language and aversion to overwrought metaphors that Rosaline and the Princess share with Berowne, undermines the conventional justification of women's intellectual inferiority for the King's men-only admissions policy. It frames his oath not as a reasonable response to feminine inadequacy but as an opportunistic securement of male social advantage.

The dramatic action of the play stems from the decision of the Princess and ladies to use reading and interpretation, as men in the play do, to pursue their interests. At her initial meeting with the King, the Princess relies on word choice and a kind of tit-for-tat rhythm of phrasing to challenge his attempt to dismiss her: "King. Hear me, dear lady. I have sworn an oath – / Princess. Our Lady help my lord! He'll be forsworn" (2.1.96–7). By turning the patronizing phrase "dear lady" into an appeal to "our lady," the Princess upsets the valuation assigned to those words and with it the King's attempts to classify her according to the weaker term of the binary lord/lady categories; in her parlance, "dear lady" becomes "our Lady," the Queen of heaven who reigns over and above "my lord," the King of France. Invoking the Virgin in her challenge to the King's exclusive claim to academic authority, the Princess symbolically reinstates the image of Mary as teacher over the chair of the humanist pedagogue when she mockingly threatens to take his place in the classroom: "But pardon me, I am too sudden-bold. / To teach a teacher ill beseemeth me" (2.1.106–7). Her sarcastic apology for attempting to "teach a teacher" disputes the notion that instruction is for men alone and subverts the implied correlation between binary categories, the notion that lord is to lady as teacher is to student as bookman is to book.

In the anti-masque staged in response to the King's masque, the Princess and her friends directly undertake to teach the teachers a lesson that will confound the terms on which the men have based their assertions of self-superiority. As Katherine Maus observes, the ladies "perform the equivalent of a bed-trick on the level of a signifier."[130] "The effect of my intent," the Princess explains disingenuously, "is to cross theirs. / They do it but in mockery-merriment, / And mock for mock is only my intent" (5.2.137–9). After Boyet informs them of the King's plot to pay them a visit dressed as "Muscovites or Russians," the Princess, Rosaline, Maria, and Katherine all exchange the tokens (pearls, a jewel, a glove, etc.) that they had received from their respective suitors and put on masks. When the men arrive disguised in Russian costumes, they address their oaths of love to the wrong women. The men reappear dressed in their usual clothes and the women reveal that they are all mismatched; the King is now committed to Rosaline, Berowne to the Princess, Longaville to Katherine, and Dumaine to Maria.

The women's Mock for Mock exposes to ridicule the men's use of bookish language to assert their superiority over others. Berowne humorously abjures the "speeches penned," "the motion of a schoolboy's tongue," "taffeta phrases," "silken terms," "three-piled hyperboles," and "figures pedantical" which he acknowledges have blown him full of "maggot ostentation" (5.2.402–3, 406–9). "Henceforth," he promises, "my wooing mind shall be expressed / In russet yeas, and honest kersey noes . . . My love to thee is sound, sans crack or flaw." "Sans 'sans,' I pray you," Rosaline responds (5.2.412–14, 16). This light repartee between Rosaline and Berowne draws attention to the men's use of the language of the academy as an exclusionary tactic. But just as "a jest's prosperity lies in the ear / Of him that hears it, never in the tongue / Of him that makes it" (5.2.838–40), so too the scholars can use their knowledge to diminish others only if those on the receiving end of their three-piled hyperboles are suitably impressed by them. Instead, the women turn deaf ears to the Muscovite's "penn'd speech" (5.2.146) and the Princess to the King's pedantical figures. "I understand you not," she tells him, "My griefs are double" (5.2.734). This firm answer, along with the women's indifferent silence and Rosaline's rejoinders, blocks the men's ability to use bookish erudition to tip the social scale in their favor.

The masque also undermines Berowne's equation of women with texts. "The ladies did change favours," Berowne realizes, "and then we, / Following the signs, wooed but the sign of she" (5.2.468–9). The effect of the women's prank is to repudiate the idea that they are "the books, the arts, the academes" of which Berowne waxed poetic, that they are inert signifiers to be interpreted by others. In swapping favors, the women assert that each "she" which the men read as a sign is a reader in her own right, one capable of construing meaning. They further prove themselves as readers by reversing the men's attempt to nullify the contractual document that they all had vowed, in writing, to uphold. While the men would like to be able to claim, even after having violated their signed pledge, that their love is nevertheless "lawful" and their faith "not torn," the women prove the men to have broken both their word and their faith (4.3.281). "To our perjury to add more terror," Berowne admits, "We are again forsworn, in will and error" (5.2.470–71). In vain does the King appeal, "Construe my speeches better, if you may" (5.2.341).

Those few words, the deferential qualifying phrase, "if you may," in contrast with the militant oath of the first scene, suggests that the Princess' anti-masque has altered relations between the sexes and reclaimed interpretation as a shared prerogative. With his entreaty, it seems that the King has ceded to the Princess the right to construe meanings by which he and his men, exiled by the women they once

banished, will have to live. It is in this respect that the play presents its
strongest challenge to prevailing attitudes about gender and literacy. Yet
Love's Labour's Lost also perpetuates the restrictions that it satirizes. At
the end, submitting to the punishment determined by the women,
Berowne puts a distinctly Spenserian gloss on events by defining the
women's power over him as that of beauty, not interpretation: "Your
beauty, ladies, / Hath much *deformed* us, *fashioning* our humours / Even
to the opposèd end of our intents" (5.2.738–40; italics added). Perhaps
Berowne has understood the Princess' point that a woman can be a
teacher; if so, however, the image of the female instructor he seems to
have in mind is that of Acrasia or Circe deforming men, not of Anne or
Mary teaching Christ his letters.

Despite the play's contradictory messages about women's place in
educational institutions, the staging of *Love's Labour's Lost* and other
contemporary plays did give women the position of consumers, if not
producers, of literary works. For early modern women, the exclusionary
provisions of actual grammar school statutes closed access to higher
education as categorically as those of Navarre's fictitious oath. But the
door to literary culture, at least, was set ajar in the English public
theatre. Plays may have been written and acted exclusively by men, but
female audience members had to be counted among the cash-purchasers
of theatre seats and play quartos. The Epilogue who appears at the end
of *Henry VIII* indicates as much. "All the expected good we're like to
hear / For this play at this time," he says, "is only in / The merciful
construction of good women" (lines 8–10). The number of prefaces in
printed quartos of plays that address women further corroborates the
impression that female playgoers made their presence felt.[131] In exchange
for their commercial support, the theatre offered women contact with
literary works that would have been otherwise incomprehensible to the
vast majority of them. Most women, even those proficient in reading the
black-letter type of printed psalters, would have been unable to decipher
a playwright's foul papers. The theatre translated that manuscript, a
scribal text written for an elite like a poem circulated in a courtly coterie,
into a performance medium accessible to literate and illiterate, writers
and readers, men and women, alike.

Love's Labour's Lost concludes without resolving the competition
between opposing readings of the contract; it also leaves the four pairs of
lovers unmarried and the audience in suspense about their eventual
union. This non-ending, unique among Shakespearean comedies, underscores that ideas about gender and literacy were in dispute and at play in
sixteenth-century England. The next four chapters concern some of the
inner conflicts, as well as social antagonisms, that sex-specific prescrip-

tions for reading and writing aroused. Early modern readers and writers, both characters in the drama and historical men and women, were faced with a dilemma. In their acts of interpretation and expression, they had to reconcile the imperative to model themselves after humanist exemplars with the urge to follow their own interests and desires. And the drama of certain plays, the drama of certain lives, I will argue, is exactly that drama.

Enter Hamlet reading on a Booke.[1]

Hamlet and Ophelia both read on stage. "The poor wretch comes reading," the Queen says of Hamlet. Gertrude attributes Hamlet's reading to his melancholy state of mind. His absorption in a book accentuates his chosen isolation from the rest of the court. Polonius examines Hamlet about his reading because its subject or title might shed insights into his mental state. With characteristic evasion, Hamlet deflects the question. Asked to identify his book, "What do you read, my lord?" he answers only, "words, words, words."

Unlike Hamlet, Ophelia reads what is handed to her. She is told by her father, "Read on this book." The book, we presume, is a religious text since he describes her as "devotion's visage." This perception is confirmed by Hamlet's greeting: "Nymph, in thy orisons / Be all my sins remember'd."[2] For Polonius and Hamlet, the sight of Ophelia with a book conjures the image of a female reader from out of the pages of *The Instruction of a Christian Woman.* She appears as a figure of the chaste woman who holds her tumultuous thoughts in check by the habitual reading of devotional texts. For them, she is an icon, not an agent. She is Devotion itself.

Shakespeare's *Hamlet* holds a mirror up to the male and female reader and displays, refracted in their images, the form and pressure of humanist practices for shaping identity through sex-specific literacies. Implicit in Hamlet's and Ophelia's practices of reading are models of the male and female subject: the "outstretch'd hero" (gendered male) versus "devotion's visage" (gendered female). The notebook method of constructing identity through the assimilation of aphoristic fragments teaches the male reader to imitate the male heroes in his books. The female reader learns to define herself by personifying the virtues of an ideal figure of womanhood and by differentiating herself as sharply as possible from the anti-ideal. Yet neither Hamlet nor Ophelia embraces, in a straightforward manner, the male heroic or female iconic function that he and she are assigned. Both struggle to define selves that exceed those of the model readers they are called to replicate.

Though the play scrutinizes the constraints that humanist pedagogy places on both Hamlet and Ophelia, its narrative is constructed around the particular predicament faced by the male reader. Shakespeare questions the validity and feasibility of imitation as a method of male self-fashioning by enacting the perverse effects of that procedure on Hamlet. We witness Hamlet, prince of the realm and acknowledged heir to the throne, faced with a contradictory set of imperatives: he is asked to display masterful agency and, at the same time, to follow blindly patterns and precedents set by others. Expected to imitate a panoply of masculine heroes, even at the cost of his life, Hamlet repeatedly fails to do so. He marks his independence and is embarrassed by his recalcitrance. By staging the dilemma faced by Hamlet, a privileged subject constrained to subordinate his needs and survival as a condition of that privilege, Shakespeare exposes a fundamental weakness in the structure of masculine domination of which humanist pedagogy was an important component part.

I

Polonius. What is the matter, my lord?
Hamlet. Between who?
Polonius. I mean the matter that you read, my lord. (2.2.193–5)

Learning to read was not only a matter of a child assimilating the sounds and meanings of a set of signs, but also one of the child grounding his or her identity upon discursive differences. James Cleland served as a tutor to Sir John Harrington, a favorite friend of Prince Henry. In *The Institution of a Young Noble Man*, Cleland writes that every young nobleman should learn "to spel & read with a sweet accent, not pronouncing verse as prose, or prose as verse, nor reading with a sharpe shril voice as a woman, or with a rough and huske voice, as an old man doth, but with a pleasaunt harmonie, reading at the beginning with leasure, pawsing at the ful period, & taking his breath at the broken points, lifting or basing his voice as the subject requireth, and the admiration or question offereth."[3] Boys from the poorest families and nearly all girls did not have the experience of writing and presenting themes, debates, letters, and poems for a tutor or grammar school master; as a consequence, they would not, in most cases, be capable of achieving the textual mastery implied by Cleland's description of a "sweet accent." Creating a "pleasaunt harmonie" in reading aloud, a skill which requires a technical knowledge of prosody and a familiarity with diverse texts, becomes yet another way of asserting one's superior social position. The register on which the educated boy learns to locate vocal pitch is not neutral; the range within which his voice will fall is "sweet" while the higher range within which a woman's voice falls is "sharpe" and "shril"; the voice of an old man is "rough" and "huske." As he identifies his vocal characteristics with the pitch designated as optimal on a scale between high and low, masculine and feminine, young and old, the boy learns to recognize the signs of his status, the promise implied by his gender and his youth, in the sound of his voice.

For boys who aspired to a high social status, reading involved a set of complex skills: translating multiple languages (Latin and Greek as well as English), responding to questions about the content of reading, and forming judgments about structure and form. Above all, it served as a preparative for expression. Students learned to turn their reading into "matter" for essays and speeches through the practice of keeping a commonplace book. In *Ludus Literarius: Or, The Grammar School* (1612), writer and schoolmaster John Brinsley maintains that a boy will easily achieve a facility for expressing himself once he has compiled an adequate supply of quotations: "And when you have the matter throughly in your head, words will follow, as waters out of a fountaine, even almost naturally, to expresse your mind in any tongue, which you studie in any right order."[4] The operative metaphor for describing the masculine mind is that of an empty or full vessel. Reading fills the mind with matter, and words stream out in elegantly-formed, polished phrases. Montaigne invokes this image ironically when he refers to the impossible task assigned to the Danaïd sisters in the underworld – transporting water in jars riddled with holes. Montaigne says that he draws from the works of Plutarch and Seneca "like the Danaïds, incessantly filling up and pouring out."[5] The commonplace book was meant to insure that quotations, collected in the process of reading, did not simply slip through a student's consciousness as water through a sieve. The student was an empty vessel that would fill to the brim as the blank pages of his paper book became replenished with pithy aphorisms.

Guarino Guarini, the most prominent educator of fifteenth-century Italy, reminded his contemporaries that Pliny and other classical authors had systematically compiled notebooks of quotations taken from their reading. At Guarini's school in Ferrara, students first received rigorous grounding in the formal rules of Latin; then they were taught to collect examples from their reading and to inscribe them in indexed notebooks.[6] In England, the practice spread through the efforts of educators such as William Lily who advocated in *Carmen de moribus* that boys write sayings down in notebooks rather than on loose pages. In *The School-*

master (1570), Roger Ascham instructs students to keep "a booke, thus wholie filled with *examples* of *Imitation*."[7] In *The True Order and Method of Writing and Reading Histories* (1574), Thomas Blundeville recommends noting examples down by category in order "to make our selves more wyse, as well to direct our own actions, as also to counsell others, to sturre them to vertue, and to withdrawe them from vice, and to beautyfie our owne speache with grave *examples*, when we discourse of anye matters, that therby it may have the more authoritie, waight, and credite."[8] Brinsley similarly advises that grammar school students keep "Common place books . . . therein at least to have references, wherby to turn of a sodaine to matters of all sorts, in the most exquisite and pure Poets: to have some direction both for matter and *imitation*."[9]

The key terms in these passages are "example" and "imitation." The word "example" could denote both witty *sententiae* and the heroes to which the *sententiae* often referred, an edifying turn of phrase as well as an inspiring figure from literature or history (Aeneas was as valid an example as Caesar or Alexander). An example could be a model for forceful writing or for virtuous action. Petrarch advanced the concept of heroic exemplarity in a series of biographies titled *De viris illustribus* (1337). With the rise of humanism in the fifteenth-century Italian city-state, teachers and literary critics developed sophisticated approaches to the use of examples as models of admirable conduct. Cristoforo Landino, the author of an influential commentary on Virgil published in 1488, wrote that Virgil "feigned and represented Aeneas – the perfect man in every way – so that we might all take him as the sole exemplar for the living of our lives."[10] The notebook method – "gathering" and "framing" textual fragments in commonplace books – was meant to construct the self according to the teachings of humanists such as Landino. As Mary Thomas Crane notes, "The student learned to gather what was already framed as a saying, it framed his character, and he, in turn, reframed it in his own writing as a sign that he had received the prescribed education."[11] Heroic figures in commonplace books corresponded to models of the ideal man: Thomas Elyot's Governor, Castiglione's Courtier, Richard Brathwait's English Gentleman.

The example, once belittled by Saint Thomas as the least valid form of proof, derived its newfound importance from humanist theories of imitation.[12] In humanist discourse, the word "imitation" invoked questions about education and the self: could Christians imitate models from pagan antiquity in good conscience? To what extent should imitation preclude individual expression? In *Timber, or Discoveries*, Ben Jonson addresses these dilemmas by defining imitation in paradoxical terms as a procedure involving both replication and innovation:

The third requisite in our poet, or maker, is imitation: to be able to convert the substance or riches of another poet to his own use: to make choice of one excellent man above the rest, and so to follow him till he grow very he, or so like him as the copy may be mistaken for the principal – not as a creature that swallows what it takes in crude, raw, or undigested, but that feeds with an appetite, and hath a stomach to concoct, divide, and turn all into nourishment; not, to imitate servilely, as Horace saith, and catch at vices for virtue, but to draw forth out of the best and choicest flowers with the bee, and turn all into honey, work it into one relish and savour, make our imitation sweet, observe how the best writers have imitated, and follow them: how Virgil and Statius have imitated Homer; how Horace, Archilochus; how Alcaeus and the other lyrics; and so of all the rest.[13]

The paradox offered by Jonson, the notion of imitation as creation, turns reading into a form of production rather than one of passive consumption; the reader "converts," "digests," "concocts," and "divides" the words on the page before him. On the one hand, the reader is supposed to become indistinguishable from the writer he emulates so that "the copy may be mistaken for the principal." On the other hand, he may be as different from the writer he models himself after as Virgil was from Homer or Horace from Archilochus. Jonson attempts to bridge the discrepancy between these two approaches by invoking the classical metaphor of the bee. The bee takes pollen from the choicest flowers, and creates honey from it; similarly, the male reader/writer converts "the substance or riches of another poet to his own use." It remains difficult in reading the passage, however, to distinguish between creative and servile imitation. As Jonson's nod to Horace suggests, the male reader depends on models to authorize his expression and identity. His autonomy has limits. He is not at liberty simply "to make choice of one excellent man above the rest, and so to follow him." Jonson qualifies that initial statement in which he emphasized the young man's choice and admonishes him, instead, to "observe, how the best writers have imitated, and follow them." It is understood that the singularly excellent man whom the male reader attempts to copy will be chosen from among the limited set of authors, Homer, Virgil, and Horace among them, whose words were recorded in commonplace books by every grammar-school boy.

Humanist pedagogy made the imitation of examples imperative not only for writing, but for action itself. Masculine agency was enlarged and defined in terms of the feats of martial courage, rhetorical brilliance, and moral virtue performed by male heroes of the literary-historical past. Male subjects laid claim to that history and to their place in it by emulating heroes from books: Hercules and Aeneas, Alexander and Caesar, Richard the Lionheart and Henry V. For schoolboys in this period, reading was a two-step process: imitation followed inscription:

"The pupil read about a laudable action and copied down a maxim in order to fix the action in his memory. He was then expected to imitate the deed when the opportunity arose."[14] After recording an example, the male reader was supposed to incorporate it literally through the actions of his body. As James Cleland writes in *The Institution of a Young Noble Man*, when a student reads of "the continencie, valour, and Eloquence of Alexander, Casar, & Scipio; he must thinke them, as so manie patternes sympathising with his own minde, & that hee will rather imitate their perfections with his hands, then heare them with his ears."[15] The instruction given the student was to translate the abstract ideals embodied by classical heroes into concrete actions, to imitate examples physically as well as mentally. "He shall not so much say his lesson," Montaigne declares, "as do it."[16]

Imitation was supposed to make boys into gentlemen. In practice, however, individual readers might choose examples or modes of imitation that their schoolmasters would have frowned upon. In his study of Renaissance exemplarity, Timothy Hampton cites the case of Girolamo Olgiati, one of three conspirators in the 1476 murder of the Milanese tyrant Galeazzo Maria Sforza. Olgiati, who attended a humanist school, read Sallust's history of the plot by Cataline to seize control of Rome. It was his reading, Olgiati suggested, that spurred him to participate in the conspiracy. Though Sallust's account is critical of Cataline, Olgiati took the assassin to be an exemplar of virtuous opposition to tyranny. As Hampton observes, "Olgiati's attack on the Milanese tyrant in imitation of a Roman model is, in the largest sense, an act of reading. It constitutes an attempt to interpret ancient history and apply it to action in the world, to move beyond word to flesh."[17]

In the brutal fifth act of *Titus Andronicus*, Shakespeare stages a strangely similar moment in which an act of reading turns into one of homicide. Like Olgiati, Titus is motivated to commit murder by an example from a text. As though in the role of a humanist pedagogue, Titus questions Saturninus about the figure of Virginius: "Was it well done of rash Virginius / To slay his daughter with his own right hand, / Because she was enforced, stained, and deflowered?"[18] When Saturninus responds affirmatively, Titus confirms the exemplary value of Virginius' murder of his daughter and assaults his own daughter:

> A reason mighty, strong, effectual;
> A pattern, precedent, and lively warrant
> For me, most wretched, to perform the like.
> Die, die, Lavinia, and thy shame with thee,
> And, with thy shame, thy father's sorrow die.
> *He kills her*   (5.3.36–38,43–47)

His coda to the deed, "With thy shame, thy father's sorrow die," is the kind of pithy phrase that a grammar-school student might copy into his commonplace book as a means of remembering Titus himself as an example. The moment is at once horrible and laughable. However it is staged, as an act of tragic dimensions or as a disturbingly funny lampoon of humanist pedagogy, the murder of Lavinia suggests the centrality of standardized practices of reading to the formation of the male subject. Brinsley had proposed that male readers store examples inside their minds: "Let them have first the most excellent patterns, & never to rest until they have the very patterns in their heads."[19] For Titus, the pattern established by Virginius inspires and authorizes his movement from word to flesh, from remembering a passage in a book to stabbing Lavinia.[20]

II

The victim of Titus' reading, Lavinia is herself a reader. Because she reads aloud to her nephew Lucius, she is compared to Cornelia, a mother praised by humanists for her role in the education of her sons. In the play, Lavinia's reading is important because it exposes the fact of her rape. Though her tongue was cut out by her attackers, she is able to testify about the assault by opening the book of Ovid's *Metamorphoses* to the rape of Philomela. Shakespeare's Lavinia is a figure for the contradictions inherent in humanist recommendations for female reading.[21] Humanists did advocate educating women so that they, like Cornelia, would be able to read moral and religious texts to their children. Yet the same writers argued vociferously against allowing women to read secular texts, in particular the erotic poems of Ovid, as Lavinia has done. Many conduct manual authors went so far as to equate reading about carnal acts with committing them. From this skewed perspective, Lavinia's transgressive reading could be seen as the cause of her violation. Thomas Bentley, author of *The Monument of Matrons* (1582), conflates crimes allegedly committed by women – adultery, promiscuity, sorcery, disobedience, greed, verbal impertinence, and impiety – with not reading, reading incorrectly, or reading the wrong texts. Virtuous readers are warned to "conforme" themselves to examples of good women and wicked readers to expect the punishments meted out to their counterparts in history and the Bible: being deposed, divorced, run through with a sword, thrown from a window, eaten by dogs, raped to death, chopped into pieces, burnt to ashes, or cast alive into hell.[22]

In *The English Gentleman* (1630), Richard Brathwait argues in a similar vein that female readers of *Venus and Adonis* deserve to be excoriated along with the most infamous temptresses and murderers:

To what height of licentious libertie are these corrupter times growne? When that Sex, where Modesty should claime a native prerogative, gives way to foments of exposed looseness; by not only attending to the wanton discourse of immodest Lovers, but carrying about them (even in their naked Bosomes, where chastest desires should only lodge) the amorous toyes of *Venus and Adonis*: which Poem, with others of like nature, they heare with such attention, peruse with such devotion, and retaine with such delectation, as no Subject can equally relish their unseasoned palate, like those lighter discourses . . . I will not insist upon them, but leave them, to have their names registred amongst those infamous Ladies; Semphronia, Scribonia, Clitemnestra, Cleopatra, Faustina, Messalina, whose memories purchased by odious Lust, shall survive the course of time; as the memory of those famous Matrons, Octavia, Porcia, Cæcilia, Cornelia, shall transcend the period of time.[23]

This image of the female reader stashing erotic poems in her bosom exemplifies the demonization that writers of didactic treatises employed in their campaign to regulate female literacy more strictly. Yet if the sexual images Brathwait introduces of "exposed looseness," "wanton discourse," "immodest Lovers," "naked Bosomes," "amorous toyes," "delectation," and "Lust" are meant to chasten the English Gentlewoman (to whom he addresses a second volume), they also seem intended to titillate his English Gentleman reader. Ironically, Brathwait invites his male readers to take moral satisfaction from engaging in the very kind of reading for which the women in his text are castigated, to inveigh against the sensuality of the female reader even as they partake in the erotic thrill of imagining her exposed and naked breasts.

For Juan Luis Vives, reading is a salutary alternative to a range of other activities in which women might engage: playing cards, thinking lustful thoughts, or talking with their gossips. In *The Instruction of a Christian Woman* (1529), he asserts that reading is an even better disciplinary technique than sewing or spinning because it occupies the mind as well as the hands. An account of Anne Boleyn's life by William Latymer, a classical scholar and friend of Erasmus, uses the same language to refer to a disobedient female reader uncovered among the queen's ladies. Latymer recounts that the Queen summoned Mary Shelton, the unfortunate noblewoman who had written "certeyne ydill poeses" in her prayerbook, and "wonderfull rebuked her that wold permitte suche wantone toyes in her book of prayers, which she termed a myrroure or glasse wherin she might learne to address her wandering thoughtes."[24]

While reading or writing "ydill poeses" signifies "wandering," the act of reading a prayerbook, an occupation emblematic of confinement, connotes chastity. In Cyril Tourneur's play *The Revenger's Tragedy*, a devotional text functions as the sign of a rape victim's virtue. After Lord

Antonio's wife (she is not named in the play) commits suicide, her corpse is found with "a prayer book the pillow to her cheek," and in her right hand a second book ("with a leaf tucked up") open to the Latin tag, "Melius virtute mori, quam per dedecus vivere."[25] Described by Latymer as a mirror in which women should learn to address their wandering thoughts, a prayer book fittingly cushions the dead wife who chose the strait confinement of a grave over life stained by the imputation of transgression. Reading, as with the Roman Cornelia, is associated with female virtue; the verbal restraint of Tourneur's wife, her choice of silent communication by means of printed words, parallels her sexual continence. Instead of preparing one to speak or write eloquently, reading takes the place of expression.

Vives, whose ideas influenced later writers such as Brathwait, places severe restrictions on women's access to books. He stipulates that women read no romances or poetry (except for the work of Christian poets such as Prudentius), no grammar, logic, or history, and no political science, mathematics, theology, or moral philosophy.[26] While Brinsley was so concerned about saving his students time that he recommended that schoolmasters provide them with a supply of quotations to use in their writing assignments, Vives tells his female readers to read and reread his book. Maids, wives, and widows are instructed to read the whole book and not only the sections that pertain most to them: "Lest a mayde shuld thynke that she nede to rede but onely the fyrst boke, or a wyfe the seconde, or a wydowe onely the thyrde. I wyll that every of them shall rede all."[27] The point of their reading is to take up time: women are to read continuously on holidays and in their spare time on working days; they are to read the gospel and the day's epistle before going to church and devotional works upon returning home. Giovanni Michele Bruto, the author of an Italian conduct manual published in a trilingual English-French-Italian edition titled *The Education of a Young Gentlewoman* (1598), likewise grants permission to women to read the Bible, Plutarch's accounts of famous women, and treatises by learned men, although not "amorous and impudent verses, or fables and newes" such as Boccaccio's tales. Bruto asserts that edifying texts such as these will inform the young gentlewoman about "the notable actions and glorious enterprises of famous & renowmed women, wherewith shee may increase the notable vertues by nature liberally bestowed upon her."[28]

Reading was meant to isolate women and to minimize their contact with other women, at least when they were of an impressionable age. "A woman," Vives dictates, "shall lerne the vertues of her kynde all together out of bokes."[29] According to the view he presents in *The Office and*

Duty of an Husband (1553), women derive their flaws – vanity, insolence, and weakness – from the influence of their mothers: "for lacke of good learning, they love & hate that only, the whiche they learned of their unlearned mothers, & examples of the evill, leaning to that part only, that the ponderous and heavy body is inclined and geven unto."[30] Vives and Bruto rationalize their concerns about women acting as mentors by associating real-life female mentors with the flesh, "the ponderous and heavy body," and with "soil" and "filthinesse."[31] Representations of women from the Bible and history were to substitute for actual women as counselors and teachers. Bruto suggests that Lord Silvestre Cataneo commissioned him to write a conduct manual for his daughter out of fear that "her tender and budding vertues . . . not having as yet taken deep root, might lose their forces by the over great tendernesse of her Grandmother." In place of the model once supplied by her grandmother, Cataneo's daughter is told to "diligently collect and gather togither" a collection of examples of famous historical and biblical women that will "serve her for an aule to prick her forward to will and desire vertue, and to dispise & abhorre all vice and filthy abomination." Young gentle-women, Bruto contends, "shall never read of such women of renowme, as Claudia, Portia, Lucretia, & Octavia, without being stirred up with a noble desire to follow their steps, dispising and wholly dispraising those that by the contrary means have passed the course of this their mortal life."[32]

This system for fashioning female selves worked by confronting the reader with a dual set of models: good women for her to emulate and bad women for her to repudiate. Addressing the reader of *The Mirror of Modesty* (1579), Thomas Salter recommends that she read or have her maidservants read to her "the examples and lives of godly and vertuous ladies, whose worthy fame, and bright renowme yet liveth and still will live for ever, whiche shee shall make choice of, out of the holy Scripture, and other histories, both auncient and of late dayes." He says that texts of this nature will encourage virtue: "for you shall never repeate the vertuous lives of any suche Ladies as, Claudia, Portia, Lucretia, and such like were, but you shall kindle a desire in them to treade their steppes, and become in tyme like unto them."[33] The allegedly evil woman in the text – Julia, Fulvia, Cleopatra, Messalina, Clytemnestra, Jezabel, or Delila, among others – was also supposed to serve as a mirror. Thomas Bentley refers to his *Monument of Matrons* as "a Mirrour for all sorts of wicked women, as in a cleere glasse . . . perfectlie to see their shamelesse pride, cruelite, idolatrie, and contempt of religion" and "a Mirrour contrariwise for all godlie and vertuous women."[34] Bentley's division of women into two contrasting groups (godly and virtuous women versus shameless and wicked ones) is a common topos in books addressed to female audiences. In his *Palace of Pleasure* (1566), William Painter attacks the morals of contemporary women, and then tries to repair the damage by acknowledging that there are as many Lucrece-like women as there are lascivious Julias among the female sex: "But if I list to speake of women of this age, from noble to unnoble, from an Emperors Daughter to a Ploughmans modder, whose lives do frame after Julia hir lore, my pen to the stumpes would weare, and my hand be wearied with writing. And so likewise it would of numbres no doubt in these dayes that folow the trace of Lucrece line, that huswifely and chastly contrive the day and nights in pure and Godly exercise."[35]

While the male reader was challenged to copy an admirable classical writer (Caesar or Virgil) or heroic figure (Alexander or Aeneas), the female reader was threatened with categorization as *being* an evil anti-model (Julia or Cleopatra) if she were found not to epitomize a virtuous model (Lucrece or Octavia). This is Richard Brathwait's advice to the female reader of *The English Gentlewoman* (1631): "Set alwayes before your eyes, as an imitable mirror, some good woman or other, before whom you may live, as if she ey'd you, she view'd you."[36] The exemplary woman in the text is "an imitable mirror," a representation of what the reader looking at her image should herself be. That mirror does not simply project a static image; if the female reader follows instructions and imagines that she is being evaluated by the reflection in the mirror, it also serves an oversight function. The female reader never really closes the book on the characters she reads about; she is asked to maintain a constant vigilance to see that she is, at all times, as different from Julia and Cleopatra as she is like Lucrece and Octavia.[37]

The male reader learned to imitate both the writers of texts and heroic characters, to wield words and swords with the grace that Caesar showed in doing both; the female reader was taught to epitomize female characters passively, to personify the exemplary ideal represented in the book before her. Brathwait, for instance, lectures his female reader to reject the example of the unruly Fulvia and to embrace that of submissive Octavia: "Be you all Octavia's; the rougher your crosse, the richer your Crowne."[38] Whereas Cleland asks male readers to read about Roman heroes and to "imitate their perfections with his hands," Brathwait instructs female readers to "be" various Roman matrons. What the conduct manuals set out are two distinct modes of reading and of self-fashioning: active imitation, for male readers, and emblematic representation, for female readers.

Imitation is a technique for achieving future perfection. Jonson does not expect a male youth to put down the *Aeneid*, pick up his pen, and write as Virgil wrote. It is precisely because Jonson imagines the creation of a male self as an extended process that he recommends *lectio* to young men. Jonson requires them to undertake a program of extensive reading because one cannot simply "leap forth suddenly a poet by dreaming he hath been in Parnassus, or having washed his lips, as they say, in Helicon. There goes more to his making than so."[39] The making of a male subject, like the making of a poem, involves repetition, failure, error, correction, and renewed effort. When a conduct manual author uses the term "imitation" to refer to a woman's emulation of models in a text, it does not have the individuating function that Jonson assigns the term. Jonson invites his male readers to develop identities that are both patterned after a common tradition and emphatically individualized. He instructs them to note "how Virgil and Statius have imitated Homer; how Horace, Archilochus; how Alcaeus and the other lyrics; and so of all the rest." Bentley does admonish women "to become even from their youth more studious imitators, and diligent folowers of so godlie and rare examples in their vertuous mothers," but he tells his readers to imitate godly women so that "they may shine also together with them on earth, as burning lampes of verie virginitie."[40] In contrast to Jonson's description of imitation, which culminates with a list of the proper names of luminary male writers, Bentley's ends with an image of depersonalized burning torches, "lampes of verie virginitie." While her male counterpart is assigned to store up memorable passages for use in some future test of courage, integrity, or eloquence, the female reader is measured by her performance in the reading process itself. Bentley praises women who pray, meditate, and read devotional works "daie and night continuallie and incessantlie, either silentlie in hart with Hanna, or openlie in mouth with Marie."[41] The female reader is asked to attain a state of being, not to master a repertoire of skills. She is either Octavia or Cleopatra. Falling short of the ideal turns her into the anti-ideal.

This is Ophelia's story. She enters the play as Devotion's Visage and departs it as the nymph/prostitute Flora; in her madness, she rejects devotional reading, with its disciplinary implications for women's behavior, in favor of oral culture.[42] Her initial role, that of the exemplary female reader, is a solitary one. While Laertes and Hamlet attend universities in France and Germany, she sews alone in her closet. She turns her correspondence over to her father for him to inspect. Unlike Hamlet who imagines his memory as a commonplace book that he can erase or inscribe, Ophelia considers hers to be bolted shut by a male guardian of her chastity. "'Tis in my memory lock'd," she tells Laertes, "and you yourself shall keep the key of it" (1.3.85–6). The task Brinsley sets his students is to learn to write or speak of any matter; the diverse quotations boys collected in the course of their reading were meant to enable them to assimilate echoes of classical authors in eloquent speeches and essays. By comparison, Ophelia's expression seems to have been informed by the practice of reading-as-sewing. Her speech, so long as she remains lucid, is cross-stich dull. She repeats stock phrases or makes helpless sounding pleas to heaven: "Good my lord, / How does your honor for this many a day? . . . My lord? . . . What means your lordship? . . . O, help him, you sweet heavens. . . Heavenly powers, restore him" (3.1.90–1,104,106,135,143). She blandly agrees with what others say. Hamlet complains about the brevity of the players' prologue, and Ophelia concurs, " 'Tis brief, my lord" (3.2.148). At other times, her voice is muffled altogether. "How now, Ophelia?" her father says, "You need not tell us what Lord Hamlet said, / We heard it all" (3.1.180–2).

The task of personifying abstract female virtue turns Ophelia's identity into that of Devotion's Visage. Polonius directs Ophelia to read so that Hamlet will not be suspicious about finding her alone: "Read on this book, / That show of such an exercise may colour / Your loneliness." "The image of a solitary woman with a book," Bridget Lyons notes, "was conventionally interpreted as representing an attitude of prayer and devoutness, just as a man walking with a book, as Hamlet does earlier, was assumed to be melancholy and philosophical."[43] In this scene, Ophelia's book is merely a stage-prop for her tableau-like role.

Emphasis on the iconography of Ophelia makes her seem like an opaque surface. References to her as a picture out of an emblem book (Devotion) or a biblical example of female virtue (Jephthah's daughter) suggest that there is only a veneer of personality to her character. The epithets addressed to her, "the fair Ophelia," "pretty Ophelia," "the most beautified Ophelia," similarly draw attention to her outside (3.1.89, 4.5.56, 2.2.109–10). That concentrated focus on Ophelia's exterior masks anxieties on the part of her father, brother, and lover about her internal self. All three men express concern that her book and somber attitude may be merely trappings and suits for show, that her devotional posture may hide deceitful inclinations. Though Polonius himself puts Ophelia in the position of having to dissemble, having to answer the question, "Where's your father?", with a lie, "At home, my lord," he hypocritically warns her against duplicity (3.1.130–1). Devotion's Visage, he moralizes, can conceal the devil himself. In fact, Ophelia's pious appearance is a front not for Lucifer but for Polonius. Unmindful of the contradiction, he reproaches her for using her book, in all obedience, exactly as he has instructed her to do, as a theatrical device in his ruses.

Laertes also links Ophelia with a stereotype of female falseness when he informs her that, "the chariest maid is prodigal enough / If she unmask her beauty to the moon" (1.3.36–7). The implication of the maxim is that one can, at best, keep a maid indoors and occupied, whether reading and sewing, out of range of the stray moonbeam, but that the chariest maid is always in danger of turning into her unchaste twin. In fact, there are hints that Ophelia's approach to reading is not wholly in keeping with the prescriptions of conduct manuals. Her recollection of the words that Hamlet addressed to her reveals that she does not read a line of verse with the automatic reflex with which one sews a hem. Ophelia remembers the "sweet breath" and "perfume" of Hamlet's words. She says that she "suck'd the honey of his music vows" (3.1.98, 99, 158). The synesthesia of this description emphasizes the sensual pleasure – olfactory, gustatory, aural – that Ophelia experiences in language. However, while Polonius looks for the devil within Ophelia, the play suggests that her undisciplined, passionate reading simply shows her to be more human than a one-dimensional icon from out of an emblem book.

Act four. Enter the prodigal maid that Laertes said was latent in his sister:

Enter Ophelia. [Q2]

Enter Ophelia distracted. [F]

Enter Ofelia playing on a Lute, and her haire downe singing. [Q1]

The folio stage direction for Hamlet and the first quarto direction for Ophelia – *Enter Hamlet reading on a book, Enter Ophelia playing on a lute, her hair down singing* – put in relief educational discrepancies that divided men and women in the early modern period. In his first entrance after learning of his father's murder, Hamlet reads a book, mulls over the teachings of philosophers, composes academic themes out of fragments from his reading. Ophelia's father, too, is murdered. Following her next entrance, she sings ballads, recalls the morals of folk tales, distributes bits of colloquial wisdom. His reading is consonant with his formation as a normative male subject, her singing a rejection of the print culture that helped shape her as an icon of piety.

In the role of Flora, a bestower of flowers known for her ambiguous past, Ophelia has come full circle. Carelessly distributing buds and blossoms to all present, scandalizing the court with uninhibited winks, nods, and gestures, she epitomizes the woman whose wandering thoughts are not held in check by devotional reading. In contrast to the prayerful female reader of the first half of the play, the mad weaver of garlands of the fourth act herself claims authority as an interpreter of signs. Her words move hearers to collection; her brother, the King, and the Queen all try to construe the meaning of her songs and speech. Laertes finds that her "nothing's more than matter" (4.5.172). "Alas, sweet lady," Gertrude asks at another point, "what imports this song?" (4.5.27). For the first time, Ophelia does not just answer questions as they are put to her. When Claudius interprets one song as a "conceit" referring to her father, she disagrees with his explication, "Pray let's have no words of this, but when they ask you what it means, say you this," and sings her Valentine ballad as a gloss on the previous song (4.5.46–7). She contradicts her auditors, keeps them off-balance, directs them to sing the refrain "a-down, a-down," fills the stage with swirling snatches of verse (4.5.169).

Ophelia's use of ballads and old tales upsets the correlation stipulated in conduct manuals between gender categories and models of behavior. She speaks the parts of both men and women, switches the genders of singing parts, and voices thoughts and words that should be unsayable for a woman. In the first song, the ballad of a pilgrim who is asked whether he has seen a man's "true love" on the way back from visiting a shrine, Ophelia sings both parts, the part of the pilgrim and that of the lover, and she shifts the gender of the lover from male to female: "*How should I your true love know / From another one? / By his cockle hat and staff / And his sandal shoon –* " (4.5.23–6). Ophelia's changes turn the ballad into a retelling of her experience of being forsaken in love. To the queen's question about the meaning of her ballad, Ophelia sings, "*He is dead and gone, lady, / He is dead and gone –* " (4.5.29–30). These words invite confusion about whether the speaker is the pilgrim or Ophelia herself. It is unclear whether the lines are sung either as a continuation of the ballad, the pilgrim answering the lover's question about the whereabouts of her love, or as a direct response to the queen who called Ophelia "lady" and may be being addressed in return as "lady" by Ophelia.

The fluidity of the persona in these lyrics enables Ophelia to bypass norms for appropriate female expression. She uses earthy language, continues singing after the King has interrupted her, swears two oaths in the same breath with which she promises not to swear. In another verse of the pilgrim ballad, she reverses the meaning of a line by adding the word "not": "*Larded with sweet flowers / Which bewept to the grave did not go / With true-love showers –* " (4.5.38–40). By rephrasing the line in the negative, Ophelia may be referring to Gertrude's failure to properly mourn her first husband, to her father's rudely appointed burial, to her own ambivalence about the lover who wooed and rejected her. The argument that even in madness Ophelia "has no voice of her own, only a discord of other voices and expectations, customs gone awry" assumes that illogic and cacophony denote the absence of agency.[44] This is to overlook the response of Ophelia's onstage audience to her utterances. They may get the meaning wrong as they "botch the words up fit to their own thoughts" (4.5.10), but they trust that those lines, however jumbled, issue from Ophelia. "How if I answer no?" Hamlet asks (5.2.167). Ophelia answers "not." The metrically jarring extra syllable signals the presence of an "I" behind the verses which, although fragmented and polyphonous, has a more emphatic presence than that of the sane, monovocal Ophelia who tells Polonius, "I do not know, my lord, what I should think" (1.3.104). Connections between signifier and signified, the flower and the person to whom Ophelia hands it, imply a kind of critique which the dutiful daughter sewing or reading her prayerbook in her chamber would not have been able to make. Do the fennel and columbine, signifying flattery and infidelity, go to the Queen, and the rue, emblem of repentance, go to the King? Or is it the opposite? Ophelia engages those on stage, along with her modern critics, in evaluating the behavior of the King and Queen through a system of signs at least as available to female members of the audience as to their male counterparts. In act three, Ophelia listened meekly to Hamlet's exposition of *The Murder of Gonzago*. In act four, drawing on folk-tales and flower lore, Ophelia sets forth, for the theatre audience as well, her own variant reading of events and characters.

III

Except for that brief scene, the perspective expressed in Ophelia's folk ballads is obscured from view. What counts, in the play as in the culture, is Hamlet's erudition. For the play's privileged male subjects, book learning offers initiation into a network of acquaintances in universities and the outside world. It also elevates their status, as Marcellus indicates by deferring to Horatio on account of his superior education. "Thou art a scholar," the sentry says admiringly, "speak to it, Horatio" (1.1.45). When Hamlet watches *The Murder of Gonzago* with Ophelia, his literary knowledge puts her at a disadvantage; he refers to the Italian source for the play, identifies the name of a character, and reveals the next turn of plot. To Ophelia's query about the significance of the dumb show, "what means this, my lord?" Hamlet responds with a Spanish phrase that she cannot understand without his help: "Marry, this is miching malicho. It means mischief" (3.2.135). In exchanges such as these, Horatio and Hamlet can rely on their university educations to speak and intervene in place of perceived inferiors. However, their sophisticated training also imposes constraints.

The problem of masculine agency in *Hamlet* arises from a contra-diction at the heart of the humanist program for forming gentlemen. On the one hand, the privileged male subject has the power to step in to alter the course of events. On the other hand, his very claim to the position of agent depends on his acceptance of controls on his behavior and decision-making. Modelling himself after past heroes adds weight to his words and deeds as it simultaneously limits his scope for action. In order to show that he is a member of an exclusive elite, Hamlet has to subject himself to limits that the structure of domination imposes, to undergo a process of self-fashioning based on normative models. In his essay "La domination masculine," Pierre Bourdieu argues that the dominant can only dominate within a given structure that constrains them as well. A man's claim to privilege depends upon a constant affirmation of his virility, a task that imposes on him the burden of continually differen-tiating himself from everything feminine.[45] As Beate Krais comments, "this characteristic of the process of acquiring gender identity – that it is a process of narrowing, of cutting off, of suppressing ambiguities – has the paradoxical result that *both* genders, women and men, are restricted in their potential; and it is in this sense that the dominants are themselves dominated by their domination."[46] It is important, of course, to add that domination is very different for those in charge and those under that charge; suffering the effects of own's own dominant position is altogether unlike the experience of subordination. Nonetheless, this situation grants women a kind of negative privilege; the exclusion of women from positions of authority affords them a critical perspective. Paulina makes the point in *The Winter's Tale* when she affirms, over the cowed silence of Leontes' male counselors, that the position of dissenter and truth-sayer is gendered female: "The office / Becomes a woman best. I'll take't upon me. / If I prove honey-mouthed, let my tongue blister" (2.2.34–6). This does not mean that a skeptical attitude is not possible for an insider such as Hamlet, but rather that questioning the essential beliefs and institutions that ground his social identity leaves him paralyzed and self-divided.

The importance of humanist instruction in Hamlet's maturation is particularly evident in the ingenious use Hamlet makes of his reading in the soliloquies. "Essayes," John Florio comments in introducing his 1603 translation of Michel de Montaigne's *Essays*, "are but mens school-themes pieced together; you might as wel say, several texts. Al is in the choise & handling."[47] In his soliloquies, texts Hamlet pieces together out of phrases gleaned from books, all *is* in the choice and handling. His most famous soliloquy, for instance, concerns a topic that was commonly assigned as the subject of themes in school. The specific term, "question," in the phrase, "to be, or not to be, that is the question," signals that Hamlet is beginning a kind of disputation familiar in academic settings and in the moots of the inns of court (3.1.56). "For all their brilliant use," Harold Jenkins notes, "the ideas of the speech are for the most part traditional."[48] Hamlet might have culled the outline of his argument from Augustine, the parallel between death and sleep from any number of authors such as Cicero, Socrates, Montaigne, Plutarch, and Cardan, the analogy of death as the country from which no traveler returns from Catullus, Seneca, Job, The Wisdom of Solomon, Cardan, and Marlowe. Maxims in his other soliloquies derive from similar sources. Hamlet's observation that reason is the essential point of distinction between man and beast is also made by Cicero and Pico della Mirandola; his phrase "thinking too precisely" comes from Florio's translation of Montaigne, as does his comparison of the glory of the heavens, "this goodly frame," to the insignificance of humanity; finally, his description of "man," "like an angel . . . how like a god," echoes Pico della Mirandola (4.4.41, 2.2.298, 2.2.306). In turning this pastiche of cliché maxims into authoritative discourse, Hamlet conveys the impression of a courtier-soldier-scholar who has realized the promise of his humanist formation.

If Hamlet's mastery of textual fragments identifies him as a typically educated male reader, so too does his practice of recording passages in a commonplace book. Erasmus contends that "it is not enough simply to relate moral sayings which deter the student from vice or incite him to honest actions; they must be drilled in, they must be plowed in, they must be hammered in, and other memorable forms, such as a sententia, a fable, metaphors, examples, apothegms, or proverbs, must be carved on rings, fastened to tables, inscribed on charts."[49] Hamlet follows this counsel with respect to his own self-fashioning. After having seen his father's ghost and heard its call for revenge, he allows the words of the heroic male figure to penetrate his consciousness by inscribing them in a notebook he carries with him:

> Remember thee?
> Ay, thou poor ghost, whiles memory holds a seat
> In this distracted globe. Remember thee?
> Yea, from the table of my memory
> I'll wipe away all trivial fond records,
> All saws of books, all forms, all pressures past
> That youth and observation copied there,
> And thy commandment all alone shall live
> Within the book and volume of my brain,
> Unmix'd with baser matter. Yes, by heaven!
> O most pernicious woman!
> O villain, villain, smiling damned villain!

My tables. Meet it is I set it down
That one may smile, and smile, and be a villain –
At least I am sure it may be so in Denmark. [*Writes*.]
So, uncle, there you are. Now to my word.
It is 'Adieu, adieu, remember me.'
I have sworn't.   (1.5.95–112)

Here Hamlet demonstrates his competence as a reader. He purposely
drills in the sayings that will incite him to "honest actions," in this case,
to kill his father's killer, by copying the commandment, "Adieu, adieu,
remember me," in the metaphorical commonplace book of his memory,
and in an actual notebook. Much as a grammar-school boy would
attempt to shape himself after the image of Caesar by copying an
aphorism of his, Hamlet inscribes the words of his father's utterance. He
responds to his father's imperative "remember me" (i.e. "kill Claudius")
by rephrasing the command as a rhetorical question to which he three
times responds positively: "Remember thee? . . . Remember thee?" "Ay
. . . Yea . . . Yes, by heaven!" Hamlet's affirmative "ay," "yea," and
"yes, by heaven" constitute the swearing of an oath that he puts in
writing before confirming, "I have sworn't." Gertrude also asks to be
remembered by her son: "Have you forgot me?" (3.4.13). However, for
Hamlet, the task of memorizing and memorializing remains an affair
between men. He vows that his promise to a father, solemnized by verbal
oath and written text, will be the sole phrase inscribed in his brain,
displacing all that had been copied there previously.

By ascribing to "youth" the collection of quotations, memories, and
impressions written on the table of his memory, Hamlet presents the act
of erasing everything from his mind except the ghost's commandment as
a step toward manhood. He frames the meeting with the ghost as that of
his acceptance of adult responsibility, the moment at which Hamlet
becomes Hamlet, when the son steps into his father's place and takes on
his identity. Before writing down his father's words, Hamlet had added
an aphorism of his own composition to his notebook: "One may smile,
and smile, and be a villain." Jonson writes that "multiplicity of reading
. . . maketh a full man, not alone enabling him to know the history or
argument of a poem and to report it, but so to master the matter and
style as to show he knows how to handle, place, or dispose of either with
elegancy, when need shall be."[50] The "full man" described by Jonson is
one who cannot only recollect the material he has studied but also
"master," "handle," "place," and "dispose" its style and content. The
active verbs chosen by Jonson indicate that the full man is one who
demonstrates, by the way he acts upon what he has read, a capacity for
purposeful agency. In devising his own moral saying, Hamlet is follow-

ing, with an ironic twist, Jonson's counsel. Like the Jonsonian "full man," Hamlet asserts he is equipped to replace the "saws of books" with his own words, that he is ready to compose memorable lines of his own.

This image of Hamlet as a compliant reader "apt" (to use the ghost's term) for further instruction, sets up expectations that Hamlet will carry out the part of the obediently heroic son and put duty to father and state before all else. In that same passage, however, Hamlet qualifies his compliance so as to cast doubt upon the whole humanist project of shaping masculine identity through the inculcation of select aphoristic fragments. His self-consciousness about exhibiting the appropriate reader-response to the apparition borders on sarcasm. He might again be mimicking Polonius when he calls theatrically for his commonplace book ("My tables") and voices smug approbation about the importance of his own words ("meet it is I set it down"). The dark laughter of Hamlet's quips, "at least I am sure it may be so in Denmark," further undercuts the seriousness of the inscription of the commonplace book. The generalization copied with such care turns out to be of limited value, valid perhaps only in Denmark, and to issue from Hamlet's personalized anger at Claudius rather than from the universal truth to which aphorisms are supposed to refer.

Hamlet's equivocal humor is consonant with the disturbing tone of his soliloquy in which to remember means to kill, to inscribe to efface, and to attain maturity to become Hamlet, a dead man, a ghost. It discloses Hamlet's ambivalence about the erasure of self implicit in the notebook method for constructing masculinity. In sonnet 122, a poem also about memory and male bonds, a commonplace book prompts the poet-persona to reveal contradictory feelings about the shaping influence of his beloved patron-friend:

> Thy gift, thy tables, are within my brain
> Full charactered with lasting memory,
> Which shall above that idle rank remain,
> Beyond all date, even to eternity;
> Or at the least so long as brain and heart
> Have faculty by nature to subsist,
> Till each to razed oblivion yield his part
> Of thee, thy record never can be missed.
> That poor retention could not so much hold,
> Nor need I tallies thy dear love to score;
> Therefore to give them from me was I bold,
> To trust those tables that receive thee more.
>   To keep an adjunct to remember thee
>   Were to import forgetfulness in me.

The overt argument of the poem is that the poet has given away his friend's commonplace book, "thy tables," because their contents are now safely inscribed or "character'd" within his mind. The commonplace book, that "poor retention," cannot register as much text as the poet's brain; moreover, allowing its "tallies" to "score" the words of the friend would sully their love with mercantile connotations; it is an "adjunct," a crutch to memory, that imputes "forgetfulness" to the poet. He proves his devotion by becoming a blank page for his friend to write upon.

Yet the sonnet also suggests that inscription is a vexed procedure. The jubilant pledge made in the first quatrain that the contents of the commonplace book will survive in the poet's memory "beyond all date, even to eternity" is undercut completely by the pessimistic second quatrain. In those lines, "Eternity" is arbitrarily redefined to mean "at the least, so long as brain and heart / Have faculty by nature to subsist, / Till each to raz'd oblivion yield his part / Of thee." The patron's notebook, then, is not to be confused with the poet's powerful rhyme of sonnet 55. Instead of outlasting marble and gilded monuments, it will be consigned to "raz'd oblivion." Only for the short span of a man's life, its "contents never can be miss'd." The assurance is hardly reassuring; the line suggests that the notebook will be readily locatable, but also, perhaps, that it will not be missed personally by the poet, that its loss does not pain him. The persona's nonchalance about having given away the intimate gift he received from his friend recalls Othello's rebuke to Desdemona about her missing handkerchief: "To lose't or give't away were such perdition / As nothing else could match" (3.4.65–6). Whatever anxieties the persona's ambiguous language arouses about his fidelity are not offset by the subsequent assertion that he himself gave the "tables" away: "Therefore to give them from me was I bold."

In the final couplet of the sonnet, the persona makes the practice of keeping a commonplace book itself suspect: "To keep an adjunct to remember thee / Were to import forgetfulness in me." According to the persona, the commonplace book is a superfluous device for remembering someone he could not under any circumstances forget. For Hamlet, it is a testament to filial duty. Both the persona and Hamlet iterate the need to demonstrate and deny, even within the same line, the depth and force of their loyalty. Like the persona, Hamlet qualifies his promise to the ghost by saying that he will remember the ghost only "whiles memory holds a seat in this distracted globe," a claim that sounds especially dubious at the moments at which Hamlet's madness is most convincing. The term "distracted" is linked with insanity, and it is only a few lines later that Hamlet begins to speak in what Horatio describes as "wild and whirling words" (1.5.139).

The conflicted language of the sonnet and Hamlet's soliloquy brings into relief a nexus of concerns about reading, identity, and masculinity. Stephen Greenblatt writes that in Tyndale's *Obedience of a Christian Man*, "we may watch the fashioning of the Protestant discourse of self out of conflicting impulses: rage against authority and identification with authority, hatred of the father and ardent longing for union with the father, confidence in oneself and an anxious sense of weakness and sinfulness, justification and guilt."[51] In the sonnet and in Hamlet's encounter with the ghost we are witness to a similar struggle between self-assertion and self-abnegation. Reading as a method of male self-fashioning involves erasure as well as encryption. Both the persona and Hamlet undergo a kind of self-obliteration when they are "character'd" by the utterances of a male figure, patron-friend or father, who stands in hierarchical relation to them. (Laertes' father instructs him similarly: "these few precepts in thy memory / Look thou character" (1.3.58–9)). The persona of the sonnet says that the tables of his friend "are within my brain / Full character'd with lasting memory." The word "full" functions here both as an adverb, conveying that the notebook has been copied in its entirety, and as an adjective referring to the brain now so crowded with the friend's text that it is too "full" to contain anything else. Hamlet must "wipe away" all other memories and texts so that his father's "commandment alone shall live / Within the book and volume" of Hamlet's brain. The idea expressed in both texts is that the self can be inscribed only after having been expurgated, that male identity emerges as a consequence of being subsumed.

The commonplace book epitomizes tensions that such contradictions trigger in Hamlet, the trained reader forced either to be an inadequate reader or not to *be*. In the remainder of the play, Hamlet's recalcitrant submission to masculine inscription registers as an unwillingness to follow the expected procedure for reading the examples before him. He voices the understanding that each example should register indelibly on his consciousness and provoke him to an act of imitation. However, throughout the course of the play, Hamlet's process of reading is short-circuited. He repeatedly fails to act upon the example before him, even when doing so makes him feel ashamed and inadequate. Paradoxically, there is an inverse relation between Hamlet's valorization of masculine paradigms and his willingness to be fashioned by them. He critiques heroic exemplarity most severely, conveying his antagonism in mordant jibes, at the very moment that he is preparing, at the end of the play, to sacrifice himself on its altar.

Like Nathaniel in *Love's Labour's Lost*, who suffers stagefright in the role of Alexander the Great ("A conquerer and afeard to speak"),

Hamlet finds himself "o'erparted" when made to play his father.[52] His inability to imitate King Hamlet, a longstanding theme in psychoanalytic discussions of the play, has been explicated with particular force by Janet Adelman. As she observes, Gertrude's "failure of memory – registered in her undiscriminating sexuality – in effect defines Hamlet's task in relation to his father as a task of memory: as she forgets, he inherits the burden of differentiating, of idealizing and making static the past . . . As his memory of his father pushes increasingly in the direction of idealization, Hamlet becomes more acutely aware of his own distance from that idealization and hence of his likeness to Claudius, who is defined chiefly by his difference from his father."[53] This account of the play is important to this chapter, especially as it concerns the development of Hamlet's growing unease about the difficulty of sustaining his extreme idealizations. My reading, however, locates Hamlet's unsuccessful attempts to emulate his father within an additional (historical) context, namely that of the organization of literacy along gender lines in early modern England. From this perspective, Gertrude's apparently blasé "failure of memory," Ophelia's poignant refuge in oral tradition, and Hamlet's ambivalent reliance on a notebook for remembering his father refer to cultural and historical conflicts of society at large as well as to the psychosexual dynamics of a family. The fissures that rive the psyches of Gertrude, Ophelia, and Hamlet also issue from a culture in which memory was defined as a masculine property, a commodity displayed by ownership of a commonplace book, a form of social capital whose acquisition was fraught with hierarchical implications.

"Examples gross as earth exhort me," Hamlet says (4.4.46). His world is peopled by masculine heroes. In his eyes, his father is a combination of Hyperion, Jove, Mars, and Mercury:

> See what a grace was seated on this brow,
> Hyperion's curls, the front of Jove himself,
> An eye like Mars to threaten and command,
> A station like the herald Mercury
> New-lighted on a heaven-kissing hill,
> A combination and a form indeed,
> Where every god did seem to set his seal
> To give the world assurance of a man.   (3.4.55–62)

Hamlet defines Claudius, and by implication all men including himself, in relation to that dazzling figure with curled locks from one god, the forehead of a second, the piercing regard of a third, and the bearing of a fourth god pictured as standing nearly in heaven. The collocation of these divinities in one person gives "the world assurance of a man." This procedure of measuring one's manhood against towering figures from the literary or historical past guides Hamlet's estimation of his own worth; he denigrates himself for falling short of the god-like father he has put together, much as he composed his soliloquies, from fragments out of books.

The first of the series of examples confronted by Hamlet is the "fair and warlike form" of his father's ghost (1.1.50). As David Scott Kastan notes, "The imitator runs the risk of being overwhelmed by his model, trapped in and by the excellence he admires."[54] If the male subject risks being trapped by excellence when presented with an exemplar such as Jove, the danger may be even greater when the model of imitation is his own father. Hamlet knows that he must measure up to the great military hero whose exploits remain the talk of admiring sentries who still refer to the king as "our valiant Hamlet" (1.1.87). As with their names, the identities of father and son should be interchangeable. Yet the closest Hamlet comes to imitating his father at the beginning of the play is when he parodies the ghost and frightens Ophelia. By her report, Hamlet accosted her, "Pale as his shirt . . . And with a look so piteous in purport / As if he had been loosed out of hell" (2.1.81–3).

The second example is that of Aeneas. After greeting the company of players, Hamlet begins to recite Aeneas' tale to Dido, a speech he "chiefly lov'd" in a previous production the company staged. He gets as far as a description of the murderer Pyrrhus. Then one of the players continues the rest of the speech in which Aeneas describes the murder of Priam and Hecuba's subsequent grief. The scene prompts Hamlet to contrast himself with the player who simulated, with such apparent feeling, Aeneas' grief and rage in recounting the bloody murder and its aftermath:

> Is it not monstrous that this player here,
> But in a fiction, in a dream of passion,
> Could force his soul so to his own conceit . . .
> Yet I,
> A dull and muddy-mettled rascal, peak
> Like John-a-dreams, unpregnant of my cause,
> And can say nothing . . .   (2.2.545–7, 561–4)

Hamlet presents himself as "unpregnant" of his cause, the antithesis of the Jonsonian "full man," empty of the matter that facilitates expression, unfit by comparison with the player who imitates Virgil's hero successfully. Hamlet is unable to "force his soul so to his own conceit," and so fails to emulate Aeneas. Indeed, he makes a slip in remembering his lines which suggests that he identifies with the feminine character in the story – Dido.[55] This is how Hamlet begins Aeneas' speech:

If it live in your memory, begin at this line – let me see, let me see –
The rugged Pyrrhus, like th'Hyrcanian beast –
'Tis not so. It begins with Pyrrhus –
The rugged Pyrrhus, he whose sable arms . . .   (2.2.444–8)

Speaking in the voice of Aeneas, Hamlet mistakenly compares the murderous Pyrrhus to a Hyrcanian beast: "The rugged Pyrrhus, like the Hyrcanian beast." In Virgil's epic, the phrase that Hamlet mistakenly uses, "Hyrcanian beast," belongs to Dido. After realizing that he has misspoken, Hamlet recites the correct line: "The rugged Pyrrhus, he whose sable arms."

Hamlet's memory lapse is significant, for Aeneas was one of the principle heroes whom male readers were supposed to imitate. Sidney alludes to this convention when he appeals to his reader in *An Apology for Poetry*: "Only let Aeneas be worn in the tablet of your memory, how he governeth himself in the ruin of his country, in the preserving of his old father, and carrying away his religious ceremonies, in obeying the god's commandment to leave Dido, though not only all passionate kindness, but even the human consideration of virtuous gratefulness, would have craved other of him."[56] Aeneas' filial duty, his "preserving of his old father," makes him an even more appropriate model for Hamlet to invoke after having inscribed his father's command on "the table of [his] memory." In reciting Aeneas' speech, Hamlet is speaking in the voice of the classical hero who carried his father away on his back as fire engulfed Troy. Aeneas, Cassius remembers in *Julius Caesar*, "Did from the flames of Troy upon his shoulder / The old Anchises bear" (1.2.115–16). It is Hamlet's task to follow Aeneas in putting his duty to his father ahead of his own fate, ahead of "even the human consideration of virtuous gratefulness." Yet after the inscription of his memory, Hamlet resists imitating Aeneas. Instead of acting as Aeneas did in honoring his father and obeying received orders, Hamlet recalls the abandonment Dido suffered when Aeneas chose country, father, and religion over "passionate kindness." In the *Aeneid*, Dido asserts that Aeneas is so heartless that he must have been suckled by Hyrcanian tigers.[57] Hamlet's slip of the tongue shows that he aligns himself subconsciously with the queen, contrary to the instructions of *De Copia*, and not, as he should, with the Virgilian masculine hero.

The next examples that Hamlet encounters are more permutations of his ghost-father. In *The Murder of Gonzago*, King Hamlet returns as the Player King. The play within Shakespeare's play is not meant only to provoke Claudius to implicate himself in his brother's murder. It is also designed to provoke Hamlet, to enact the murder of his father and seduction of his mother so that he himself will be forced to witness it, to inscribe those events so indelibly on his consciousness that he will be compelled to act. Hamlet becomes so absorbed in the play that he even urges the murderer to commit the regicide: "Begin, murderer. Leave thy damnable faces and begin. Come, the croaking raven doth bellow for revenge" (3.2.246–8). While Horatio later says that he "did very well note" Claudius, Hamlet's whole attention appears focused on the players (3.2.284). That it is Ophelia, not Hamlet, who voices a reaction when the King stands up, further corroborates the impression that Hamlet is transfixed by the spectacle of poison and corruption before him.

From the gaunt military hero in act one to the emblem of trusting virtue in the players' Italian drama, King Hamlet undergoes another transformation when he turns up again as the ghost in Gertrude's bedchamber. This time, according to the stage direction in the first quarto, he arrives not in plated armor but in a nightgown. Hamlet further emphasizes the foolishness of the ghost's appearance with the line he speaks upon the ghost's arrival. "Immediately before Hamlet refers to Claudius as a 'king of shreds and patches,'" Margaret Ferguson points out, "the ghost appears, or rather reappears, with a dramatic entrance that allows the phrase 'king of shreds and patches' to refer to the ghost as well as to Claudius."[58] The ambiguity of the reference turns the ghost, the primary exemplar of the play who has just had all the attributes of Hyperion, Jove, Mars, and Mercury heaped upon him, into a figure of ridicule, a ragged jester: "A king of shreds and patches – / Enter GHOST – " (3.4.103). In answer, the ghost insists upon the solemnity of his visit, explaining that he has returned to goad Hamlet's memory: "Do not forget. This visitation / Is but to whet thy almost blunted purpose" (3.4.110–11). And he reiterates his earlier injunction, "remember me," with the negative command, "do not forget." For Hamlet, not forgetting, in this context, does not mean simply recalling his father's command; it entails re-membering the father himself by acting as a martial hero in his place.[59] But all that Hamlet fights back in this scene are his own tears. He testifies that the vision of the ghost would make stones capable of courageous deeds; that is not, however, its effect on him. The ghost's "piteous action," some kind of gesture akin to the "passionate action" exhibited by the Player Queen in the dumb show, threatens to convert his stern effects, to move him not to kill but to weep.

After King Hamlet and Aeneas, the final heroic figure encountered by Hamlet is that of Fortinbras. Hamlet pointedly defines the youthful soldier-prince leading his troops into battle against Poland as the kind of "example" students were enjoined to follow:

> Examples gross as earth exhort me,
> Witness this army of such mass and charge,
> Led by a delicate and tender prince,
> Whose spirit, with divine ambition puff'd,
> Makes mouths at the invisible event,
> Exposing what is mortal and unsure
> To all that fortune, death, and danger dare,
> Even for an eggshell.   (4.4.46–53)

Hamlet emphasizes that the examples confronting him do not require extraordinary interpretive skill; they are self-evident, "gross as earth." Here again, Hamlet mixes conventional truisms with cutting ironies. He takes pains to draw the correct lesson from the model hero. Observing how the contrast between the delicacy of Fortinbras' physique and the massive size of his army accentuates his daring, Hamlet pronounces a suitable aphorism: "Rightly to be great / Is not to stir without great argument, / But greatly to find quarrel in a straw / When honour's at the stake" (4.4.53–6). After pointing out the contrast between himself and Fortinbras, as he did earlier with the actor playing Aeneas, Hamlet voices his sense of failure and "shame" for falling short of the ideal represented by the rival prince. But in the same lines he disrupts the valorizing effect of his commonplace with an image of hollowness. The ideal Hamlet is unable or unwilling to exemplify in his actions is shown to be a fantasy and trick of fame. All the epic pageantry of the Norwegian army and their youthful general marching off to death cannot conceal the meaninglessness of the conflict for which they will die. Their honor is an eggshell.

This sense of the absurd only grows in Hamlet as he begins, at the end of a long struggle, to move from inscription to imitation. The task facing Hamlet has always been that which Claudius puts to Laertes: "What would you undertake / To show yourself in deed your father's son / More than in words?" (4.7.123–5). In conversation with Horatio, Hamlet suggests that his journey to England was a turning point in his attempts to emulate his father. The initial act of writing in his commonplace book was meant to turn him into his father. By copying out the words of the ghost, he was aiming, in Jonsonian terms, "to follow him, till he grow very he: or so like him, as the copy may be mistaken for the principal." Hamlet invokes the Jonsonian metaphor directly when he describes having sealed a letter condemning Rosencrantz and Guildenstern to death. Luckily, he explains, "I had my father's signet in my purse, / Which was the model of that Danish seal" (5.2.49–50). Hamlet uses the original signet that was the "model" for the official seal on Claudius' letter. He "folded the writ up in the form of th'other, / Subscrib'd it, gave't th'impression, plac'd it safely" (5.2.51–2). Like the ghost, he inscribes instead of being inscribed; he is himself a model for others to emulate and capable of giving the document his "impression." Hamlet's letter is indistinguishable from the letter of the King.

Yet in the process of mastering imitation, Hamlet became uncertain about its value. He had made an equivocal statement on the subject early on in the play. "Ambition [is] of so airy and light a quality . . . it is but a shadow's shadow," Rosencrantz had told him. "Then," answered Hamlet, "are our beggars bodies, and our monarchs and outstretch'd heroes the beggars' shadows" (2.2.261–4). Hamlet's insight is that if ambition is unsubstantial, then monarchs and heroes reach fruitlessly to exemplify a grandiose illusion, a shadow's shadow: ambition. By this logic, to imitate heroic exemplars is to seek oneself to become a shadow. Beggars, men untrained in humanist imitation, are substantial compared to princes foolishly trying to become Aeneas and Alexander, Mars and Mercury. Hamlet came back from England more bitter. He meditates in the churchyard cemetery about the futility of modelling one's self after dead men: "Dost thou think Alexander looked o' this fashion i' th'earth? . . . Why, may not imagination trace the noble dust of Alexander till a find it stopping a bung-hole? . . . Alexander died, Alexander was buried, Alexander returneth to dust, the dust is earth, of earth we make loam, and why of that loam whereto he was converted might they not stop a beer-barrel?" (5.1.191–2, 196–8, 201–5). In this passage, Hamlet puts to rest the notion that humanist imitation of classical heroes inspires greatness in English schoolboys; rather, as his parody of an exercise in Latin grammar suggests, it prompts automatic responses rehearsed by rote.

In *Henry V*, Fluellen's comic allusion to Alexander the Pig, a bungled analogy between Alexander the Great (or Big) and the English king, parodies humanist idealization of Alexander to similar effect. The clumsiness of the Welsh captain's parallel, which extends to include the birthplaces of Alexander and Henry, exposes example-based hermeneutics as an exercise in arbitrary connections: "I tell you, captain, if you look in the maps of the world, I warrant you sall find, in the comparisons between Macedon and Monmouth, that the situations, look you, is both alike. There is a river in Macedon, and there is also moreover a river at Monmouth. It is call'd Wye at Monmouth, but it is out of my prains what is the name of the other river – but 'tis all one, 'tis alike as my fingers is to my fingers, and there is salmons in both" (4.7.19–25). In the dramatic narrative, this tongue-in-cheek critique of humanist exemplarity is set between two grim scenes showing Henry V issuing the command, contrary to the accepted rules of war, to kill all of the French prisoners. "Pity it was," Holinshed writes of the slaughter, "to see how some

Frenchmen were suddenly sticked with daggers, some were brained with poleaxes, some slain with mauls, other had their throats cut, and some their bellies paunched."[60] By underlining the absurdity of Fluellen's comparison of Alexander the Great and Henry V, Shakespeare also highlights an incongruity between Henry's glorified image and the gruesome deeds he performs in pursuit of glory. The grand analogies of humanist schoolmasters turn out to obscure hypocrisy and cruelty. The exalted figure of Alexander, compared to a pig in *Henry V*, devolves to dirt in *Hamlet*. In contrast with the heaven-directed process by which Hamlet constructed his father as a god-like exemplar poised on-high, his thoughts now incline downward. The bone-littered ground of the church cemetery makes the emulation of heroic figures seem akin to what Montaigne termed "imitation meurtrière."[61]

This is the position in which Hamlet finds himself in the fifth act: stripped of all options other than that of heroic imitation, a course of action with lethal consequences. The predicament is captured uncannily in a preface appended to Jacques Du Bosq's conduct manual *The Complete Woman*. In a lengthy digression away from the topic of the book, the preface comments on the inadequacy of exemplarity as a principle of self-fashioning. Published several decades after *Hamlet*, when humanist habits of thought were beginning to lose their hold, the preface argues that the "weaknesse of examples" follows from the fact that actions singled out for imitation are extracted from the context in which they first occurred. The obligation to emulate deeds from the past, regardless of what one's own position would otherwise dictate, reduces the scope for action available to the male reader and introduces an element of irrationality to his decision-making. In the end, the author observes, "we follow not the judgement of those great men, nor but our own" and we are left "not having a full fredome of choice" in circumstances that call for strategic calculation. The author describes the constraints that exemplarity imposes:

Because he is forced and tied as it were to imitation, that he is prevented by an example which captivates him, through the great esteme we have thereof. And that the desire we have to become like to some goodly model, and to do a thing like to another which hath been applauded of all, shuts up the eyes of our reason, and lets it not consider at leasure, the time and places and other circumstances, which make an action good or ill.[62]

In all of the instances previously cited in which he fails to live up to the models of masculine bravura presented to him in the persons of Aeneas, Fortinbras, and his own father, Hamlet must respond to a dramatic situation and at the same time emulate established examples. He is incapacitated not by a morbid state of mind, as A. C. Bradley would have it, but by the impossibility of reconciling the contrary demands placed upon him.[63] Hamlet, as Polonius points out, may walk "with a larger tether" than may be given to Ophelia (1.3.125); nonetheless, what differentiates Hamlet and Ophelia is the degree of constraint imposed on each and not the constraint itself. Hamlet, too, is "forced and tied as it were to imitation." The situation calls for political cunning and maneuvering. Yet Hamlet is made to prove his physical courage in a duel in which the deck is stacked against him, sword and wine laced with poison, and his prowess cannot save him. For Hamlet, humanist models of identity and techniques of reading are neither liberating nor enabling; they pave the way to his death.

While Fortinbras, like Virgil's Aeneas, unhesitatingly puts father and country before all else, Hamlet still harbors the suspicion that doing so is a betrayal of himself. "How all occasions do inform against me," he says, "And spur my dull revenge" (4.4.32–3). Earlier he self-deprecatingly rejected a comparison of himself with lofty Hercules; in the cemetery even that idol has fallen. "Let Hercules himself do what he may," he says, "The cat will mew, and dog will have his day" (5.1.286–7). The impotence Hamlet attributes to Hercules describes his own conformity in submitting to the example of his father. Previously, he agreed to the ghost's command with shouts of affirmation: "Ay . . . Yea . . . Yes by Heaven!" Later, unable to follow through on his initial impulse, he posed the question: "How if I answer no?" (5.2.167). It is not until the end of the play that Hamlet is able, like the player, to "force his soul" to the imitation of a heroic model, to carry out the second stage of the reading process. Only at that point does Hamlet begin to act on the examples he has been recording. He presents himself as a martial contender, "in the same figure like the King that's dead" (1.1.44). Horatio now might say of the two Hamlets, as he once said of King Hamlet and the ghost, "these hands are not more like" (1.2.212). Hamlet is now similar enough to Hamlet to be mistaken for him. Force of example turns young Hamlet into *un exemplaire*, a duplicate, a copy. The self that declares itself in the first-person is evacuated of its singularity by the same paternal identification that bodies it forth. He steps into a grave with a cry from the dead: "This is I, / Hamlet the Dane" (5.1.250–1).

Hamlet's birth, as we know from the first gravedigger, coincided with his father's duel with King Fortinbras. The duel that he himself fights marks that anniversary ironically. The occasion turns Hamlet into a corpse and his father's ghost. Challenged by Laertes, the resigned Hamlet of act five answers as his father did when "dar'd to the combat" by King Fortinbras and agrees to a duel. He begins to speak in the royal "we": "We defy augury" (5.2.215). He walks into a trap set by his father's murderer and by the son of the man he himself murdered with the nonchalance of the soldiers he observed going to their graves as if to their beds. In that final scene, he must appear to the assembled audience, "Officers *with cushions* . . . KING, QUEEN, LAERTES, [OSRIC], *and all the* State" as King Hamlet himself did in the duel that he fought over the fate of the kingdom (5.2.221). Informed against, betrayed, Hamlet fulfills his oath by killing Claudius and is himself killed. He knew that the risk of imitating dead heroes was that he might become one of them. His corpse is now an example for others. Fortinbras himself issues the command that equates Hamlet with past military heroes, Aeneas and King Hamlet among them: "Bear Hamlet like a soldier to the stage" (5.2.401). Imitation turned out to be, as Hamlet suspected, a method not only for creating the self but also for expunging it.

The reluctance that Hamlet evinces in this play shows that resistance can come from members of a dominant class when circumstances bring their own inclinations or preferences into conflict with prevailing values and practices. By contrast, Ophelia reminds us that the dominated, even when they seem least capable of action, can assert their independence by resorting to alternative cultural forms. A society, as Michel de Certeau observes, is "composed of foregrounded practices organizing its norma-tive institutions *and* of innumerable other practices that remain 'minor,' always there but not organizing discourses and preserving the beginnings or remains of different . . . hypotheses for that society or for others."[64] The meanings of Ophelia's flowers, like the stories of the master's daughter or the baker's daughter, are multiple, overlapping, part of a folkloric tradition available to the daughter of the Lord Chamberlain as well as to the daughter of the fishmonger. Like the royal ghost, Ophelia presumes to inscribe the memory of others. "There's rosemary," she tells Laertes, "that's for remembrance – pray you, love, remember" (4.5.173–4). While the ghost tells Hamlet to recall his obligation to submit to paternal and state authority, Ophelia brings back to our memory buried beliefs and stories subversive of that order, the remains of a different hypothesis for early modern society and for Shakespeare's play.

Fig. 6   Portrait of Mary Sidney, Countess of Pembroke. Simon van de Passe, 1618.

3 She reads and smiles

Enter Modestia reading in a book.[1]
Enter Valdaura, reading to her selfe.[2]
Enter Celia wth a Booke in her hand.[3]
Enter Vittoria with a booke in her hand.[4]
Enter Queene Mary with a Prayer Booke in her hand, like a Nun.[5]
Enter Matilda, in mourning vaile, reading on a booke.[6]
Enter a Page deliuering a letter to Sopho. which shee priuately reads.[7]
*Enter Second Lady, who curtsies to all, but Salandine, they to her; then
  she sits on the Rushes, and takes out a book to read.*[8]
Enter Lepida in her night attire with a Booke and a lighted Taper.[9]
*Enter Charmia in her night gown, with a prayer Book and a Taper, boults
  the door and sits down.*[10]
She sits downe hauing a candle by her, and reades.[11]
She reads and smiles.[12]

For Hamlet, a woman holding a book is a cliché figure for female virtue:
a nymph in her orisons. The fact of her sex alone classifies her perusal of
a text as an exercise in piety. Hamlet's response to the sight of Ophelia
reading stems from dictates that also informed assumptions about female
readers off-stage. In 1597, Nicholas Breton praised Mary Sidney in terms
that could have been taken from any conduct manual: "Vertue is her
love, Truth is her studie, and Meditation is her exercise."[13] The plaudit,
as much prescription as description, assumes that female virtue is
inseparable from pious reading. It commends Sidney not as an accomplished scholar, which her work shows her to have been, but as a
practitioner of the chastity-through-busy-work form of literacy recommended by Juan Luis Vives and Richard Hyrd as a technique for female
self-fashioning. In spite of her achievements in classical learning and
poetic composition, Sidney's ultimate value, her reputation for chastity,
derives from her immersion in the same basic program of reading-only
literacy set as a requirement for all women alike.

At first glance, the Simon van de Passe portrait of Sidney with an open
book in her right hand appears only to complement Breton's description

of the Countess as Devotion's Visage (fig. 6). She is identified in the 1618 engraving by a Latin inscription encircling her face and upper body and translated underneath into English: "The Right Honorable and most vertuous Lady MARY SIDNEY, wife to the late deceased Henry Herbert Earle of Pembroke &c." Once again, female virtue, supplemented by proofs of social status, is represented through the iconography of woman and book. The significance of the engraving shifts, however, once the viewer becomes aware of a small detail. Inscribed in minute letters along the edge of its open pages is the title of the book: "Davids Psalmes."

By picturing Sidney with the Book of Psalms she was celebrated for translating, van de Passe redeploys the conventional iconography of the female reader to create an unorthodox portrait of a female author. The book in the engraving still functions metonymically as a sign of exemplary female devotion, but the virtue it denotes is not predicated on silence, the mute expression of the wife in *The Revenger's Tragedy* who decorously commits suicide after having been raped, communicating an explanation voicelessly through a passage marked in her prayer book. Mary Sidney revised the forty-three psalms her brother had completed at his death and translated the remaining one hundred and seven herself; her experimentation with a dazzling array of verse forms influenced poets such as John Donne and George Herbert. While the book in Tourneur's play illustrates the wife's chosen muteness, the book of "Davids Psalmes" in the engraving symbolizes the most inspired song of which the human voice is capable. As Samuel Daniel put it in addressing Mary Sidney, "Those Hymns that thou doost consecrate to heaven, / Which Israels Singer to his God did frame: / Unto thy voyce eternitie hath given."[14] The irony implicit in the portrait is that Sidney's standing as articulate Protestant writer depends upon her being seen as a reticent female reader. Her literary production is authorized only to the extent that it can be understood also as participating in the feminized occupation of reading devotional texts: psalms from the Bible.

The portrait's double vision of Sidney as a writer hidden in the figure of a devout reader was one that Sidney herself cultivated. Her public persona as a reader, along with her elevated rank and financial means, enabled her to maintain her respectability even as she broke with convention by acting as a patron, editor, and author. The ambiguity of her position is captured in titles, most famously in *The Countess of Pembroke's Arcadia*, in dedications that identify her as an esteemed reader, and in prefaces that hint, to varying degrees, at a role for her in the production of those works as well.[15] The slippage between Mary Sidney's roles as passive consumer and active creator is explicitly raised in the edition of her brother's romance published under her aegis. The

1593 preface unpacks the double entendre of the possessive case used in the book's title, *The Countess of Pembroke's Arcadia*. Foregrounding Mary Sidney's "honourable labor" in repairing the "ruinous house" of Philip's unfinished manuscript, the preface concludes that the work "is now by more than one interest *The Countesse of Pembroke's Arcadia*: done, as it was, for her: as it is, by her."[16] Only the architectural metaphor affixes a saving qualification to the astonishing claim that the *Arcadia* is "by her." Mary Sidney does not build from the ground up but repairs an existing structure to stand as a monument to her family name. Her exertion can be considered honorable because it is offered in service to a brother's memory and literary reputation, not her own.

Mary Sidney exploits the subject position of reader to similar effect in her work as a translator. She established credibility by rendering into English texts associated with the Protestant cause, most notably the Psalms but also the Huguenot tract *Excellent discours de la vie et de la mort*. When Mary Wroth wrote original fiction and poetry, the romance *Urania* and sonnet sequence *Pamphilia to Amphilanthus*, she had Mary Sidney's translations brandished at her as a reproach. Conveniently forgetting Sidney's contribution to *The Arcadia* and her translation of Petrarchan poetry, Lord Edward Denny lectured Wroth to stop writing "lascivious tales" and to follow instead the "rare, and pious example of [her] vertuous and learned Aunt, who translated so many godly books and especially the holy psalmes of David."[17] Yet composing an English version of a foreign language devotional work was not necessarily so innocuous as Denny implies. As Margaret Hannay and Anne Lake Prescott, among others, have observed, early modern women often subtly altered or undermined texts in the process of translating them.[18] The practice offered a socially sanctioned opportunity for female expression because it could be absorbed within an orthodox framework. In Mary Sidney's case, the respectability that she accumulated within the sector of religious literature offered her a measure of protection for ventures into more secular domains.

Even in recent decades, however, the image of Sidney as pious reader has obscured from view the significance of her non-devotional writing, in particular that of her important translation of Robert Garnier's *Marc Antoine*. Her publication of *Antonius: A Tragedy* brought her into conflict with at least two contemporaries, Samuel Brandon and Samuel Daniel, drew Shakespeare into the fray as a mediator, and put her work at the center of a debate that played out over several decades on the stages of the English public theatre. The unfolding of the confrontation can be read in a string of related plays that followed the appearance of Sidney's Cleopatra play: Daniel's *Tragedy of Cleopatra* (1594), Brandon's

Tragicomedy of the Virtuous Octavia (1598), Shakespeare's *Antony and Cleopatra* (c. 1607), and Daniel's revised *Tragedy of Cleopatra* (1607). The care with which Brandon, Daniel, and Shakespeare read Sidney's play testifies to the force of her critique. Through her own labor of literacy, Mary Sidney challenged the humanist model of the ideal woman as a figure of virtuous passivity, Chastity on a monument reading psalms, and valorized in its place a model of action not alabaster, Cleopatra toiling physically to raise the dying Antony to the top of a building for a last embrace, passion exemplified in a feat of heroic exertion. By offering this revisionary reading of the character of Cleopatra and by assuming the anti-conventional role of writer-translator, Sidney took a public stance against the constriction of the exemplary woman to chastity icon and against the reduction of female literacy to chastity exercise.

I

Antonius: A Tragedy can be read as a proleptic answer to the admonition – "Be you all Octavias" – that Richard Brathwait would address to female readers four decades after Sidney's translation first appeared.[19] While conduct manuals defined female identity through contrasting figures of goodness and badness – Lucrece and Helen, Virginia and Clytemnestra, Octavia and Cleopatra – Sidney's translation presented a direct challenge to that Una-Duessa schema for constructing female subjectivity through reading. Robert Garnier's *Marc Antoine* unsettled rigid dichotomies by depicting Cleopatra as a complex heroic subject worthy of emulation. By translating his play, Sidney undermined prevailing dicta about what counted as a positive example for the female reader. Her *Antonius* introduced to the canon of published English literature a female anti-example recast in positive terms as a stage heroine. With that public endorsement of Cleopatra as a model for the English gentlewoman, an alternative to the Octavia praised in conduct manuals, Sidney risked undermining the image of herself as a devotional reader on which her public persona was founded.

We saw in the previous chapter that the female reader was taught to epitomize feminine virtue by identifying herself with ideal figures and distancing herself from their anti-ideal opposites. Her task did not extend to original composition or public action. She was assigned to meditate on the text as an end in itself. This procedure of devotional contemplation differs most from the technique of humanist imitation taught to school-boys in that its end was mainly metaphysical. While the male reader was challenged to emulate valiant men (Aeneas and Caesar) through his actions, the female reader was told to distinguish herself from lascivious women (Julia and Cleopatra) and to align herself with chaste women (Lucrece and Octavia) on the basis of her mental outlook, the purity of her thoughts.

Dedicated to Mary Sidney's mother, the epistle to Geoffrey Fenton's *Tragical Discourses* (1567) recapitulates these sex-specific instructions for reading. Fenton justifies his translation of Bandello's novellas by claiming that it will teach the male reader to participate in civic life and to promote the welfare of his country. To the female reader, it offers a "stoare of examples" that will "instructe her in her dutie, eyther for the maried to kepe her fayth to her husband, with Lucretia, or the unmaried to defend her virginitye, with Virginya."[20] Her lesson is to die in the event of rape; her examples are female corpses, Virginia and Lucrece.[21] Fenton extrapolates on these separate approaches to reading by providing each sex with a "diversitie of examples in sondrye younge men and women." Model female subjects are "patternes of chastetye" characterized by a willingness to die to preserve their virtue unsullied. They have no scope for action except to choose between the "daunger" of illicit sexuality and the supposed "felicitye" of death. Exemplary male subjects, on the other hand, are "maisters of theym selves." They achieve distinction through active self-discipline; "bridlynge wythe maine hande, the humour of theyr inordinate luste," these praiseworthy men "vanquished all mocions of sensualytye, and became maisters of theym selves" (8). Verbs such as "use," "commande," "bridle," and "vanquish" link exemplary masculinity with control over one's self and others. This contrast between the qualities of a virtuous woman and those of a virtuous man, between a state of being and a capacity for action, between the epitomization of chastity and the enactment of mastery, points to the gender differences that humanist practices of reading were intended to instill.

The epistle addressed to Mary Sidney's mother is an instance of the continual pressures that operated on members of the Sidney household to follow examples from life and literature. After Mary Sidney's brother Philip left home to study at Oxford, her father instructed his younger son Robert to imitate his absent brother: "Follo the dyrectyon of your most lovyng brother . . . Imitate hys vertues, exercyses, studyes, & accyons; he ys a rare ornament of thys age, the very formular, that all well dysposed young Gentlymen of ouer Court, do form allsoe thear maners & lyfe by . . . Ons agayn I say Imytate hym."[22] Philip Sidney became the object of even more intense veneration when he died on the battlefield fighting for the Protestant cause. In a Latin treatise titled *Nobilis* ("The Noble Man"), Thomas Moffett detailed Philip's perfections "by way of an example to [Philip] Sidney's most honorable nephew William Herbert."[23] Decades later, the sermon preached at the funeral of Herbert, Mary Sidney's son, who died in 1630 at the age of fifty, held him up as an example for his younger brother. Thomas Chaffinger informed Philip Herbert that his behavior would be judged by standards set by his brother and his uncle: "men are big with the expectation of you; and blame them not that they should be so, especially of you, who . . . have had so pious and religious an Aeneas to your brother, and so famous and valiant a Hector to your Uncle."[24]

While examples were pressed upon both men and women in the family, the expectations and penalties invoked by Chaffinger in referring to Aeneas and Hector were very different from those implied by alluding to Virginia and Lucrece. The funeral sermon exhorts Philip Herbert, the new Earl of Pembroke, to perform statesmanlike deeds in the conduct of his life; the dedicatory epistle warns Mary Dudley Sidney to refrain from extramarital sex on penalty of death. A man who acted recklessly in his youth, as did William Herbert, who refused to marry the lady-in-waiting pregnant with his child, could still be praised as an Aeneas at his funeral. Yet a woman even suspected of trespass, no matter how sterling her comportment, was liable to be derided as a passion-ridden Dido, the figure to whom Mary Sidney was compared in a 1603 letter from Dudley Carleton to John Chamberlain alleging that she had once loved Raleigh.[25] Sidney's standing as "a chaste matrone," as John Harrington refers to her in a letter to Lucy Harrington, Countess of Bedford, did not shield her from salacious allegations, even rumors of perversion, that circulated about her name.[26] Her good image as well as the insinuations that threatened it derived their strength from the classical models of female virtue and vice that inspired them. Sidney could never take her standing for granted. While Frances Meres complimented her with a comparison to the worthy Octavia in 1598, Sidney's choice of Cleopatra as a subject of reading put her in danger of being classified with the reviled seductress instead.

Sidney took that chance in choosing the French tragedy *Marc Antoine* as the text for her translation. The play rewrites Roman history, offering a particularly revisionary view of Cleopatra, in disregard of its own sources. At first, Garnier's Cléopâtre appears to be merely a conventional temptress. Over the course of five acts, however, she emerges as a multi-faceted character – queen, lover, mother, wife, and classical hero – captivating for her courage as well as her constancy. Through his staging of the story of Cleopatra and Antony, Garnier revisits the Dido and Aeneas myth, putting in question the radical gender differentiation it supports. In the *Aeneid*, Virgil represents Dido's love with images that recall fires lit in the Trojan war. In Garnier's play, the same metaphor operates to describe Antoine's ardor. The Egyptian philosopher Philostratus compares the passion burning in Antoine with the fire of war threatening Egypt: "Amour dont on se jouë, et qu'on dit ne s'esprendre / Que dans nos tendres cœurs, met nos villes en cendre" [The love we take lightly, thinking it kindles / Our fond hearts only, leaves our cities in ashes].[27] He warns that it was that same ardor, the love of Paris for Helen, which set Troy ablaze.

Borrowing from a French tragedy about the Carthaginian queen, Garnier underscores the tie between her story and that of her Egyptian counterpart by reassigning words spoken by Dido to Cléopâtre. In her final soliloquy, Cléopâtre restates and then revises Dido's description of herself as "heureuse et trop heureuse" [happy and too happy].[28] Happiness is not merely past but also present for Cléopâtre: "je suis heureuse, en mon mal devorant" [I am happy, in my consuming pain] (5.1962). The phrase echoes and confirms the chorus' earlier paradoxical assessment of her and Antoine: "Heureux en son malheur Antoine, / Et bien heureuse nostre Royne" [Antoine, happy in his unhappiness, / And very happy our queen] (3.1326–7). Their unhappy happiness is to suffer defeat and separation in this world only to find one another again in the next. In Cléopâtre's dying vision, the Ptolemaic kings are absent and the couple walks alone along an underworld river lined with cypress trees:

> Or meurs donc Cleopatre, et plus long temps n'absentes
> Antoine, qui t'attend aux rives pallissantes;
> Va rejoindre son ombre.   (5.1904–6)

> Je mourrois tout soudain, tout soudain je mourrois,
> Et ja fugitive Ombre avec toy je serois,
> Errant sous les cyprés des rives escartees,
> Au lamentable bruit des eaux Acherontees.   (5.1970–3)

> [Die then, Cleopatra, and stay no longer
> From Antony who waits for you by the pale shores [of Acheron];
> Go join his ghost.]

> [I would die instantly, instantly I would die,
> And be with you soon a fleeting shadow,
> Wandering under the cypress trees on distant shores,
> By the mournful sound of Acheron's stream.]

These verses and those of the chorus summon images from Virgil's epic of Aeneas' failed encounter with Dido in the underworld. In book six, Aeneas attempts to justify himself to her: "I swear by heaven's stars, by the high gods, / By any certainty below the earth, / I left your land against my will . . . The gods' commands drove me to do their will." The dissimilarity between the epic and Garnier's play is that Virgil depicts Dido, "the burning soul, savagely glaring back," as answering Aeneas' sorrowful plea by turning her back and fleeing his presence "his enemy still."[29] In the course of Cléopâtre's soliloquy, the first image of Antoine waiting alone by the river Styx is succeeded by that of Cléopâtre walking alongside him, the yearning aroused by his absence translated into the contentment of satisfied union. While Virgil's Aeneas becomes a hero by abandoning Dido and founding an empire, Garnier's Antoine is ennobled by remaining with Cléopâtre and dying in her arms.

This revision of Virgil fits into the larger scheme of the play, which upsets the hierarchy of exemplary models and their opposites to question fundamental assumptions about gender identity. Garnier's play elevates Antony above Aeneas; it also entails a reconsideration of Cleopatra as the female anti-ideal counterpoised against the ideal of Octavia.[30] Garnier sets Cléopâtre in the company of Portia and Cornelia, the Roman matrons for whom he named the first two plays in his civil war trilogy, a gesture that puts him at odds with Plutarch who sees Octavia and Cleopatra as antithetical. Plutarch portrays Octavia as a female paragon whose shining worth ought to have brought Antony into line and Cleopatra as the harlot who extinguished Antony's best qualities and magnified his worst. According to Roman historians, even Plutarch who described her intellect admiringly and depicted her death with pathos, Cleopatra was a ruthless temptress who destroyed Antony in pursuit of her own ambitions. Dio presents Cleopatra as plotting to induce Antony's suicide through news of her death: "He had an inkling that he was being betrayed, but his infatuation would not allow him to believe it . . . Cleopatra was fully aware of this and hoped that if he should be informed that she was dead, he would not prolong his life but meet death at once."[31] In the early modern period, writers drew upon these classical historians to create Cleopatra as a symbol of female infamy in the conduct literature of a century to come. In Castiglione's *The Courtier*, Octavia and Cleopatra are named in the debate pitting Julian, the defender of women, against their detractors, Gaspar and Phrisio. While Julian places Cleopatra in the company of other women rulers who conquered foreign lands and erected great edifices, Phrisio names her as an example of lasciviousness.[32] In Brathwait's *English Gentlewoman*, Cleopatra is only one in a series of examples of "odious Lust."[33]

Undoing that construction of Cleopatra is a preoccupation of Garnier's play. In the long soliloquy that fills the entire first act of the play, Antoine describes Cléopâtre in terms taken from Garnier's Latin sources, as a treacherous sorceress with a penchant for poisoning men, and adopts the moralistic tone of those texts, blaming his downfall on his attachment to her. However, the remaining four acts of the play work to dismantle the one-dimensional representation of Cléopâtre set up in that initial scene. The factual and philosophical claims made in the soliloquy (Cléopâtre is false; therefore all women are false) are contradicted as Garnier redeploys the very language used to decry Cléopâtre in testimony to her abiding constancy. And yet, remarkably, Garnier valorizes Cléopâtre without turning her into the figure of virginal or matronly chastity defined as the female ideal. Rather, she is by turn regal, maternal, defiant, loyal, physically courageous, candidly sensual. For at least one female reader of *Marc Antoine*, Françoise Hubert, the achievement of the play was this reinvention of its female protagonist:

> Malgré du Temps le perdurable cours,
> Ton nom caché dedans l'onde oublieuse,
> Reflorira, Cleopatre amoureuse,
> Ayant GARNIER chantre de tes amours.[34]

> [In spite of the ceaseless passing of time,
> Your name, obscured by the waters of forgetfulness,
> Will flourish again, amorous Cleopatra,
> With GARNIER, the bard of your loves.]

The resurrection of Cleopatra celebrated by Hubert, the poet who had married Garnier three years before, entailed redefining the anti-ideal invoked by writers such as Boccaccio and Castiglione. Through his novel characterization of Cleopatra, Garnier offered the female reader an alternative to that of reading in order to epitomize "chastity." And he included the poem of Françoise Hubert in the printed edition as further evidence that a female reader, like the female protagonist of the play she praised, could be not only a lover, mother, and wife, but also a subject: queen or poet.

Residue of the anti-Cleopatra discourses infiltrates Antoine's initial soliloquy. In that speech, Antoine enumerates a list of complaints against Cléopâtre, culminating with the hackneyed misogyny of the concluding quatrain:

> *Inhumaine*, traistresse, ingrate entre les femmes,
> Tu trompes, parjurant, et ma vie et mes flammes.   (1.17–18; italics added)

> Pensant garder son sceptre, et rendre la Fortune
> Adversaire à toy seul, qui doit estre *commune*.   (1.137–8)

> Bien d'elle je me plains de ne m'estre loyale,
> Et de n'avoir *constance* à ma constance *egale*.   (1.141–2)

Mais quoy? le naturel des Femmes est *volage*,
Et à chaque moment se *change* leur *courage*.
Bien fol qui s'y abuse, et qui de *loyauté*
Pense jamais trouver compagne une beauté.   (145–8)

[Inhuman, treacherous, ungrateful among women,
You betray, by breaking faith, both my life and my love.]

[Meaning to keep her scepter, and to make Fortune
Adversary to you alone, which should be shared in common.]

[Rightly I accuse her of not being loyal to me,
And of not showing constancy to my constancy equal.]

[But then? women are by nature fickle
And continually change in their hearts.
Foolish indeed is the one who mistakenly hopes
Ever to see beauty accompany loyalty.]

By extending his indictment of Cléopâtre to the entire female sex,
Antoine turns a personal grievance into an inquiry into the nature of
women generally.

However, these clichés of the aggrieved lover turned woman-hater,
like the rantings of Shakespeare's Posthumus, are not left unquestioned. Parallel to the first act soliloquy of Antoine is the second act
soliloquy of Cléopâtre. Her speech repeats themes from his. She echoes
his anti-Cleopatra rhetoric when she faults herself, over the objections
of Eras, for all that Antoine has suffered: "Ma beauté trop aimable est
notre adversité" [My too pleasing beauty is our downfall] (2.430). She,
too, laments her losses – kingdom, liberty, children – and expresses her
resolve to die, matching Antoine's "il me convient mourir" [it is fitting
I die] with an expression of equal resolve, "il n'y a que la mort" [only
death remains] (1.7; 2.426). Just as Antoine declares his willingness to
relinquish everything to César, empire and all, in return for the love of
Cléopâtre, Cléopâtre says that his love was to her "plus cher que
sceptre, enfans, la liberté, le jour" [more dear than scepter, children,
liberty, the light of day] (2.410). The structural equivalence established
between the two soliloquies, congruent expressions of devotion and
despair on the part of hero and heroine, makes echoes of the first
speech resonate more powerfully in the second. Antoine's terms of
opprobrium turn against themselves as Cléopâtre recontextualizes
them:

Te quitter, te tromper, te livrer à la rage
De ton fort ennemi? que j'aye ce *courage*?   (2.391–2)

Tu as donc estimé que mon ame Royale
Ait couvé pour te prendre une amour *desloyale*?
Et que, *changeant* de cœur avec l'instable sort,
Je te vueille laisser pour me rendre au plus fort?   (2.399–402)

Tu verras, mort et vif, ta Princesse te suyvre:
Te suyvre, et lamenter ton malheur importun,
Qui m'est, ainsi qu'estoit ton empire, *commun*.   (2.544–6)

Sans telle affection je serois *inhumaine*.   (2.552)

Je ne serois *volage*, inconstante, infidelle.   (2.583)

[To leave you, betray you, give you up to the rage
Of your great enemy? could I have such a heart?]

[You believed, then, that my royal soul
To lure you harbored disloyal love,
And that, changing heart with shifting fate,
I would leave you to give myself to one stronger?]

[You will see, in both death and life, your princess follow you,
Follow you, and lament your untimely doom,
Which is for me, as was your empire, ours in common.]

[Without such affection I would be inhuman.]

[I would not be fickle, inconstant, unfaithful.]

Words from Antoine's soliloquy – "commune," "constance," "egale,"
"inhumaine," "volage," "courage," "loyauté" – ricochet and rebound in
Cléopâtre's soliloquy and later scenes. Cléopâtre's actions, Antoine's
friend Lucile argues, show her heart to be "*Egalement* touché de l'amour
qui vous ard" [Equally affected by the love that inflames you] (3.907).
Dircet describes Cléopâtre hoisting Antoine up to the monument "de ses
femmes aydee, et d'un coeur si *constant*" (4.1655). Cléopâtre's own
outraged rebuke to Charmion for urging her to abandon Antoine, "je
serais inhumaine," counters Antoine's charge that she is "inhumaine,
traitresse, ingrate entre les femmes." So too, his reproach that she left
him alone to face Fortune which should have been their *common*
adversary is undermined by her insistence that their destiny, like the
empire they ruled, is theirs to share in *common*.

This tactic of recapturing the words that Antoine used to chastise
Cléopâtre and taking the sting out of them reverses our initial impression
of the play's heroine. But its consequences reach further. By having
Antoine extrapolate generalizations about the nature of all women from
the example of Cléopâtre, Garnier lays the groundwork for interpreting
her character in a representative fashion. He prepares the audience to
consider how the transformation of Cléopâtre, from the crude emblem of

female treachery of act one to the psychologically and morally compelling subject of act five, engages the problem of female fashioning more generally. By challenging the assessments that Petrarch and Dio, the two sources named in the play's argument, provide of Cleopatra, Garnier puts in question the way in which his own contemporaries were drawing upon classical history as a storehouse of negative and positive examples for female readers. The valorization of military heroes, Caesar, Alexander, and Aeneas, as models for men, and of Roman matrons, Lucrece, Virginia, and Octavia, as models for women, supported the notion that men achieve virtue through action, women through inaction. The undermining of this principle could have been reason enough for the English humanists who read Garnier's play in translation to find its representation of the Egyptian queen so galling. Cléopâtre demonstrates her virtue not by an immobile display of chastity but by the arduous feat of raising Antoine from the ground to the top of the monument. Moreover, while Cléopâtre wins praise for her actions, Antoine is lauded only in death as the passive object of his mistress' eulogies.

Cléopâtre undermines sex-specific definitions of virtue through her sensuality as well. When pressed to justify the utility of her eternal love for Antoine, Cléopâtre tells Charmion exactly upon which value she bases her decision to die: "C'est dessur la vertu, le seul bien de ce monde" (2.644) [It is on virtue, the only good in this world]. She puts conventional notions of female virtue in question through the varied roles that she assumes. Garnier's Cléopâtre is very much a queen. The sorrow of the Egyptian chorus over her predicament and the loyalty of her servants testify to her following among her people. Her refusal, in an extended stichomythia dialogue with Charmion, to blame her destiny on the gods further emphasizes her regal dignity. But she is also, unlike her Shakespearean analogue, a mother. The final act presents her saying farewell to her children. The parting, so painful it almost kills her, indicates the suffering she is willing to endure for the man she loves. Even when Euphron forces Cléopâtre to visualize the fate awaiting her children, the executioner's knife pressed to their throats, she still refuses to betray Antoine. Yet the role of lover comes first for Cléopâtre. The joy in sadness she expresses in the throes of death is imbued with desire:

> Non, non, je suis heureuse, en mon mal devorant,
> De mourir avec toy, de t'embrasser mourant,
> Mon corps contre le tien, ma bouche desseichee,
> De soupirs embrasez, à la tienne attachee.   (5.1962–5)

> [No, no, I am happy, in my consuming pain,
> To die with you, to kiss you as I die,

My body against yours, my parched mouth
Burned by sighs, to yours attached.]

The images Cléopâtre conjures of physical union, her body joined to
Antoine's, constitute the very form of thought that devotional reading
was meant to suppress in women. In Garnier's Cléopâtre, virtue is
coupled with passion.

This view of Cléopâtre as an example of virtue, in all her varied
incarnations, can be sustained only if the term itself is redefined. This is
what Garnier sets about to do in transferring qualities usually associated
with admirable men over to Cléopâtre instead. In the scene in which
Dircet reports to César the elevation, literal and figurative, of the dying
Antoine, Cléopâtre displays the kind of *virtù* typically reserved for male
heroes:

> [Cléopâtre] n'ouvrit la porte, ainçois une corde jetta
> D'une haute fenestre, où l'on l'empaqueta;
> Puis ses femmes et elle à mont le souleverent,
> Et à force de bras jusqu'en haut l'attirerent.
>   Jamais rien si piteux au monde ne fut veu:
> L'on montoit d'une corde Antoine peu à peu,
> Que l'ame alloit laissant, sa barbe mal peignee,
> Sa face et sa poitrine estoit de sang baignee;
> Toutesfois tout hideux et mourant qu'il estoit
> Ses yeux demy-couverts sur la Roine jettoit,
> Luy tendoit les deux mains, se soulevoit luy mesme,
> Mais son corps retomboit d'une foiblesse extréme.
> La miserable Dame, ayant les yeux mouïllez,
> Les cheveux sur le front sans art esparpillez,
> La poitrine de coups sanglantement plombee,
> Se penchoit contre bas, à teste recourbee,
> S'enlaçoit à la corde, et de tout son effort
> Courageuse attiroit cet homme demy mort.
> Le sang luy devaloit au visage de peine,
> Les nerfs luy roidissoyent, elle estoit hors d'haleine.
>   Le peuple, qui d'abas amassé regardoit,
> De gestes et de voix à l'envy lui aidoit:
> Tous crioyent, l'exitoyent, et souffroyent en leur ame,
> Penant, suant ainsi que cette pauvre Dame:
> Toutesfois, invaincue, au travail dura tant,
> De ses femmes aydee, et d'un cœur si constant
> Qu'Antoine fut tiré dans le sepulchre sombre,
> Où je croy que des morts il augmente le nombre.   (4.1630–57)

[[Cleopatra] did not open the door, but instead, from a high window,
Threw down a rope in which he was bundled;
Then her women and she lifted him upwards,

And by the strength of their arms pulled him to the top.
   Never in the world was anything so pitiful seen:
Antony being raised slowly by the rope,
His soul leaving him, his beard unkempt,
His face and chest soaked with blood;
Nonetheless, moribund and hideous though he was,
He kept his half-shut eyes on the queen,
Held out both hands to her, raised himself up,
But his body fell back from extreme weakness.
The miserable lady, her eyes wet,
Her hair disordered on her brow,
Her chest bloodily scourged by blows,
Leaned down, her head bent low,
Clasped the rope, and with all her might,
Courageously pulled up that half-dead man.
Blood streamed down her face in the exertion,
Her sinews stiffened, she was out of breath.
   The mass of people who watched below,
Encouraged her unrestrainedly by gesture and by word:
All shouted, urged her on, and suffered in their souls,
Toiling, sweating, just like that poor lady:
Yet, unbeaten, she strove at such length,
Aided by her women, and by a heart so constant,
That Antony was drawn into the dark tomb
Where I think he now adds to the number of the dead.]

The images of Antoine and Cléopâtre that appear in this passage could not be more at odds with the examples of model men and women cited by Fenton, "maisters of theym selves" (gendered male) and "patternes of chastetye" (gendered female). Antoine, far from being the subject of all agency, is supine, "d'une foiblesse extrême." All he can do is to open his arms and momentarily lift himself to greet her. And unlike the patterns of chastity extolled by Fenton, women left to be raped or die first, Cléopâtre is not helpless to act. At first, the activity of lifting Antoine is described in impersonal terms, "L'on montoit d'une corde Antoine." Then, the agent doing the lifting is identified: "La miserable Dame . . . courageuse attirait cet homme demy mort."

Adjectives such as "courageuse" and "invaincue" cast Cléopâtre's act of raising Antoine as the feat of a hero. Erasmus writes in *De Copia* that the example of Hercules teaches us that "by sweat and helping others immortal fame is gained."[35] Like Hercules, whose seven labors Antoine previously enumerated, Cléopâtre demonstrates her courage through an act of endurance. Hercules, Antoine recalls, "le ciel souleva de son espaule forte" [lifted the sky with his strong shoulder] (3.1213). Dircet recounts that Antoine is raised, with Eras and Charmion helping

Cléopâtre, "à force de bras." Garnier uses the same verb, *soulever*, to describe the lifting performed by Cleopatra and Hercules alike; in both exploits, the source of wonder is the individual's muscular strength. While raising Antoine to the monument might seem not to compare with Hercules holding up the sky, Garnier invests her action with grandeur. All the attention in the narration is on her body in pain. Dircet carefully details the self-inflicted marks of grief on her bloodied chest, her posture bent in effort, her sinews taut, the flush of exertion visible in her face, her shortness of breath. The source of this extraordinary stamina is her unswerving loyalty: "De ses femmes aydee, et d'un cœur si constant / Qu'Antoine fut tiré dans le sepulchre sombre." The cause and effect structure of narrative's climactic sentence definitively negates the misogynist rhyme of act one: "Mais quoy? le naturel des Femmes est volage, / Et à chaque moment se change leur courage." Antoine was lifted to the heights of the monument precisely because Cléopâtre's heart was so entirely constant. In the course of proving her virtue, in the feminine sense attached to the word, her unchangeable devotion, she has also inflected the term with connotations of masculine *virtù*. Garnier's Cléopâtre confounds gender categories by demonstrating her fidelity through an act signifying moral courage and physical strength.

II

Mary Sidney's *Antonius* is a material trace of an act of reading. In translating *Marc Antoine* into English, Mary Sidney made a record of the specific words and images that the French play suggested to her. Her text reveals a mind absorbed in an involved, analytic procedure far removed from the mechanical processing of meaning prescribed for women (embracing good female examples, abjuring bad ones). As an inventive and rigorous translator, Sidney flouts the notion that women should read only passively and only for the purpose of being instructed. She corrects Garnier's history, clarifies his allusions, adjusts his metaphors, and conjures the mental states described in his soliloquies. Her text of *Antonius* also marks an act of authorship. Its publication, sanctioned by "The Countess of Pembroke" named on the title page, established Sidney in the public eye as an up-to-date textual critic informed about the latest trends in literary circles on the Continent and about current developments in verse and dramatic form in her own country. Her selection of a work by Garnier, the leading tragedian of sixteenth-century France, aligns her with the movement for classically-inspired vernacular literature promoted by the Pléiade poets who celebrated him. At the same time, her use of unrhymed lines indicates her independent judgment. In spite of her proven ability in elaborate versification, Sidney puts only the choruses into rhyme. The rest of *Antonius* (1592) is written not in the stylized couplets of the French original but in the rougher blank verse of Christopher Marlowe's *Tamberlaine* (1590).

Translation carved out for Sidney, as for other women in early modern England, an intermediary zone between reading and writing in which it was possible for her to claim position as an author. Gender mattered differently in that gray area; while a woman was generally limited to translating subject matter that she would have been permitted to read, she could be praised for translating a work that she would have been censured for having composed herself. In the epistle to his translation of Montaigne's *Essays*, which is dedicated to the Countess of Bedford and her mother Lady Anne Harrington, John Florio went so far as to differentiate between original composition and translation on the basis of gender, to define the first activity as masculine and the second as feminine. He considers his last book "masculine" because it was a work of his own imagination, while he labels his more recent translation of the *Essays* a "defective edition (since all translations are reputed femalls)."[36] This claim is misleading if it is construed to mean that translation came to be associated primarily with women and depreciated in importance as a consequence. A fifth of all books printed in Elizabeth's reign were translations.[37] The propaganda wars waged in post-Reformation Europe heightened commercial demand for translation; economic and political factors alone would have militated against its feminization.

Women did compose an important segment of the market for vernacular versions of foreign language texts. Some 163 books, in approximately 500 editions, were addressed to women between 1475 and 1640; a fifth of these female-oriented books were translations.[38] In the late Middle Ages, women had traditionally traded in vernacular books; of 186 women throughout Europe known to have owned books between 1300 and 1500, two thirds owned translations.[39] Women also wrote translations. Among these female translators was a late medieval precursor to Mary Sidney; Eleanor Hull translated the seven penitential psalms from French and Latin to English in the fifteenth century.[40] In early modern England, most translations by women treated religious themes: Margaret More Roper's *A Devout Treatise on the Pater Noster*, Queen Elizabeth's *The Glass of the Sinful Soul*, Anne Cooke's *Apologia Ecclesiae Anglicanae*, and Elizabeth Cary's *The Reply of the Most Illustrious Cardinal of Perron to the Answer of the Most Excellent King of Great Britain*. However, such work was not stigmatized as feminine. Respected male writers and translators, among them Thomas Wyatt and Philip Sidney, Thomas Hoby and Arthur Golding, also shared in the

same task of devotional translation that occupied and distinguished
Mary Sidney. In addition to his famous translation of Castiglione's
Courtier, Hoby published an English version of a religious text in the
same vein as one published by his wife, Elizabeth Cooke. Hers was *A
Way of Reconciliation Touching the True Nature and Substance of the
Body and Blood of Christ in the Sacrament*; his was *Martin Bucer's
Gratulation of the Most Famous Clerk M. Martin Bucer . . . unto the
Church of England*.[41] Paradoxically, value accrued to such texts and the
women who wrote them to the extent that translation remained a
lucrative, influential, and largely masculine business.

The important point about Florio's dedicatory epistle is that the
partition of literary activity according to gender put a strain, to differing
degrees, on how both sexes defined their roles as readers and writers. In
her preface to *The Mirror of Princely Deeds*, a translation of a book-
length Spanish romance, Margaret Tyler felt the need to answer detractors ("ill willers") who would compel her "either not to write or to write
of divinitie" with a spirited defense of women's prerogative to write,
whether in translation or not, on any subject they pleased.[42] She risked a
loss in status by stepping across the generic boundary marked out for her
as a female reader-translator. But her actions also affected the self-
perceptions of male counterparts. The participation of women in the field
of translation as writers and readers, specifically the role of his patron
Lucy Russell in the production of his own book, triggers anxieties of
emasculation in Florio. He asserts defensively the masculinity of his
earlier book, which had a male patron, in order to counter the subordination he experienced as a translator under the tutelage of Lady Russell,
whom he describes alternately as an Indian chief, a stern king, a Spartan
mother, a cannibal captor, a siren mermaid, and the goddess Diana
whom he imagines having inscribed the condition of his thralldom on a
collar set about his neck.

The parameters that shaped and circumscribed the translation work of
men and women such as Florio and Tyler were contingent. At the turn of
the century, Margaret Beaufort could translate *The Imitation of the Life
of Christ* in collaboration with a male colleague, publicly commission
William Caxton to publish the French romance *Blanchardyn and Eglan-
tyne*, and be praised at her death by Bishop John Fisher for her roles as a
translator and "a veray Patroness."[43] Moreover, it was even possible for
Caxton, in his preface to that romance, to charge that women "studye
over moche in bokes of contemplacion" and would benefit from reading
a romantic adventure story instead.[44] However, by the time that Tyler
published her translation in 1578, the lines were being redrawn to contain
women solely within the sphere of religious devotion. Tyler describes the

constraining effects of humanist prohibitions on female reading and candidly disputes them. She argues that male authors have dedicated all kinds of works to female patrons and readers, "some stories, some of warre, some Phisicke, some Lawe, some as concerning government, some divine matters," and that women therefore should be allowed to write books on a equally wide range of subjects.[45] Tyler's preface shows that humanist strictures had to be enforced, at times in the face of strenuous opposition, not simply decreed from on-high. The threat of social stigma served to pressure both Florio and Tyler to conform to changing gender/ genre norms.

These, then, were the straits that Mary Sidney had to negotiate when, in addition to the Psalms, she took up French drama. The impact of her *Antonius* can be measured by the response it provoked. The two plays written directly in answer, Samuel Daniel's *Tragedy of Cleopatra* (1594) and Samuel Brandon's *Tragicomedy of the Virtuous Octavia* (1598), indicate that Sidney's reading, particularly of the character of Cleopatra, was too contentious for certain of her contemporaries to let stand. Garnier/Sidney had portrayed Cleopatra as a gender-bending wife-hero capable of both "female" and "male" forms of virtue, a rival to Roman matrons (Portia, Cornelia) worthy of theatrical representation, a female exemplar too complex and faceted to be reduced to an emblem. It was this turnabout that both Samuel Daniel and Samuel Brandon would try to reverse. In their 1594 and 1598 plays, Daniel and Brandon rewrote *Antonius* with the purpose, the obsession in Brandon's case, of dismantling Garnier/Sidney's Cleopatra and reassembling its parts to fit the prototype of female badness found in Garnier's original sources.

The relation between *Antonius* and other neo-classical plays is not a new topic of study. As early as 1924, Alexander Witherspoon elaborated the theory that Sidney published the play to lead a concerted campaign against the barbarism of the popular stage. The claim for an organized movement is based on evidence that is slender at best: a few letters that passed between Gabriel Harvey and Edmund Spenser in 1579 and the text of Philip Sidney's *An Apology for Poetry* which Witherspoon treats as an index to views also held by Mary Sidney. His conspiracy theory aside, Witherspoon does make an important observation: seven English writers, taking Garnier's seven tragedies as models, wrote twelve plays in around twenty-five years, plays that resemble each other strongly. To these plays, including works by Thomas Kyd, William Alexander and Elizabeth Cary as well as Daniel and Brandon, we can add the play by Fulke Greville about Antony and Cleopatra that he later burned. The plays in this group share all the following characteristics of French neo-classical drama: emphasis on philosophical contemplation over action, experimentation in a single work with different verse forms, and Senecan devices such as stichomythia and choruses. However, the trend set by *Antonius* is evidence of Sidney's intellectual influence, not of a secret cabal. Her translation, which appeared in quarto in 1592 and was reprinted in octavo in 1595, was among the books that William Drummond of Hawthornden listed as belonging to his library in 1611. Gabriel Harvey wrote in praise of her "furious Tragedy *Antonius*" and William Clark, in 1595, of her "well graced Antonie."[46] Shakespeare, another reader of the play, paid his own tribute to Sidney in *Antony and Cleopatra*, written over a decade later.

In fact, the preconceptions Witherspoon brings to his analysis of Sidney's translation stem from the Renaissance stereotype of the female devotional reader. He views Sidney as a "virtuous lady," a translator who stuck too closely to the original French text, a robotic and uninspired interpreter of Garnier's verse. Disregarding numerous changes Sidney introduced, Witherspoon alleges that she "adds only one couplet to the original, and omits only one line."[47] At the same time, while he criticizes Sidney for staying too close to the original in her translation of the play, he also criticizes her for making alterations to the argument: Garnier's "expression to the effect that, at the battle of Philippi, 'la liberté Romaine rendit les derniers soupirs,' becomes, in the English lady's version, 'the libertie of Rome being now utterly oppressed.' Likewise, virtuous lady as she was, she did not think it needful or edifying to dwell on the charms of Cleopatra, and where the Frenchman had written with some animation of 'la singulière beauté de Cléopâtre, Roine d'Egypte, arrivée en Cilice en royale magnificence,' she dismisses the fair Egyptian with a curt phrase, 'Cleopatra Queene of Aegypt'."[48] These passages cited by Witherspoon do hint at what Sidney was after as a translator. She writes here, as in the body of the play, with keen political awareness; the defeat of Brutus and Cassius at Philippi is for her the downfall of republican government, the creation of a new institutional order whose imposition she does not soften, as Garnier does, by personifying "liberty" as an organic being breathing its last breaths. As Witherspoon notes, Sidney also omits description of Cleopatra's first meeting with Antony.[49] In Garnier's argument, it appears as though the events of the play directly follow the defeat of Brutus and Cassius. It would seem from his version that Antony was married to Octavia (rather than Fulvia) before meeting Cleopatra and that the climactic war with Rome occurred soon after that first encounter. Garnier suppresses mention of events that occurred between the initial meeting of Antony and Cleopatra in Cilicia and Octavius' much later decision to declare war.

By reordering the narrative sequence in Garnier's argument, Sidney restores Plutarch's chronology and focuses attention on the precise dramatic situation in which Antony finds himself. Taking a cue from Plutarch, Sidney describes Antony's mental state as he travelled eastward: "the places renewed in his remembrance the long intermitted love of Cleopatra Queene of Aegipt: who before time had both in Cilicia and at Alexandria, entertained him with all the exquisite delightes and sumptuous pleasures, which a great Prince and voluptous Lover could to the uttermost desire."[50] Sidney added this sentence to the argument. Her nonmoralistic evocation of Antony as an ardent lover should put to rest the allegation of prudishness. Her adjustments to the argument stem not from misplaced decorum, as Witherspoon would have it, but from her interest in historical and psychological precision. In her version, the depth of Antony's attachment to Cleopatra pulls him ineluctably eastward. The drama of his return to Syria has an altogether different quality to it than that of his first encounter with Cleopatra described in Garnier's argument. Sidney's version highlights the specific moment enacted by the play: the occasion of the campaign Antony undertook against the Parthians following the death of Crassus. She puts more emphasis on the lovers alone by attributing the cause of Antony's rage to jealousy, by passing over the details of his suicide, and by omitting the suicide of his servant altogether. Also, just as she probed Antony's psychological state on his return to Syria, Sidney similarly departs from Garnier's text to assign Cleopatra a motive for her refusal to open the monument doors. Whereas Garnier simply says that the doors were closed, Sidney elaborates with the phrase, "which she not daring to open least she should be made a prisoner to the Romaines, and carried in Caesar's triumphe cast downe a corde from an high window." In the last two lines of the argument, Sidney adds a stage direction not found in the original and leaves out Garnier's reference to the virulently anti-Cleopatra historian Dio: "The Stage supposed Alexandria: the Chorus, first Egiptians, and after Romane Souldiers. The Historie to be read at large in Plutarch in the Life of Antonius."

The critical spirit evident in Sidney's modification of the argument infuses the rest of her translation as well. While her attention to the details of the original French text suggests a profound appreciation of Garnier's imagination and craft, Sidney shapes *Antonius* according to her own poetic sensibility and knowledge of classical sources. One important difference between the translation and the original is the use of concrete rather than abstract terms. Sidney translates "geniture" (progeny) (1.122) as "tender babes" (1.123). In describing the climactic moment of the battle of Actium, Garnier writes that Antoine followed Cléopâtre in flight "comme si son ame / Eust esté attachée à celle de sa Dame" [as if his soul / Had been attached to that of his lady] (2.439–40). Sidney embellishes Garnier's description of Antoine's pursuit of Cléopâtre away from the battle by introducing the image of a chain stretching between his soul and hers "(as if his soule / Unto his Ladies soule had bene enchain'd)" (445–6). To an extended description of the Nile, Sidney appends an additional descriptive phrase: "thy Skie-coullor'd brookes" (800). This alertness to the possibilities of figurative language brings Sidney to embellish metaphors developed incompletely by Garnier. In one passage, Antoine compares the "fire" of his torment ("le feu qui te brusla") to burning embers ("brandon") that scorched the soul of Orestes after he killed his mother and fled from her specter: "Il fuyoit son forfait, qui luy pressoit le flanc, / Empreint en sa moüelle, et la fantôme palle" [He fled his crime, which pressed him on / Printed in his marrow, and the pale ghost] (1.55, 56, 60–1). Sidney extends and enriches the metaphor of fire by changing the verb "printed" to "kindled": "He fled his fault which folow'd as he fled / Kindled within his bones by shadow pale" (1.61–2).

Sidney also makes Garnier's highly academic text accessible to a larger audience. She glosses mythological references, substituting arcane terms with more readily comprehensible ones. In her translation, she changes "Canopides ondes" (1.110) to "Nilus streames" (1.111) (Canopus was an island town on the mouth of the Nile famous for its luxury), "la laine Canusienne" (4.1742) to "wolle of finest fields" (4.1761), "Edonides folles" (2.314) to "Bacchus priests" (Edonides were Thracian women who followed Bacchus) (2.318), and "Dindyme" (2.376) to "Cybels sacred hill" (the mountain of Dindymus in Phrygia was sacred to Cybele) (2.381). These examples demonstrate both Sidney's knowledge of history, geography, and mythology and her unwillingness to allow erudition to obscure a text's meaning. In other instances, she substitutes proper names with descriptive adjectives so that "Aquilon" (1.151) becomes "the Northern blast" (1.153), "l'Acheron" (2.541) "joyles lake" (2.548), "la gente Philomele" (2.329) "wood-musiques Queene" (2.333), and "les Elysiennes plaines" (3.1341) "swete fields" (3.1354).

Though Sidney adds some phrases to the original, her preference throughout is for concision. In analyzing Sidney's translation of Philippe de Mornay's *Discours de la vie et de la mort*, Diane Bornstein observes that Sidney eliminates superfluous words and lengthy syntactic structures.[51] The same is true of *Antonius*. If Sidney can reduce three lines to two, she does so:

       Que ceux lamentent par compas,
       Qui telles miseres n'ont pas,
       Que celles que j'endure.   (2.384–6)

In measure let them plaine:
Who measur'd griefes sustaine.   (2.390–1)

In her translation of these lines from the chorus of act one, Sidney excises
the confusing shift in subject from an impersonal third person to an
unidentifiable first person, the "je" ("I") that appears out of nowhere to
interject his/her personal suffering into the collective lament of the
chorus. Sidney's decision to edit out this non-sequitur and compress the
passage is characteristic. Her style is pithy, direct and clear.

Tracing just one term from Garnier's text, the word "vomir," through
Sidney's translation illustrates how exactly she chose her words. Since
"vomir" (to vomit) has a more metaphorical meaning in French, Sidney
does not translate the term literally, except in the one instance in which
its meaning is literal. In that case, Antony is describing the death he
would have liked to have suffered in battle, after having killed a world of
soldiers, his guts punctured by a lance: "Je vomisse la vie et le sang au
milieu / De mille et mille corps abbatus en un lieu" (3.1090–1). This
Sidney translates verbatim: "My bodie thorow pearst with push of pike /
Had vomited my bloud, in bloud my life, / In midd'st of millions felowes
in my fall" (3.1100–2). By limiting the use of the term "vomit" to
Antony's graphic description of war's brutality, Sidney heightens the
effect of that passage. She keeps the term from becoming trite by
substituting more exact language in three other instances in which its
meaning is more figurative. In Garnier's text, after committing suicide,
Eros "vomit sang et ame, et cheut à ses pieds morts" (4.1602); in Sidney's
version, Eros "ending life fell dead before his fete" (4.1619). Garnier has
Cléopâtre say that she can no longer cry because her tears are "con-
sommez de la braise / Que vomist ma poitrine" (literally, "consumed by
the coals / That my chest vomits") (5.1984–5); Sidney's Cleopatra states
that her tears are "consumed by the coales / Which from my breast, as
from a furnace, rise" (5.2007–8). In this last example, Sidney does away
with a mixed metaphor, the image of Cléopâtre vomiting coals, by
introducing in its place an image of smoldering coals in a furnace whose
rising smoke vaporizes her tears. Finally, Sidney chooses against a literal
translation of Cléopâtre's dying words, "mon ame vomissant" (5.1999),
the last phrase of Garnier's text, ending *Antonius* instead with the lyrical
line, "fourth my soule may flowe" (5.2022).

Another of Sidney's preoccupations as a translator is with the first
person voice. Rather than attempting to reproduce the polished surfaces
of Garnier's highly stylized rhyming couplets, Sidney strives for a more
naturalistic quality. In a speech spoken by Octavius Caesar, for instance,
she replaces the phrase "jumeaux d'adultere" (4.1420) (twins of adultery)

with "Cleopatras bratts" (4.1437). Sidney makes the bloodthirsty Caesar not only promise massacres but use cruder language to reflect the rough violence of his thought. Verse is reserved for the elegiac commentary of the Egyptian chorus that follows the first three acts and for the Roman chorus that follows the fourth. As Coburn Freer asserts, Sidney strove early on, unlike the authors of other contemporaneous plays such as *Gorboduc*, to make the language of characters reflect their mental states.[52] One alteration that Sidney repeatedly makes to Garnier's text is to elide relative pronouns and conjunctions. Instead of ideas or events being listed one after the other, with the coordinating conjunction "et" ("and") between them, the hypotactic structure introduced by Sidney allows for relationships between ideas and events to be elaborated. One of many possible examples is her translation of the instructions Cléopâtre gives Diomède to announce news of her death to Antoine:

> Conte luy *que* mon ame, ardant impatiente
> De son amour perdue, a pour marque constante
> De sa fidelité, laissé mon faible corps,
> *Et que* j'accrois le nombre innombrable des morts.

> (2.679–82; italics added)

> Tell him, my soule burning, impatient,
> Forlorne with love of him, for certain seale
> Of her true loialtie my corpse hath left,
> *T'*encrease of dead the number numberlesse.　(2.686–9)

In Garnier's version, an imperative introduces two subordinate phrases joined by a conjunction, "tell him that . . . and that . . ." Sidney eliminates both subordinating terms, putting additional emphasis on "my soule" and on the verb and object of that subject – "left" and "corpse" – so that there is no doubt about the action represented: *My soul hath left my corpse*. She breaks one modifying phrase, "impatient / de son amour perdue," into two short ones, "impatient, / Forlorne with love of him." The tempo of these lines, unhindered by cumbersome subordinating clauses, makes Cleopatra's impatience audible. In place of the conjunction and relative pronoun introducing the verb, "et que j'accrois," Sidney inserts an infinitive: "T'encrease." In the English version, Cleopatra is too agitated to subordinate her phrases as she does in the more controlled and dispassionate French lines. Sidney's translation evokes the anguished state of mind of a woman preparing to die.

Such passages indicate that far from promoting the slavish imitation of foreign verse, Sidney was intent on developing the more colloquial idiom of English blank verse. Her interest in the potential of the form, particularly to convey the psychological dimensions of a character's predicament, shows through in her translation of lines like this one: "Si moy qui fus son cœur, qui fut sa chere amie" [if I who was his heart, who was his dear beloved] (2.580). Sidney's version of the line, particularly in the context of the passage in which it appears, conveys an entirely different tone:

> If I, whome alwaies more then life he lov'de,
> If I, who *am* his heart, who *was* his hope,
> Leave him, forsake him (and perhaps in vaine)
> Weakly to please who him hath overthrowne?   (2.586–9)

Both verbs in Garnier's version of this line ("fus"/"fut") locate Antoine's affection in the past; in Sidney's version, the altered tense of one verb, highlighted by the line's iambic rhythms, points to the disparity between Antony's enduring passion and lost faith ("who *am* . . . who *was*"). In this scene, Cleopatra impels Eras and Charmion to consider the enormity of the betrayal they propose. Sidney disrupts the placid surface of Garnier's line to convey the heroine's inner turmoil. The change of tense inserted by Sidney dramatizes what is at stake for Cleopatra in her decision, no less than the endurance of her tie to Antony. What to her the attachment means, the precarity and preciousness of it, is movingly apparent in that unexpected, single-syllable present tense verb: "I, who *am* his heart."

To take another example of Sidney's departure from Garnier's text, a passage from one of Antoine's soliloquies, is to see how deliberately she worked to make speech reveal a character's frame of mind:

> Je l'aime, *ainçois* je brusle au feu de son amour,
> J'ai son idole *faux* en l'esprit nuict et jour,
> Je ne songe qu'en elle, et tousjours je travaille,
> Sans cesse remordu d'une ardente tenaille.
> Extreme est mon malheur, mais je le sens plus doux
> Que le cuisant tison de mon tourment jaloux:
> Ce mal, *ains* ceste rage en mon ame chemine,
> Et dormant et veillant incessamment m'espine.   (3.910–17)

> I love, *nay* burne in fire of her love:
> Each day, each night her Image haunts my minde,
> Her selfe my dreames: and still I tired am,
> And still I am with burning pincers nipt.
> Extreame my harme: yet sweeter to my sence
> Than boiling Torch of jealouse torments fire:
> This grief, *nay* rage, in me such sturre doth kepe,
> And thornes me still, both when I wake and slepe.   (3.921–8)

In Garnier's version, Antoine uses Cartesian reasoning to diagram the state of his inner turmoil: "I love; therefore I burn." Beginning with the initial statement "Je l'aime" ("I love her"), Antoine develops an account centered on a composed first person subject: "I love her, thus I burn . . . (I have her image . . . I think . . ."). This repetition of the first person pronoun allows Antoine to elaborate on his pain in a logical fashion, to proceed from a diagnosis of *why* he suffers to a description of *how* he suffers. By contrast, Sidney's hero evinces as well as describes distress. Where Antoine is analytic, Antony is volatile and conflicted. Antoine reflects methodically upon the cause of his affliction ("I love her") and its consequence ("thus I burn in the fire of her love"). Antony gives us not philosophical reflection but the image of himself as love's martyr, a reverse Dido, a Roman general burning with desire for his queen.

Antony speaks of emotion with emotion. Six lines after Sidney replaces "ainçois," which elaborates and extends the preceding idea, with "nay," which vehemently contradicts and qualifies what has come before, she does the same with "ains" ("as well as"). Inner division wrenches the syntax of Antony's speech, interrupting the sequence of his thoughts ("I love, nay burn"; "this grief, nay rage"). He moves from an initial assertion ("I love") not to a series of first person statements ("I have her image . . . I think only of her") but to the immediate experience of suffering: "Each day, each night her Image haunts my minde, / Her selfe my dreames: and still I tired am." The shift in subject introduced by Sidney enacts the psychological condition Antony describes. Thoughts of Cleopatra so literally dominate his mind that she becomes the subject rather than him. While Garnier's Antoine makes a statement, "J'ai son idole faux en l'esprit nuict et jour," Sidney's Antony reveals his distress in his phrasing and diction. His repetition of words, "each day, each night," his double reference to Cleopatra, "her Image" and "her selfe" (two neutral terms for the single noun modified by a pejorative adjective, "idole faux," in the French text), and his use of the strong verb "haunts" (Cleopatra *haunts* his *mind* and *dreams* rather than simply being "in" his "spirit" as the French text has it) create the impression of a man whose mental world is wholly preoccupied with thoughts of his lover. It is only after invoking this experience of grueling psychic torment that Antony returns to the first person: "And still I tired am." The colon that introduces the phrase in the 1592 octavo edition marks an interval in Antony's speech. He communicates his exhaustion not only in words but also in that pause for breath, that missed beat.

Sidney also subtly marks her translation as that of a female author by tampering with genders in the text. Among the changes she introduces is her addition, at three different moments in the text, of the word "mother." In the first case, she replaces the term "parricide" (1.58) with "mother-murdering" (1.59) to describe Orestes' crime of killing his mother, Clytemnestra. This correction could be chalked up to her sense of exactitude when it comes to classical references, her unease with a matricide being termed a parricide. However, in two other instances, she inserts the word "mother" when no similar such imperative applies. She translates "flots mariniers" (2.797) as "Mother Sea" (2.806) and "la terre" (4.1400) as "Mother Earth" (4.1418). Beth Wynne Fisken notes that Sidney developed the image of the Earth as "an aging mother, once again pregnant" in her translation of Psalm 104.[53] Sidney's ascription of femaleness to the sea and earth recalls Elizabeth's rendition of the term "pere" ("father") as "mother" and "espouse" (spouse) as "wife" (having first written and crossed out "husbande") in the translation of Marguerite de Navarre's *Miroir* that she presented to Catherine Parr.[54] In these instances, Sidney and Elizabeth both make of the devotional text, conceived by humanist pedagogues as an enclosure for wandering female thoughts, a space in which it is possible to reorder hierarchy, invert categories, even re-gender the world.

This sweeping reevaluation of sex roles and stereotypes epitomizes the most innovative aspect of Sidney's translation: her decision to enhance Garnier's portrayal of Cleopatra as a figure of heroic stature. While she might have mollified potential critics by minimizing Cleopatra's importance, Sidney instead shifts the focus away from Antony and foregrounds Cleopatra's role in the monument scene. This insistence upon keeping Cleopatra in central view is apparent both in the preliminary argument to the play and in Dircet's long monologue. In the argument, Sidney diverges from the original text by making Cleopatra, rather than Antony, the subject of this dramatic episode:

[Antoine] ainsi fut tiré tout sanglant par Cleopatre et ses deux femmes, puis couché honorablement sur un lict, et enseputuré. ("Argument," 40–1)

[The doors of the monument] which she not daring to open least she should be made a prisoner to the Romaines, and carried in Caesars triumphe, cast downe a corde from an high window, by the which (her women helping her) she trussed up Antonius halfe dead, and so got him into the monument. ("The Argument")

In Garnier's version, greater emphasis is placed on veneration of the dying Antoine. All the verbs in the sentence refer to his body as it is raised up, laid to rest, and then entombed. In Sidney's version, Cleopatra plays a larger role than in the original. It is she who tosses down the rope with which to raise Antonius and she who "trussed up Antonius halfe dead, and so got him into the monument." Eras and Charmion are relegated to parentheses.

Evidence that this enlargement of Cleopatra's role was deliberate comes in the second description of the same scene found in Dircet's account of Antony's death. Again, as in her translation of the argument, Sidney places more emphasis on Cleopatra than Garnier does in the orginal text:

> [Cléopâtre] ainçois une corde jetta
> D'une haute fenestre, où l'on l'empaqueta;
> Puis ses femmes et elle à mont le souleverent,
> Et à force de bras jusqu'en haut l'attirerent.   (4.1630–3)

> [Cleopatra] kept close the gate: but from a window high
> Cast downe a corde, wherin he was impackt.
> Then by hir womens helpt the corps she rais'd,
> And by strong armes into hir windowe drew.   (4.1647–1650)

In the French text, Cléopâtre and her women pull together equally. In the English translation, Cleopatra alone is the grammatical subject, the person primarily responsible for lifting Antony, with Eras and Charmion merely lending a hand. In the French, the phrase "à force de bras" describes how Antoine got up to the window, specifying that he was raised by physical effort rather than by some other means. Sidney turns that explanation into testimony of Cleopatra's strength: "the corps she rais'd, / And by strong armes into hir windowe drew." The female third person pronoun and female possessive pronoun that bracket the phrase, "by strong armes," call attention to Sidney's transgressive linkage of a heroic demonstration of physical vigor with the gender of the queen.

The corporeal vitality that Sidney celebrates in Cleopatra is sexual as well as muscular. In contrast to other contemporary English writers, Sidney does not shy away from representing her heroine as having a body.[55] Her representation of Cleopatra's physicality is especially striking in the monument narration and in the last scene of the play. Sidney chooses not to downplay but rather to heighten the eroticism of the queen's final soliloquy:

> No, no, most happie in this happles case,
> To die with thee, and dieng thee embrace:
> My bodie joynde with thine, my mouth with thine,
> My mouth, whose moisture burning sighes have dried:
> To be in one selfe tombe, and one selfe chest,
> And wrapt with thee in one selfe sheete to rest.   (5.1985–90)

In the English translation, as distinct from the original French, Cleopatra mentions her mouth twice instead of once and refers to its "moisture" as well as its dryness. Risking calumny herself, Sidney has Cleopatra imagine aloud the pleasure of physical union with reference to her own body: "My bodie . . . my mouth . . . my mouth." In focusing attention on her mouth, even the wetness of her mouth, and on the contact between her body and Antony's, she articulates the experience of sexual longing unfearfully.

The frankness of Sidney's language in this soliloquy has been downplayed on the grounds that the "eroticization of death was hardly novel in a period when 'to die' signified the act of intercourse" and that Cleopatra's sexual impulses are confined "to an expression of desire for death."[56] This appraisal overlooks the fact that Sidney herself introduced the sexual pun on dying to the text. In Garnier's version, Cléopâtre laments the possibility that she will die without being reconciled with Antoine: "Ainsi preste de voir la Carontide nasse, / Je n'auray ce plaisir de mourir en ta grace" (2.411–12). In Sidney's translation, the more formal term "grace" is replaced by "love" which gives "dying" its sexual connotation: "So ready I to row in Charons barge, / Shall leese the joy of dying in thy love" (2.418–19). What Cleopatra desires is not death but sex with Antony. Sidney's Cleopatra has no immortal longings; loss moves her to desire Antony physically and to imagine making love to him, in the grave even. This is the impression she sustains through the last lines of the soliloquy:

> I spent in teares, not able more to spende,
> But kisse him now, what rests me more to doe?
> Then lett me kisse you, you faire eies, my light,
> Front seate of honor, face most fierce, most faire!
> O neck, ô armes, ô hands, ô breast where death
> (O mischief) comes to choake up vitall breath.
> A thousand kisses, thousand thousand more
> Let you my mouth for honors farewell give:
> That in this office weake my limmes may growe,
> Fainting on you, and fourth my soule may flowe.   (5.2013–22)

In the original French text, Cléopâtre maintains a formal tone as she showers kisses on the body of Antoine: "Que de mille baisers, et mille et mille encore, / Pour office dernier ma bouche vous honore" (5.1996–7). She is still speaking the language of funereal ritual. The emphasis is on the homage being paid Antoine; the last "office" her mouth performs is to honor him. In Sidney's translation of those lines, Cleopatra addresses Antony more intimately: "A thousand kisses, thousand thousand more / Let you my mouth for honors farewell give." In the translation, Cleopatra speaks familiarly, "let you give" instead of from a remove, "My mouth honors you." Sidney has shifted the verb from "honor" to "give" and doubled the locus of agency. It is unclear whether Antony or Cleopatra is the subject or object of kissing. The sentence can be construed so that either "you" (Antony) or "my mouth" (Cleopatra) gives or receives kisses, so that its meaning is either "Allow my mouth to give you a thousand kisses" or "Let you give my mouth a thousand kisses." Combined with images of arousal and climax in the final two lines, "my limmes may grow," "fainting," "my soule may flowe," the confusion of subject and object evokes images of reciprocal erotic expression. It is to a return to a physical life shared with Antony that Cleopatra's desires bend, not to death.

III

Two years after the publication of *Antonius: A Tragedy*, Samuel Daniel's *Tragedy of Cleopatra* first appeared in print. It was republished a total of six times between 1594 and 1609. In a dedicatory poem, Daniel presents the play as a sequel to Sidney's translation commissioned by the Countess herself. However, a tension emerges in the poem between his praise of Sidney as a patron and his criticism of her as an author:

> Madam, had not thy well grac'd Anthony,
> (Who all alone having remained long,)
> Requir'd his Cleopatras company.
>
> Who if she heere doe so appeare in act,
> That for his Queene & Love he scarce wil know her,
> Finding how much shee of her selfe hath lackt,
> And mist that glory wherein I should shew her,
> In majestie debas'd, in courage lower;
> Yet lightning thou by thy sweet favouring eyes,
> My darke defects which from her sp'rit detract,
> Hee yet may gesse it's shee, which will suffise.[57]

Daniel begins with a compliment to Sidney, referring to her "well grac'd" translation, and a romanticized vision of the relation between the two plays, picturing them as figures for Antony and Cleopatra themselves, once separated and now reunited. Yet the metaphor of complementarity breaks down as Daniel acknowledges that his representation of Cleopatra diverges significantly from that of Sidney. By his own admission, the discrepancy between the two is so great that Daniel's Cleopatra would not be even recognizable to (Sidney's) Antony.

In *The Tragedy of Cleopatra*, Daniel confesses, Cleopatra has lost her glory, her majesty been "debas'd," her courage brought "lower." He uses his play as a vehicle to reinscribe the discourses negated by Sidney in which Cleopatra stands as a potent negative symbol. Placed in that position, a protégé caught correcting his patron, Daniel refigures his disagreement with Mary Sidney by comparing it to Cleopatra's separation from Antony. His proposed solution to the conflict is that Sidney herself "lighten" what is "dark" in his depiction of Cleopatra by maintaining a pleasant demeanor. He weights his request for forgiveness emotionally by suggesting that Antony will remain "all alone," unable to recognize Cleopatra, unless Sidney is a good sport about Daniel's correction of her play and imbues the queen with some of that cheerfulness. Sidney must either accept the terms of his critique or be put in the ungenerous position of parting Antony from Cleopatra.

In spite of the ambiguity of his dedication and patent differences between the two plays, recent critics have taken Daniel at his word when he depicted his play as a sequel to *Antonius*.[58] They have based their view on the supposition that Garnier's play (hence the translation based upon it) is incomplete and ends without Cleopatra having committed suicide. Yet although there is no stage direction in *Marc Antoine* to relay the specific details, there is ample reason to think that Cléopâtre applies the asps to her body when she announces dramatically, "Or meurs donc Cleopatre," (5.1904), that she feels the effects of the poison when she states, "je suis heureuse, en mon mal devorant, / De mourir avec toy," (5.1962–3), that she expects to live only moments longer when she refers to the "office dernier" that her mouth will perform, and that she dies as she utters the last lines of the play, "mon corps affoiblissant / Defaille dessur vous, mon ame vomissant" [[let] my weakening body faint on you, expelling my soul] (5.1998–9). Garnier's play begins with the two main characters announcing their resolution to die and ends with their deaths. To readers of Sidney's *Antonius*, the resurrection of Cleopatra in Daniel's play could only have come as an astounding anti-climax. Plainly, Daniel's claim that Sidney's play is incomplete without the addition of his *Tragedy of Cleopatra* is strategic rather than candid. The imperfection Daniel finds in *Antonius* is not in its narrative structure but in its content. What he has undertaken to write is less a sequel than a revision.

In his play, Daniel controverts the complexity of Garnier/Sidney's representation of Cleopatra and reinstalls instead the straightforward categories of female badness and virtue found in didactic treatises. Drawing upon the highly negative account of Cleopatra by Dio, the source named by Garnier in his argument and omitted by Sidney in hers, Daniel stages the universal condemnation of Cleopatra as an example of lust, vanity, and inconstancy. Only then, having definitively framed her as an anti-ideal, does Daniel move Cleopatra from the bad to the good example column. In the fifth act, he turns Cleopatra into an exemplary figure by showing that she has learned to embody, through her suicide, the examples of Virginia and Lucrece. Like those paradigms of female virtue, Cleopatra cleanses herself of sexual stigma through death. While shades of stoicism also color her decision to take her life, making it partly a triumph over state authority, Daniel portrays the act primarily as a testament to her submission to dominant gender ideology. For Daniel, suicide is the length to which Cleopatra must go to escape negative categorization.

The opening soliloquy in the first scene of *The Tragedy of Cleopatra* makes clear that Daniel has set out to recast Sidney's *Antonius* completely. Whereas *Antonius* is constructed as a refutation of Antony's suspicions, Daniel's play begins with a startling revelation: Cleopatra did not love Antony while he was alive. Her assertion that she has come to do so now that he is dead hardly lessens the enormity of the deceit that Daniel assigns to her. Cleopatra says that suffering taught her love:

> And next is my turne, now to sacrifize
> To Death, and thee, the life that doth reprove mee,
> Our like distress I feele doth sympathize,
> And even affliction makes me truly love thee.
> Which Anthony, (I must confesse my fault,)
> I never did sincerely untill now;
> Now I protest I doe, now am I taught,
> In death to love, in life that knew not how.   (1.133–40)

Daniel's heroine picks up the language of funereal rites from Garnier/ Sidney's Cleopatra, speaking of sacrificial offerings, but the similarity ends there. This Cleopatra did not know how to love Antony and, as she now confesses, only pretended that she did. Even after claiming that she has now found it in her heart to love Antony, she delights in her ability to attract the Roman Dolabella as a suitor: "hath my face yet powre to win a Lover?" (4.1071). (Garnier/Sidney's Cleopatra calls on her women to join her in marring their features to show that they are no longer concerned with their appearance.) In a scene based on Dio's account of Cleopatra's failed seduction of Octavius Caesar, Cleopatra shows the Roman conquerer letters she received from Julius Caesar and speaks flirtatiously to him about the favors he could have received from her: "For looke what I have beene to Anthony, / Thinke thou the same I might have been to thee" (3.661–2).

Cleopatra's licentiousness is the main topic of conversation in the play. All of the characters harp on the motif of her place as an anti-model in the exemplary scheme of things. Unlike Garnier's Egyptian chorus that sees the affliction of the nation fatalistically as part of an eternal order and expresses sympathy for their queen, Daniel's chorus blames their predicament wholly upon Cleopatra:

> And CLEOPATRA now,
> Well sees the dangerous way

Shee tooke, and car'd not how,
Which led her to decay.
And likewise makes us pay
For her disordred lust.   (1.210–15)

The chorus exults in noting that Cleopatra has received her come-
uppance; her lust was her decay. They express their outrage with
redundant references to "the hidious face of sinne" (1.191), "the bed of
sinne reveal'd," and "the luxury that shame would have conceal'd"
(1.231–2).

Even Cleopatra speaks in the same register. There is a moment in *1
Henry VI* that resembles the spectacle of Cleopatra berating herself for
her supposed sexual crimes. After persuading Burgundy not to join
enemy invaders in ravaging his own country, Joan undercuts her
eloquent protest of English brutality with an oddly out-of-character
aside: "Done like a Frenchman – [*aside*] turn and turn again" (3.8.85).
The jarring non-sequitur puts an English nationalist slur into Joan's
mouth for the propaganda-effect of making the patron saint of French
nationalism denigrate the French. Daniel's Cleopatra, like Joan in that
scene, is made to denounce herself. Only hers is not a momentary lapse
but a one-track discourse on the topic of her worthlessness spread out
over five acts. In the first scene, she refers to her life as "foule" (1.4), to
her court as "my lascivious Courte" (1.145), and even to her children as
"th'ungodly pledges of a wanton bed" (1.82). The only difference
between the tedious moralizing of the chorus and that of Cleopatra is her
use of the first person. When Caesar arrives for a visit, she tells him that
her shame is so great that she prefers not to be seen but to hide "in
darknes, my disgrace t'inclose" (3.596). Even in the final scene of her
death, she belabors the theme of her sexual transgressions: "Heere I
sacrifize these armes to Death, / That Lust late dedicated to Delights"
(5.1541–2).

The overarching moral of this play replete with pious maxims is that of
the stories of Virginia and Lucrece. In Cleopatra's words, "My death . . .
is all the world hath left t'unstaine me" (1.171–2). Daniel's Cleopatra
does not die to rejoin Antony but rather to decontaminate herself. Death
offers absolution, "cleere fame" (5.1437) and "cleere glory" (5.1571).
Unlike Sidney's Cleopatra, focused on the memory of Antony's body to
her last breath, Daniel's Cleopatra disparages the physical world. She
sees her body as "the prison" of her soul, the "cage" that has entrapped
her like a captive bird, and death as a welcome release (3.1151, 54).[59] In
regard to this aspect of the play, Daniel can be seen as contributing to
the corpus of *ars moriendi* literature that Sidney had helped to promote
through her own translations, not only of *Marc Antoine*, but also of

Petrarch's *Trionfo della morte* and Philippe de Mornay's *Discours de la vie et de la mort*. As Mary Ellen Lamb suggests, Sidney's translations of these works, underwritten by a Stoic belief in the need to face hardship with fortitude, offer the female reader models for achieving heroism without directly opposing patriarchal authority. For Lamb, Daniel follows Sidney by depicting in Cleopatra's death a socially sanctioned means of resisting domination.[60] According to this interpretation, Cleopatra is challenging masculine prerogatives when she contradicts Caesar's wishes and determines to die: "So shall I act the last of life with glory, / Dye like a Queene, and rest without controule" (4.1187–8). Reading the passage in this way, however, obfuscates the extent to which the speeches of Daniel's Cleopatra resemble the dicta of conduct manuals. While certain lines in the play do raise the possibility of women surmounting earthly constraints, they are no more questioning of the prevailing order in this respect than official sermons or didactic treatises. It is precisely by reducing women's scope of action to defending their reputations through suicide that such works coerce women into limiting their expression and behavior generally.

The limits of any subversive potential that might be ascribed to Daniel's play are quickly apparent in the account Nuntius provides of Cleopatra's off-stage death. Her thoughts are confined to repentance for her former life and anticipation of her imminent transcendence. In her final speech, Cleopatra has more to say about the divinity of snakes than she does about Antony whom she mentions only in afterthought (5.1615). Nuntius recounts how Cleopatra delivered a long address to the asp, declared that she would sacrifice her arms to death, "bares her arme, and offer makes / To touch her death, yet at the touch with-drawes" (5.1545–6), experienced an inner struggle between honor and life, reproved her rebellious flesh for conspiring with Caesar, strengthened her resolve, suffered the deadly touch of the asp, affirmed that she was really going to die for "here ends / This act of life" (5.1609–10), reacted suddenly to the poison, progressively weakened, and finally, at last, died with a happy expression on her face, "telling death how much her death did please her" (5.1636). The scene narrated, with its false starts, theatrical posturing, and smiling female cadaver, reinscribes Sidney's heroic Cleopatra within the innocuous script of pious melodrama.

IV

Samuel Brandon's objective is more radical. He does not seek to rehabilitate Cleopatra. Instead, he grabs all of Cleopatra's good parts and globs them onto Octavia. Everything that distinguishes Cleopatra in

Sidney's *Antonius* Brandon reassigns to the title character of his *Virtuous Octavia*: her regal aura, her claim to eloquence, her maternal love, her conjugal constancy, her courage to die. This celebration of Octavia as a female ideal is supposed to reestablish the equivalence between chastity and virtue that Sidney's unorthodox representation of Cleopatra helped to unsettle. Brandon's gesture enacts the chastisement of the female reader threatened with disgrace for choosing the wrong books or interpreting them in the wrong way. *The Tragicomedy of the Virtuous Octavia* appeared in 1598, six years after the publication of *Antonius: A Tragedy*. By shaping a virtuous alternative to Cleopatra, using Sidney's own text as raw material, Brandon implies that Sidney is unable to distinguish between ideal and anti-ideal and is, therefore, herself in need of correction.

Brandon's idealization of Octavia has an altogether different cast to it than Sidney's heroization of Cleopatra. For instance, while Sidney uses Cleopatra as an example of constancy to confute Antony's prejudicial views of women, Brandon holds up Octavia as an anomaly to highlight the inconstancy of other women. This is the gist of Caesar's comment to Octavia: "Well sister, then I see that constancie / Is sometimes seated in a womans brest: / Your strange designes even from your infancie, / Can never without wonder be exprest."[61] Octavia is exceptional rather than representative. Like a saint, she has inspired wonder from earliest childhood. Her constancy, one of her "strange designes," sets her apart from other women rather than connecting her to them. Over the course of five acts, Brandon enumerates her perfections in a seemingly inexhaustible supply of epithets. Octavia is "heavens day-starre," "piller of our blisse," "peerelesse paragon," "natures pride," "faire cabinet, where wisdomes treasure lies," "Earth's glory," "heavens beloved bride," "Rich seate of honor," "vertues paradize," "mirrour of our age," "fayer issue of renoun'd Octavius race," "bright lamp of vertue," "honors living flame," "perfect virtue gracing woman kinde," "the paragon of natures pride" (sigs. A6v, B2v, B3v, B4r, E1v, E2v, E3v, E7v). Brandon's tactic is one familiar from conduct manuals: damning with excessive praise. In Jacques du Bosq's *The Complete Woman*, the preface defends the author against charges that he overpraised women in the first edition of the book. Du Bosq's extravagant praise, the preface explains, is actually a highly sophisticated and effective form of critique:

It was needfull then to set another face upon it, to disguise a Precept under the habit of a Praise, to embellish Women with all the perfections which they want; to praise them for all the vertues [the author] would perswade them to; and making their pictures somewhat handsomer and fairer then they, to shew them ingenuously their faults, and withall to procure a desire in them to correct them.

To enkindle within their hearts a longing to become like so goodly an Image, and by this meanes insensibly to oblige them to a change of life, and to reforme themselves according to this modell.[62]

Brandon's contribution to the chain of *Antonius* spin-offs lies in his use of a neo-classical play, in a more explicit way than Daniel attempted, to perform the exact function of a conduct manual, to expose women's defects and prod them to self-correction. As Du Bosq would do some forty years later, Brandon cloaks his precepts in praises so as to change women "insensibly," on a level at which they are only partly aware. To female readers, Brandon offers Octavia as a mirror of feminine perfection in which to see their own imperfections reflected, "to oblige them to a change of life, and to reforme themselves according to this modell."

For evidence that Brandon wrote his play as a judgment on Mary Sidney, we have only the text of his play and its dedicatory apparatus. "Concerning his life," in the words of the *Dictionary of National Biography*, "no particulars whatever are preserved." There is the verse dedication in which Brandon pointedly refers to Lady Lucia Audelay as "Rare Phoenix," an appellation which was associated with Mary Sidney and might well have been addressed to another noblewoman as a slight to Sidney. Another poem, titled "All'autore" and signed "Mia," praises Brandon for surpassing Orpheus. While the Thracian poet could not move women to remorse, "Mia" asserts that Brandon has succeeded in "winning that sexes grace, which did refuse / By hearing Orpheus, to relent their rage" (A2v). The suggestion is that female readers who reject the text resemble the Maenads who tore Orpheus apart limb from limb. But the most interesting hint comes in a third poem by Brandon that includes the title of Sidney's play:

> When barking envie saw thy birth,
> it straight contemnd the same:
> And arm'd his tongue, to give a charge,
> thy weakenesse to diffame.
> But seeing honors golden hooke,
> so linckt to vertues lyne:
> He fled away as halfe afraid,
> yet ceast not to repine.
> But feare not Momus, make returne,
> and haply for thy paine
> Thou maist *Antonius* coullors beare
> when he revives againe.   (A3r)

As Brandon tells the story of its reception, his play was dogged with controversy from the outset. He associates "Momus," the Greek god of ridicule banished from heaven for his continual fault-finding, with "barking envie," those hostile to his play, and with "Antonius." While Brandon refers to the Roman triumvir as "Antony" and "Marke Antony" in the play's argument (the text that follows this poem on the verso side of the same page), his name is given in Latin as "Antonius" in this poem to recall the title of Sidney's play. Brandon baits his detractors by inviting Momus to return, this time as a champion of Sidney's play adorned in "Antonius coullours," and denigrates them by association with the god of ridicule. For Brandon, the controversy touched off by his play is a struggle between virtue and envy, honor and slander, his play and *Antonius*.

Brandon also signals his revisionary intentions in the argument to his play by conspicuously quoting from Sidney's argument. If we recall, Sidney narrates a sequence of events beginning with the defeat of Cassius and Brutus at Philippi and ending with the double-suicide of Antony and Cleopatra. She adds a sentence to the text of Garnier's argument: "But comming in his journey into Siria, the places renewed in his remember-ance the long intermitted love of Cleopatra Queene of Aegipt." Brandon picks up this wording as if to highlight the differences between the narratives of Sidney's play and his own:

Antony going to make warre with the Parthians, and comming into Syria: the place *renewed the memory*, and the memory revived *the long intermitted love*, he once bare to *Cleopatra the Queene of Ægipt*: he therefore wholy subjecting himselfe to the desire of this Cleopatra: forsaketh his vertuous wife Octavia. Whereupon, hir brother Caesar disdaining that she should suffer so great an indignitie: maketh warre upon Antony, and overcometh him, first at Actium, and then at Pelusium, to the utter ruine and destruction, both of Antony and Cleopatra. (A3v–A4r; italics added)

From the dreamy divagations of Antony's thoughts, aroused to memory of Cleopatra by Eastern landscapes, the text shifts disjointedly to critical evaluation: Antony's passion is judged as subjugation. Drawing upon many events portrayed in *Antonius*, Brandon transforms a tragic love story set among the ruins of civil war into a morality play of trans-gression punished: "the utter ruine and destruction, both of Antony and Cleopatra." This, in Brandon's view, is a happy ending, not tragedy but tragicomedy.

In *Antonius*, Sidney decoupled chastity from female virtue. Cleopatra's sensuality in constancy defies conduct manual categorization. In *The Tragicomedy of the Virtuous Octavia*, Brandon firmly refastens chastity to female virtue by dissevering ideal from anti-ideal, matron from harlot, Octavia from Cleopatra. All of the play's energies are spent on making one point about Cleopatra vis-à-vis Octavia: "Shee be but comparable any way" (D4r). His plot has as an organizing principle only that

Octavia completely eclipse Cleopatra. Brandon assigns Octavia female companions, Julia and Camilla, who exceed Cleopatra's Iras and Charmion in piling praises upon their mistress. He emphasizes the lightness of Octavia's skin relative to Cleopatra's, literalizing Daniel's reference to "darke defects," by darkening the Petrarchan pink and white complexion of Garnier/Sidney's Cleopatra to a "sun-burnt" hue. And though there is no precedent for doing so in any source he might have consulted, Brandon gives Octavia a status better than queen: "life-saving Empresse" and "Roomes glorious Empresse" (B2v, E1v). Octavia herself draws attention to her imperial status as if to emphasize how greatly she outdoes Cleopatra's majesty: "Am I an Empresse still thus disobay'd?" (B6v) and "Thou wrongst an Empresse and a Romaine queene" (C1v).

The stones Brandon casts against Sidney's heroine are actions, words, and images from *Antonius* itself. In a scene that reprises Cleopatra's sad farewell to her children, Brandon depicts Octavia's eviction from Antony's house, in the company of all of her children, in effect upstaging Cleopatra in her enactment of maternal sorrow. After failing to persuade Caesar to desist from war with Antony, Octavia swoons and has to be revived by Caesar. In another scene, Brandon's Octavia addresses a plea, "O sisters deare" (E3v), to the fates. This request for pity to the legendarily pitiless fates is a misplaced echo of words that Sidney's Cleopatra addressed to on-stage female companions: "My Sisters, holde me up" (5.1906). Brandon even creates a Dido-like moment for Octavia parallel to Cleopatra's rehearsal of the Carthage queen's suicide speech. To admonish Antony for his heartless eviction of his family, Octavia paraphrases Dido's reproach to Aeneas: "O Antony, borne of no gentle Syre, / Some cruell Caucasus did thee beget . . . More milde then thee, I find each cruell beast" (F2v).

Reiterating the language of purity and defilement used by Daniel, Octavia also gestures toward suicide, as though to challenge Cleopatra in that arena as well: "Ile rather dye the world unspotted myrrour, / And with my faith surmount his injurie" (D3v). The image of the chain joining Antony with Cleopatra "as if his soule / Unto his Ladies soule had bene enchain'd" (2.445) first inserted by Sidney into her translation, multiplies in Brandon's play into "heart-enchaining wordes" (B1r) and "the loving chayne, / That from your highnesse dooth his minde divorce" (B7r). In these instances, Brandon downgrades Sidney's description of Antony's and Cleopatra's linked souls by playing upon associations of the word "enchain" with enslavement and dependence. "Tis not affection," Octavia condescendingly remarks, "that enchaines my minde" (D3r). In another passage, Brandon depreciates Cleopatra's vow of love by associating her words with lies. In *Antonius*, Cleopatra adamantly refuses to betray Antony:

> Soner shining light
> Shall leave the daie, and darknes leave the night:
> Sooner moist currents of tempestuous seas
> Shall wave in heaven, and the nightlie troopes
> Of starres shall shine within the foming waves,
> Then I thee, Antonie, leave in depe distres.   (2.540–5)

Brandon's Octavia reclaims Cleopatra's oath as one of Antony's broken promises to her: "Did not he say, the starres from heaven should fall, / The fishes should upon the mountaines range, / And Tyber should his flowing streames recall: / Before his love should ever thinke on change" (B8v–C1r). It is not enough for Brandon to exalt Octavia; he must also darken and diminish Cleopatra.

What seems to have most incensed Brandon about *Antonius* was that Cleopatra, in spite of her erotic nature, stakes a claim to virtue. When Eras challenges her, saying, "Your dutie must upon some good be founded," her mistress answers that it is grounded "on vertue . . . the onlie good" (650–1). Cleopatra's austere rejoinder makes her sexual purity or impurity irrelevant to her virtue. In *The Virtuous Octavia* and in the dedicatory verses that precede it, Brandon hammers on the word "vertue" as if mind-numbing repetition alone could secure its definition. It appears a total of sixty-two times in his text.[63] Through compulsive iteration, Brandon wraps the word "vertue" in a sticky web of connotations. References to symbols of awe (lamp, flame, laws, monarchs, altar, paradise) and lofty attributes (nobility, harmony, sacredness, brightness) coat the word with elevated associations at the same time as it is being linked with the titular roles of empress, queen, and lady. The trade-off implied is that in return for accepting the subordinate position of wife, a woman will be made the object of reverent admiration.

To limit further the meaning of "vertue" to its conduct manual definition, Brandon connects the word with the conventional good female example of Octavia and its obverse with the conventional bad female example of Cleopatra. Brandon cannot, without violating the neo-classical principle of unity of place, include Cleopatra as a character in a play set in Rome. But this does not stop him from staging the stigmatization of Octavia's rival. Brandon introduces a made-up character extraneous to the plot – "Sylvia, a licentious woman" – to occupy Cleopatra's position as anti-ideal on stage (A4v). The second act in which Sylvia debates the relative value of chastity with Camilla and Julia has no place in the narrative Brandon outlined in his argument. It exists

purely as a vehicle for making the point that sexual purity should be the
be-all and end-all determinant of a woman's social standing. After
learning that Antony has been living with Cleopatra, Octavia affects a
pose of righteous acceptance. Antony's disgrace, she affirms, will fall on
his own head and her virtue install her in heaven. The scene ends with
Octavia appealing to virtue to repulse her foes with its all-mastering
shield. Enter Sylvia. "Well," says licentious Sylvia, "let them talke of
vertue, those that list . . . I know what would touch him to the heart"
(C2r). As Julia and Camilla listen silently, Sylvia argues that Octavia
should avenge Antony's betrayal by taking lovers of her own. Describing
her delight in flitting from lover to lover like a bee sampling different
flowers, Sylvia defines constancy as an evil:

> the thing that workes all womens fall.
> Why constancie is that which marreth all.
> A weake conceipt which cannot wrongs resist,
> A chaine it is which bindes our selves in thrall,
> And gives men scope to use us as they list.
> For when they know that you will constant bide,
> Small is their care, how often they do slide.   (C2v–C3r)

In this proto-feminist discourse, chastity is an instrument for inducing
female subjugation and justifying a sexual double standard.

Only after Sylvia has dismissed marriage vows as unimportant, does
Camilla step foward to castigate her as a "wicked woman," "foule
monster," "stain of thy sexe," and "leawd creature" (C5r). The scene
ends with Camilla's dismissal of Sylvia and an ode to chastity:

> O Chastity bright vertues sacred flame,
> Be never woman lovely wanting thee.
> Be never woman wrong'd adorn'd with thee.
> Be all disgrac'd that merit not thy name.   (C5v)

Octavia is set on a pedestal as an example of chastity while Sylvia/
Cleopatra is left to burn in hell. This is the play's true denouement,
though it comes as early as the second act. The report of Antony's death
at the end of the play is an anti-climax, a matter merely of just deserts:
"she that taught him first to swim in sinne: / Was even the first that
drown'd his life therein" (F3v). Cleopatra's death is not mentioned. By
the end of the second act, Cleopatra's presence already had been
expunged from the play in Camilla's repudiation of Sylvia/Cleopatra as
the personification of sexual vice. The aim of Brandon's manipulation of
female ideal and anti-ideal was to counter Sidney's redefinition of
Cleopatra as an example of a virtuous woman. In her exchange with
Sylvia, Camilla elevates Octavia and debases Cleopatra in the same

action of asserting the dominant meaning of female "virtue": "O
Chastity bright vertues sacred flame." By this logic, chastity is virtue,
virtue chastity, and both virtue and chastity embodied as one in the
triumphant paradigmatic female example of the Virtuous Octavia.

V

The ongoing controversy over Cleopatra was reawakened when that
heroine, initially imported by Sidney from the Continent to England, was
translated again by Shakespeare to the public stage. In 1616, Robert
Anton cited Cleopatra as one of the pernicious examples of female lust
that were corrupting women in theatre audiences:

> Why doe our lustfull Theaters entice,
> And personate in lively action vice:
> Draw to the Cities shame, with guilded clothes,
> Such swarmes of wives to breake their nuptiall othes:
> Or why are women rather growne so mad,
> That their immodest feete like planets gad
> With such irregular motion to base Playes,
> Where all the deadly sinnes keepe hollidaies.
> There shall they see the vices of the times,
> Orestes incest, Cleopatres crimes,
> Lucullus surfets, and Poppeas pride,
> Virgineaes rape and wanton Lais hide
> Her Sirens charmes in such eare charming sense;
> As it would turne a modest audience,
> To brazen-facet profession of a whore.
> Their histories perswade, but action more,
> Vices well coucht in pleasing Sceanes present,
> More will to act, then action can invent.[64]

The visual impact of theatrical representations, Anton contends, is
enough to metamorphose modest matrons into whores. In his view, the
damage done by spectacles with any sexual content is so great that even a
moral example cannot be staged safely; the enactment of Virginia's rape
is as potentially damaging to the female playgoer as that of Cleopatra's
"crimes."

While there is no evidence to suggest that the sight of an actor boying
Cleopatra's greatness actually turned women into prostitutes, a play
about the Egyptian queen did have a transformative influence on one
playgoer. The changed man was Samuel Daniel. The play was *Antony
and Cleopatra*. After encountering Shakespeare's tragedy, Daniel revised
his *Tragedy of Cleopatra* in 1607 to incorporate elements of Sidney's and
Shakespeare's more sympathetic views of Cleopatra. The interconnec-

tions between these texts by Sidney, Shakespeare, and Daniel establish that in one case, at least, a woman reading and writing on an estate in northern Wiltshire was able to shape how a controversial figure of female exemplarity was presented on a London stage.[65]

While the Cleopatra debate between Mary Sidney, Samuel Brandon, and Samuel Daniel carried on through printed rather than staged plays, the theatrical context in which it unfolded is nonetheless crucial to our understanding of it. The fact that *Antonius* was probably never performed does not mean that Mary Sidney was motivated in her promotion of Senecan tragedy by a fundamental opposition to theatre itself.[66] Nor does it mean that she set out to publish a "closet drama" when she translated Garnier's *Marc Antoine*. This assumption, nearly universal in recent appraisals of the play, is based upon the mistaken notion that French neo-Senecan plays were "intended for private reading rather than stage production."[67] An earlier neo-Senecan Cleopatra play, Etienne Jodelle's *Cléopâtre captive*, took the French cultural establishment by storm when it was performed, famed actors in the lead roles, first before the King at court and again at the Collège de Boncourt in 1553. Those performances show that Garnier's imitation of Seneca's works, the only Latin tragedies extant, did not make his works unstageable. Garnier's *Marc Antoine* itself may have been performed in the year it was published. In May, 1578, a play titled *La Tragedie de Marc Antoine et Cleopatre* was acted before an audience at Saint-Maixent.[68] While there is no definitive proof that the record in question refers to Garnier's *Marc Antoine*, there is clear evidence that other plays by the dramatist were performed. The repertory for 1594 of a French acting company listing twelve plays, half of which were tragedies, includes three by Garnier: *Les Juives*, *La Troade*, and *Hippolyte*.[69]

In his famously successful *Spanish Tragedy*, Thomas Kyd, who translated Garnier's *Cornelie*, evokes contemporary reports about continental theatre. In a scene with Hieronimo, Lorenzo reports having witnessed tragedies performed "in Paris, 'mongst the French tragedians." Like these characters from Kyd's popular play, Mary Sidney would have seen neo-Senecan tragedy as a literary form that was not only the rage of the French and Italian theatre but also the most lauded dramatic genre in literary circles, "*Tragedia cothurnata*," as Hieronimo puts it, "fitting kings."[70] Her *Antonius* is less akin to Milton's *Samson Agonistes* than it is to William Gager's *Dido*, a neo-Senecan tragedy performed with "strange, marvellous, and abundant" stage effects at Oxford in 1583.[71] Closer to home, a play connected with the Sidney circle, Samuel Daniel's neo-Senecan *Tragedy of Philotas*, was acted by a professional theatre company, the Children of the Queen's Revels, on January 3, 1605.[72]

Sidney's stipulation of a stage as the locus of action, "the stage supposed Alexandria," suggests that she envisioned *Antonius* in a theatrical setting. To see Sidney herself in that context, we have only to turn to the dedication to *Ulysses Redux* that Gager addressed to her in 1592: "Wherefore I ask of you, most noble Countess, that, like another Penelope, you extend your hand to be kissed by this Ulysses arriving, not at Ithaca, but now for the first time onto the stage."[73] Gager sees Sidney presiding over the playing space, her hand extended to the playwright with her patronage. The platform he envisions in his dedication is no doubt a scaffold set up at a university for a visiting courtly audience, not that of a public playhouse. However, it is significant nonetheless that it is a stage that Sidney occupies in his imagination and no closet.

The contemporary stage also played a role in Samuel Daniel's eventual reconciliation with Mary Sidney. With the publication in 1607 of a thoroughgoing revision of *The Tragedy of Cleopatra*, inspired in part by Shakespeare's recent play, Daniel recanted his previous representation of Cleopatra as a lying seductress. The conversion of Daniel indicates that the theatre could, as critics suspected, unsettle dogmas and modify mentalities.[74] Through the public theatre, a medium in which the limits of gendered codes could be probed, Daniel and Sidney were able to negotiate their conflict over the definition of female virtue and the limits of female literacy on different terms. Sidney's role in the controversy, once that of chastised reader, turned to that of authorial source. Shakespeare's *Antony and Cleopatra*, performed at the Globe in the first decade of the seventeenth century, brought Daniel to pick up Sidney's book again, fifteen years after its first publication, and to reinterpret its female subject from a strikingly more positive perspective. Having once criticized his patron for casting the sexual-virtuous Cleopatra as a good example, Daniel corrected his earlier interpretation in the light of Sidney's text, carrying out, in the process, the most extensive revision of a published work in his career.

There is little doubt, Ernest Schanzer concludes, that "Shakespeare had read the Countess of Pembroke's *Antonius* shortly before or during the composition of *Antony and Cleopatra*."[75] Echoes of Sidney's translation reverberate in the text of Shakespeare's play: the knot meant to hold Antony and Caesar in perpetual "amity," Cleopatra's answer to Antony that she "dare not" open the doors of the monument, Antony's comments about Caesar's ignorance of warfare, the metaphor of Antony's eyes serving Venus or Mars, Antony's abrupt assertion that he must "from this enchanting Queene breake off," references to the Nile's "slime" and the abundance promised by its swelling tide, Antony's "I can no more," the scene in which Cleopatra loses consciousness and has to be revived by her women, Cleopatra's insistence upon giving Antony his "due rights" of burial, and the "haunt" that Antony says will be his and Cleopatra's as they walk hand in hand through the underworld.[76] Beyond verbal echoes, the two plays are connected by similarities between characters. The soul-searching of Shakespeare's Antony, for example, is suggested not by Plutarch but by *Antonius*. So too, are aspects of Shakespeare's Cleopatra: her certain love, her regenerative sexuality, her eloquence as Antony's eulogist. The critique of Virgil that Shakespeare develops with references to Dido and Aeneas also is implicit in *Antonius*.[77] Most importantly, the unconventional structure of Shakespeare's denouement derives from Sidney; in her *Antonius*, as in Shakespeare's play, the hero dies in act four and the heroine is left to preside alone over the final act.

Shakespeare did not simply plunder Sidney's translation for what was of use to him but read it with great attention. One telling example of his insights into her text is his use of the final lines of *Antonius*:

> A thousand kisses, thousand thousand more
> Let you my mouth for honors farewell give:
> That in this office weake my limmes may growe,
> Fainting on you, and fourth my soule may flowe.   (2019–22)

Shakespeare literalizes the interchangeability of subject and object in that passage by dividing Cleopatra's last words between Antony and Cleopatra. In Shakespeare's enactment of the monument scene, Antony rehearses the bid by Sidney's Cleopatra to bestow thousands of kisses on her lover. The words now issue from the dying Antony as he waits to be lifted to the monument:

> I am dying, Egypt, dying. Only
> I here importune death awhile until
> Of many thousand kisses the poor last
> I lay upon thy lips.   (4.16, 19–22)

After the stage direction, "*They heave* ANTONY *aloft to* CLEO-PATRA," Cleopatra answers him: "And welcome, welcome! Die when thou hast lived, / Quicken with kissing. Had my lips that power, / Thus would I wear them out" (4.16.39–41). In these lines, Cleopatra takes up the second half of the last quatrain from *Antonius* by suggesting that, if her lips had the power to resurrect Antony, she would wear them out with kissing him. Shakespeare borrows from Sidney at the same time as he reverses her image of Cleopatra feeling her own life ebb away as she kisses Antony. He transforms the pure pathos of her heroine into the exuberant grief of his. In the reunion of Antony and Cleopatra, first separated spatially by the distance between the stage and the gallery above, Shakespeare enacts the mutual embraces, unstageable in Garnier's neoclassical theatre, evoked by Sidney through the ambiguous syntax of her verse.

Shakespeare, to a lesser degree, also had consulted Daniel's 1594 *Tragedy of Cleopatra*. In 1607, Daniel repaid the favor by adding material from Shakespeare's play to his revision. Daniel took from Shakespeare the idea of the countryman bearing figs (though in Daniel's play he is really the noble Diomedes in disguise) and the staged enactment of Cleopatra's death in which Eras and Charmion feature prominently, "not onely / Spectators in this Scene, but Actors too."[78] Perhaps the most intriguing connection between the two plays is an apparent reference to the stage mechanics of Shakespeare's monument scene; Daniel testifies to the visual impact of the scene by including in his narration the detail that Eras and Charmion "tugd at the pulley" to lift Antony from the ground (sig. G8v). However, the narrative form of the scene and its meaning derive from Sidney's *Antonius*. Daniel follows Sidney in turning the episode, missing from his 1594 play, into an occasion for Cleopatra to negate accusations of faithlessness with an irrefutable demonstration of loyalty and love.

As we saw earlier, Daniel's dedicatory poem to his 1594 version of *The Tragedy of Cleopatra* gives the impression of a troubled relation between himself and Sidney. This suggestion of a rift is confirmed by external biographical evidence which shows that their estrangement, dating from about 1593, coincides with Daniel's denigration of Sidney's Cleopatra, and, likewise, their renewed ties with his positive reevaluation of her Cleopatra in 1607. In addition to the 1594 dedication, the poem in which he confesses to having "obscur'd" the "worth" of Sidney's Cleopatra, Daniel's prefaces to other published works confirm these approximate dates of the initial split and later reconciliation between patron and protégé.

Daniel's early triumph as a sonneteer had been associated with Mary Sidney, and he dedicated his acclaimed *Delia* to her in 1592. In 1593, however, Daniel appears to have become embroiled in the quarrel between Fulke Greville and Sidney over who would assume the role of her brother's literary executor. Greville had published an edition of the *Arcadia* left to him by Philip with corrections in the author's hand. It was this edition that Mary Sidney termed "disfigured" when she published her own edition in 1593.[79] In 1595, a year after publication of *The Tragedy of Cleopatra*, Daniel was under the protection of Greville who interceded on his behalf with the queen. Daniel did not only benefit from the attentions of Sidney's antagonist during this period of tension over the *Arcadia*; in the same year, he snubbed Sidney by publishing his *Civil*

Wars, the "greater taske" that he acknowledged in the 1594 preface having undertaken at Sidney's urging, with a dedication to Charles Blount, Lord Mountjoy, instead of to her and later, in 1601–2, with a dedication to Elizabeth.[80] Greville's assistance did not procure Daniel a position at court, and he was left to take refuge instead in the household of Mountjoy.[81] In the dedicatory epistle to his 1599 *Poetical Essays*, Daniel attests to his abandonment and thanks Blount for having received the "tempest-driven, fortune-tossed" poet to his shores.[82] This lavish expression of gratitude to his newfound patron in 1599 implies a residual bitterness on Daniel's part toward Sidney for having left him solitary and resourceless.

His resentment, however, did not prove permanent. Daniel's publication of the revised *Tragedy of Cleopatra* in 1607 accompanied, and may have helped to accomplish, a rapprochement with Sidney. He had already made a conciliatory gesture toward her in the 1603 dedication of his *Defence of Rhyme* addressed to her son, William Herbert, the new Earl of Pembroke, in which he remembered "having been first incourag'd or fram'd" in his literary career by Herbert's "most Worthy and Honourable mother."[83] In the period after this dedication, Daniel may have been spurred to appeal directly to his earlier patron by new financial necessity. Following the scandal that erupted in 1605 over *Philotas*, whose dramatization of the downfall of a court favorite was read as an allegory for the Essex affair, Daniel lost both his position as a licenser for the Children of the Queen's Revels and his favor with Mountjoy, whom he clumsily implicated in the affair. Daniel expresses dejection in a written apology to Mountjoy, which he pitifully terms "the last sute I will ever make," and in a similarly downbeat letter to Robert Cecil, chief minister to James I, in which he offers to withdraw publication of *Philotas* in exchange for enough money to leave court and "bury" himself out of the way.[84] Fortunately for Daniel, however, both Anne of Denmark and Mary Sidney stepped into the breach. In 1607, Daniel found financial security in the Queen's service as a groom of the Privy Chamber. A preface published two years later indicates that Sidney also provided financial assistance. Daniel dedicated the work that he considered to be his crowning achievement not to the Queen but to the patron who first had encouraged him in the endeavor. His long delayed dedication of *The Civil Wars* to Mary Sidney came in 1609. In a prefatory epistle to the work, he describes himself as "revived" by Sidney's "Goodnes." Book 8 of the epic opens with Daniel offering the work, "my last," to Mary Sidney, "who had the first of all my labours past."[85]

The way for this reconciliation was prepared in 1607 by Daniel's revision of *The Tragedy of Cleopatra*, which is dedicated to Mary Sidney on the title page. In an epistle printed in the 1611 edition, Daniel lauds Sidney as an example to others based on her intellectual influence:

> Great sister of the Muses glorious starre
> Of femall worth, who didst at first disclose
> Unto our times, what noble powers there are
> In womens harts, and sent example farre
> To call up others to like studious thoughts.[86]

Although he qualifies the compliment with a courtly flourish, locating her powers in her heart rather than her mind, Daniel nevertheless acknowledges Sidney's more capacious definition of the female subject by suggesting that "femall" worth might inhere not only in a woman's restraint from misconduct but also in her active contribution to the literary culture of her day.

The changes that Daniel made to his *Tragedy of Cleopatra* similarly reflect the broadening of perspective on female virtue that Sidney had advocated and Shakespeare nourished in each of their characterizations of Cleopatra. In his "newly altered" version of the play, Daniel recants his 1594 theory that Cleopatra never loved Antony while he was alive. His new Cleopatra, like Sidney's and Shakespeare's, reciprocates Antony's passion. In describing her last moments with Antony, she tells how her clothes became stained with his blood as she held "his struggling limmes in his last extasie" (sig. G7v) and refers to him as "my Antony," "my Lord," "my spouse," and "my love" (G7v). By contrast, in the 1594 version of the play, Cleopatra says nothing of the manner in which he died, only that he "lyes falne, confounded, dead in shame and dolors" (1.19). In the second scene of the revised play, Dircet confirms Cleopatra's account of how Antony slew himself, was raised to the monument, and died in Cleopatra's arms. Dircet refers to Cleopatra as Antony's "love" and "his royall Cleopatra" and to Antony as "her love" (G7v). He describes how she tended Antony's wound, "Calles him her Lord, her spouse, her Emperor / Forgets her owne distresse, to comfort his, / And interpoints each comfort with a kisse" (H1r).

In the second act of Daniel's tragedy, as in the second act of *Antonius*, Eras and Charmion try and fail to persuade Cleopatra to make a deal with Octavius. In *Antonius*, Lucilius assures Antony that there are many proofs which "Do plaine enough her heart unfained prove, / Equally toucht, you loving, as you love" (917–18). Similarly, in the revised *Tragedy of Cleopatra*, Cleopatra asserts, "My constancy shall undeceive their mindes, / And I will bring the witnesse of my blood / To testifie my fortitude, that binds / My equall love, to fall with him I stood" (H4v). Unlike her 1594 prototype who dwelt obsessively on her unworthiness, the 1607 Cleopatra subordinates mention of her faults ("Defects I grant I had, but . . ." (H4v)). She puts the emphasis instead on her constancy and "equall love." Most significantly, this Cleopatra, like Sidney's and Shakespeare's, seeks death only in order to rejoin Antony: "I bring my soule, my selfe, and that with speed, / My selfe will bring my soule to Antony" (K1r).[87]

Daniel's reworking of the character of Cleopatra to conform to Sidney's vision is most apparent in his narrated description of the final reunion with Antony. In his dedication to the 1594 version of the play, he had acknowledged having depicted Cleopatra "in courage lower." Daniel's revised version restores Cleopatra to her former stature by recounting, as does Sidney, the monument scene as a demonstration of the queen's valor. In *Antony and Cleopatra*, the mechanical act of lifting Antony's body, aided by some kind of crude machinery, is more comic than heroic.[88] Shakespeare's Cleopatra uses the situation as an occasion for making sexual puns, "How heavy weighs my lord!," and ascribes the physical strength required for lifting Antony to male gods rather than herself; if she had Juno's power, she says, she would compel Mercury to raise Antony to the heavens. "O, come, come, come," she cajoles. After that little effort follows the stage direction, "*they heave ANTONY aloft to CLEOPATRA*" (4.16.38). The unclear pronoun reference may refer to the way the action was staged; the stage machinery seems to have made Cleopatra's actual part in lifting Antony appear gratuitous.

With regard to this key event in the play, Daniel imitates Sidney rather than Shakespeare. All the emphasis in his 1607 *Tragedy of Cleopatra* is on Cleopatra's role in the physical work of the scene:

> There Charmion, and poore Eras, two weake maids
> Foretir'd with watching, and their mistresse care,
> Tugd at the pulley having n'other ayds,
> And up they hoise the swounding body there
> Of pale Antonius, showring out his blood
> On th'under lookers, which there gazing stood.
>   And when they had now wrought him up half way
> (Their feeble powers unable more to doe)
> The frame stood still, the body at a stay,
> When Cleopatra all her strength thereto
> Puts, with what vigor love, and care could use,
> So that it mooves againe, and then againe
> It comes to stay. When shee afresh renewes
> Her hold, and with r'inforced power doth straine,
> And all the weight of her weake bodie laies,
> Whose surcharg'd heart more then her body wayes.
> At length shee wrought him up, and takes him in.   (G8v–H1r)

Daniel takes from Sidney the notion that it is Cleopatra's "vigor love and care" that enable her to perform a feat of physical endurance that would have been otherwise impossible. He contrasts Cleopatra's "r'inforced power" with the "feeble powers" of her "weake" maids. Echoing Sidney's description of "strong armes," he emphasizes that "Cleopatra all her strength thereto / Puts" and summons through her passion the last measure of force necessary to raise Antony to the monument. Inevitably, Daniel adds exaggerated details, such as that of Antony's blood raining down on unprepared spectators, and employs melodrama for emotional impact. It is not enough that Cleopatra "enlast hir in the corde, and with all force / This life-dead man couragiously uprais'de" (4.1663–4) as Sidney puts it in her translation. Daniel draws out the scene. Eras and Charmion undertake to lift Antony but stop when he is only half-way up so that Cleopatra must come to the rescue; she too struggles until, as in *Antonius*, with strength renewed by love, she lifts Antony at last triumphantly to her window. There can no longer be any concern, as Daniel raised it in his 1594 dedication, that Antony will not recognize the Cleopatra of this play for the heroine she is, "that for his Queene & Love he scarse will know her." Transfigured by the 1607 revisions, Daniel's queen is in this scene irrefutably once again Mary Sidney's Cleopatra.

Building on Garnier's depiction of Cleopatra, Sidney had imagined a female subject dignified by strength and desire as well as faith. Her vision, in turn, animated Shakespeare's complementary view that "vilest things / Become themselves in her, that the holy priests / Bless her when she is riggish" (2.2.243–5). Like Samuel Daniel, Shakespeare's Caesar is brought to reevaluate Cleopatra on Mary Sidney's terms. The Roman emperor's final assessment of the woman whom he had earlier dismissed as a whore is a tribute to her unfathomable complexity. The sight of Cleopatra in death moves Caesar to remark that "she looks like sleep, / As she would catch another Antony / In her strong toil of grace" (5.2.336–8). Compressed in the last three words of Caesar's lines are all the traits of infinite variety that conduct manuals deemed irreconcilable and that Cleopatra nevertheless exemplifies: sexual energy, heroic action, spiritual depth. The phrase is an oxymoron and a theological crux; in the Protestant lexicon, grace is a freely-bestowed dispensation from heaven, not a reward for effort. A "toil of grace" is beyond the bounds of ordinary human action. "Toil" means "net" as well as "labor." It refers both to Cleopatra's allure, her power to attract Antony, and to her physical and intellectual resourcefulness in reaching her own ends, lifting Antony to the heights of the monument, frustrating Caesar's schemes, controlling the circumstances of her death. "Grace" suggests both a corporeal presence, the elegance of her bearing, and proximity to the divine, the holiness of her passion.

The proliferation of Cleopatras that first issued from Mary Sidney's *Antonius* is part not only of the history of the theatre, but also of the history of reading. In publishing the play, Sidney intervened in the debate over what paradigms and what practices would guide female interpretation and, through the daring craft of her translation, reformulated the relation between reading and a woman's character. She tested the parameters of acceptability that defined in narrow ways the contents of books, the forms of interpretation, and molds of selfhood set aside for her sex. Because she recast female exemplarity in unorthodox terms, her act of translation exposed her to criticism and rebuke. Yet her characterization of the Egyptian queen as a complex heroic figure was validated a decade and a half later when Shakespeare's *Antony and Cleopatra* brought Sidney's influence to the world of the public theatre. The interest that this Cleopatra saga continued to generate into the seventeenth century, inspiring Fletcher and Massinger's "prequel" about the queen's early affair with Julius Caesar as well as Thomas May's and eventually John Dryden's versions, shows that sex-specific models of identity, patterns of comportment taught through habits such as reading and playgoing, were at the same time hugely important and vigorously contested.[89]

As the author of *Antonius*, Mary Sidney offered the theatre an alternative model of Cleopatra and offered women an alternative model of virtue. Even as the writer-translator of the volume of the Psalms she holds in her portrait, Mary Sidney rejected conduct manual strictures while insisting upon her claim to social standing, to the name of the "Right Honorable and most vertuous Lady Mary Sidney." The portrait she commissioned superimposes the image of learned author on that of pious reader. It depicts her in the static and immobile posture of a devout woman of unyielding virtue. Only the hand holding her book open conveys any hint of physical animation. Her slightly tensed fingers draw attention not just to the title of the book, which identifies Sidney as an author, but also to her writing of its manuscript pages as a bodily act. The viewer of the 1618 portrait of Mary Sidney is left with that incongruous double image, a discrepancy smilingly concealed, the contradiction of her strong toil of grace.

4   Writes in his tables

Enter one with a pen and inke.[1]
Balurdo drawes out his writing table, and writes.[2]
As he is writing an Angel comes & stands before him.[3]
They seat themselves at a Table severally, and fall to writing.[4]
Writes in his tables.[5]

It has become a commonplace of Tudor–Stuart drama criticism: the plays and the dominant discourses of this period represent men as writers and women as texts to be inscribed. "Was this fair paper, this most goodly book, / Meant to write 'whore' upon?", Othello asks of Desdemona.[6] In posing the question, Valerie Wayne points out, Othello is "himself writing the body of misogynist discourse onto Desdemona's 'book'."[7] Yet if women in this period were likened to paper and books, so too were men. With his death imminent, King John compares himself to a scribal text: "I am a scribbled form, drawn with a pen / Upon a parchment, and against this fire / Do I shrink up" (5.7.32–4). Richard II speaks of "the very book indeed / Where all my sins are writ, and that's myself" (4.1.264–5). The metaphor, however, functions differently depending upon the gender of the person depicted. When it refers to a woman, her sexual transgressions and hidden crimes surface as alphabetic characters. In the case of a man, it is his soul that is textualized, in all its dimensions, contradictions, and instability. The female version of the metaphor is linked with shame and legibility, the male version with secrecy and inscrutability.

Shakespeare's representation of both Lucrece and Tarquin as texts in *The Rape of Lucrece* illustrates this point. Lucrece, imploring Night to conceal her, imagines the fact of her rape as engraved in words on her person:

Make me not object to the tell-tale day.
The light will show charactered in my brow
The story of sweet chastity's decay,
The impious breach of holy wedlock vow.

138

> Yea, the illiterate that know not how
> To cipher what is writ in learnèd books,
> Will quote my loathsome trespass in my looks.   (806–12)

In this passage, Lucrece expresses her anticipation of social disapproval, being made the "object" of reproachful gazes, through the image of herself as a public text to be read by everyone. Daylight will expose what is now hidden: the narrative "charactered" on her forehead. In the course of five lines, the actual content of that narrative shifts from "sweet chastity's decay," to "the impious breach of holy wedlock vow," and finally to "my loathsome trespass." "Decay" implies a process beyond Lucrece's power, a "breach" an act committed deliberately by Tarquin or herself, and "my loathsome trespass" a crime for which she alone is responsible. Lucrece's movement toward self-inculpation coincides with her self-description as a book for the illiterate. The act of imagining herself as a text readable by all-comers, lasciviously accessible even to the uneducated masses, brings her to blame herself for Tarquin's violence.

There are examples in other works from this period of allegedly promiscuous women being read as texts. The sin of their illicit love, Claudio says in *Measure for Measure*, "With character too gross is writ on Juliet" (1.2.132). In *Much Ado About Nothing*, Leonato asks rhetorically of Hero, "Could she here deny / The story that is printed in her blood?" (4.1.120–1). In Philip Sidney's *Arcadia*, Philoclea falls in love only to discover that the ink in which she inscribed a promise of virginity has become smudged; for her, the text is a graphic replica of her stained chastity: " 'Alas,' said she, 'fair marble, which never received'st spot but by my writing, well do these blots become a blotted writer'."[8] A page blotted with ink, as an image for the female self, implies error, pollution, contact with dangerous fluids; ink, blood, semen. The only story such a text could contain is that of sexual transgressions printed in boldly visible letters.

Shakespeare attributes Lucrece's vulnerability to her failure to decipher Tarquin's "meaning":

> But she that never coped with stranger eyes
> Could pick no meaning from their parling looks,
> Nor read the subtle shining secrecies
> Writ in the glassy margins of such books.   (99–102)

Described as an activity parallel to "coping" (wrestling), reading has a sexual connotation; in this sense, Lucrece's inability to read Tarquin is evidence of her purity. It is important to note, however, that the metaphorical text in this passage is Tarquin. He is referred to in the same terms as La Fin, a character in George Chapman's *Byron's Conspiracy*, whose indecipherability is compared to illegible writing: "those strange characters writ in his face / Which at first were hard for me to read."[9] Unlike the text engraved on Lucrece, the writing associated with Tarquin is presumed to be in his own hand, an obscure marginal comment written on the page of a book. The "glassy" appearance of the page refers literally to the surface of the paper used for printed books, which was more likely to smear when written upon than writing paper, and metaphorically to the changeable foundations of Tarquin's personality.[10] The abstruse quality of the writing is also significant. Reading or writing a scribal text required initiation into what writing master David Brown termed "rare secrets of art."[11] One of Castiglione's courtiers argued that writing should be deliberately esoteric because "if the woordes that the writer useth bring with them a litle (I will not saie diffycultie) but covered subtilty . . . they geve a certain greater aucthoritye to writing."[12] In the case of Tarquin, Shakespeare implies that such "subtle shining secrecies," marks and dashes blurred on glossy paper, are hard to read, and yet at the same time enticing, shining with allure, precisely by virtue of their difficulty and elusiveness.

A page blotted with ink, as an image for the male self, connotes self-expression and self-fashioning. One thinks of the Bordeaux copy of Montaigne's *Essais*: a book interlineated with the author's handwritten additions; printed words crossed out, punctuation altered, lowercase letters changed to uppercase; Montaigne's italic script spilling over from the margin to the bottom of the page, one word replaced by another, lines scratched through in the intensity of composition, the train of thought continuing past the cross-outs, new formulations left to stand.[13] What Margaret Cavendish remarked of her husband can be extended to the humanist-instructed male subject: "He creates himself with his pen."[14] "My selfe am the groundworke of my booke," writes the Montaigne of Florio's translation.[15] The reverse might also be said to be true. His book is the groundwork of his self: "The book emerges as the locus of the self, the space where Montaigne finds and founds his sense of being."[16] Text and self mutually define and determine the other.

This is a notion that finds echo in Shakespeare's sonnets. The persona repeatedly draws attention to the handwritten text of the sonnets as a material trace of his interiority. In a rhetorical question posed to his friend, the persona asks, "What's in the brain that ink may character / Which hath not figured to thee my true spirit?" (sonnet 108). He voices the wish that he could find the mental presence of his friend "in some antique book / Since mind at first in character was done" (sonnet 59). The implication is that one's true spirit can be figured in ink and the mind done in character. The idea is a sixteenth-century one, composition ("inditing") previously having been separate from the act of transcription ("writing"), an idea difficult to recover for readers of texts published in the ages of mechanical and electronic reproduction. For Shakespeare, the scribal form of the "sugared Sonnets," circulating in manuscripts "among his private friends," is central to their meaning.[17] When he false-coyly asks not to be remembered, "If you read this line, remember not / The hand that writ it" (sonnet 71), he calls particular attention to the handwritten poem as an artifact of the self. Sonnet 74 invokes the metaphor in even more literal terms:

> When thou reviewest this, thou dost review
> The very part was consecrate to thee.
> The earth can have but earth, which is his due;
> My spirit is thine, the better part of me.

The persona is not saying here, as he does in sonnets 32 and 71, that the marks made by his hand will revive his memory after he is dead. "This," the text written in the poet's hand, occupies the same grammatical position in the poem as "the very part consecrate to thee," his soul. When the poet's friend reads one, he reads the other. The bold claim made in these lines is that self and autographical text are interchangeable.

This assertion, proposed as an axiom in the sonnets, becomes the object of sustained inquiry in *Richard III*. In that play, Richard exempli-fies the masculine subject formed through writing: complicate, rhetori-cally agile, obsessed with self-signification. He enacts humanist practices of writing by replicating copies and appropriating texts to achieve mastery over others. But Richard's manipulation of writing for self-advancement, even to carry out and validate regicide, contradicts the humanist assumption that instruction in penmanship and composition necessarily produces reliable subjects to serve hierarchy and state. As he uses writing to co-opt the widow of a man he murdered, kill his own brother, and hide his illegal execution of a subject, Richard recalls the claims for an equivalence between self and text posited in the sonnets and Montaigne's *Essays*. In Shakespeare's play, the correspondence between the counterfeit documents that Richard contrives and his studied self-construction invites the audience to interrogate sceptically the scribal foundations of male identity.

I

Writing was vaunted in early modern England as a vehicle for masculine self-realization. As William Higford sums it up, "Reading maketh an able man, Discourse a ready man, and writing a perfect man."[18] The boy who has learned to write beautifully, Richard Mulcaster argues in *The Training Up of Children* (1581), "hath purchased those two excellent faire winges, which will cause him [to] towre up to the top of all learning, as Plato in the like case of knowledge, termeth Arithmetick and Geometrie his two wings wherwith to flie up to heaven, from whence he doth fetch the true direction of his imprisoned ignorant [soul]."[19] In Mulcaster's fanciful image, the grammar-school boy sprouts one wing after learning to read. It is only after learning to write, however, that he acquires a second wing and, with it, a capacity for flight. Thomas Dekker draws on the same image of the quill pen to suggest that writing endows the writer with wings: "How many fly higher, and spread a more Noble wing with that one feather, then those Butter-flies do, that stare up and downe in the eyes of a kingdome, with all the painted feathers of their riotous pride."[20] The exalted status of writing depended, in part, on excluding women from access to it. Even as late as 1638, a letter-writing manual titled *The Secretary of Ladies* had to defend itself against the criticism that writing was not meant for women because "it ill becomes their sexe." According to its "advertisement to the Reader," the book would convert those "who cannot yet consent that Gentlewomen should write."[21] Whether educators prohibited women from writing altogether or, like Vives, recommended that they acquire the skill for the limited purpose of copying morally salutary texts, the basic premise was the same; "the gender bias implicit in the term 'penmanship' was not fortuitous: writing was largely a male domain."[22]

This notion that writing was essentially masculine, like the Renaissance pun on pen and penis, was invoked to make cultural difference (writing/lack of writing) appear as congenital as genital difference. The aim was to represent a phenomenon of post-Reformation social history, the radically unequal distribution of literate skills based on gender, as an invariable fact of nature. By the time of the English Civil War, signatures collected for the Protestation Oath of 1641, for the Vow and Covenant of 1643, and for the Solemn League and Covenant of 1644 indicate a signature-literacy rate of 30 percent for men and 10 percent for women. Throughout the early modern period, as Keith Thomas emphasizes, literacy implied a spectrum of gradated skills ranging from the highest competence conferred by a full humanist program of study, the ability to read and write Latin (among other languages) in a range of scripts, to the most narrow form of literacy, the ability to read (but not write) texts printed (not handwritten) in black-letter (not roman) type. The lopsided three-to-one ratio of men versus women able to sign their names masks a far larger discrepancy between the numbers of each sex possessing the full complement of literate skills necessary for participation in government, commerce, law, or divinity.

Though signatures remain the sole quantifiable source of data for establishing rates of writing-literacy in this period, social historians have drawn on other evidence, in particular wills, inventories, publishing data, court records, school curricula, letters, private journals, and literary works, to argue that the number of women who could read far exceeded the small number who could sign their names. "Even well-to-do women were notoriously bad at writing," Keith Thomas notes, "and their spelling was often dreadful. But they were not necessarily any worse at reading than the men."[23] Literacy was not sex-specific; the forms of its acquisition and transmission were. In early modern England, as Jennifer Monaghan has documented was the case in colonial New England, prevailing social policies were aimed not at excluding women from print culture wholesale, but at limiting their access to writing specifically.[24]

Writing was intended to produce model masculine subjects. First the student traced the outlines of the alphabet, his stylus guided either directly by the hand of his teacher or by the grooves of a wax tablet in which the letters were carved.[25] Then he attempted to copy the model before him without any help. As Donne suggests in a sermon comparing the crucifixion to a schoolboy's copy text, the act of duplicating a text enabled one to incorporate its contents literally through the action of one's body: "His death is delivered to us, as a writing, but not a writing onely in the nature of a peece of Evidence, to plead our inheritance by, but a writing in the nature of a Copy, to learne by; It is not onely given us to reade, but to write over, and practise."[26] The virtues which writing was supposed to instill corresponded to the social roles that boys were being trained to perform. "For the male side," Mulcaster elaborates, "that doubt is long ago out of doubt, that they be set to schoole, to qualifie themselves, to learne how to be religious and loving, how to governe and how to obey, how to forecast and prevent, how to defende and assaile."[27] Schooling was supposed to cultivate both obedience and authority, to accomplish the boy's integration into a hierarchical society in which, unlike his female counterpart, he was to enact the roles both of subject and of master. The contradiction imposed by these dual positions is embodied in the task of learning to write. Allowing his hand to be guided in set patterns, assimilating the aphorisms imposed as copy texts by the schoolmaster, accepting correction when he made errors, the boy was supposed to learn submission. Manipulating pen, ink, and paper through controlled techniques, insinuating himself into different scripts and languages, deploying the arts of persuasion in school essays, he was also supposed to learn mastery. In training to copy authorized models with template-like precision and also to differentiate his hand by swerving from the same models, the male student was discovering self-signification as a scribal practice. He formed his identity in writing.[28]

A letter by Richard Croke to Cardinal Wolsey testifies eloquently to the shaping force which humanist educators attributed to writing. Croke, an eminent scholar of Greek, was appointed tutor to Fitzroy, the Duke of Richmond and the illegitimate son of Henry VIII. Apparently, George Cotton, who later became the governor of Richmond's household, had contradicted Croke's instructions by teaching Richmond to use the secretary hand. Croke wanted Wolsey to insure that the boy write only in italic, only in Latin, only to noble or royal correspondents, and only at times when Croke could be there in person "to dyrecte and forme his said hande and stile." Croke's objective was that Richmond "more fermely imprynte in his mynde both wordes and phrases of the Latten tonge, and the soner frame hym to some good stile in wrytinge whereunto he is now very ripe." The transitive verbs employed by Croke, "forme," "frame," "imprynte," depict writing as an action of which the writer himself is on the receiving end. It is through the process of shaping a text, Croke implies, that the boy himself is formed, framed, and imprinted.[29]

Jonathan Goldberg's *Writing Matter: From the Hands of the English Renaissance* is the most extensive study of writing manuals from this period published to date. Goldberg contends that the imposition of a uniform italic script, the hand favored by humanists such as Richard Croke, participated in the constitution of the modern individual as a docile body. Instruction in the italic hand formed or aimed at forming the student according to the model of the impersonal, standardized script he was copying: "Writing italic, he is to be firmly imprinted by what he prints, styled and framed (like the hands in the copybooks) by his *stilus graphicum*."[30] Goldberg's argument that the disciplined acquisition of writing produced direct and congruent changes in students' comportment depends upon accepting the views of humanist pedagogues at face value. In his account of the production and transmission of handwritten manuscripts, *Scribal Publication in Seventeenth-Century England*, Harold Love criticizes Goldberg for presenting claims about handwriting on the basis of printed simulacra rather than on scribal manuscripts. In practice, Love points out, an extraordinary range of hands originated in the seventeenth century. Instead of a straightforward movement from variety to conformity, he discerns "repeated attempts to impose conformity subverted by new assertions of diversity."[31] The mixed hand, a free-form combination of italic and secretary hands rather than a standardized script, dominated in most spheres until the end of the seventeenth century when "round hand," a business script, eventually prevailed. In contrast to Goldberg's position that writing instilled submission, Love presents a view of "script as the medium of freedom, intimacy and individuality, and of the scribal text's essential evasiveness and indeterminacy."[32] For Goldberg, writing entailed the inculcation of set paradigms; the practice of imitating the tutor or schoolmaster's italic script, down to the details of spacing and form, imbued in students the uniform conformity characteristic of the duplicate texts they learned to produce. Love contends that writing enabled individuals to circumvent constraining paradigms; in his view, the practice of engaging in emendation as play, of circulating variant versions of single works, gave writers the same limitless possibilities for transformation as the multiply divergent, indeterminate texts they revelled in creating.

An account of writing that is adequate to the rich qualities of scribal manuscripts that survive from this period, warrants and decrees, letters and diaries, sonnets and plays, must draw on the perspectives both of Goldberg and of Love to consider structure as well as agency, the prescriptions codified by humanist pedagogues as well as the actual practices of those who took pen in hand and wrote, the fixed simulacra printed in writing manuals as well as the idiosyncratic handwritten notations often found in those texts. [33] The owner of one copy of *A Book Containing Divers Sorts of Hands* (1571), a book more aptly titled than its author probably had intended, did not follow either the spelling or the flourishes of the writing master's text exactly. Most striking is the contrast between the quirky "g" and "y" penned by the book's owner and the standard italic equivalents of those letters printed on the same page; departing from the copy text, the book's owner turned the descenders of those letters into curlicue coils.[34]

Contemporary plays are important to this inquiry into gender and literacy because they offer evidence about the significance of writing in the culture at large. As a skill that was new to the vast majority of the population, writing appeared both as a new form of bodily discipline and as a means to acquire status, as an instrument for reinforcing unequal social relations and for enabling self-expression.[35] Manuscripts (and printed books) became the objects of a new economy in which texts licensed and constrained action to a larger extent than before. Those who were able to inform what was being written, by virtue of their authority and technical mastery, could assert their presence and their positions. Writing not only enabled them to impose their will; it also gave them the means to construct a social identity and a private inwardness. Early modern playwrights explored the concerns that writing elicited as its selective diffusion appeared to give certain individuals greater power over others and the ability to fashion themselves as complex and inscrutable subjects. This potential for manipulation and self-aggrandize-ment implicit in writing brought Thomas Dekker to describe the quill pen as "a pyneon puld from the left wing of the devill."[36] Shakespeare's Richard III, the penman with a withered arm, incorporates some of these darker and demonic aspects of writing. In the educational treatise of schoolmaster Richard Mulcaster, the boy who learns how to write becomes an angel-like creature with wings; in Shakespeare's play, he turns into Richard III.

II

Unlike Talbot, the cartoon hero of *1 Henry VI*, Richard III has depth, that is to say, secrets. He appears "round" and the other characters "flat" by comparison.[37] In *3 Henry VI*, Richard precociously anticipates the psychological realism of *Richard III* in a soliloquy that invokes childhood trauma to explain his lust for power. It is, Janet Adelman comments, "an extraordinary moment: in it we hear – I think for the first time in Shakespeare – the voice of a fully developed subjectivity."[38] The distinctive subjectivity that emerges in that charged moment belongs, not coincidentally in my view, to the Shakespearean character most obsessed by writing. Handwritten texts circulate at his instigation in *Richard III* and drive the dramatic action.[39] Their number and importance in the plot draw our attention to the conjuncture between new models of subjectivity and new practices of writing. With the expansion of literacy in the sixteenth century, scribal culture was no longer associated primarily with a clerical elite: "Writing now concealed an 'I' and no longer a 'he'."[40] Yet while writing was extended into secular domains, access to it was still restricted, serving to divide not clerks and laity, but rich and poor, men and women. The social position and masculine identity of that scribal "I" assumed a new importance.

In *Richard III*, Shakespeare invents a character to personify the link between the male subject and the scribal first person. The play portrays with striking ambivalence, by turns valorizing and questioning, a form of self-isolated identity that is specifically correlated with masculinity and with writing. Writing, in this discussion, does not necessarily imply the composition of more or less original texts. It refers to the way in which Richard exploits his knowledge of writing to exert force over others. Richard operates as a kind of master scribe who inscribes himself and others through the shrewd deployment of handwritten documents. Over the second half of the play, however, his supremacy is gradually overwhelmed by female invective. The triumph of the women's curses, though ironized by their absorption within the teleology of More/Hall/Holinshed's written chronicle, nevertheless upsets the humanist fantasy of omnipotent male writing, and, in its place, conjures one of unlettered female rage erupting to topple courtiers and kings.[41]

Richard employs texts – a cynical Petrarchan poem, an outdated death warrant, a counterfeit treason indictment – for purposes of seduction, murder, and legitimation. In the process, he signifies himself. The lyric poem demonstrates his virtuosity in rhetoric, the death warrant his cleverness in subterfuge, the indictment his mastery in inciting terror. These multiple shifting registers of Richard's personality, at odds at times with his own self-descriptions, define him in terms of complexity and illegibility, attributes associated with the male scribal subject. Richard makes the connection explicit when he invokes an image of himself engaged in writing. Following Hastings' execution, Richard depicts Hastings as the blank book in which he had trustfully inscribed his secrets:

> So dear I lov'd the man that I must weep.
> I took him for the plainest harmless creature
> That breath'd upon the earth a Christian;
> Made him my book, wherein my soul recorded
> The history of all her secret thoughts.[42]

The dramatic irony of this passage is amplified by what the audience knows about Richard's use of writing. Orsino may tell Viola (disguised as a male page), "I have unclasped / To thee the book even of my secret soul" (1.4.12–13). In *Twelfth Night*, the scribal text, in this case a blank book filled with the writing of its owner, stands as a metaphor for a man's true interior being. In *Richard III*, the same figure has dark resonances. The reference to Hastings as a paper book, a text inscribed with the history of Richard's soul, recalls the handwritten death warrant that circulated in an earlier scene as an actual stage prop. In a later scene, Elizabeth taunts Richard to woo her daughter by engraving the names of the two murdered princes on a pair of bleeding hearts (4.4.271–3). The image of Richard engaged in writing connotes not self-disclosure but violence and betrayal.

Erasure, the correlative to inscription, is also part of Richard's scribal repertory. He tells the London citizens whom he has connived into supporting his bid for the crown, "Your mere enforcement shall acquittance me / From all the impure blots and stains thereof" (3.7.232–3). Shakespeare's choice of theatrical terms in this scene emphasizes that it is Richard, along with Buckingham, who writes the scene in which he plays the "maid's part" (saying "nay" to an offer he willingly accepts) and displays clergymen as "two props" to create an impression of piety.

Richard wants both to write the scene and to absolve himself from the act of composition, the traces of blots and stains it leaves behind, to expunge the material proof of the theatrical script he composed and performed.

Stanley and Hastings envisage Richard's power over them as that of erasure. Stanley's servant tells Hastings that Stanley has fled because "he dreamt the boar had razed off his helm" (3.2.11). Stanley takes his dream as a warning that Richard, figured by the boar, his heraldic emblem, is after Stanley's life. Before being executed, Hastings generalizes the threat evoked in Stanley's dream to apply to himself as well: "Stanley did dream the boar did raze our helms" (3.4.82). The line derives from More/Hall/Holinshed's chronicle which recounts that Stanley left court because "he had a fearfull dreame in the whiche he thought that a bore with his tuskes so rased them bothe by the heades that the bloud ran aboute bothe their shoulders, and for as much as the protectour gave the bore for his cognisaunce, he ymagined that it should be he."[43] The key to Shakespeare's use of this passage is in the verb "rase" (modernized as "raze" in current editions of the plays). In the chronicle, "rase" means "lift"; in *Richard III*, the statement "the boar lifted his helm" makes no sense with the detail about the boar's tusks missing. Shakespeare borrows the word "rase" and turns its meaning from "raise" to "erase."[44] The chronicle recounts a dream in which danger is represented literally as a physical assault that leaves the two men with blood streaming down their shoulders. But in Shakespeare's version of Hastings' dream, the danger evoked is more subjective. The reference to Richard's heraldic sign draws attention to the emblematic significance of Hastings' helmet as well. A drawing of one's helmet (shaped according to the rank of the knight and topped by a distinctive crest) was placed above the coat of arms; the three elements, helmet, crest, and coat of arms, are termed the "armorial achievement." Both versions of the dream convey the threat of Richard's murderous intentions. In Shakespeare's play, however, Stanley expresses his fear as that of symbolic self-annihilation: "The boar had razed off his helm." The phrase suggests the erasure of the emblem of Stanley's helmet, a key component of his heraldic symbology.

This is the meaning that Bolingbroke assigns to the word "raze" when he protests Richard II's usurpation of his lands:

> Whilst you have fed upon my signories,
> Disparked my parks and fell'd my forest woods,
> From my own windows torn my household coat,
> Razed out my imprese, leaving me no sign,
> Save men's opinions and my living blood,
> To show the world I am a gentleman.   (3.1.22–7)

Bolingbroke substantiates the general charge that Richard II has mis-
appropriated his estates (signories) by listing a series of specific acts: the
plundering of his lands, chopping down of his trees, smashing of his coat
of arms from window panes, the obliterating of representations of his
heraldic device. Within a few lines, Bolingbroke's attention shifts from
the destruction of his property (signories, parks, woods) to the vandalism
of heraldic self-inscriptions (household coat, imprese, sign). The tempo
of this passage, beginning slowly with an end-stopped line, quickening
with the alliteration of disparked parks and forests felled, building
momentum through the repetition of possessive pronouns, "my" and
"my own," and climaxing with an enjambed phrase that spills over two
and a half lines, suggests that Bolingbroke's claims are listed in ascending
order of importance. The emphasis is not on his material loss but on the
terror of being left signless. Stanley and Hasting's use of the term "raze"
alludes to Richard's scribal mastery, his ability to obliterate them
symbolically as well as physically, to leave them without any mark to
show the world they are gentlemen.

The play, while focusing on Richard's conniving self-inscription, does
concede that writing, in theory, could form virtuous males as humanist
educators promised. Edward's first-born son embodies the exemplary
writing-literate schoolboy. As he is being led off to the Tower to die, the
young prince critiques Richard's misuse of writing:

> *Prince.* I do not like the Tower, of any place.
> Did Julius Caesar build that place, my lord?
> *Buckingham.* He did, my gracious lord, begin that place,
> Which since, succeeding ages have re-edified.
> *Prince.* Is it upon record, or else reported
> Successively from age to age, he built it?
> *Buckingham.* Upon record, my gracious lord.
> *Prince.* But say, my lord, it were not register'd,
> Methinks the truth should live from age to age,
> As 'twere retail'd to all posterity,
> Even to the general all-ending day.
> *Gloucester.* [Aside.] So wise so young, they say, do never live long.
>
> (3.1.68–79)

The prince, a foil to Richard in this respect as others, emphasizes the
salutary effects of writing. Offering a naive view of history belied by the
Tudor bias of Shakespeare's own sources and plays, he warns Richard
that his control over the written record, the registering of certain events
and omission of others, will not keep the truth from being revealed. As
though repeating a school lesson, the prince further points out the
discrepancy between Richard and another soldier-writer, Julius Caesar,

who "With what his valor did enrich his wit, / His wit set down to make his valor live" (3.1.85–6). Caesar, celebrated both for performing and for writing down virtuous deeds, is a model for the prince's self-conception. The nephew speaks here as the dutiful student who has copied out passages from Caesar's texts; fittingly, he concludes the speech with an aphorism: "Death makes no conquest of this conqueror, / For now he lives in fame, though not in life" (3.1.87–8). The prince's statement of his intention to follow Caesar in conquering France "or die a soldier, as I liv'd a king," indicates that he has successfully internalized humanist teachings by acting to emulate masculine heroes from his reading (3.1.93).

As for Richard's image of Hastings as a paper book, the audience knows that the credulous nobleman was never a receptacle for Richard's inner reflections. If Richard had such a book, the audience would be it, or so he flatters us to think. In the play's initial lines, he begins to divulge the history of his soul's secret thoughts in the first of a series of soliloquies. He appears to pluck out the heart of his mystery, to lay out the splayed enigma of his soul for the theatre audience to comprehend. The secret he promises to reveal is his motive for treachery. "Rudely stamp'd," "cheated of feature," "deform'd," "unfinish'd," "scarce half made up" (1.1.16, 19, 20, 21), he is too ill-formed to join in the peace-time recreations of dancing and seduction. "And therefore," he says, as though it followed logically, "since I cannot prove a lover . . . I am determined to prove a villain" (1.1.28–30). Richard beguiles the audience by making us witness to his self-construction, his efforts to complete the fashioning process left unaccomplished at his birth. "I clothe my naked villainy," he says, "With odd old ends stol'n forth of Holy Writ" (1.3.336–7). The texts, in this case tags from the Bible, which Richard says that he uses to hide his (villainous) self from view are also central to his creation of that self. It is his dexterous negotiation of texts, not an essentially evil core, that creates Richard after his own multiple images.

This adroit use of writing to shape himself and others emerges in the play's second scene. In that famously staged seduction, Richard adopts the role of love poet and makes Anne into the object of Petrarchan discourse. Richard wants to wed Anne and to recuperate Henry's corpse. Marrying the widow of the former prince of Wales and wresting away her guardianship of the dead king's body (it is en route to Chertsey when he takes control and redirects it to Whitefriars) would enable Richard to appropriate two still potent symbols of the former regime. But Anne displays the rhetorical agility to frustrate Richard's initiative; in contrast to Clarence, Brakenbury, and Hastings who treat Richard with servility in the preceding scene, she answers him with angry dignity. She spurns

his lies with quick-witted retorts and inverts the terms of his discourse:
"Lady" / "Villain"; "Fairer than tongue can name thee" / "Fouler than
heart can think thee"; "I did not kill your husband" / "Why then he is
alive" (1.2.68,70,81,83,91). After arguing that Richard is the devil, she
adroitly maneuvers him into placing himself in that category:

> *Anne.* No beast so fierce but knows some touch of pity.
> *Richard.* But I know none, and therefore am no beast.
> *Anne.* O wonderful, when devils tell the truth!   (1.2.71–3)

Anne enters this scene as a righteous victim. She is Antigone, lamenting
the lacerated body of a male kinsman, interposing herself physically to
protect his corpse, defying the authority of the state when the men beside
her fearfully obey. She names Richard as the agent of the murders of her
father-in-law and husband. Anne, not Margaret, utters the play's first
curses; it is she who initially invokes the images of wolves, spiders, toads,
serpents, and aborted fetuses that cluster around Richard over the course
of the play.

By the end of the scene, however, her role as brave dissident has
devolved into that of a court lady ripe for seduction. Abruptly, Anne
acquiesces: "I would I knew thy heart" (1.2.196). Richard accomplishes
her capitulation through a deft play on poetic conventions. Buried within
Richard's seemingly improvised conversation with Anne are fragments of
love poems. Like the sonnets of the 1590s vogue that circulated primarily
in manuscript, these verses are scribal texts:

> *Gloucester.* I never sued to friend nor enemy:
> My tongue could never learn sweet smoothing word;
> But now thy beauty is propos'd my fee,
> My proud heart sues, and prompts my tongue to speak.
>   *She looks scornfully at him.*
> Teach not thy lip such scorn; for it was made
> For kissing, lady, not for such contempt.
> If thy revengeful heart cannot forgive,
> Lo here I lend thee this sharp-pointed sword,
> Which if thou please to hide in this true breast,
> And let the soul forth that adoreth thee,
> I lay it naked to the deadly stroke
> And humbly beg the death upon my knee.
>   *[Kneels;] he lays his breast open; she offers at [it] with his sword.*
>   (1.2.171–82)

Drawing on the logic of traditional love lyrics, Richard argues that it is
in fact he who is the victim of Anne's beauty and Anne who is an
accessory to murder. He speaks in Petrarchan clichés. Her eyes are like
the sun. Her lips are made for kissing; her beauty a source of torment.

His heart is enclosed in her breast. He is her servant. He will die at her command. Richard uses end rhymes: enemy/fee; thee/knee; Henry/me. He injects into the exchange the sonneteer's language of paradox: "This hand which for thy love did kill thy love, / Shall for thy love kill a far truer lover" (1.2.189–90). In the face of such trite versifying, Anne responds by enacting tableau-like illustrations of the aloof mistress, alternately striking proud poses and aiming a sword at her suitor's heart. Richard, the murderer, has switched places with his victim through a rhetorical sleight of hand.

The courtly love tradition, by a willful suppression of actual social inequalities, reimagines woman's relation to man as that of a domineering mistress who dooms the defenseless poet-servant to despair by her disdain. Richard, the warrior kingmaker backed by all the force of the state, succeeds in framing his relation to Anne, the resourceless widow to the heir of a defeated house, in those inverted terms by adopting the role of sonneteer. So positioned, he maneuvers Anne into the accompanying role of the haughty lady deserving of contempt for not gathering her rosebuds while she may: "Teach not thy lip such scorn; for it was made / For kissing, lady, not for such contempt." According to the poet of courtly love, a woman who does not return the poet's passion is not fulfilling the end for which she and her lips were created. In this scene, the role of Marvell's coy mistress is rejected by Anne as the only alternative to that of Richard's wife.

For Richard to exploit Petrarchan conceits to coerce a woman into his bed is conventional, not exceptional. What is remarkable is the extent to which his behavior undermines the deep psychological portrait he offered of himself only one scene earlier. If anyone believed the rationale he provided for his villainy in the play's opening soliloquy, his demonstration of his skills of seduction is a bewildering reversal. He appears deliberately to confound his self-description as a sexual outcast driven to revenge because his deformities make him disgusting to women. After his seduction of Anne, we could expect him to announce, "Since I have proven a lover, I no longer have reason to prove myself a villain." Instead, Richard repeats his plan to kill Clarence. In contrast to the pasteboard villain of the opening scene, charming his listeners with claims of transparency, Richard begins to engage the audience with the puzzle of his unintelligibility.

The complexity of Richard's subjectivity is invariably connected with its textualization. Utilizing a mode of deception possible only through writing, he artfully deploys an expired death warrant to murder and dissociate himself from murder. The death warrant is a visual token of the evasiveness that typifies, to use one of Richard's puns, both the moral and alphabetic characters of the play's men. (As Richard puts it, "without characters fame lives long" (3.1.81)). In Tudor–Stuart England, the monarch, parliament, and courts depended on written texts, validated either by seals or by signatures, for the execution of their will: "The king's word might be law but his warrant was required before action could be undertaken by his servants."[45] Once out of Edward's hands the warrant on Clarence's life becomes a free-floating signifier that passes from Richard's pocket ("I have it here about me," he says) to the murderers (who use it to gain access to Clarence), to Brakenbury (Clarence's guard) and apparently back to Edward (Brakenbury states that he will bring it to him). The fact that the "order was revers'd" has no bearing on the efficacy of the text itself (1.4.344, 2.1.87). It functions autonomously from the king as an absolute sign of his intention. It opens the door to the prison, absolves the murderers of criminal liability, conceals Richard's plan to kill Clarence behind Edward's signature.

This traffic in texts occurs only between male characters. The Archbishop of York, at risk to his own life, does hand over the great seal to Elizabeth before she goes into sanctuary. But in Elizabeth's hands, the seal appears to lose its efficacy. It is mentioned only once. There is no Hamlet-like ruse on Elizabeth's part to authenticate a forged execution order of her own. We hear only second-hand that she has claimed sanctuary with her younger son; soon after we see both of her sons being escorted to the tower under Richard's malevolent watch. Brakenbury's easy capitulation before the written warrant carried by the first murderer contrasts with his rebuff of the entourage of royal and noble women who seek entry to the tower when the two princes are imprisoned there. "Let him see our commission," the murderer says of Brakenbury, "and talk no more" (1.4.89–90). The point, amplified by the murderer's tone of patronizing assurance, is that only the scribal documents circulated between men have the force to compel silence and submission.[46]

As it passes from hand to hand, the death warrant symbolizes the avoidance of accountability that unites the male characters. "Are you now going to dispatch this thing?" Richard asks the murderers. "We are, my lord," they tell him, "and come to have the warrant / That we may be admitted where he is" (1.3.341–3). The language of innuendo they speak ("this thing" is understood to refer to a murder and "he" to the unnamed victim) shows the murderers playing along with Richard's prevarication. The warrant, here, functions not as an authorization, but as a euphemization of the killing. Brakenbury, when he receives the warrant from the murderers, focuses on how he can carry out its directions without being held responsible for having done so:

> I am in this commanded to deliver
> The noble Duke of Clarence to your hands.
> I will not reason what is meant hereby,
> Because I will be guiltless from the meaning.   (1.4.91–4)

A hermeneutic of unreasoned reading is meant to exculpate Brakenbury of the murder, to leave him guiltless from the meaning of the warrant. His assertions of non-comprehension, however, work precisely to expose the clarity of his comprehension; his feigned use of neutral terms of observation exposes the self-awareness with which he participates in the crime as he gives over Clarence to be killed: "there lies the Duke asleep; and there the keys" (1.4.95). The second murderer acknowledges being afraid, "not to kill him – having a warrant – but to be damned for killing him, from the which no warrant can defend me" (1.4.107–9). Even this character, more candid about the implications of the act he is about to commit, emphasizes the power of the signed document to protect him from terrestrial judgment. All the characters through whose hands the warrant passes look to scribal texts to shelter them. King Edward, who signed the warrant, seeks to disavow his guilt by saying that he had later revoked it.

"Power effaces its hand," observes Jonathan Goldberg, "and has others write for it."[47] In his manipulation of the death warrant, Richard uses effaced writing, writing he traces without leaving any trace of his hand. He confesses in the opening soliloquy, archly confident in the silence of the theatre audience, that he has successfully plotted to have Clarence (whose first name is George) imprisoned by spreading rumors of a prophecy "which says that G / Of Edward's heirs the murder shall be" (1.1.39–40). A little over a dozen lines later, Clarence explains that he has been arrested because the King "hearkens after prophecies and dreams, / And from the cross-row plucks the letter G" (1.1.54–5).[48] The cross-row is the alphabet printed in black-letter on hornbooks (a wood paddle covered with a thin layer of horn to protect the letters, syllables of words, and The Lord's Prayer printed on a sheet of paper); it takes its name from the image of the cross placed at the beginning of the alphabet. Richard's confession followed by Clarence's misapprehension establishes a pattern. Richard plucks a letter from the cross-row and the letter kills; responsibility for the writing, meanwhile, and for the killing, is displaced onto someone else.

Richard's project of effaced writing is never so fully realized as in that moment when he, the real author of Clarence's death, flaunts Edward's signature on the warrant to his face. Clarence "by your first order died," Richard says, "And that a winged Mercury did bear; / Some tardy cripple bare the countermand" (2.1.88–90). He makes the observation with a kind of glee. Though Richard, the figure in whom winged Mercury and tardy cripple combine, is the one to blame, Clarence died by Edward's order. Richard exploits the fact that unlike earlier signs of identity (coats of arms, badges, seals) which could be affixed by others, the signature is a non-transferable manifestation of a unique self. As Erasmus remarks, "A man's handwriting, like his voice, has a special, individual quality."[49] Edward's signature is proof of his physical participation in the act of condemning Clarence to death; his own hand traced the sign of his irreducible presence and responsibility.[50] By hiding behind the royal signature, Richard displays his versatility in manipulating texts to shift blame. At the same time, he makes the strategic use of writing seem like a normative masculine procedure. He shows a whole circle of men, ranging from the lowest criminal to a courtier to a king, signing, reading, obeying, and circulating scribal texts to finesse their complicity in murder.

In the two instances cited so far, Richard appropriates texts, in one case from Petrarch and in the other from King Edward, to seduce and to kill. After Hastings' execution, Richard himself commissions a scribal text. His aim this time, with his authority now greatly expanded, is to legitimate an illegal execution committed by the state. The scrivener hired to copy the document comes on stage to describe its inscription as an artisanal technique:

> Here is the indictment of the good Lord Hastings,
> Which in a set hand fairly is engross'd,
> That it may be today read o'er in Paul's . . .
> Eleven hours I have spent to write it over,
> For yesternight by Catesby was it sent me;
> The precedent was full as long a-doing.
> And yet within these five hours Hastings liv'd,
> Untainted, unexamin'd, free, at liberty.   (3.6.1–3, 5–9)

The scrivener's soliloquy is based on an observation offered by the narrator of More/Hall/Holinshed's chronicle about the transparent imposture of the treason indictment. The formal "set hand" used in "fairly" inscribed legal documents endows them with value, authority, truth. The chronicle, more detailed in its description of the document than Shakespeare's play, notes the care given to the formation of individual characters and the choice of parchment, a material requiring time-consuming work, in place of paper. While Hastings had been free from suspicion only five hours earlier, the indictment charging him took two scriveners at least twenty-two hours to inscribe. The very elegance and neatness of the text exposes its fraudulence.

The production of that legal document adds a new facet to the persona that Richard selectively discloses. Previously, he appropriated texts for their instrumental function: Petrarchan verse for seduction, an (expired) warrant for murder. Here, Richard draws on a text, expertly drafted by the scrivener, for its symbolic value. His post-facto commission of the indictment is less about exhibiting his rhetorical skill or cleverness in blameshifting than it is about his ability to enforce compliance through fear. Unlike the death warrant, the indictment is conspicuously fake. The effectiveness of the type of coercion described by the scrivener depends on the audience at St. Paul's silently comprehending the discrepancy between the event of Hastings' death and the official description of it. "Who is so gross / That cannot see this palpable device?" the scrivener asks rhetorically, "Yet who's so bold but says he sees it not?" (3.6.10–12). That the device is a sham must be both "palpable" and unsayable for each listener to be made fully aware of the extent of Richard's power over them.

III

| *Richard.* Give me some ink and paper. | (5.3.50) |
| *Richmond.* Give me some ink and paper. | (5.3.41) |

Margaret. Cancel his bond of life . . .	
That I may live and say "The dog is dead."	(4.4.77–8)
Richmond. The bloody dog is dead.	(5.5.2)

Richard III, like a musical score, is divided into two movements: the first dominated by Richard and handwritten inscription, the second by the play's women and oral invective. Anne, Elizabeth, Margaret, and the Duchess provide the only blocking action of the play until Richmond appears in the final act. If it were not for the female characters, the action of the play would consist only of Richard killing victims – Henry VI, Clarence, Rivers, Grey, Vaughan, Hastings, the prince of Wales, little York, Anne, and Buckingham – in a kind of lurid true crime story. Instead, the play's women, beginning with Anne in act one, attempt to stop Richard, ineffectually at first from the margins of the play, forcefully in act four when Elizabeth, Margaret, and the Duchess raise a chorus of maledictions from center stage. As the force of the women's curses becomes apparent, Richard is stripped of his former allure and his exquisite complexity revealed as a pose. The play's ending foregrounds Richard and Richmond as virtually indistinguishable and equally disenchanting models of the scribally constructed male subject.

Women's exclusion from writing surfaces obliquely when Richard accuses the Queen and Jane Shore of witchcraft:

> Then be your eyes the witness of their evil.
> Look how I am bewitch'd! Behold, mine arm
> Is, like a blasted sapling, wither'd up!
> And this is Edward's wife, that monstrous witch,
> Consorted with that harlot, strumpet Shore,
> That by their witchcraft thus have marked me.   (3.4.67–72)

In the chronicle version of this story, Richard charges the women with having "wasted" his body.[51] Shakespeare's replacement of "waste" with the term "mark" locates Richard's accusation within the discourse that denied women writing in order to deny them scope for action. The charge is that the women have, in a sense, taken pencil in hand and presumed to inscribe instead of being inscribed. Indeed, Margaret proclaims that sin, death, and hell have set their "marks" on Richard; alternatively, that he is "mark'd" by elves. Speaking Richard's language of scribal control, she orders the contractual document or bond of Richard's life to be canceled (1.3.292, 227, 4.4.77). Elizabeth threatens to have Richard branded as a murderer, that is, of having his skin seared with an iron shaped in the letter "M," of writing the sign of his crimes upon his flesh (4.4.140–3). In his speech about the women, Richard conflates witchcraft, illicit sexuality, and female writing as though to ward off the possibility of being marked himself, of becoming a book or paper to write "murderer" upon. His move is to make potential criticism inutterable by accusing others of the very action of crippling inscription in which he himself is engaging. Though everyone knows his arm was withered at birth, Richard turns the transparently false claim that he has been marked by the women into proof that he alone possesses the power to mark and dominate others, to inscribe Elizabeth and Jane Shore as witch and whore.

Richard's lithe improvisation in moments such as this forces attention. He infiltrates himself into every corner and conversation. He spins off a seemingly inexhaustible supply of public personae – faithful lover, devoted brother, obedient son, loyal subject, pious Christian, honorable statesman – while simultaneously addressing the audience privately through a dialogue of flippant asides. The scribal qualities of Richard's character, his incalculable mastery and enticing encryptedness, are what make his stage presence compelling. But as the women's curses begin to permeate the play, Richard stops confiding in the audience. He speaks his last extended asides in the fourth act when the stability of his rule appears increasingly precarious and he begins to fear he shall but "wear these glories for a day" (4.2.5). Richard diminishes in standing in inverse proportion to the female characters; correspondingly, writing loses in value what oral invective gains. As the curses that fell on deaf ears in the first act gather momentum in the third and fourth acts and fix the outcome of the final act, male writing allies itself with serial murder, female voices with the working out of divine justice.

"Why should she live, to fill the world with words?" Richard said of Margaret at the end of *3 Henry VI* (5.5.44). In *Richard III*, Margaret returns, this time in company of Anne, Elizabeth, and the Duchess, to fill the stage with words: "hell-hound," "carnal cur," "bottled spider," "foul bunch-back'd toad," "abortive, rooting hog" (4.4.48, 56,81, 1.3.227). The play is haunted by her presence. Old, outcast, bitter: she is the figure of a witch. Curses originate in grievances; in *Macbeth*, it is the refusal of a sailor's wife to share her bowl of chestnuts with one of the weird sisters. Margaret's injury is the loss of husband, son, and crown. The historical Queen Margaret had been dead a year at the time that this scene would have occurred. Shakespeare upsets the chronology of historical events in order to bring Margaret back from the grave as the force with which Richard must reckon. The play contains no surprising turns of plot; it is simply a working-out of the predictions made by Margaret in act one: King Edward's death by "surfeit," Prince Edward's death by "untimely violence," Elizabeth's loss of glory, the premature deaths of Rivers, Dorset, and Hastings, Richard's betrayal of Buckingham, the loss by blood of all that Richard had won by blood (1.3.197, 200–1, 241–3, 299–303, 272).

By staging the realization of Margaret's predictions to coincide with the denouement, Shakespeare dispels Richard's aura of magnetism. The agency that formerly inhered in Richard's writings is reassigned to an old woman's curses. "The day will come," Margaret tells Elizabeth, "that thou shalt wish for me / To help thee curse this poisonous bunch-back'd toad" (1.3.245–6). "Remember this another day," she warns Buckingham, "When he shall split thy very heart with sorrow, / And say, poor Margaret was a prophetess" (1.3.299–301). The last three acts trace the downfall of those who had joined in flouting Margaret in the first act. One by one, they step forward to acknowledge the truth of her predictions:

> *Grey.* Now Margaret's curse is fall'n upon our heads,
> When she exclaim'd on Hastings, you, and I,
> For standing by when Richard stabb'd her son.   (3.3.15–17)

> *Hastings.* O Margaret, Margaret, now thy heavy curse
> Is lighted on poor Hastings' wretched head.   (3.4.92–3)

> *Queen Elizabeth.* Go: hie thee, hie thee from this slaughter-house,
> Lest thou increase the number of the dead,
> And make me die the thrall of Margaret's curse.   (4.1.43–5)

Buckingham. Thus Margaret's curse falls heavy on my neck:
"When he," quoth she, "shall split thy heart with sorrow,
Remember Margaret was a prophetess!"   (5.1.25–7)

The incantatory quality of these professions, especially those uttered by
the three men in the extremity of their impending executions, depends
upon repetition – repetition of Margaret's name, pronounced six times in
these eleven lines, repetition of the word "curse," repetition of the exact
phrasing of her speech. Her words are imagined as having weight,
pressing down the men's heads and necks, as though her utterance, not
the executioner's axe, could kill. Convicted traitors were supposed to
praise, even as they prepared to die, the monarch who condemned them
and thereby to legitimate the established order. The evocation of
Margaret's name, in place of Richard's, by the condemned men vests her
words with charismatic authority.

In act four, with Anne and the two princes dead, Elizabeth pleads with
Margaret, fulfilling another of Margaret's prophecies. "O thou, well
skill'd in curses, stay awhile," Elizabeth asks, "And teach me how to
curse mine enemies" (4.4.116–17). Margaret's words from the first act
echo here again as Elizabeth recalls the exact wording of her curses:
"bottled spider" and "foul bunch-back'd toad." Three women, Margaret, the Duchess, and Elizabeth, dominate the scene with their triangu-
lated presence. None is now "a queen in jest, only to fill the scene"
(4.4.91). They take possession of the stage, sitting down upon it in show
of mourning, and fill its space with curses. The confrontation that
follows when the Duchess and Elizabeth block Richard's path, inter-
cepting him in his expedition as he puts it, is the climax of the play. It is
the moment at which the countercurrent of female invective overwhelms
the current of male writing. The curse of Richard's mother, withheld
until now, picks up where Margaret's curses left off and presents, as in a
map, the end of all, the defeat of Richard at the conjuration of his
victims' spirits:

Therefore, take with thee my most grievous curse,
Which in the day of battle tire thee more
Than all the complete armour that thou wear'st.   (4.4.188–90)

In place of the crafty politician bragging about clothing his naked villainy
with biblical texts, an infantilized Richard returns to being dressed by his
mother. Her curse becomes a garment, heavy as metal plating, both to
"attire" and to "tire" him, to weigh him down, to deplete his vitality.
This is literally what happens when the spirits of Richard's victims,
conjured by the Duchess in her curse, keep Richard from resting before
the battle (while they bid Richmond to sleep a quiet sleep).

Having predicted the events which will conclude the play, the three women withdraw, clearing the stage for Richmond to appear. Some critics see his arrival to do battle with Richard, in the absence of other oppositional figures, as an allegorical encounter between the forces of God and Satan. This interpretation, however, overlooks Shakespeare's insistent conflation of the two figures. To begin with, the similarity between the names Rich-ard and Rich-mond is deliberate. While the chronicle also refers to Richard's rival as "Henrie earle of Richmond," "the earle Henrie," or "king Henrie the seaventh" (even before he has won the Battle of Bosworth Field), Shakespeare calls Henry by his title and Richard by his proper name to underline their sameness.[52] In Shakespeare's play Richmond even mimics Richard's propensity for shape-shifting by sending out multiple impersonations of himself to the battlefield. While Hall had depicted Richmond as eagerly seeking combat with Richard, Shakespeare portrays Richmond as attempting to avoid his nemesis altogether. An indignant footnote in the Arden edition unwittingly calls attention to the calculation on Shakespeare's part in departing from the chronicle version: "This surprising information is Shakespeare's invention . . . the stratagem, while suitable enough for the sly Henry IV, hardly seems appropriate in the heroic Richmond."[53] Instead of clarifying the supposed differences between them, Richard's slyness as opposed to Richmond's heroism, the structural parallelism of act five stresses their similarities. In rote speeches, the ghosts of Richard's victims address both Richard and Richmond before the two men go to bed. Both Richard and Richmond give lackluster orations to their men on the morning of the battle. Both men swear by the same saint. There is not a single memorable line in either speech, and if heaven has sided with Richmond its reasons for doing so are not clear. The distinction between Richard and Richmond as sly Macchiavel versus courageous leader has collapsed definitively. Instead of antithetical foes, the two characters appear more as duplicate versions of a new character: the cunning, if colorless, Rich-ard-mond.[54]

Rich-ard-mond speaks the same line twice. Both in the guise of Richard and in that of Richmond, he calls for writing instruments: "Give me some ink and paper" (5.3.50, 41). The image of the two men sitting in their tents writing, again emphasizing the similarity between them, has an anachronistic quality to it. The efficacy of writing has been exhausted, and Richmond's victory foreordained by Margaret and the Duchess. Yet Richard and Richmond continue to act as though the battle plans they are putting down on paper matter to the outcome. Later in the same scene, Norfolk steps forward with a rhyme he found stuck to his tent: "Jockey of Norfolk, be not so bold: / For Dickon thy master is bought and sold" (5.3.305–6). The crude lines are one more piece of evidence that Richard has lost the ability to exert force through writing. While he once controlled all the texts produced and circulated on stage, bits of paper carrying seditious rhymes now attach themselves to his followers' tents. That scene is the last in which we see anyone with a text or pen in hand. Writing has made its last appearance.

The duel which follows is entirely banal. It lacks any of the spectacular effects of the mortal combat between Hotspur and Prince Hal in *1 Henry IV*. In *Richard III*, Antony Hammond, the editor of the Arden edition, is forced to intervene in a footnote in order to rewrite the anti-climax as a climax. This time he corrects the sparse stage directions found in the quarto by writing his own extensive instructions. It takes stylized entrances and exits, additional trumpets, special gestures (the removal of Richard's crown from his corpse), and the help of pall bearers, but Hammond manages to stage the scene as the victory of virtue over villainy:

This, the most physically exciting moment in the play, is badly served by the Q stage-directions. The minimum to make it actable has been added here, but the director ought to feel free to improvise to make this wordless encounter between Good and Evil as symbolically effective as possible. Catesby and Richard must leave at one door; trumpets maintain the tension, then the antagonists appear through separate doors. They fight, Richard is killed, the retreat is sounded (as Q says) and Richmond exits. Richard's body is still on-stage, and, as we learn from Stanley's remarks and the direction (lines 4–7), the crown is removed from Richard's head off-stage, it is necessary to assume that the stage-keepers acted their routine part as bearers-of-the-dead, and carried him off. The stage is thus clear for the triumphal return of the victor with Stanley, no doubt Oxford, Blunt, and Herbert, and as many supers as available . . . Richard's death is thus the single act of destruction necessary to purge the kingdom of its accumulated ills.[55]

These are all the editor's additions. The quarto text itself contains no speeches between the two rivals, no cosmic imagery, no prolonged sword play, no dying words, no display of generosity by the victor, just a plain stage direction: "*Alarum, Enter Richard and Richmond, they fight, Richard is slain.*"

In keeping with the mood of anti-climax, Richmond's final speech does no more than reinscribe him as Richard's double. The ingeniously scripted nature of his claim to the throne, like that of Richard's, discloses as a fabrication the Tudor propaganda argument that one man is a more lawful king than the other. Both characters, using the same words, called for pen and ink before battle. For both, writing is instrumental in achieving strategic aims. Both Richard, as a character in the play, and Richmond, as a figure in history, the founder of a new political dynasty, deploy texts to bolster their legitimacy and enforce their will. In Richmond's case, one such text is that of Shakespeare's play itself which, with some ironic qualifications, shares in the post-facto historical revisionism of its sources, writers in the employ of the Tudor state as the scrivener was in Richard's: Thomas More, Edward Hall, and Raphael Holinshed.

Shakespeare participates in the mythmaking enterprise of those Tudor historians even as he exposes fabrications in their accounts. At the end of his play, when Richmond proposes that "Richmond and Elizabeth, / The true succeeders of each royal House, / By God's fair ordinance conjoin together" (5.5.29–31), the audience has heard such assertions about rightful lineage before. Richard, too, demanded, "What heir of York is there alive but we?" (4.4.471). The rejoinder to Richard's specious claim, an epithet hurled at him by his mother, is a fitting answer to Richmond's as well: "Thou toad, thou toad, where is . . . Clarence? / And little Ned Plantagenet his son?" (4.4.145–6). Rather than allowing Clarence's children to be forgotten, Shakespeare earlier brought young Edward and Margaret Plantagenet onto the scene after their father had been killed; he returned Margaret to the stage a second time, with Anne holding her hand, when the princes were imprisoned in the tower. In Richmond's victory speech, the effort to suppress the existence of Clarence's children calls attention to attempts by contemporary historians to suppress evidence unfavorable to the Tudors in their chronicle retelling of the War of the Roses. It also brings to mind the deeds of Richmond's prototype. The historical Henry VII, as Shakespeare's contemporaries surely were aware, signed an order to execute little Ned in 1499. Using violence and marriage to usurp the crown, Richmond is not the prince in shining armor some critics have made him out to be, but a copy of his predecessor, formed by the same stylus.

IV

By staging *Richard III* as a competition between male writing and female curses, Shakespeare exposes the strategic underpinnings of discourses that linked writing with masculinity. The play depicts social structures, based on a selective distribution of literate skills, as shaping and positioning subjects; at the same time, it enacts the resourceful maneuvering of those subjects inside imposed limits. With great effectiveness, the play's women resist the strictures that would make their lack of writing concomitant with a lack of agency. In doing so, they put in question the axiom that writing is an instrument of omnipotent power before which women have only to lay down their bodies for violent inscription. Margaret, Anne, Elizabeth, and the Duchess strive tirelessly with Richard over common stakes, both over physical sites – the church, the tower, the stage – and over bodies, those of Henry VI, the young princes, young Elizabeth, and that of Richard himself. Sequestered from writing, they assert their autonomy and cast the outcome of events through curses. Blotted Page, they demonstrate, is not the only alternative subject-position to that of Writer.

Strategic choices, not a passive observance of rules, also characterize Richard's exercise of writing. The theatrical medium provides insight into how a paradigm such as that of man-as-writer might have affected people in practice. The metaphor gives Richard an image for describing himself and for reflecting on his relationship to other men. His enactment of the role of writer allows him to delineate ties to male peers and subordinates, verbally assault female opponents, and force people of both sexes into troubling concessions. And yet, while his aggressive use of writing enhances his status, both in relation to other characters and to the audience, it also reveals his susceptibility. In his last soliloquy, the complicated subjectivity that seemed so movingly real when Richard spoke his first lines has eroded into a parody of itself:

> What do I fear? Myself? There's none else by;
> Richard loves Richard, that is, I and I.
> Is there a murderer here? No. Yes, I am!
> Then fly. What, from myself? Great reason why,
> Lest I revenge? What, myself upon myself?
> Alack, I love myself. Wherefore? For any good
> That I myself have done unto myself?
> O no, alas, I rather hate myself
> For hateful deeds committed by myself.
> I am a villain – yet I lie, I am not!   (5.3.183–92)

This repetitive questioning shows Richard trapped in inventing contrary personalities: murderer and judge. He claims to fear himself, love himself, and hate himself; he makes assertions and confesses to lying, acknowledges his guilt and absolves himself of it with schizophrenic double-speak, imaginations of multiple personalities, Richard the murderer as a separate being whom Richard the speaker can attack or escape or haul to court: "All several sins . . . throng to the bar, crying all 'Guilty, guilty!'" (5.3.199–200). A textual crux in the soliloquy underlines this instability in Richard's self-presentation. The statement of double personality found in the version of his soliloquy printed in the first quarto – "I and I" – directly contradicts the assertion of integral selfhood that appears in the second quarto: "I am I."[56] These discrepancies, between quarto texts and between the various narrative accounts of More, Hall, and Holinshed, reinforce the play's larger point about Richard, that his persona is an effect of amalgamated textual constructions.

Fractured by the same deletions and contradictory interlineations that mark the scribal manuscript, Richard's identity is exposed in this speech to be no more than one in a series of self-formulations that the male subject is at work in writing. The startling "I" of the first soliloquy has been fatally overwritten by the transparently contrived "I" of the last. Ironically, Hastings' and Stanley's nightmare of obliterated signs is also the ending that the chronicles assign to Richard. After Richard's death, Hall writes, "The proude braggyng white bore (whiche was his badge) was violently rased and plucked doune from every signe and place were it myght be espied."[57] The foundations of Richard's identity were vulnerable to appropriation and erasure. The acquisition of writing, while confirming the elevated position of the scribally initiated man, also made him dependent on writing for his being as his social inferiors were not. He was left, as Richard says of his kingdom, standing on brittle glass.

5   She writes

Enter Hospitalitie while she is a writing.[1]
Enter Leucippe (reading) and two Maids at a Table, writing.[2]
Enter Countesse, she writes a little, throwes downe the paper and departs.[3]
*Enter Bellafronte with a Lute, pen, inke and paper being placde before
    her. Shee writes.*[4]

In the winter of 1574, Mercy Harvey wrote a series of letters answering
the solicitations of a married nobleman. The correspondence is preserved
by virtue of her brother's interpellation into the humanist program for
masculine self-fashioning. Gabriel Harvey, Mercy's brother, claims to
have copied the letters into his commonplace book. According to
Gabriel, Mercy initially rebuffed all of the nobleman's advances. The
nobleman prevailed on her to meet him at a malt house, but on the
appointed day he encountered in her place the woman's mother and
sister and some of their servants. When P., the nobleman's serving-man,
later reproached Mercy for having made his master undertake a tiring
journey in vain, she promised to explain herself in a letter. P. came the
following night for the letter only to be told it was unfinished. He came
the next day but failed to speak to Mercy. On the third day, the letter
was waiting for him. In it, she excuses her absence as unavoidable; she
also questions what reason a nobleman might possibly have for wishing
to speak to her. "I have hard mie father saie," she writes, "Virginitie is
the fairist flower in a maides gardin, and chastitie the ritchist dowrie a
pore wench can have."[5] The letter is signed "Pore M." and concludes
with a postscript asking the nobleman to destroy the letter after he has
read it. In answer, the nobleman justifies his choice of her, "nature hath
delt better in fashioning the then with any other here about," and vows
his love in similarly ambiguous terms: "nether can I be of that dissem-
bling nature to profes great loove where I do not like" (83).[6] Mercy
answered two days later with another aphorism: "Chastitie, they say, is
like unto time, which, being ons lost, can no more be recooverid" (83). In
Hamlet-like terms, she asserts that it "is no showe of chastitie, as your

165

Lordship imagins, but chastitie indeede, that I care for" (83). The nobleman responded by sending her a gold ring.

In her next letter, Mercy goes to the heart of the dilemma, masked by the lord's Petrarchan language, that a woman in her situation faced: "Milord, if youre sute were as honest as it is ernest, truly you shuld not be so reddie to make it, but I wuld be willing to graunt it" (84). No matter how discreet he might be about the matter, it would "brust owte in the end" and she would be left as used goods on the marriage market. "Then," she asserts, "were I, pore wench, cast up for hawks meate" (85). Her fears were not unfounded. When they met next, the nobleman attempted to force her into bed. P. had persuaded Mercy to speak to his master the day after Christmas in a nearby house. She arrived to find the nobleman "reddie in a litle parlour in his dublet and his hose, his points untrust, and his shirt lying out round about him. And after a short salutation, and a twoe or thre kisses would needs have laid the maide on the bedd" (87–8). To his dismay, he was prevented from doing so by the woman of the house whom Mercy had instructed beforehand to interrupt them with an urgent summons for her to return home.

Events took a decided turn after another missed appointment. In Mercy's next letter, she refers self-consciously to her decision to address him in verse: "Therefore, in steade of a leiser gift, / I bequeath you this paper for a shift. / You se I am disposid to rime, / Though it be cleen out of time" (90). Nearly half of her letter consists of evasive poems in which she blames her refusals on her family: "The truth is, I am not mine owne maide, / My frends to disobey I am afraide" (91). Excusing herself for failing to meet the nobleman as she had promised brings her to make new concessions. Instead of rebuffing his requests, now Mercy herself concocts an elaborate scheme for extending their correspondence. She asks that he have P. deliver his letters to a certain poor woman's house. Then a second messenger, "on that cannot reade himself," should deliver the letters to her. If someone sees them being delivered, she will say that she had written the letters to send to her brother at Cambridge but forgot them at the poor woman's house. So that she will be believed, she suggests that he seal the letters and "write thus in the backside, in a small raggid secretary hand, – To mie loving brother, Mr. G. H., on of the fellowes of Pembrook hall, in Cambridg" (92).

It is after the nobleman inscribed the outside of his next letter, following Mercy's instructions, that Mr. G. H., the teller of the story, came to play a part in it. The last letter inscribed in Gabriel Harvey's commonplace book is one that he himself wrote to the nobleman. In it, Gabriel recounts having met a country fellow who told him that he had a letter for him in his pocket but that he could not give it to him. His mistress, he said, told him that nobody should see it. "Whie, foole," said Gabriel Harvey, "I am nobodie, thouh I see it, thou maist say, and vowe too, if need be, nobodie hath seen it" (94). As though unaware of the nobleman's designs on his sister, Gabriel describes the contents of the nobleman's own letter to him: "a verie amorous and glosing discours touching her suddain departure, her speedie return, the want of her praesens, the pleasure taken in reading her letters, the possession of her according to prommis" (95). "The subscription," he notes, "was in your lordships owne name, as I remember me, thus, – Thine more then his owne, PHIL." (95). With that same touch of exaggerated innocence, Gabriel concludes his letter: "Thus it was mie hap, Milord, by a meere chaunce, to liht on sutch a letter and tokin, sent, not from you, as I take it, but in your L. name, from I knowe not whome, to a sister of mine. Whereuppon I was sumwhat straungly affectid on the suddaine, musing greatly whoe this lustie suter should be, and what should be ment by the loftie subscription within, and the suttle superscription withoute" (96–7).

What is most salient in this exchange of letters between a nobleman and the daughter of a rope-maker comes down to a subject and verb: Mercy wrote. She could write and did write in spite of blocks in her way. While her letters come to us through the filter of her brother's commonplace book, colored by the prurient relish with which he narrates her story, other inscriptions bear direct witness that some early modern women, from the lower as well as upper echelons of society, relied on scribal proficiency to defend claims or advance their positions. Marked by two competing assertions of ownership, the flyleaf of a copy of Edward Cocker's writing manual, *Arts Glory. Or The pen-man's treasurie* (1657), preserves one such piece of writing (frontispiece). The first inscription reads, "John Lycoris His Booke / Bought ye 2th of February / and Cost 18 d. Anno / Domine [sic] 1658." A second inscription, in a different hand, then follows: "Anne Licoris / Her Booke / Nouember ye 29th / 1664." (John and Anne both sign the same family name, but John spells the first syllable with a "y" (Lycoris) while Anne spells it with an "i" (Licoris)).[7] In this case, it seems, a seventeenth-century sister took for her own use a writing book purchased by her brother. If sex-specific prohibitions along with practical and material constraints (limited access to books, writing supplies, schools, and careers) kept the number of women able to write to a minimum and shaped the form and content of what that minority wrote, they did not keep women from seeking or exercising scribal skills altogether. There is no way to know how John Lycoris felt about Anne Licoris' use of the writing manual he had purchased, but published authors from the period communicated their fears over women's appropriation of scribal privileges in vivid terms. This chapter draws upon Thomas Dekker's *Whore of Babylon* and the autobiographical works of Grace Mildmay and Anne Clifford to explore masculine anxieties about female writing dramatized on stage as well as the practical uses to which actual women put pen and ink.

Female-authored manuscripts from early modern England testify both to women's participation in scribal activity and to the educational differences that marked their compositions and hands. Documents written by men and by women display significant discrepancies in levels of scribal competence. For early modern men, the perceived inferiority of women's handwriting, along with other signs of second-rate schooling, was an identifiable sex characteristic that confirmed masculine privilege. In describing the nobleman's letter to his sister, Gabriel Harvey calls attention to the contrast between "the loftie subscription within, and the suttle superscription withoute," that is, the stylish signature inside the letter and the cramped non-descript writing used to record the address on the outside. Both inscriptions were actually penned by the nobleman. The latter, however, was forged, according to Mercy's instructions, "in a small raggid secretary hand" that she presumes will pass for a woman's writing.

This assumption expresses a widespread cultural belief that there was an inherent link between gender and quality of handwriting. John Winthrop, who later became governor of Massachusetts, recalls the impression that his wife's unpracticed handwriting and spelling made upon him. He "observed the scribbling hand, the mean congruity, the false orthography and broken sentences, etc; and yet found [his] heart not only accepting of them, but delighting in them, and esteeming them far above more curious workmanship in another."[8] Erasmus offers a less sentimental and more overtly condescending opinion of female handwriting when he turns a dialogue about the importance of good penmanship, defined according to the regularity of characters and of the intervals between them, into an occasion for a chauvinist gibe. When "Ursus" declares that nothing is uglier than messy writing, unevenly spaced and "scattered about like the Sybil's leaves," "Leo" answers, "Yet this is just how my wife writes!"[9] In effect, Erasmus ridicules women for failing to achieve a skill attainable only through the instruction from which he sought to exclude them.

According to Harvey's account, the correspondence between his sister and the nobleman is assymetrical. There are differences in the character of the handwriting, in the content of the letters, and in the method and ease with which each correspondent is able to send and receive mail (Mercy's part in the exchange is affected by the supervision placed on her contacts with non-family members). One rationale for sequestering women from writing was that it was necessary to do so in order to protect their chastity. While printed texts such as bibles and psalters were produced for reading-consumption, scribal texts were the medium of communication. A woman with reading-only literacy could be restricted to assimilating devotional texts printed in black letter type. A woman initiated into writing, even with a knowledge of scripts greatly inferior to that of her brother, was equipped to evade strictures on her contact with the world outside. This practical concern for safeguarding female virtue informed the selective education of women at every level of society.

Yet even more disturbing to humanist pedagogues and male writers than the thought of women using writing to circumvent social control was the thought of them using writing to usurp male authority. In the seventeenth century, the phenomenon of women writers prompted Richard Lovelace to imagine them grabbing pens away from their husbands. Such a scene, he feels sure, would have horrified Ben Jonson:

> How would thy masc'line Spirit, Father Ben,
> Sweat to behold basely deposed men,
> Justled from the Prerog'tive of their Bed,
> Whilst wives are per'wig'd with their husbands head.
> Each snatches the male quill from his faint hand
> And must both nobler write and understand,
> He to her fury the soft plume doth bow,
> O Pen, nere truely justly slit till now![10]

The act of a woman writing necessarily implies the loss of "Prerog'tive" for men. The pen is the crowning symbol of male dominion and potency. The husband who has lost his "male quill" has been "deposed" from a position of superiority, left emasculated and "faint." Underlying the poet's invective is terror at the prospect of ceding to women this instrument with all its correlative powers, its potential for violence, deception and secrecy, its reach into the inner recesses of heart and mind.

I

While reading skills appear to have been distributed fairly equally between men and women, knowledge of writing was statistically far less prevalent for women. Writing or a lack of writing therefore constituted a significant line of demarcation between the sexes. Existing inequalities could be systematized and objectified in terms of this differential in practical skills. As Keith Thomas notes, "The uneven social distribution of literacy skills greatly widened the gulf between the classes . . . The same was true of women."[11] Sources of evidence for such an imbalance include parish registers, marriage contracts, wills, court depositions, loyalty oaths, apprentice agreements, laws regulating education, school curricula, autobiographies, funeral sermons, and literary works. Preliminary analysis of these documents suggests a widespread pattern of reading-only literacy centered on women: "Parish registers, marriage contracts, and wills throughout the early modern period generally reveal that about twice as many men as women from similar social classes could sign their names, and that women's signatures are more poorly written than the men's, so that their name might have been the only thing these women ever wrote."[12] Since reading and writing were taught consecutively, in that order, incidence of reading-only literacy also can be attributed to economic considerations; the children of agricultural laborers, for instance, were likely to be removed from school around the age of seven. Just when their more privileged peers were learning to manipulate pen and ink, these children took up farm implements. However, unlike boys in this situation whose access to education was narrowed mainly by economic, geographic, and demographic circumstances, girls of all social backgrounds were the object of purposeful, concerted efforts at restricting their access to full literacy.[13]

Jennifer Monaghan and Judith Walter have demonstrated that sex-specific forms of literacy were institutionalized in colonial America. Requirements for parents to educate their children in reading were written into law in Connecticut (1650), New Haven (1655), New York (1665), Plymouth (1671), and Pennsylvania (1683); parents who failed to provide their children with instruction could lose custody of them. In 1660, New Haven authorities added the stipulation that writing was mandatory as well, but only for boys: "To the printed law, concerning the education of children, it is now added, that the sonnes of all the inhabitants within this jurisdiction, shall (under the same penalty) be learned to write a ledgible hand, so soone as they are capable of it." A 1703 Massachusetts law reiterated the need to assure that masters of apprentices provide "for the instructing of children so bound out, to read and write, if they be capable." Some parents may have taken advantage of the gender-inclusive language of this provision in order to have their daughters taught writing; it would seem so, for legislators amended the law seven years later to make the teaching of literate skills sex-specific: "males to read and write, females to read."[14]

Children who were neither acquiring a trade nor learning to read could be removed from their parents and apprenticed to someone else. As with legislation on involuntary apprenticeship, the terms of voluntary apprenticeship agreements were sex-specific with regard to literacy. Walter has studied the agreements involving 267 apprentices, of whom 32 were girls. Some kind of educational provision was specified for only 31 apprentices. For boys, indentures usually mandated that the boy be taught to read, write, and cipher. James Chichester, apprenticed at ten, was to be sent to school "until he can write a leagable hand." Hopestill Chandler, apprenticed to a blacksmith in 1658, was to be taught to read the Bible and "to write enough to keep book for his trade." For girls, on the other hand, indentures left out the second half of the literacy equation: the 1674 agreement for Sarah Joye of Salem stipulated that she be taught only her catechism and "to read English, [and] the capital laws of the country" while Sarah Braibrok was apprenticed in 1656 to a couple who were responsible for teaching her "to reade the English Tongue" and provide her with religious instruction. None of the agreements for female apprentices includes a provision for writing.[15]

Puritan New England imported its pedagogical methods and its school texts (hornbooks, primers, psalters, and bibles) from England. A similar approach to education, drawing upon Latin-language versions of the same essential texts, held sway in Counter-Reformation France. In their study of French literacy from the sixteenth through the nineteenth century, François Furet and Jacques Ozouf conclude that "there was undoubtedly a specifically Counter-Reformation approach to education, aimed primarily at girls and excluding writing."[16] To spread its message, the French Counter-Reformation placed an emphasis on devotional reading similar to that of the English Reformation. Religious orders such as the Béates, founded in 1688, were dedicated to imparting reading-only literacy to girls. Though its effects were not uniform in all regions, or even within a given country, the attempt to instill piety and proper comportment through the reading of religious texts did shape curricula in many parts of Europe. In some areas, this specialized form of reading-only instruction, a product of the religious and social conflicts of the sixteenth century, remained the mainstay of female education into the industrial age.[17] In the mid-nineteenth century, at a school run by the Béates in the Massif Central, girls followed a program of instruction that began at seven in the morning in the summer and eight in the winter: "right until evening, this timetable made no provision for writing: nothing but lacemaking, hymns, recitation and reading."[18]

In early modern England, the eroticization of female writing helped to stigmatize the acquisition of scribal techniques by women. According to *The Education of a Young Gentlewoman* (1598), women who know how to write are likely to engage in illicit affairs: "there is no lesse danger that they will sooner learne to be subtil & impudent lovers, than learnedly to write verses, poetrie, ballads and songs."[19] *Asylum Veneris, Or A*

Sanctuary for Ladies (1616) testifies that some girls were prohibited from writing by their parents on the grounds that "the Pen must be forbidden them as the Tree of good and evill, and upon their blessing they must not handle it. It is a Pandar to a Virgine Chastitie, and betrayeth it, by venting foorth those amarous Passions, that are incident to hotter bloods, which otherwise, like fire raked up in embers, would peradventure in a little space be utterly consumed."[20] Often those women who did learn to write were subject to social opprobrium. Of the famed lyric poet of ancient Greece, Stephen Gosson says that "Sappho was skilfull in Poetrie and sung wel, but she was whorish."[21] As Lovelace puts it, the female poet "Powders a Sonnet as she does her hair, / Then prostitutes them both to publick Aire."[22]

Attacks on women who took up the pen were complemented by efforts to regulate the content of their writing. The different uses to which writing could be put became gendered. Even though the lines of demarcation were not immovable, as we saw in chapter three, original composition generally was construed as masculine whereas other kinds of writing, chiefly the transcription and translation of devotional texts, could be considered as appropriate feminine tasks given a proper pedagogical justification. In the conduct manuals that did not prohibit it altogether, writing was presented as a means of enabling women to deepen their devotion and strengthen their virtue. Women were encouraged to copy texts that would cultivate in them the desired traits of restraint and modesty. "Whan she shall lerne to write," Vives prescribed in his *Instruction of a Christian Woman* (1529), "let nat her example be voyde verses nor wanton or tryflyng songes: but some sad sentence prudent and chaste taken out of holy scripture or the sayenges of philosophers: whiche by often writyng she may fasten better in her memory."[23] In *The Pen's Excellency or The Secretary's Delight* (1618), Martin Billingsley advised women to write in order to compensate for the deficiencies of their memory "especially concerning matters of moment." In this way, they could "commit many worthy and excellent things to Writing, which may, occasionally, minister unto them matter of much solace."[24] Elizabeth Brooke, praised for her uncommon piety, was remembered at her funeral as a disciplined note-taker in church: "she used a mighty Industry to preserve what either instructed her Mind, or affected her Heart in the Sermons she had heard . . . she wrote the Substance of them, and then digested many of them into Questions and Answers, or under Heads of common Places; and then they became to her Matter for repeated Meditation."[25] Copying texts or sermons was seen as a self-fashioning technique. While transcribing passages, as we have seen, was supposed to prepare men for exemplary action, it was meant to make women, with the same efficacy as reading, into models of virtuous passivity.[26]

As with different modes of writing, different scripts became associated with each sex, although such identifications could be reassigned as the status of the secretary and italic hands changed. When Mercy Harvey advised the nobleman to imitate her handwriting, she specified that he should write the address on the outside of the letter in "a small raggid secretary hand." Her instructions suggest that a native secretary script, as opposed to the imported italic, would be perceived as the work of a woman's hand. Apparently, it was not only the crude execution of the hand that marked it as feminine but the type of script as well. In her analysis of the influence of humanism on male and female education, Alice Friedman suggests that the difference in scripts used by sister and brother Margaret and Francis Willoughby of Nottinghamshire, born in the same decade as Mercy and Gabriel Harvey, reflects a larger cultural divide. While Margaret (b. 1544) joined the service of the Duchess of Suffolk and later of Princess Elizabeth, her brother (b. 1546) received a classical humanist education: "He even learned to write in the humanist script, the clearer and more modern Italian hand which was gradually replacing English secretary – even his handwriting distinguished him from his sister and those of lower social status."[27] When it was first introduced to England, "italic was undoubtedly the hand of greater prestige, being preferred for material to be presented to royal or aristocratic readers."[28]

By the late sixteenth century, however, a shift seems to have occurred in the valuation accorded to the different hands. The secretary hand came to be coded as specifically masculine. For famed penman John Davies, marks dashed across the page in executing this complex and highly individualized script denote male vigor and native English virility. "Never saw I yet a woman that could write our English secretary hand lively," he asserts, "though the Romane or Italian handsomly: because they naturally lack strength in their hand to perform those full strokes, and (as it were) to bruise a letter as men can do."[29] Writing masters rationalized a sex-specific distinction between italic and secretary on the basis of women's presumed mental inadequacy as well as physical weakness. Martin Billingsley testified that italic "is usually taught to women, for as much as they (having not the patience to take any great paines, and besides phantasticall and humorsome) must bee taught that which they may instantly learne."[30] While some educated women in the seventeenth century wrote in secretary, most do seem to have learned italic alone as Billingsley recommends; by contrast, educated men acquired both scripts and also improvised a "mixed hand" that combined the two. The complexity of the secretary hand, the speed with which it could be written, and its habitual use in the business of government meant that proficiency in the script remained an important qualification for masculine social advancement. Different hands and different scribal practices gained and lost value according to the dynamics of social distinction between groups and individuals.[31] This competition to acquire and preserve status through literate practices was not only a matter of concern for humanist pedagogues but also material for drama for contemporary playwrights.

II

In his play *L'Ecole des femmes*, Molière shows how the guardian of a young woman tries to prevent her from learning to write on the grounds that "a woman who writes knows more than is appropriate."[32] In order to prepare Agnès to become his wife, Arnolphe offers her a conduct manual titled *Maxims on marriage, or the duties of the married woman with her daily practice*. Aside from maintaining modesty and chastity in seclusion, the other wifely duty mentioned in the manual is refraining from writing. The seventh maxim stipulates that only husbands should have access to the equipment necessary for writing: "Even if it should vex her, among her furnishings / There should be no writing desk, ink, paper or pens. / The husband must, according to good custom, / Write everything that is written in his house."[33] For Arnolphe, Agnès is wax to be molded into the ideal wife through the repetitive tasks of sewing his clothes and reading his maxims. He explicitly juxtaposes the innocence of a woman schooled in reading-only literacy with the suspect sophistication of women writers. All of their verses, novels, letters, love notes, and learning, he says, are not worth the honesty and chastity that ignorance preserves in a woman. In spite of all his precautions, however, Agnès learns to write in order to correspond with a younger man who wins her love. Arnolphe's fears about women writing are confirmed when he comes upon a letter that Agnès has sent to his rival. Subsequently, he berates her not for her inconstancy but for her skill with a pen: "Now you see, minx, what purpose writing serves; / It was against my design you were instructed in that art."[34]

In contemporary English plays, fears about the dangers of turning over the instruments of scribal culture to women emerge in scenes in which female writing is linked with sex and violence. In *Titus Andronicus*, Shakespeare enacts the spectacle of Lavinia writing the names of her rapists in the sand by holding a stick in her mouth and guiding it with her stumps. Her brother's reference to her rape as a "bloody deed" also applies to Lavinia's attempt to write using her hacked-off arms: *"She takes the staff in her mouth, and guides it with her stumps, and writes – "* (4.1.82,78). In *Bussy D'Ambois*, George Chapman stages a scene in which Tamyra, the adulterous wife of Montsurry, is forced at knife point to write her lover a letter that she inscribes in her own blood:

> *Montsurry.* Why write you not? . . .
> Write! for it must be; by this ruthless steel . . .
> Speak! Will you write? . . . *Stabs her* . . . .
> Till thou writest,
> I'll write in wounds, my wrong's fit characters,
> Thy right of sufferance. Write! . . . *Stabs her again* . . . .
> *The FRIAR ascends with a sword drawn.*
> *Friar.* What rape of honor and religion!
> Oh, wrack of nature! *Falls and dies.*
> *Tamyra.* Poor man! Oh, my father!
> Father, look up! Oh, let me down, my lord,
> And I will write . . .
> *Montsurry.* Write, write a word or two.
> *Tamyra.* I will, I will.
> I'll write, but in my blood, that he may see
> These lines come from my wounds, and not from me.
>
> *Writes.*[35]

For the friar, who dies from the shock of witnessing the spectacle, Montsurry's act of writing in wounds on Tamyra's body is equivalent to a rape. The scene also may be meant to suggest a logical punishment for the adulterous woman who conducted her affair by writing letters to her lover, Bussy D'Ambois. Now she is made to write not to arrange another assignation but to lure D'Ambois into the trap set for him, to pour out her blood on the page so that her husband may spill that of her lover.

The defensive stance of Arnolphe, not the mocking skepticism of Molière, informs Thomas Dekker's *The Whore of Babylon*. Dekker's representation of the danger inherent in placing the power of the pen into the hand of a woman amplifies humanist prescriptions. In his play, written three years after the death of Elizabeth, Dekker focuses on the queen as a locus for male anxieties about loss of control. As Katherine Eggert has shown, many works written ostensibly in adulation of Elizabeth "show the stresses of resentment against female rule: while they praise the queen, they also question and seek to limit the operation of her feminine nature, by bringing poetic authority to bear against royal authority, the male pen against the female crown."[36] By staging the moment in which Elizabeth signs a death warrant to authorize the execution of Essex, Dekker validates the threat posited in the works of contemporary pedagogues with a frightening embodiment of the female writer as dominatrix. Unlike *Richard III*, which dramatizes the prevalence of textual corruption as an intrinsic condition of coercive regimes, *The Whore of Babylon* presents the danger inherent in writing as one of unchecked female power. It confirms the truth of conduct manual warnings by channeling resentments about the former queen's rule into a critique of female insubordination through writing. The play, which Dekker terms a "dramatical poem," is supposed "to set forth, in tropical and shadowed colors, the greatness, magnanimity, constancy, clemency, and other the incomparable heroical virtues of our late Queen, and on the contrary part the inveterate malice, treasons, machinations, underminings, and continual bloody stratagems of that purple whore of Rome."[37] In fact, the characters of the Fairy Queen Titania (Queen Elizabeth) and of the Empress (the Whore of Babylon) converge. The "bloody" aspect of the Empress' schemes is mirrored in images of slaughter evoked by Titania's signing of an execution order. Both Titania and the Empress, moreover, wield their power through the pen, a symbol of royal as well as poetic authority. As Dekker puts it in a pamphlet titled *The Dead Term*, a dialogue between the cities of London and Westminster, "a Pen in a princes hand commaunds with as ample force as his Scepter, with it doeth he give Pardons for life, or the heavy doom of death." [38] In *The Whore of Babylon*, the stresses of resentment against female rule crystalize around the specter of female writing.

Dekker's preoccupation with writing is evident in two set pieces, "A Paradox in praise of a Pen" and "Invective against a Pen," contained in *The Dead Term*. On behalf of the pen, Dekker argues that it "carries in it such power, such Conquest, such terror, such comfort, and such authority" that even great subjects are humbled by it. Even in praising the pen, it seems that Dekker, like Shakespeare, cannot help but evoke the potential danger it represents; any "comfort" it might bring is far outweighed by the conquest and terror it presages. In speaking of lawyers, for instance, he diverges altogether from the task of offering praise to note that while pens, in the hands of good lawyers, can be swords of justice, "in the handes of badde and unconscionable Lawyers, Pens are forkes of yron, upon which poore Clients are tossed from one to another, till they bleede to death."[39] The "Invective against a Pen" extrapolates from this sort of grim image to conjure a vision of all the world's evils dripping down from the tip of a quill pen. "A Pen!" Dekker exclaims, "The invention of that, and of Incke hath brought as many curses into the world, as that damnable Witch-craft of the Fryer, who tore open the bowels of Hell, to find those murdering engines of mankind, Guns and Powder." The pen is to blame for the deceptions wives inflict on their husbands: "By help of this, Wives practise to abuse their Husbands, by the Witch-craft of Amorous passions, (which are conjurd out of a Goose-quill)." The pen barters away castles, sows schisms and heresies, and foments treason; "the Tragedies of so many of our Ancient Nobility, were never acted on Scaffoldes, but a Pen was chiefe Actor in their deaths and downefals." It spews forth venom like a poisonous toad. It "draweth bloud where it once fastneth." So malevolent an instrument is the pen that when Elizabeth had to sign an execution order, Dekker claims, she would say, "Would to God wee had never beene taught how to write."[40]

In *The Whore of Babylon*, this same line is pronounced by the character of Titania as she signs a death warrant on stage. That such a climactic moment should foreground writing is not surprising in the context of a play in which books and scribal texts figure so prominently. The proliferation and exchange of texts for the competing purposes of treason and international conspiracy, on the one hand, and, on the other, punishment and the exercise of legitimate authority, enact the paranoid fantasy of *The Dead Term* for a theatre audience. At the center of that maelstrom of manuscripts and warrants and gilded books is the figure of the woman ruler. The preponderance of texts in the play flows from the Empress and Titania. The Empress exerts her might by issuing edicts and by writing letters to plotters against Titania's throne. She inscribes Campeius' name in her "tables" and sets her mark on his forehead (2.2.55). Titania signs a pardon and a death warrant on stage. Dekker invests this image of the woman scribe with ominous meanings by associating female writing with illicit behaviors and unnatural deaths.

Jean Howard observes that "in elaborating his allegory of Protestant plainness and Catholic deceit, Dekker employs an implicit debate structure throughout the text, pitting Titania against her opponents in ways probably meant to engender a sense of dramatic conflict, but which ironically end up destabilizing the binary oppositions upon which the play's whole polemical strategy rests."[41] The play's dichotomous structure breaks down because Dekker's aversion to female appropriation of the masculine pen ultimately proves stronger than his interest in sectarian polemics. While Dekker sets the Empress against Titania, he introduces sexual slanders against the Empress that recall similar ones made against Elizabeth, Titania's prototype. The Empress is incensed that Titania and her fairy lords call her the "Whore of Babylon." They "give out that I am common," she says indignantly, "that for lust and hire / I prostitute this body" (1.1.93, 95–6). During her reign, Elizabeth was referred to as the Empress of Babylon by her detractors. She also was accused of committing fornication with various members of her court and of burning the offspring of those liaisons.[42] In *The Alchemist*, first performed in 1610, Ben Jonson makes this connection between Elizabeth, Titania, and unbridled sexual appetite explicit by staging the impersonation of the Fairy Queen by a London prostitute to whom the alchemist pays mock tribute.[43] In the last decades of Elizabeth's reign, her courtiers were ridiculed by foreign visitors for lavishing praise on the fresh beauty of the no longer youthful queen.[44] One of the kings in the Empress' court implicitly points to this connection between the Empress and Elizabeth when he says that the Empress' critics "say you can throw mists before our eyes / To make us think you fair" (4.4.67–8).

These hints about the correspondent promiscuity of the Empress and Titania bolster a more important parallel between them: the use that both queens make of their pens to draw blood. The letter that the Empress writes to Paridel and the privileges she grants him have the sole end of killing Titania. People say that her purple robes and scarlet mantles, as one king tells the Empress, are "dyed so deep with blood upon them spilt; / And that all o'er y'are with red murder gilt" (4.4.45–6). The Empress confirms the impression in the orders she issues to the Armada: "burn, batter, kill, / Blow up, pull down, ruin all: let not white hairs / Nor red cheeks blunt your wrath; snatch babes from breasts, / And when they cry for milk let them suck blood" (4.4.128–31). Dekker attributes a comparable thirst for blood to women generally in a seemingly gratuitous remark that Plain Dealing makes about surgeons who "before a thousand people, rip up the bowels of vice in such a beastly manner, that like women at an execution, that can endure to see men quartered alive, the beholders learn more villainy than they knew before" (2.1.131–5).

These lines refer to Holinshed's description of the women who thronged to attend the gruesome execution of the men convicted in the Babington plot. According to his version of events, there was "no lane, street, allie, or house" in the city or suburbs of London that was not crowded with people of both sexes "contending to the place of death for the advantage of the ground where to stand, see, and heare what was said and doone." Holinshed draws particular attention to the macabre curiosity of women. He reports that after the traitors were drawn and quartered, their hearts burned in the fire, their heads and quarters carried away in baskets, and the spectators returned home, "the fields were frequented all that daie of the weaker sex, as womenkind, with the yoonger and tenderer sort: who albeit they could not with wished opportunitie see the execution of these traitors, when it was at the quickest: yet they satisfied their eies with beholding the fier wherein their bowels were burned, and the scaffold stained with the tincture of their bloud."[45] The analogy made by Plain Dealing compares these female spectators, gawking at the grisly after-effects of a group execution, to surgeons tearing open bodies before mass audiences. In *The Dead Term*, Dekker connects this same image of bodily evisceration to writing by comparing the invention of pen and ink to the discovery of gunpowder by a Friar who "tore open the bowels of Hell."[46]

This collocation of images linking writing, women, and blood converges in the climactic moment in which Titania signs a death warrant to send a nobleman to the block. In that scene, the figures both of the surgeon who disembowels human bodies and of the female spectator drawn to witness such acts combine in the person of Titania. Dekker's enactment of the signing of the death warrant in *The Whore of Babylon* changes the meaning of the anecdote narrated in *The Dead Term*. In the pamphlet, Dekker says that Elizabeth, when faced with signing a death warrant for any nobleman, would wish aloud that she had never learned how to write. The quotation is cited simply as one more in a series of examples of the danger of writing. In dramatizing Elizabeth's pronouncement, however, Dekker turns that evil from a generalized threat to a specific one posed by women in power. The scene in the play shows Titania hesitating over the execution order that her counselor urges her to sign:

> *Titania.* What comes this paper for?
> *Fideli.* Your hand . . .
> *Titania.* Must we then
> Strike those whom we have loved? Albeit the children
> Whom we have nourished at our princely breast
> Set daggers to it, we could be content
> To chide, not beat them, might we use our will.
> Our hand was made to save, but not to kill.
> *Florimell.* You must not, 'cause he's noble, spare his blood . . .
> *Titania.* We must the surgeon play and let out blood.
> Every peer's birth sticks a new star in heaven;
> But falling by Luciferan insolence,
> With him a constellation drops from thence.
> Give me his axe – how soon the blow is given!
>   *Writes.*
> Witness: so little we in blood delight,
> That doing this work, we wish we could not write. (4.2.1–2, 12–18, 33–9)

Titania's speech invokes female ruthlessness through a distorted image of breastfeeding. As we have seen, the Empress, who attributes her clemency toward her subjects to "a mother's holy love," orders her army to make the children of Fairy Land suck blood instead of mother's milk. In another scene, a king tells two other kings to drink treason, sedition, and heresies at the Empress' breast so that they may spew forth interdictions, excommunications, bulls, and patents to kill lawful rulers. The dichotomy between the Empress' poisoned breast and Titania's nourishing one collapses as Dekker shows both women to be agents of death. Like Lady Macbeth, Titania is capable of killing the infant, or lover in this case, whom she "nourished at [her] princely breast." This image of Titania as a nursing mother and of the condemned man as a helpless infant sets political authority in opposition to female nature and recasts the warning against the abuses of writing in general as a cautionary admonition against women's use of the pen in particular.

A woman's hand, which is to say, her writing, was not created by nature to exert force. It "was made to save, but not to kill." From the first line in which the unsigned warrant is presented to Titania, the material nature of both writing and execution is emphasized. The "hand" that will sign the paper is also the one that will swing the ax. Even the decision to cure the body politic by sacrificing a disloyal peer is couched in these terms. Titania uses the concrete image of a surgeon handling a patient to describe her action. Like the doctors mentioned by Plain Dealing who assist in torture-executions, Titania "must the surgeon play and let out blood." Though she expresses reservations about authorizing the execution, her action of signing the warrant shows her to be no more faint-hearted than the women who Plain Dealing notes can endure to see men quartered alive. John Davies, if we recall, held that women lack the strength "to bruise a letter as men can do." Writing bruises. For the master calligrapher, the act is by definition violent. Its instruments are the wings and skins of slaughtered animals, its agent the knife-wielding penman who draws his weapon to cut the point of his quill.[47] Dekker can only convey his full horror at the thought of female penmen by invoking gruesome images of women delighting in the sight of human guts. He writes as though a woman who writes has not broken a rule, arbitrarily construed, but ruptured arteries, organs, the hidden integrity of the body itself. In the context of these images, redolent with blood and bowels, Titania's final pronouncement, "Doing this work, we wish we could not write," has an entirely different valence. It does not simply express compunction about the value of a prisoner's life. It registers the playwright's unease about female writing as a woman's own fear that by transgressing the limit of reading-only literacy, she has violated something inviolate, the commandment against murder, an elemental taboo.

III

The actual part that women played in scribal culture was both more mundane and more complex than a reading of Dekker's play would have

one believe. The contents of a commonplace book kept by Anne Southwell, probably from around 1588 to 1636, include a copy of a letter she
wrote to the lord deputy Falkland of Ireland, a hymn to Christ, a
paraphrase of Seneca's *Book of Providence*, quotations from Augustine's
City of God, poems titled "Giving no Inch of ground to Jeopardy,"
"Blessed Life," and "Anger," meditations on the Ten Commandments,
epitaphs on Cassandra MackWilliams, the King of Bohemia, and the
Countess of Somerset, an inventory of her goods ("A feather bed &
bolster, a matt, A payre of new canvas sheetes, A white Rugg . . ."), a
catalogue of her extensive library, and a lively series of descriptions of
animals ("The Rhinoceros is of a monstrouse shape and of a beawtifull
coulle[r] for he is yellow speccled with purple his feet are like an
Elaphants").[48] A widow writing about her life between 1577 and 1632,
Martha Moulsworth inscribes the margins of her autobiographical poem
with biblical citations that testify to her immersion in the study of holy
scripture. Yet while she imbues the text of her poem with sacred
teachings, she characterizes her experience of writing it as a moment of
self-formation. Composing verses on her birthday, she draws a parallel
between the text and her self: "This season fitly willinglie combines / the
birth day of my selfe, & of theis lynes." Her verses contain more than a
diligent recording of events cast in a Protestant framework. From them
emerges a distinct first-person voice: "the Virgins life is gold, as Clarks us
tell / the Widowes silvar, I love silvar well."[49]

Moulsworth's pleasure in her independent status as widow and her use
of poetry to convey her satisfaction suggest that while humanists
generally taught writing to female charges as a means of inculcating
passivity and self-effacement, some women nevertheless turned writing
into a means of developing and expressing their own autonomy. On the
whole, as Caroline Bowden has documented, influential women in
Elizabeth's court were equipped with advanced literate skills. Out of
sixty-six women who appear in a book recording personal gifts made by
the queen to members of her Privy Chamber, fifty-three signed their
names and one wrote her initials. Most were noblewomen, though some
were listed under the title "Mistress" and as "women to the Lady." The
majority used italic script; eight used secretary or a combination of the
two. Citing numerous cases of women using correspondence to pursue
their interests or those of their friends, Bowden observes that "the ability
to write their own letters gave the women concerned an active role in
political and social life and expanded their influence significantly beyond
the household."[50] Women who managed to acquire writing-literacy, in
spite of strictures that made it more difficult for them to do so, were
advantageously positioned to seek privileges and curry favor, to obtain

benefits for dependents, to intercede on behalf of condemned relatives, to defend their legal rights in courts of law, to act as patrons, and to participate in intellectual exchanges.

Two of the most compelling personal narratives written by women from this period, the autobiographical works of Grace Mildmay and of Anne Clifford, show that the practice of writing was, for them, not only a disciplinary technique but also an instrument of self-discovery and social contestation. Both women were disinherited and deployed their own texts to counter the wills of their fathers. Their writings incorporate transcriptions of biblical verse, in accordance with humanist precepts, as well as narratives of their own composition. Mildmay's eighty-five page autobiography precedes a longer compilation of spiritual meditations; the scriptural passages that she copied and paraphrased constitute most of this second part of the volume. Clifford's later memoir, which includes events also related in her diary about the years 1616–19, is interlaced with biblical citations. In both Mildmay's and Clifford's writings, the stories of their lives, including acts on their part of disobedience, become part of a narrative of divine intervention on the side of the devout female author.

Grace Mildmay (1552–1620), the second daughter of Sir Henry Sharrington and Ann Paggett of Lacock Abbey in Wiltshire, authored her autobiography sometime between 1617 and 1620. (In view of the controversy associated with a woman's use of the secretary hand, it is interesting to note that Mildmay wrote the text in italic but added revisions and corrections in a secretary hand also clearly identifiable as hers.)[51] Her autobiography recounts episodes from her childhood, her marriage to Anthony Mildmay at the age of fifteen in 1567, the twenty years she spent in the household of her father-in-law, Walter Mildmay, Chancellor of the Exchequer from 1566 to 1598, and subsequent years. However, the focus of the text is on one event in particular, the plot by her sister and other members of her family to slash her inheritance. The story, as Mildmay tells it, bears a striking resemblance to the plot of *King Lear*: "My father Sr Henry Sharington of Laycot in Wiltshire Knight / Had onely three daughters then living, and / vpon our Maryages he diuided his land into / three partes."[52] Of the three daughters, Ursula, Grace, and Olivia, the eldest died before her father. During the last days of her father's life, the youngest, Olivia, conspired with other members of the family to deprive Grace of the portion originally allotted to her. On Henry Sharrington's deathbed, Olivia arranged for a new will to be drawn up granting her the two portions previously allotted to Grace and to Ursula; Grace was to receive only the poorest third formerly willed to Olivia. When Grace Mildmay came to pay her final respects to her father, the co-conspirators tried to hide the evidence of the legal transaction being performed. "Vpon the sight of mee," Mildmay recounts, "they scattered / one from another & put away the bookes and / parchmentes" (64).

Books and parchments of another kind, religious texts and the manuscript of her own *Meditations*, exercised a formative influence over Mildmay over the course of her life. In her middle sixties, she advises her family "to beginn wth the S[c]riptures to read them / with all diligence & humility as a disciple continually euery day" (39). This habitual reading of devotional texts beginning in childhood, along with the supervision of her governess and later of her in-laws, appears to have shaped her into the model woman depicted in conduct manuals. Her praise of Mrs. Hamblyn, the governess, echoes the same criteria for judging female virtue found in didactic treatises: "She proued very religious, wyse, & chaste, & all good / vertues that might be in a woman were constantly / settled in her, (for, from her youth she made good / vse of all things that euer she did read, see, or / heare)" (45–6). Mrs. Hamblyn schooled Mildmay in the use of writing as a technique for self-fashioning; when, for instance, Mildmay encountered a common-law couple "of impudent behauior," the governess assigned her the task of composing verse inveighing against illicit unions. "And this shee did for myne instruction," Mildmay explains, "to take / heed of the lyke, & to abhorre & despise the same" (48). Mildmay testifies that the writing of her *Meditations* and the copying of biblical passages "hath beene the exersise of my / mynde" beginning in those early years (42). The precepts she internalized in the process of this meditational reading and writing directed the conduct of her whole life. Her fear of exposure to negative influences was so great that she isolated herself in her house: "I spent the best part of my youth / in solitarinesse, shunning all opportunities to / run into company least I might be inticed & / drawen awaye by some euill suggestions to / stayne myne vnspotted garment, & so be robbed / of myne innocencie, for I durst put no confi- / dence in my selfe for myne owne defence" (58). Like the model female subject depicted on the title page of Brathwait's *English Gentlewoman*, Mildmay feels compelled to hide from the world, reading alone in her chamber in order to safeguard her virtue.

And yet, the docile female self that Mildmay presents to the reader is fractured by resentment and self-assertion. In the clash with her family precipitated by the revision of her father's will, Mildmay found inner strength through the relationship with God that she had developed through her meditations. She drew on her knowledge of Scripture to legitimate her claims and castigate her enemies. God was on her side, of that she was certain. "God did behold myne innocencie," she writes,

"and my / naturall & faithfull hart to my father, and / forgatt it not
according vnto the scriptures" (64). She confronts her sister with a
warning of divine intervention: "yf you haue laboured my father by all /
meanes to worke, & bring to passe this vnnaturall / wrong towards me, I
commit my whole cause / into the hand of God, & doe most earnestly /
desyre him to be judge betwixt you & mee, & / to right & defend my
Cause" (66). While Mildmay repeatedly emphasizes her filial love and
sense of duty toward her father, she is unable to hide her anger at his
betrayal. "When my father dyed," she recollects, "he / was perswaded to
alter his mynde, & to / forget that my sister & I proceeded both / from
one father & from one mother, & that / I had euer beene his obedient &
louing daugh- / ter" (63). Cancelled by her hand in the manuscript is an
even stronger criticism of her father's action; she originally wrote and
crossed out that her father accepted not only to change his mind but also
"to breake his couenant towards me." Sermons preached from every
pulpit dictated that Mildmay see her father as a surrogate for God and
submit obediently to him, irregardless of how he disposed of his
property, as a religious duty. Instead, she depicts God as a stand-in for
her father, "setting himselfe as it / were in person, against all myne
opposites in theyr / strong & strange oppositions" (69). She believes that
her divine father, her ally and champion, directly intervened to kill her
earthly father before he was able to complete the last paperwork
necessary to disinherit her: "God the lord of lyfe & father of our fathers /
preuented & frustrated theyr purposes when / he cut off my father 24
houres of tyme & suffred him not to liue to doe / me hurt" (69).

Devotional practices of reading and writing have the paradoxical effect
of validating Mildmay's self-construction as an author. While she
acknowledges the untutored quality of her writing, which she attributes
to her lack of "vniversitie Learning" (50), she also claims divine authority
for it:

> This book of my Meditations
> is the consolation of my soule, the joye of my
> hart & the stabilitie of my mynde.
>
> As they are approued by the word of God,
> & as I doe approoue them in myne owne con-
> science by the same word:
>
> And I have not sett them down for osten-
> tation or vanitie, as God himselfe is witnesse
> but with the zeale of my hart.   (49)

Mildmay finds a rationale for recounting the story of her clash with her
family in the duty of every Christian to stand as witness to God's mercy

and righteousness. Even her disobedience to paternal authority, in violation of basic legal and religious precepts, becomes part of her latter-day scriptural narrative of persecution and redemption. She introduces the whole episode of her father's will by framing it as an example of divine intercession on behalf of the faithful: "And further I must not let slippe out / of my mynde What God hath done for me in / myne owne perticular inheritance" (63). The figure to whom she compares herself is not Virginia or Lucrece but King David. After defying her sister, Mildmay echoes the words of the psalmist, "I went into a place by my selfe alone, & / powred out my hart vnto God" (66). In her plea to the reader to receive her work charitably, she adds a note in the margin in which she speaks in the same voice: "And my self will say wth the Prophet David. / psalm 119: Accept, I beseech thee etc." (50). Any obligation that she has as a daughter is superseded when she steps into the role of the psalmist; for Mildmay, as for David, the one crucial relationship that shapes and sustains her life's narrative is that between the singer and God.

This slippage between devotional practice and real-life imperatives that enables Mildmay to give expression to her experience also operates in the autobiographical works of Anne Clifford (1590–1676).[53] In Dekker's representation of Titania's relation to writing, her act of signing the execution order is a moment of high drama. Clifford makes a similarly climactic scene the central event in her diary and memoir, but, contrary to Dekker's queen, she distinguishes herself by her refusal to sign the official parchment presented to her. Fifteen at her father's death, Clifford spent decades of her life defying her father, her uncle, her two husbands, and her King in a legal battle over the provisions of her father's will. George Clifford (1558–1605), the third Earl of Cumberland, left Anne only 15,000 pounds and the reversion of his properties in the event that his brother should die without a male heir. Yet the entail placed on the lands by Edward II decreed that the Clifford properties should pass to the most direct descendant, in the event of either a male or female heir; Clifford's father had to break the entail in order to disinherit Anne in favor of her uncle.[54] On the basis of the terms of the original settlement, Anne laid claim to her father's lands and titles: castles and estates in Craven, Appleby, Brougham, Brough, and Pendragon, along with the Barony of Clifford in Yorkshire and the office of Sheriff of Westmorland.[55]

In her writings, Clifford narrates her repeated refusals to sign a legal document relinquishing her claims to her father's property in exchange for a cash settlement as stipulated in the will. Burdened by debts, Richard Sackville, her first husband, used blackmail and threats, even banishing her to the countryside and taking away her daughter, in order to pressure Anne to concede to the Cliffords' demands. On April 12, 1616, she records in her diary, "I told my Lord how I had left those writings which the judges & my Lord wou'd have me sign & seale behind with my mother."[56] On April 18, she writes that a messenger "came hither & brought me a letter from my Lord to let me know this was the last time of asking me whether I wou'd set my hand to this award of the Judges."[57] Her entry for January 18, 1617 gives a vivid account of the meeting in which King James himself confronted her with a paper to sign. Writing in her memoir after having regained her lands, at the remarkable remove of nearly six decades, Clifford stresses the importance of that moment from her past by recalling it once more in her entry for January 18, 1676:

The 18th day I remembered how this day was 59 years (since) I went with my first Lord, Richard Earle of Dorset, before King James, into his Inner Drawing Chamber at Whitehall where ye King earnestly desired mee to subscribe to an award which hee intended to make betwixt mee & my said Lord on the one part, & my Uncle of Cumberland & his Son Henry Lord Clifford on the other part, concerning the lands of my antient Inheritance in Craven & Westmorland. But (by God's Grace) I began to deny it, it being the first time I was ever before that King. Eccles. 3; 8.6. Prov. 20.24.[58]

Clifford justifies her refusal to "subscribe" or put her signature to the document by testifying to the part that God took in the altercation. By her account, her disobedience to the king's command was enabled "by God's Grace" and authorized by holy Scripture. The citations from Ecclesiastes and Proverbs refer to the ultimate control that God exerts over human affairs and to the need to meet adversity with patience and faith. Following her second marriage in 1630, Clifford would call on the same sources of scriptural authorization in defying her new husband, Philip Herbert, Mary Sidney's son and the Earl of Pembroke, when he attempted to marry his son to Clifford's youngest daughter, in spite of the fact that the young woman was "extreamly averse from that match." "At length it pleased God," Clifford writes in her autobiography, that Isabella married a different man.[59]

A series of four consecutive diary entries for April, 1617 attests to the importance of literate skills in Clifford's daily life:

Upon the 16th my Lord & I had much talk about these businesses he urging me still to go to London & to sign & seal but I told him that my promise was so far passed to my mother & to all the world that I wou'd never do it whatsoever became of me & mine . . .

Upon the 17th in the morning my Lord told me he was resolved never to move me more in these businesses, because he saw how fully I was bent.

Upon the 18th being Good friday I spent most of the day in hearing Kate
Burton read the Bible & a book of the Preparation to the Sacrament.

Upon the 19th I signd 33 letters with my own hand which I sent by him to the
Tenants in Westmorland.[60]

Three months after the strained confrontation with King James, Clifford
was still facing relentless pressure from her husband to relinquish her
lands. While she steadfastly refused to "sign and seal" the papers
prepared for her on the sixteenth, she "signed 33 Letters" with her own
hand only three days later. She withheld her signature from a legal
document that would license her dispossession but inscribed it on a series
of letters that confirm her position of authority over the lands her father
once ruled.

Clifford used the inscription, accumulation, and deployment of texts in
legal, managerial, and political activities as well as in her scholarly
pursuits, devotional exercises, and personal reflections. In 1649, six
months after Charles' execution, Clifford finally was able to claim her
estates at last. Since her cousin, Henry, the fifth Earl of Cumberland, had
died without issue, the lands reverted to her according to the original
terms of her father's will. On July 11, Clifford left London to embark on
a voyage to reclaim, one by one, the family properties over which she had
fought for control: Skipton Castle, Barden Tower, Appleby Castle,
Brougham Castle, the Castle of Pendragon, and Wharton Hall.[61]
Through her memoir, Clifford consigns to history the experience of
reclaiming her inheritance as well as the thoughts it inspired in her: "so
the 8th day of August in 1649 I came into Appleby Castle ye most
auncient seat of myne inheritance, and lay in my own chamber there . . .
So various are ye pilgrimages of this human life. Eccles. 3.5."[62] Clifford
immediately began renovating the castles, churches, bridges, and schools
under her jurisdiction; as Sheriff of Westmorland, she convened courts to
hear complaints and punish offenders. On each of the five castles, on
Barden Tower, and on the seven churches she repaired, she installed a
plaque inscribed with one of her favorite passages from Isaiah: "And
they that shall be of thee shall build the old waste places; thou shalt raise
up the foundations of many generations, and thou shalt be called the
repairer of the breach, the restorer of paths to dwell therein" (Isa.
58.12.).[63] She built Saint Anne's Almhouse in Appleby, erected a new
bridge over the River Eden, and endowed a trust with land at Temple
Sowerby to restore the village bridge and church and to erect a new
grammar school. She also cracked down on refractory tenants, removing
the cattle of those who refused to pay back rent.[64] Beyond the boundaries
of her estates, her influence extended to political involvement. The entry
in her memoir for April 25, 1660 shows Clifford's engagement in national

Fig. 7.   *The Great Picture of the Clifford Family.* Attributed to Jan van
Belcamp, *c.* 1647.

affairs: "a New Parliament began to sitt at Westminster wherein were
chosen, most part by my means, Knights of the Shire of Westmerland
[sic], my two Cozens – Sir Thomas Wharton and Sir John Lowther of
Lowther, Knight and Barronett; and for Burgesses of the Burrough of
Appleby my Cozen Sir Henry Chomely and Christopher Clapham
Esq."[65]

The famous triptych that Clifford commissioned around 1647 recalls
for the viewer all the varied uses to which Clifford put writing in her roles
as pious gentlewoman, combative litigant, able administrator, family
chronicler, and political claimant. Attributed to Jan van Belcamp, "The
Great Picture of the Clifford Family" is nine feet tall and eighteen feet
long (fig. 7). Its central panel depicts Anne's parents and her two

brothers, both of whom died in childhood; portraits of herself at age fifteen and fifty-six appear on the left and right panels respectively. In the first panel, a young Clifford is pictured with her lute and with a series of books arranged meticulously on shelves above her. In the last panel, a middle-aged Clifford stands underneath books piled in disorderly stacks on the shelves as though in the process of being consulted. Her right hand rests prominently, in a gesture of ownership, on two other books placed over a long piece of parchment inscribed with her personal history. That manuscript, which unfurls over the edge of a table, symbolizes the voluminous body of texts that Clifford wrote in her lifetime: letters, official documents, biographies of each of her parents, massive genealogical chronicles, texts on monuments and epitaphs on tombs, in addition to her diary, autobiography, and memoir. Both through its pictorial representations and through the minutely painted texts incorporated into its composition, the triptych stands as an artifact of contemporary conflicts over gender and literacy that have been the theme of this book. As such, it indexes themes, personalities, and texts discussed in previous chapters.

The left-hand panel of the triptych brings us back to the efforts of humanists in the early sixteenth century to stake out education as a masculine sphere. In Clifford's painting, a picture of Anne as teacher, not the saintly figure but Ann Taylor, Clifford's governess, has been instated alongside that of Samuel Daniel, the humanist pedagogue and poet who served as Clifford's tutor. Parallel frames and placement of the two portraits put the male and female instructors on equal footing. This refutation of the humanist bias that motivated the demotion of female teachers in favor of male schoolmasters accords with Clifford's rejection of other limitations placed on women's social roles and legal rights following the Reformation. In her genealogical chronicle, she cites the remarkable case of a thirteenth-century female ancestor, Isabella de Clifford, who held the office of Sheriff of Westmorland: "Very remarkable it is in the life of this Isabella that in the time of her Widdowhood she had the Honor to execute the same office in her own person & satt herself upon the Bench as Hereditarie Sherriff of Westmorland upon Tryals of Life & Death an Honor which no woman in this Kingdom has hitherto attained but herself."[66]

Clifford's invocation of female examples from the chronicles, framed in deliberately gendered terms, invalidates the sex-specific prescriptions of early modern humanists on the grounds of historical precedent. Her own father, George Clifford, the Earl of Cumberland, who appears in a contemporary portrait like a knight from *The Faerie Queene*, resplendent with lance and plumed helmet, had stipulated that his daughter's studies be restricted on the basis of her sex. In a move to make her disinheritance intellectual as well as financial, Cumberland purposely denied Anne the Latin education from which he had benefitted as a student of John Whitgift, the archbishop of Canterbury and a former regius professor at Trinity College, Cambridge.[67] Yet, like the women in *Love's Labour's Lost* who out-argue the play's bookmen without recourse to Latin, Anne Clifford nonetheless found a way to dispute the legal arguments of a Renaissance king and his courtiers, her father, uncle, and husbands included, in spite of the limits of an English-only education. Even more audaciously, she acted on the example of a medieval female ancestor to assert her own right to hand down binding interpretations of the law from a seat on the judicial bench.

Clifford backs up her unusual claims to such authority with an ostentatious display of books. The triptych shows her at the center of her own Academe. The title of each volume, clearly lettered on its spine, is an unambiguous repudiation of the humanist effort, symbolized by Navarre's exclusion of women from his book-lined court, to sequester erudite knowledge for men alone. In the panel that portrays Clifford at fifteen, the twenty-five volumes pictured include works of theology, philosophy, science, history, geography, and literature: the Bible, Augustine's *City of God*, Boethius' *Consolation of Philosophy*, Gerard's *Herbal*, Camden's *Britannia*, Daniel's *Chronicle of England*, Ovid's *Metamorphoses*, Castiglione's *Courtier*, Montaigne's *Essays*, Cervantes' *Don Quixote*, Philip Sidney's *Arcadia*, and the complete works of Chaucer and Spenser. In the panel depicting her in middle-age are twenty equally varied works, among them Donne's *Sermons* and *Poems*, Antonius' *Meditations*, Plutarch's *Lives* and *Morals*, Guicciardini's *History*, Henry Wotton's *Book of Architecture*, Herbert's *Poems*, the works of Fulke Greville and Ben Jonson, and a Bible. (In the central panel, a Bible, the third in the triptych, together with the works of Seneca and a book about medicines stand on a shelf above Clifford's mother, who holds a copy of the Psalms in her left hand.) The choice of titles both supports and contradicts humanist strictures on female reading. In addition to the Bibles and devotional handbooks, the painting also includes works such as Ovid's *Metamorphoses* that women were sternly enjoined to avoid.[68] The works of piety in her library certify Clifford's respectability; at the same time, the volumes of poetry and romance fiction, science, history, and architecture found on the same shelves complicate the conventional aspect of her representation as a pious woman by showing her to have been a cultivated reader and authoritative landowner as well.

As in Shakespeare's portraits of Hamlet and Ophelia, books figure in the triptych as signs of the self. Clifford's strategic use of texts, however, offers insights into alternative possibilities for action not pursued by the fictional characters of *Hamlet*. In Shakespeare's play, Hamlet is unable to evade the edict of his father or to challenge him by insisting on his own interpretations; a good student and a good son, Hamlet seals his fate in the pages of a commonplace book inscribed with his father's words. Clifford instead counters the influence of her father's writing by authoring dissenting texts of her own. And unlike Ophelia, who retreats into oral culture and marginality to escape the role of Devotion's Visage, leaving political conflict and affairs of state to university-educated men, Clifford calls on her training in scripture, supplemented by secular reading and pragmatic acumen, as a resource in her challenge to her father and to her king.

By doing so, Clifford put in question prevailing attitudes about gender. It was said of her at her funeral, "the Subject here, Woman, we must allow to be so far figurative as . . . by a Synechdoche, under one to comprehend both Sexes."[69] A generation after Mary Sidney, Clifford offered in her triptych and in her family chronicle representations that expanded conventional notions of female exemplarity along the lines suggested by *Antonius*. Clifford, like Sidney, attributes to women, herself included, characteristics generally assigned exclusively to men. Her self-representation in the triptych she commissioned appears, quite deliberately, "to comprehend both Sexes." The central panel of the triptych presents Clifford's mother and father in traditionally gendered clothing, an ornately embroidered dress with lace ruff for her mother, a velvet coat and suit of armor for her father. The two side panels, however, make Clifford's gender appear ambiguous. On the left, in the image of her at fifteen, the delicate lace of her collar, richly worked fabric of her dress, and the roundness of her face connect her with the feminine figure of her mother whose portrait shares those traits. On the right, in the image of her at fifty-six, her bodily posture, longer face, and more severe dress align her with the masculine figure of her father. As Katherine Acheson notes, the double gender identification of Anne in the triptych parallels her written description of herself in her autobiography. "Never," Clifford asserts, "was there child more equally resembling both father and mother than myself."[70]

The secondary place given to portraits of her two husbands, relegated to small frames on the wall, and the detail of a playfully docile Italian greyhound looking up at her for attention, complete this unorthodox image of an exemplary woman beyond masculine control. The portrait of Clifford as a dowager countess, dressed somberly in black, with only a dog and cat for companions, is all the more striking given that her second husband was still living when it was painted. As Graham Parry notes, "Philip Herbert looks as if he occupied the same dimension as Richard Sackville, who had died in 1624." Herbert, however, was still very much alive in 1646, the year in which The Great Picture was commissioned, though in lodgings separate from those of his wife; he backed Parliament and she the king.[71] Remarkably, the bishop who preached the eulogy at Clifford's funeral attested to her assertion of independence in positive terms. Calling upon a singular metaphor, the model lady as helmsman of a boat, Edward Rainbow praised Clifford's self-possession: "She was absolute Mistris of her Self, her Resolutions, Actions, and Time . . . like him at the Stern, she seem'd to do little or nothing, but indeed she turn'd and steer'd the whole course of her Affairs."[72]

This conflation of gender terms, "she was . . . like him," might have crept into the bishop's text under the influence of Clifford's own writings. In inscriptions incorporated into the "The Great Painting," Clifford blurs boundaries between the sexes by attributing the same qualities, wit and judgment, both to her father and to her mother. The triptych also provides visual reinforcement of Clifford's valorization of her mother by allowing Margaret Clifford to share the central role, typically performed only by the father, of presenting the eldest son and heir to the viewer.[73] Neither text nor image accedes to the schema illustrated by the title pages of *The English Gentleman* and *The English Gentlewoman* that divided the sexes into separate domestic and civic spheres. In another inscription in the triptych, Clifford remembers her Aunt, Anne Russell Dudley, the Countess of Warwick, as "a most virtuous and religious lady, and yet an Excellent Courtier."[74] In the *Lives* that she authored about her family, Clifford writes of how Warwick intervened effectively in conflicts at court and, as a consequence, was "generally esteemed and honored through the whole court and all the said Queen's dominions . . . for she was a great freind [sic] to virtue and a helper to many petitioners and others that were in distress, that came to court for relief of their wrongs."[75] Her aunt, in Clifford's account, takes on the masculine role of chivalric champion, rescuing victims in distress, rather than a conventionally helpless feminine one. Moreover, Clifford praises her mother for acts that amounted to political dissent. She recounts that although Margaret Clifford "met with great oppositions, even from King James himself" in disputing her daughter's disinheritance, she "shewed she had a spirit too great to yeild [sic] to fortune or opposition, further than necessity compelled her to it; and so much constancy, wisdom and resolution did she shew in that business, that the like can hardly be parallelled [sic] by any woman."[76] In assigning these traits, "constancy, wisdom and resolution" to an exemplary woman, Clifford follows Mary Sidney rather than her own tutor, Samuel Daniel. (Coincidentally, the volume of Daniel's *Works* found in the triptych's left-hand panel makes *The Tragedy of Cleopatra*, along with the conflicts it provoked with Sidney, Clifford's former mother-in-law, an implicit part of the picture.)

Clifford uses the roles of patron and of historian not only to unsettle gender models but also to settle financial and personal accounts with male relatives. All four framed portraits hanging on the wall of the central panel of the triptych are of her aunts: her mother's sisters, Anne, Countess of Warwick, and Elizabeth, Countess of Bath, and her father's sisters, Margaret, Countess of Derby, and Frances, Lady Wharton; Francis Clifford, the uncle who claimed her father's lands, is pointedly left out. In her version of Clifford genealogy, she traces back an important part of the family lands and titles to the same thirteenth-century female ancestor she praised for acting as sheriff: "from the time that this most noble Lady Isabella married this Roger de Clifford being the 8th of April 1269 till the 30th of October Anno Domini 1605 when George Earl of Cumberland died which was three hundred & twenty six years [sic] the Cliffords that descended from her lawfully enjoyed the Lands of Inheritance in the County of Westmorland."[77] Drawing on documents from a period of over three centuries, Clifford reroutes the lines of inheritance leading to her own generation from a patrilineal to a matrilineal course, shifting the moral authority conferred by holding dominion over ancestral lands from an indifferent father to a farsighted and generous foremother.

Clifford's desire for textual control, evident in her compiling of chronicles seems to have extended to works published by others. In one case, her active shaping of the written record appears to have led her to destroy a text of which she disapproved. Like Mary Sidney, Clifford aroused the discomfort of male contemporaries about the precedent she set for other women. In a dedication apparently meant to flatter her, Antonie Stafford, a devotional writer, clumsily chose to use the opportunity to voice concerns about her transgressive assertiveness. "I am afraide," he acknowledged, "that (ere long) you will disable my sex, falsifie the Scriptures and make Woman the stronger vessel."[78] The evidence suggests that Clifford had the dedication containing that line destroyed. Out of all the extant copies of Stafford's book, a religious work called *Stafford's Niobe*, only one includes the entire text of his unauthorized epistle to Clifford; the offending pages were ripped out of some nine other surviving copies.[79]

This strategy of using texts for tactical ends, through authorship and censorship, is one familiar from *Richard III*. Clifford's endless repetition of variations on the phrase "sole daughter and heir" to refer to herself in her family chronicles, memoir, autobiography, and inscriptions in "The Great Picture" is symptomatic of the obsession with rewriting history to bolster one's position that Shakespeare explores in that play.[80] Yet while Richard delegated the actual transcription of scribal documents to a professional scrivener, Clifford involved herself directly in their production. Her diary entry for April 1, 1619 makes self-conscious reference to her hands-on role as a writer of history: "The first day in the morning I writ in the Chronicles."[81] Her many references to the work of contemporary historians and antiquarians and her tireless pursuit of primary documents – including inquisitions, charters, grants, and wills – show her to be a competent and informed chronicler of events.[82]

At the same time that Clifford holds the pen as Richard does, however, she also speaks the oral discourses associated with women in the play. She validates her claim to her father's lands and titles not on textual grounds alone, the reams of historical and biblical texts she knowledgeably invokes, but also on the authority of female prophecy. A dream of Margaret Clifford, akin to the premonitory visions of old Margaret and the Duchess of York, frames her daughter's ordeal as part of a providential order that requires Anne's victory in the end. As Clifford tells it, her mother had a gift for prediction:

she had a kind of prohetick [sic] spirit in her in many things; and in particular, she would often tell her only daughter, the Lady Anne Clifford, that the antient lands of her father's inheritance would at last come to be hers, what opposition soever was made to hinder it, though it would be very long first. Which many years after came to pass; and she was the rather induced to believe it by reason of a strange kind of divining dream or vision, that appeared to her in a fearfull manner in Barden Tower in Craven, when she was great with child with her third child, which told her she should be delivered a little while after of a daughter which should be the only child to her parents and live to inherit the antient lands of her father's ancestors; which after proved to be true.[83]

Clifford's position at the interstices between literate erudition and oral tradition, between practical mastery and devotional meditation, between history and prophecy make her story a case study in the variable results of forming identities through literacy instruction.

The ability to direct the course of her life and to participate in public discourse and decision-making depended not only on Clifford's birth and connections but also on her rigorous application of writing. In early modern England, scribal and interpretive proficiency was indeed a key factor in the acquisition of status and in the exercise of power. The allocation of these skills and correlated benefits was an underlying concern of male writers, authors of conduct manuals as well as playwrights, as they railed against women taking on the prerogative of writing. Their forewarning that women would usurp male authority in doing so was not pure projection on their part but a strategic move in an ongoing social conflict. Contemporary readers and writers, men as well as women, learned to define themselves and guide their actions according to prevailing models of sex-defined difference. In the process, they contested and transformed those models, documenting their struggles with each other and with themselves in writing, most vividly in works for the English public theatre. Along with the models of gender that inform them, those plays remain with us, traces of the incomplete, complicated, and contradictory ways in which humanism helped transform men and women into dissimilarly literate subjects.

Notes

1 Robert Davenport, *A New Trick to Cheat the Devil* (1639), sig. F4v.
2 While knowledge of reading and writing increased steadily throughout early modern Europe, that overall trend should not be taken as evidence of a sudden sixteenth-century shift from oral to literate culture. As M. T. Clanchy has documented, literate skills spread gradually in England between the eleventh and thirteenth centuries, spurred by pragmatic exigencies rather than the appeal of high culture, and came to co-exist with earlier social and intellectual practices; "clerical skills were gradually absorbed, insofar as they were useful, and an amalgam was formed over generations of literate and pre-literate thought" (From *Memory to Written Record: England, 1066–1307* [Cambridge, Massachusetts: Harvard University Press, 1979]). Brian Stock makes a similar point about the eleventh and twelfth centuries, arguing that the written did not simply supersede the oral; instead, a new type of interdependence arose between the two (*The Implications of Literacy: Written Language and Models of Interpretation in the Eleventh and Twelfth Centuries* [Princeton: Princeton University Press, 1983], 9). In these post-conquest centuries, he points out, "genuine literacy remained largely a monopoly of ecclesiastical culture"; literacy impacted the masses not because they could read and write but because those who ruled them could (26). Both Clanchy and Stock offer a needed corrective to the conceptions of "oral" and "written" as compartmentalized, polarized phenomena found in the work of Jack Goody and Walter Ong (Goody, *The Logic of Writing and the Organization of Society* [Cambridge: Cambridge University Press, 1986] and Ong, *Orality and Literacy* [London: Methuen, 1982]). Even in the far more literate culture of post-Reformation England, Tessa Watt points out, pre-literate and literate traditions, the oral/visual and the written, continued to interact: "The meaning of a printed ballad was not only in its text, but also in the melody of the tune it was sung to; its tempo and instrumentation; the location of the performance; the talent, character and social status of the singer; the people in the audience; the other songs sung before and after; even the other songs sung to the same tune, which resonated in the ears of the listener. The meaning could also be in the woodcuts along the top of the broadside; its location on the alehouse or cottage wall; the other ballads or painted cloths in the room; and the stained glass windows or paintings in the local church which recurred

in the mind's eye of the viewer" (*Cheap Print and Popular Piety, 1550–1640* [1991; rpt. Cambridge: Cambridge University Press, 1994], 328–9).

3 Roger Chartier, "The Practical Impact of Writing," in *Passions of the Renaissance*, v. 3, *A History of Private Life*, eds. Phillipe Ariès and Georges Duby (Cambridge, Massachusetts: Harvard University Press, 1989), 115. See also Carlo M. Cipolla, *Literacy and Development in the West* (Harmondsworth: Penguin, 1969), 56. However, this striking discrepancy between male and female levels of education should not be interpreted to mean that women were wholly illiterate. Recent scholarship has put into question low estimates of the number of women who could read in early modern England. In dispute are the statistics at which David Cressy arrived by analyzing court documents, loyalty oaths, and ecclesiastical records. Cressy concludes that only a small fraction of women could read in this period because high percentages of women made marks instead of signing their names. He notes, for example, that between 1580 and 1640, 90 percent of women in ecclesiastical court cases in London and 95 percent in the countryside could not sign their names, and concludes that the same percentage of women, more or less, could not read (*Literacy and the Social Order: Reading and Writing in Tudor and Stuart England* [Cambridge: Cambridge University Press, 1980]).

These figures are, as Keith Thomas has said, "a spectacular underestimate" ("The Meaning of Literacy in Early Modern England," in *The Written Word: Literacy in Transition*, ed. Gerd Baumann [Oxford: Clarendon Press, 1986], 103). Reading and writing were taught consecutively as separate skills; a child whose education was cut off at an early age would have learned to read but not to write. Thomas contends that the assumption that a person's inability to sign his or her name signifies an inability to read leads Cressy to underreport levels of reading knowledge among women of every social class and among lower-class men. H. S. Bennett likewise concludes "that an ability to read was widespread; that it was to be found in all ranks of society, among both men and women, and that it was powerfully increased by the products of the printing press and by the strong religious emotions provoked by the action of Henry VIII and by later monarchs and their advisers" (*English Books and Readers: 1475 to 1557* [Cambridge: Cambridge University Press, 1970], 29). For further evidence that levels of reading-literacy were vastly higher than those of signature-literacy, especially for women, see J. W. Adamson, "The Extent of Literacy in England in the Fifteenth and Sixteenth Centuries: Notes and Conjectures," *The Library* 10 (1929), 163–93, Margaret W. Ferguson, "A Room Not Their Own: Renaissance Women as Readers and Writers," in *The Comparative Perspective on Literature: Approaches to Theory and Practice*, eds. Clayton Koelb and Susan Noakes (Ithaca, New York: Cornell University Press, 1988), 93–116, Margaret P. Hannay, ed., *Silent But for the Word: Tudor Women as Patrons, Translators, and Writers of Religious Works* (Kent, Ohio: The Kent State University Press, 1985), Suzanne W. Hull, *Chaste, Silent and Obedient* (San Marino, California: The Huntington Library, 1982), Margaret Spufford, *Small Books and Pleasant Histories: Popular Fiction and Its Readership in Seventeenth-Century England* (Athens, Georgia: University of Georgia Press, 1982), Merry Wiesner, *Women and Gender in Early Modern Europe* (Cambridge: Cambridge University Press, 1993), and Louis B. Wright,

"The Reading of Renaissance English Women" *Studies in Philology* 28.4 (1931), 139–56.

4 Hilda L. Smith, *Reason's Disciples: Seventeenth-Century English Feminists* (Urbana: University of Illinois Press, 1982), 41.

5 Facsimile (Amsterdam: Da Capo Press, 1971), 174.

6 *The Complete Woman* (London, 1639), sig. C1r.

7 At the base of humanist pedagogy was the conventional notion that reading could shape the reader in fundamental ways; in the words of an Elizabethan state sermon, "That thing, which (by continual use of reading holy Scripture, and diligent searching of the same) is deeply printed and graven in the heart, at length turneth almost into nature" (*Sermons or Homilies Appointed to be Read in Churches in the Time of Queen Elizabeth of Famous Memory* [Liverpool: The Caxton Press, 1812?], 10–11). On the construction of the early modern subject through acquired bodily habits, see Norbert Elias, *The History of Manners* (1939; rpt. New York: Pantheon Books, 1978) and *Power and Civility* (1939; rpt. New York: Pantheon Books, 1982), Pierre Bourdieu, *Outline of a Theory of Practice* (1977; rpt. Cambridge: Cambridge University Press, 1987), Peter Stallybrass, "Patriarchal Territories: The Body Enclosed," in *Rewriting the Renaissance: Discourses of Sexual Difference in Early Modern Europe*, eds. Margaret W. Ferguson, Maureen Quilligan, and Nancy Vickers (Chicago: University of Chicago Press, 1986), and Peter Stallybrass and Allon White, *The Politics and Poetics of Transgression* (London: Methuen, 1986).

8 *The Society of Individuals*, trans. Edmund Jephcott, ed. Michael Schröter (Cambridge, Massachusetts: Basil Blackwell, 1991), 55. Louis Althusser, who similarly stresses the importance of social practices in the emergence of modern society, reaches back to the early modern period to illustrate his argument that habits of comportment produce and reproduce ideology, rather than the reverse. In support of that argument, Althusser cites advice given by the seventeenth-century philosopher Blaise Pascal: "Kneel down, move your lips in prayer, and you will believe" ("Ideology and Ideological State Apparatuses," in *Lenin and Philosophy and Other Essays*, trans. Ben Brewster [New York: Monthly Review Press, 1971], 168).

9 "New Historicisms," in *Redrawing the Boundaries: The Transformation of English and American Literary Studies*, eds. Stephen Greenblatt and Giles Gunn (New York: The Modern Language Association, 1992), 414.

10 Carol Thomas Neely has criticized new historicism and cultural materialism for undermining the position that there is an "area of 'femaleness' . . . that is not utterly inscribed by and in thrall to patriarchal ideology" ("Constructing the Subject: Feminist Practice and the New Renaissance Discourses," *English Literary Renaissance*, 18.1 [1988], 7). This assessment, which presumes that "constructing the subject" necessarily means viewing women as repositories of dominant beliefs, is a reductive account of what amounts to a range of approaches for understanding the formation of subjects from a literary–historicist perspective. My purpose here is to demonstrate that gender identities form through complex interactions between different groups and social actors. In this book, cultural construction does not refer to the work of a single group or of the dominant elite alone but rather to exchanges and

contests between groups and actors. Women as well as men, poor as well as rich, although unequally positioned, are nonetheless engaged in social transformation. For this reason, I do not use the term "patriarchy" in discussing gender inequality. Though important reformulations of the term have been proposed by Marxist and feminist scholars, "patriarchy" most often stands for the notion that male domination is a universal and ahistorical phenomenon based on the fact of sexual difference alone. Thus crudely defined, the term does not make allowance for distinct articulations of gender inequality in different cultures and subcultures. By assuming the subordination of women as a given, it closes off consideration of the specific mechanisms by which hierarchical relations between men and women are sustained. Finally, relying on a transcultural idea of the subject, the term evades the question of how gender inequality is related to forms of domination based on race, class, sexual orientation, ethnicity, or religion. For critiques of the concept of patriarchy, see Judith Butler, *Gender Trouble: Feminism and the Subversion of Identity* (New York: Routledge, 1990), 35, and Joan Wallach Scott, *Gender and the Politics of History* (New York: Columbia University Press, 1988), 33–5. For an ambitious attempt to theorize a more nuanced model of patriarchy based on historical analysis, see Sylvia Walby, *Patriarchy at Work* (Minneapolis: University of Minnesota Press, 1986).

11 *The Practice of Everyday Life* (Berkeley: University of California Press, 1984), xvii.

12 Jacob Burckhardt, *The Civilization of the Renaissance in Italy* (London: Phaidon Press, 1960), 240–3, Sandra M. Gilbert and Susan Gubar, eds., *The Norton Anthology of Literature by Women: The Tradition in English* (New York: W.W. Norton, 1985), 14–15, and Joan Kelly, "Did Women Have a Renaissance?", in *Women, History and Theory: The Essays of Joan Kelly* (Chicago: University of Chicago Press, 1984), 19.

13 "Moderation and its Discontents: Recent Work on Renaissance Women," *Feminist Studies* 20.2 (1994), 352.

14 *Cheap Print and Popular Piety* (1991; rpt. Cambridge: Cambridge University Press, 1994), 332.

15 Baldassare Castiglione, *The Book of the Courtier*, trans. Thomas Hoby (1561; rpt. New York: AMS Press, 1967), 368, 374.

16 On the importance of conduct manuals during this period, see Ann Rosalind Jones, "Nets and Bridles: Early Modern Conduct Books and Sixteenth Century Women's Lyrics," in *The Ideology of Conduct: Essays on Literature and the History of Sexuality*, eds. Nancy Armstrong and Leonard Tennenhouse (London: Methuen, 1987), 39–72, Ruth Kelso, "The Doctrine of the English Gentleman in the Sixteenth Century," *University of Illinois Studies in Language and Literature* 14 (1929), 1–288, and *Doctrine for the Lady of the Renaissance* (Urbana: University of Illinois Press, 1956), John E. Mason, *Gentlefolk in the Making: Studies in the History of English Courtesy Literature and Related Topics from 1531 to 1774* (Philadelphia: University of Pennsylvania Press, 1935), and Frank Whigham, *Ambition and Privilege: The Social Tropes of Elizabethan Courtesy Literature* (Berkeley: University of California Press, 1984).

17 *Of Domestical Duties* (London, 1622), sig. P3v.

18 "Historical Differences: Misogyny and *Othello*," in *The Matter of Difference: Materialist Criticism of Shakespeare*, ed. Valerie Wayne (Ithaca, New York: Cornell University Press, 1991), 165.

19 *The Stage and Social Struggle in Early Modern England* (New York: Routledge, 1994), 90. On the theatre as a site for managing and articulating social tensions, see also Stephen Greenblatt, *Shakespearean Negotiations* (Berkeley: University of California Press, 1988), David Scott Kastan and Peter Stallybrass, eds., *Staging the Renaissance: Reinterpretations of Elizabethan and Jacobean Drama* (New York: Routledge, 1991), and Louis Montrose, "The Purpose of Playing: Reflections on a Shakespearean Anthropology," *Helios* 7.2 (1980), 51–74.

20 *The Mirror of Modesty*, Sig C3r.

21 Ed. Standish Henning (London: Edward Arnold, 1965), 1.2.43–6, 49–52.

22 *Education and Society in Tudor England* (Cambridge: Cambridge University Press, 1966), 74.

23 These images, cited by Susan Groag Bell, are in the following manuscripts: *Missal*, Bayerische Staatsbibliothek, Munich MS clm. 14.045, fol. 41v; *Book of Hours*, Walters Art Gallery, Baltimore, MS 10.290, fol. 69; *Book of Hours*, Bibliothèque Royale Albert 1er, Brussels, MS IV 315, fol. 105v ("Medieval Women Book Owners: Arbiters of Lay Piety and Ambassadors of Culture," in *Women and Power in the Middle Ages*, eds. Mary Erler and Maryanne Kowaleski [Athens, Georgia: University of Georgia Press, 1988], 149–87).

24 Legends of the Virgin Mary had long described her as learned. The eighth- or ninth-century Latin gospel of Pseudo-Matthew recounts that she was educated between the ages of three and fourteen with other girls within the enclosure of the Temple: "in the praises and vigils of God none were found before her, no one more learned in the wisdom of the law of God, more lowly in humility, more elegant in singing, more perfect in all virtue." The widely popular *Golden Legend* by Jacobus de Voragine testified to Mary's precocious aptitude for reading. Her education was the subject of paintings by Pinturicchio in Italy and by Murillo and Roëlas in Spain and of a marble sculpture at Ste-Colombe-les-Vienne in France. A thirteenth-century window at Chartres depicts the Virgin attending school (Dorothy Gardiner, *English Girlhood at School: A Study of Women's Education through Twelve Centuries* [London: Oxford University Press, 1929], 10–11).

25 Myra D. Orth, "'Madame Sainte Anne': The Holy Kinship, the Royal Trinity, and Louise of Savoy," in *Interpreting Cultural Symbols: Saint Anne in Late Medieval Society*, eds. Pamela Sheingorn and Kathleen Ashley (Athens, Georgia: University of Georgia Press, 1990), 204.

26 Cited in Gardiner, *English Girlhood at School*, 74.

27 *A Myrour to Lewde Men and Wymmen*, ed. Venetia Nelson (Heidelberg: Carl Winter, 1981), 145–6.

28 *Education and Society in Medieval and Renaissance England* (London: Hambledon, 1989), 1.

29 Cited in Bell, "Medieval Women Book Owners," 163.

30 Shannon McSheffrey, *Gender and Heresy: Women and Men in Lollard Communities, 1420–1530* (Philadelphia: University of Pennsylvania Press, 1995), 58.

31 The case was presented before Bishop Tunstall in 1523 (Kenneth Charlton, "Mothers as Educative Agents in Pre-Industrial England," *History of Education* 23.2 [1994], 143).

32 Cited in Bell, "Medieval Women Book Owners," 177.

33 *Works*, v. 3 (Cambridge: Cambridge University Press, 1844), 420.

34 Urban Wyss, *Libellus valde doctus . . . multa et varia scribendum litterarum genera complectens* (Zurich, 1549).

35 Cited in Gardiner, *English Girlhood at School*, 162.

36 Pamela Sheingorn, "Appropriating the Holy Kinship: Gender and Family History," in *Interpreting Cultural Symbols: Saint Anne in Late Medieval Society*, eds. Pamela Sheingorn and Kathleen Ashley (Athens, Georgia: University of Georgia Press, 1990), 189–90.

37 *The Statutes of the Realm*, v. 2, 7 Henry IV, c. 17 (London, 1816), 158.

38 *The Statutes of the Realm*, v. 3, 35 Henry VIII, c. i (London, 1817), 896.

39 Thomas Smith provides an account of the procedure in *De Republica Anglorum: A Discourse on the Commonwealth of England* (1583; rpt. Cambridge: Cambridge University Press, 1906), 102–3.

40 J. F. Stephen, *A History of the Criminal Law of England* (London: Macmillan, 1883), 461.

41 Joyce Youings, *Sixteenth-Century England* (1984; rpt. New York: Penguin Books, 1991), 112. In Shakespeare's *2 Henry VI*, Jack Cade expresses outrage over the class bias implicit in offering benefit of clergy when he addresses Lord Say: "Thou hast appointed justices of peace to call poor men before them about matters they were not able to answer. Moreover, thou hast put them in prison, and, because they could not read, thou hast hanged them" (4.7.34–8). The practice resulted in obvious inequities as in the fifteenth-century case of Thomas Gurney who is cited in the *Paston Letters* (1464) as having tried to kill "my lord of Norwich's cousin." Convicted along with a servant who served as an accomplice, Gurney was spared as "a clerk convict" while the servant, who could not read, was hanged (W. J. Frank Davies, *Teaching Reading in Early England* [1973; rpt. New York: Barnes & Noble, 1974], 163).

42 Stephen, *A History of the Criminal Law of England*, 462, and Cynthia B. Herrup, *The Common Peace: Participation and the Criminal Law in Seventeenth-Century England* (Cambridge: Cambridge University Press, 1987). Herrup notes that "Women received the right to plead benefit of clergy in small felonies by 21 James I, c. 6, because, the law stated, 'so many women do suffer death for small causes' " (143).

43 Eileen Power, *Medieval English Nunneries c. 1275–1535* (Cambridge: Cambridge University Press, 1922), 264.

44 Gardiner, *English Girlhood at School*, 138.

45 Power, *Medieval English Nunneries*, 263.

46 After its suppression, Bedford Abbey passed into the hands of the mayor and burgesses of the neighboring town; at Sherborne residents raised funds themselves to buy the former monastic school; schools in Bruton, Reading, Chichester, and St. Albans were also reestablished after a brief interval (Michael Van Cleave Alexander, *The Growth of Education 1348–1648: A*

Social and Cultural History [University Park: Pennsylvania State University Press, 1990], 22).

47 Simon, *Education and Society in Tudor England*, 170.

48 J. J. Scarisbrick, *The Reformation and the English People* (Oxford: Basil Blackwell, 1984), 164.

49 *The Lay Folks Mass Book*, ed. Thomas Frederick Simmons (1879; rpt. London: Oxford University Press, 1968), 216.

50 Toulmin Smith, *English Gilds: The Original Ordinances of More Than One Hundred Early English Gilds*, ed. Lucy Toulmin Smith (1870; rpt. London: Oxford University Press, 1963), xxx. Lucy Toulmin Smith edited this book, published after her father's death, and wrote its introduction.

51 Michael G. Sargent, "The Transmission by the English Carthusians of some Late Medieval Spiritual Writings," *Journal of Ecclesiastical History* 27.3 (1976), 233–4.

52 Foster Watson, *Luis Vives: El Gran Valenciano (1492–1540)* (Oxford University Press, 1922), 74–5.

53 Julia Boffey, "Women Authors and Women's Literacy in Fourteenth- and Fifteenth-Century England," in *Women and Literature in Britain, 1150–1500* (Cambridge: Cambridge University Press, 1993), 161.

54 *The Book of Margery Kempe*, ed. and trans. B. A. Windeatt (New York: Penguin Books, 1985), 20.

55 See the introduction by Edmund Colledge and James Walsh to Julian of Norwich, *Showings* (New York: Paulist Press, 1978), 21. Other works that passed through similar channels were autobiographies of women, including the *Lives* of Bridget of Sweden, Elizabeth of Spalbek, Christina Mirabilis, Marie d'Oignies, and Catherine of Siena, and numerous devotional manuals. *Disce Mori*, a catechetical treatise, addresses "my best-beloved Suster dame Alice" who was most likely a nun of Sion. The beautiful Ellesmere psalter was commissioned by a woman for use by a female community; an inscription recording the transaction ("domina isabella de vernun dedit istud psalterium conventum de hampul") accompanied a miniature of Lady Isabella, the patron, offering the psalter to Mary and the Christ child (Josephine Koster Tarvers, "'Thys ys my mystrys boke': English Women as Readers and Writers in Late Medieval England," in *The Uses of Manuscripts in Literary Studies: Essays in Memory of Judson Boyce Allen*, eds. Charlotte Cook Morse, Penelope Reed Doob, and Marjorie Curry Woods [Kalamazoo, Michigan: Medieval Institute Publications, 1992], 311, 319).

56 "D'une femme, / Depuys cent ans escript"; Marguerite de Navarre, *Les Dernières poésies de Marguerite de Navarre*, ed. Abel Lefranc (Paris, Armand Colin, 1896), 230. In his article "Le 'Miroir des Simples Ames' et Marguerite de Navarre," Jean Dagens identified Porete as the author of the book mentioned by Marguerite de Navarre in *La Mystique Rhénane* (Paris: Presses Universitaires de France, 1963), 281–9. The translation of lines from this poem is mine.

57 Romana Guarnieri, ed., "Il movimento del Libero Spirito," *Archivio italiano per la storia della pietà* 4 (1965), 503.

58 "O qu'elle estoit ceste femme ententive / A recevoir cest amour qui brulloit / Son cueur et ceulx ausquelz elle parloit!", Marguerite de Navarre, *Les Dernières poésies*, 230.

59 See the editors' introductions to Elizabeth Cary, *The Tragedy of Mariam*, eds. Barry Weller and Margaret Ferguson (Berkeley: University of California Press, 1994), 1–2, and to Julian of Norwich, *Showings*, eds. Colledge and Walsh, 22.

60 Cited in Simon, *Education and Society in Tudor England*, 180.

61 Cited in Gardiner, *English Girlhood at School*, 194.

62 Alexander, *The Growth of Education*, 122.

63 Gardiner, *English Girlhood at School*, 194.

64 Ibid., 194.

65 The example of a school founded by Gilbert of Sempringham shows that maintaining institutional settings for female education was possible in medieval England given the right initiative and strong community support. After studying abroad in the early-twelfth century, Gilbert returned home and began to hold classes for boys and girls of the neighborhood; evidently, girls at the school gained some knowledge of Latin. For the chronicler William of Newburgh, this attempt to "order and instruct women," the children of townsfolk, was remarkable because they belonged to a class not usually sent to nunneries or thought worthy of education. The order of Sempringham founded by Gilbert, an offshoot of the Cistercian order, numbered 700 men and 1500 women at the founder's death. His biography describes the order as a chariot with four wheels, two of men, clerkly and lay, two of women, lettered and unlettered. Only a girl who clearly lacked aptitude for learning was given the option of becoming one of the lay sisters who worked while the others read (Gardiner, *English Girlhood at School*, 67–8).

There are other recorded instances of girls and boys being instructed in the same pre-Reformation institutions. Around 1500, a priest named Sir William Barbour ran a school for some thirty children, among them Elizabeth Garrand, the eight-year-old daughter of a London draper, whom he taught the Pater Noster, Ave, and Credo, "with ferther lernyng" (Gardiner, *English Girlhood at School*, 77 and Eileen Power, *Medieval Women* [Cambridge: Cambridge University Press, 1975], 84). The most thoroughly documented case is that of the "petites écoles" that operated in late-medieval Paris. A 1357 document setting out the responsibilities of the teachers for these schools ("maîtres et maîtresses d'école") stipulates that schoolmistresses must teach only girls. In spite of an apparent segregation of the sexes, however, both boys and girls received instruction in the elements of Latin. A contemporary account of a meeting convened in 1380, with forty-one schoolmasters and twenty-one schoolmistresses in attendance, describes the schoolmistresses as "honorable women keeping school and teaching grammar" (eds. Ghislain Brunel and Elisabeth Lalou, *Sources d'histoire médiévale: IXe–milieu du XIVe siècle* [Paris: Larousse, 1992], 605–6, and J. W. Adamson, "The Extent of Literacy in England," 190). Anecdotal evidence for co-education in this period also comes from literary sources such as the thirteenth-century English translation of the French romance *Floriz and Blauncheflur*, which describes the hero and heroine learning French and Latin togther at school, and Froissart's poem titled "Espinette Amoureuse" (*c*. 1350), in which he remembers female classmates from the school he attended in Valenciennes (Gardiner, *English Girlhood at School*, 38).

66 P. 377. Becon argues that "it is expedient that by public authority schools for women-children be erected and set up in every christian commonweal, and honest, sage, wise, discreet, sober, grave, and learned matrons made rulers and mistresses of the same, and that honest and liberal stipends be appointed for the said school-mistresses, which shall travail in the bringing up of young maids, that by this means they may be occasioned the more gladly and willingly to take pains" (*Works*, v. 3 [Cambridge: Cambridge University Press 1844], 376).

67 Gardiner, *English Girlhood at School*, 195–6. Aubrey gives an idealized description of the Wiltshire convents: "There the young maids were brought up . . . at the nunneries, where they had examples of piety, and humility, and modesty, and obedience to imitate, and to practise. Here they learned needle-work, the art of confectionary, surgery (for anciently there were no apothec-aries or surgeons – the gentlewomen did cure their poor neighbors: their hands are now too fine), physic, writing, drawing, etc." (cited in Power, *Medieval English Nunneries*.

68 Austin (London, 1637), 5.

69 *The Great Didactic of John Amos Comenius*, trans. and ed. M. W. Keatinge (London: Adam and Charles Black, 1910), 67–8.

70 It was necessary to exclude girls specifically from institutions such as St. Olave's School, Southwark (started as an elementary school in 1560); Felsted School, Essex (founded in 1564 by Richard Lord Rich); Harrow (its statutes were drawn up in 1590 and were in effect beginning in 1608); the Queen's School at Canterbury Cathedral (founded 1598–9); Tiverton School, Devon-shire (founded 1599); and a school at Uffington. In the last case, the statutes indicated that girls had been allowed to attend the school in the past. Other schools permitted girls to attend only until they had learned English and in no case beyond the age of nine or ten: Bunbury Grammar School, Cheshire (founded in 1594); three schools in Northamptonshire founded by Nicholas Latham in 1619; Thaxted School, Essex (founded in 1622); and a school in West Chiltington, Sussex founded by William Smyth in 1634 (Norma McMullen, "The Education of English Gentlewomen 1540–1640," *History of Education* 6 [1977], 91).

   Richard Mulcaster says that it was common for girls and boys to receive elementary schooling together (*The Training up of Children* [1581; rpt. Amsterdam: Da Capo Press, 1971], 167–8). There may have been instances of co-education in grammar schools as well. As evidence for this possibility, J. W. Adamson cites two pictorial representations of female grammar school students. The first is the woodcut of a seal adopted by the Oakham and Uppingham grammar schools in Rutland County, founded in 1584, that "depicts seven persons, one, which fills most of the field, being that of the schoolmaster seated at a table on which lies the birch, the customary symbol of the grammar teacher. The other six are very small figures of pupils, each holding an open book; four are boys, two, standing side by side and apart from the rest, are girls." The clothes worn by the girls, suggesting the approximate date of the seal's manufacture, are late Elizabethan or early Jacobean. The second image, also a woodcut, appeared on the verso of the title page of the 1662 and 1665 editions of Edmund Coote's *The English*

Schoolmaster: "A grammar master is seated at a table listening to a child in the foreground who is 'up to say'; eleven other children are seated at some distance from the master, whose costume is contemporary with that of his confrère in the Uppingham seal, that is to say, Elizabethan or early Jacobean. All the children wear a voluminous garment; none wears doublet and hose. All may be girls; alternatively eleven may be 'petties' of one or both sexes. But the child who confronts the master wears a skirt with a long train that sweeps the ground; I find it impossible to suppose she is not a girl" (Adamson, "The Extent of Literacy in England," 191–2).

71 In the Middle Ages, for example, reading was connected with hearing rather than seeing, and composing with dictation rather than with using a pen (M. T. Clanchy, *From Memory to Written Record*, 218).

72 *Cultural History: Between Practices and Representations* (Ithaca, New York: Cornell University Press, 1988), 12. In addition, see Roger Chartier, ed., *Pratiques de la Lecture* (1985; rpt. Paris: Editions Payot et Rivages, 1993). An emphasis on practices is also an important element of the "ideological" model of literacy put forward by Brian Street. Countering Goody's transcultural and transhistorical model, Street argues that researchers must consider that "the particular practices of reading and writing that are taught in any context depend upon such aspects of social structure as stratification (such as where certain social groups may be taught only to read), and the role of educational institutions" (*Literacy in Theory and Practice* [1984; rpt. Cambridge: Cambridge University Press, 1993], 8).

73 *Culture and History, 1350–1600: Essays on English Communities, Identities and Writing* (Detroit: Wayne State University Press, 1992), 185. Michel Foucault draws attention to the place of writing in the Greek "culture of taking care of oneself." "One of the main features of taking care," he points out, "involved taking notes on oneself to be reread, writing treatises and letters to friends to help them, and keeping notebooks in order to reactivate for oneself the truths one needed. Seneca's letters are an example of this self-exercise" ("Technologies of the Self," in *Technologies of the Self: A Seminar with Michel Foucault* [Amherst: University of Massachusetts Press, 1988], 27).

74 *Renaissance Self-Fashioning: From More to Shakespeare* (University of Chicago Press, 1980), 161.

75 "Ambiguity and Interpretation: A Fifteenth-Century Reading of *Troilus and Criseyde*," *Speculum* 54 (1979), 328.

76 *The Spiritual Exercises of Saint Ignatius*, trans. Anthony Mottola (1964; rpt. New York: Doubleday, 1989), 140–1.

77 "Margaret Porete: *The Mirror of Simple Souls*, A Middle English Translation," ed. Marilyn Doiron, *Archivio italiano per la storia della pietà* 5 (1968), 255. Subsequent references to this edition will appear in the text.

78 If the daughter reads the Song of Songs before undertaking this rigorous course of reading, Jerome writes, "she may not discern that a spiritual union is celebrated under carnal words" ("St. Jerome on Female Education," *Pamphlets Pertaining to Education*, v. 3, *Education of Girls: Institutions and Suggestions* [California Department of Public Instruction, 1861–96], 375).

79 *Nicholas Love's Mirror of the Blessed Life of Jesus Christ*, ed. Michael G. Sargent (New York: Garland Publishing, 1992).

80 See Caroline Walker Bynum, *Jesus as Mother: Studies in the Spirituality of the High Middle Ages* (Berkeley: University of California Press, 1982), 106, and *Holy Feast and Holy Fast: The Religious Significance of Food to Medieval Women* (Berkeley: University of California Press, 1987), 119, 200, as well as Ernest W. McDonnell, *The Beguines and Beghards in Medieval Culture* (New Brunswick, New Jersey: Rutgers University Press, 1954), 318.

81 Both monks and nuns were supposed to be at an equal remove from the world, but in practice the church limited the influence of female mystics and thinkers within the church by placing greater restrictions on nuns; "the history of the enclosure movement is in effect the history of an effort to add a fourth vow of claustration to the three cardinal vows of the nun" (Power, *Medieval English Nunneries*, 342).

82 For accounts of Porete's prosecution, see Robert Lerner, *The Heresy of the Free Spirit in the Middle Ages* (Berkeley: University of California Press, 1972), 68–78, Romana Guarnieri, "Il movimento del Libero Spirito," *Archivio italiano per la storia della pietà* 4 (1965), 388–9, 408–12, Henry Charles Lea, *A History of the Inquisition of the Middle Ages* (1955; rpt. New York: Russell and Russell, 1958), 574–9, and Paul Fredericq, *Corpus documentorum haereticae pravitatis neerlandicae* (Ghent: J. Vuylesteke, 1889), 155–60.

83 Cited in Anne Clark Bartlett, *Male Authors, Female Readers: Representation and Subjectivity in Middle English Devotional Literature* (Ithaca, New York: Cornell University Press, 1995), 144.

84 *Nicholas Love's Mirror of the Blessed Life of Jesus Christ*, ed. Michael Sargent, 9–10.

85 "The Life of Saint Bridget," in *The Myroure of oure Ladye*, ed. John Henry Blunt (London: N. Truübner, 1873), lv.

86 *A Myrour to Lewde Men and Wymmen*, ed. Nelson, 71.

87 *The Myroure of oure Ladye*, 65, 67, 68.

88 Out of 1,850 items sold by John Dorne in his Oxford bookshop in 1520, 150 volumes were by Erasmus, "a clear indication of the overwhelming position occupied by Erasmus in the minds of the educated of the time" (H. S. Bennett, *English Books and Readers: 1475 to 1557*, 22).

89 *De Copia*, in *Literary and Educational Writings 2: De Copia / De Ratione Studii*, ed. Craig R. Thompson, *Works* (University of Toronto Press, 1978), vol. 24, 608.

90 Ibid., 619–20.

91 Cited in Edmund Colledge and Romana Guarnieri, "The Glosses by 'M. N.' and Richard Methley to *The Mirror of Simple Souls*," *Archivio Italiano per la Storia della Pietà* 5 (1968), 379.

92 *The Faerie Queene*, ed. Thomas P. Roche (1590 [I–III] and 1596 [IV–VI]; rpt. New York: Penguin, 1987), 15. Subsequent references to this edition will appear in the text.

93 *De Copia*, 681.

94 *Instruction of a Christian Woman* (London, 1529), sigs. C3v–C4r.

95 Ibid., sig. F2r.

96 Ibid., sig. L3v.

97 *The English Gentlewoman*, 106.

98 *Instruction of a Christian Woman*, sig. L3v.

99 *Sadoleto on Education: A Translation of The De Pueris Recte Instituendis*,

trans. and eds. E. T. Campagnac, and K. Forbes (London: Oxford University Press, 1916), 15–16.

100 *A Bride-Bush, or A Wedding Sermon* (London, 1617), 43.

101 *Antony and Cleopatra* (2.2.65–8); all quotations of Shakespeare in this chapter refer to *The Norton Shakespeare*, ed. Stephen Greenblatt (New York: W.W. Norton, 1997). However, I have retained the English spellings of names from the quarto edition of *Love's Labour's Lost* ("Berowne" and "Katherine") which the Norton edition provides in French spelling ("Biron" and "Catherine").

102 *A View of the Present State of Ireland*, ed. W. L. Renwick (London: The Scholartis Press, 1934), 137–8.

103 *Renaissance Self-Fashioning*, 170, 173.

104 *English Society 1580–1680* (New Brunswick, New Jersey: Rutgers University Press, 1982), 191.

105 *The Training up of Children* (1581; facsimile rpt. Amsterdam: Da Capo Press, 1971), Dedicatory Epistle.

106 As Rosemary O'Day indicates, "education, which had been seen by many in the mid-sixteenth century as an agent of social mobility and of ease of communication, was now seen as the buttress of monopoly in many areas of human activity . . . It was important, therefore, for an aspiring élite to gain control of education and restrict access to it from among other social groups" (*Education and Society 1500–1800: The Social Foundations of Education in Early Modern Britain* [London: Longman, 1982], 142).

107 The case, which occurred in 1639, is cited in Gardiner, *English Girlhood at School*, 205.

108 *A View of the Present State of Ireland*, 142.

109 Outside the context of his official duties as a licenser responsible for "reforming" or correcting texts, Edmund Tilney, Master of the Revels under Elizabeth, uses the term "reformation" to argue for the importance of husbands achieving mastery over their wives. In a treatise on marriage published in 1568, Tilney writes that "though the civill lawe giveth man the superioritie over his wyfe, that is not to offende, or despise hir, but in misdoing, lovingly to *reforme* hir," sig. B8r (*A Brief and Pleasant Discourse of Duties in Mariage, Called the Flower of Friendship* [1568]). In *The Civil Conversation*, the first three books of which were translated by George Pettie in 1581, Stephano Guazzo advises the prospective husband to marry a very young wife, even if her parents think she is too young, so that he may have a hand in training her: "for she being yet but young, with the helpe of her good nature, he may easily, like a tender twig, make her straight if she begin to growe crooked: and with grave admonitions *refourme* her wanton mynde" (v.2, 18). Along with women and boys, religious non-conformists and rebels were said to be in need of "reformation." As he was preparing to tour the monasteries in his official capacity as visitor in 1535, Layton wrote to Cromwell about affairs in the northern counties: "There can be no better way to beat the King's authority into the heads of the rude people of the north than to show them that the King intends *reformation* and correction of religion" (cited in Madeline Hope Dodds and Ruth Dodds, *The Pilgrimage of Grace 1536–1537 and the Exeter Conspiracy 1538* [Cambridge: Cambridge

University Press, 1915], v. 71). In this instance, the sectarian connotation of the word ("reformed" as opposed to "Roman Catholic") blends with its disciplinary meaning ("reformation" as the violence inflicted on recalcitrant subjects). The term also applied to the control of expression and behavior in public places. A 1551 government edict requiring all acting troupes to be licensed called for "the *reformacion* of Vagabondes, tellers of newes, sowers of seditious rumours, players, and printers without license & divers other disordred persons." In 1592, the Aldermen wrote to the Archbishop of Canterbury to inform him of the disorders and corruptions caused by playing and to ask for his help since Tilney had been given the "authority to *reform*, exercise or suppress all manner of players, plays and playhouses." In 1601, the Privy Council blamed the city for its failure to enforce its orders for the "*reformation* of the said disorders" issued a year and a half earlier (V. C. Gildersleeve, *Government Regulation of the Elizabethan Drama* [New York: Columbia University Press, 1908], 9, 56).

110 *The Institution of a Young Noble Man*, facsimile (New York: Scholars' Facsimiles and Reprints, 1948), 49–50.

111 *Renaissance Self-Fashioning*, 170.

112 Thomas Heywood, *2 Edward IV* (1599), Q 1613, sig. T4v.

113 Richard Brome, *The Court Beggar* (1640), in *Five New Playes* (1653), sig. S3r.

114 Nathan Field, *Amends for Ladies* (1611), Q 1618, sig. D1v.

115 Anonymous, *King Leir* (1594), Q 1605, sig. E1r.

116 Henry Killigrew, *The Conspiracy* (1635), Q 1638, sig. L3r.

117 Richard Brome, *The Queen and Concubine* (1635), in *Five New Playes* (1659), sig. C3v.

118 John Fletcher and Nathan Field, *Four Plays, or Moral Representations, in One* (1612), F 1647, sig. 8E2v.

119 Walter Mountfort, *The Launching of the Mary* (1633), F 340b, lines 2129–30.

120 Thomas Heywood, *The Fair Maid of the Exchange* (1602), Q 1607, sig. G4v.

121 *An Apology for Actors* (London, 1612), sig. C3r.

122 *The Schoole of Abuse* (1579; rpt. in Arthur F. Kinney, ed., *Markets of Bawdrie: The Dramatic Criticism of Stephen Gosson* [Salzburg: Institüt für Englische Sprache und Literatur, 1974]), 89.

123 *An Apology for Actors*, sigs. G1v–G2v.

124 *The School of Abuse*, 98.

125 Ibid., 87, 92.

126 *The Academy of Love*, 99.

127 *The English Gentleman*, 195.

128 *Distinction: A Social Critique of the Judgement of Taste* (Cambridge: Cambridge University Press, 1984).

129 (4.3.326). Carol Cook observes a similar sex-based differentiation between readers and the objects of reading in *Much Ado About Nothing*: "To read others in this play is always an act of aggression; to be read is to be emasculated, to be a woman" ("'The Sign and Semblance of Her Honor': Reading Gender Difference in *Much Ado About Nothing*," *PMLA* 101 [1986], 187).

130 "Transfer of Title in Love's Labour's Lost: Language, Individualism,

Gender," in *Shakespeare Left and Right*, ed. Ivo Kamps (New York: Routledge, 1991), 218.

131 Richard Levin discerns a movement at the end of the sixteenth century toward the inclusion of women readers in quarto prefaces: "An early formula, 'To the Gentlemen Readers,' used in Marlowe's *Tamburlaine* (1590) and the anonymous *The Troublesome Reign of King John* (1591), soon disappears to be replaced by the neutral 'To the Readers' or by other ungendered headings such as 'To the Courteous Reader,' 'To the Judicious Reader,' 'To the Reader Extraordinary,' 'To the Comic Play-readers,' 'To the General Reader,' 'To the great Variety of Readers,' etc., although sometimes the text itself is directed only at men . . . There is an even more impressive piece of evidence in Humphrey Moseley's epistle, 'The Stationer to the Readers,' prefixed to the Beaumont and Fletcher First Folio, where he explains that he did not include plays that had already been published because 'it would have rendred the Booke so Voluminous, that *Ladies* and *Gentlewomen* would have found it scarce manageable, who in Workes of this nature must first be remembered.' And several of the commendatory verses composed for this Folio envision women reading it: Robert Stapylton says it will present the plays 'Both to the People, and the *Lords* that sway / That *Herd*, and Ladies whom those Lords obey'" ("Women in the Renaissance Theatre Audience," *Shakespeare Quarterly* 40 [1989], 173).

A compelling, if exceptional, case of a contemporary woman reader of Shakespeare is that of Frances Wolfreston (1607–1676/77). The remainder of her extraordinary library, which numbered approximately 960 volumes when it was put on the auction block in the nineteenth century, included *Hamlet, Othello, King Lear, Richard II*, and *Venus and Adonis* (Paul Morgan, "Frances Wolfreston and 'Hor Bouks': A Seventeenth Century Woman Book-Collector," *The Library* 11.3 [1989], 197–219). The size of Wolfreston's library makes her anomalous, but seventeenth-century women clearly represented an important segment of the market for printed plays. Nearly a fifth of the seventy-nine Shakespeare First Folios held by the Folger Shakespeare Library contain either the signatures or names of seventeenth-century women (Elizabeth Hageman and Sara Jayne Steen, "From the Editors," preface to a special issue entitled "Teaching Judith Shakespeare," *Shakespeare Quarterly* 47 [1996], v).

2   ENTER HAMLET READING ON A BOOK

1 The stage direction appears in the Folio edition, sig. 003r.
2 2.2.168, 191–5, 3.1.43–9, 3.1.89–90. References to *Hamlet* are to the Arden edition, ed. Harold Jenkins (London: Methuen, 1982). Citations of other plays by Shakespeare refer to *The Norton Shakespeare*, ed. Stephen Greenblatt (New York: W.W. Norton, 1997). For a discussion of scenes of reading and writing, in a wide range of plays by Shakespeare, see the collection of essays edited by David M. Bergeron, *Reading and Writing in Shakespeare* (Newark: University of Delaware Press, 1996).
3 *The Institution of a Young Noble Man* (London, 1607; facsimile, New York: Scholars' Facsimiles & Reprints, 1948), 76.

4 *Ludus Literarius: Or, the Grammar School* (London, 1612; rpt. Menston, England: The Scolar Press Limited, 1968), 43.

5 *The Complete Essays of Montaigne*, trans. Donald M. Frame (1957; rpt. Stanford: Stanford University Press, 1989), 107.

6 For an account of Guarini's theory and practice of education, see Anthony Grafton and Lisa Jardine, *From Humanism to the Humanities: Education and the Liberal Arts in Fifteenth- and Sixteenth-Century Europe* (Cambridge, Massachusetts: Harvard University Press, 1986).

7 *The Schoolmaster* (London, 1570), 130.

8 *The True Order and Method of Writing and Reading Histories* (London, 1574), sigs. H2v–H3r.

9 *Ludus Literarius*, 196 (emphasis added). On the habit of keeping common-place books, see Peter Beal, "Notions in Garrison: The Seventeenth-Century Commonplace Book," in *New Ways of Looking at Old Texts*, ed. W. Speed Hill (Binghamton, New York: Medieval and Renaissance Texts and Studies in conjunction with the Renaissance English Text Society, 1993), 131–47; Ann Blair, "Humanist Methods in Natural Philosophy: The Commonplace Book," *Journal of the History of Ideas* 53.4 (1992), 541–55; Ruth Mohl, *John Milton and His Commonplace Book* (New York: Federick Ungar, 1969); and Max W. Thomas, "Reading and Writing the Renaissance Commonplace Book: A Question of Authorship?," in *The Construction of Authorship: Textual Appropriations in Law and Literature*, eds. Martha Woodmansee and Peter Jasz (Durham, North Carolina: Duke University Press, 1994), 401–15.

10 As cited in Timothy Hampton, *Writing from History: The Rhetoric of Exemplarity in Renaissance Literature* (Ithaca, New York: Cornell University Press, 1990), 20.

11 *Framing Authority: Sayings, Self, and Society in Sixteenth Century England* (Princeton: University Press, 1993), 8.

12 Hampton, *Writing from History*, 16.

13 *Timber, or Discoveries*, ed. Ralph S. Walker (Syracuse: Syracuse University Press, 1953), 86–7.

14 Paul Grendler, *Schooling in Renaissance Italy: Literacy and Learning, 1300–1600* (1989; rpt. Baltimore: The Johns Hopkins University Press, 1991), 264.

15 *The Institution of a Young Noble Man*, 62.

16 *The Complete Essays*, trans. Donald M. Frame, 124.

17 *Writing from History*, 3.

18 (5.3.36–8, 42–6). According to some versions of the story, Virginius, a Roman centurion, killed his daughter to keep her from being raped; however, a version in which he killed her after the rape also is recounted by George Chapman in *Alphonsus, Emperor of Germany* (1594) and by Ludowicke Lloyd in *The Pilgrimage of Princes* (1573) and *The Consent of Time* (1590) (*Titus Andronicus*, The Arden Edition, ed. J. C. Maxwell [1961; rpt. New York: Routledge, 1991], 119).

19 *Ludus Literarius*, 209.

20 The limits of humanist exemplarity, which Shakespeare indicates in *Titus Andronicus* by showing its lesson taken to an extreme, appear to have been widely recognized by the mid- to late-seventeenth century. Steven Zwicker

demonstrates compellingly that in the years surrounding the Civil War, intellectual habits based on humanist pedagogy became "deformed and refashioned by the pressure of national political debate and conflagration." Citing Milton's response to James' *Eikon Basilike*, Zwicker argues that "contest was crucial to all the experiences of reading at this historical juncture, central to the interpretive act" ("The Politics of Reading *c*. 1649," paper presented at the Folger Shakespeare Library, 21 April 1995).

21 On habits of reading among English women, see Margaret Ferguson, "Response: Attending to Literacy," in *Attending to Women in Early Modern England* (Newark: University of Deleware Press, 1994), 265–79, Caroline Lucas, *Writing for Women: The Example of Woman as Reader in Elizabethan Romance* (Philadelphia: Open University Press, 1989), Elizabeth Robertson, *Early English Devotional Prose and the Female Audience* (Knoxville: The University of Tennessee Press, 1990), and Susan Schibanoff, "Taking the Gold Out of Egypt: The Art of Reading as a Woman," in *Gender and Reading: Essays on Readers, Texts, and Contexts* (Baltimore: The Johns Hopkins University Press, 1986), 83–106.

22 *The Monument of Matrons* sig. B2r.

23 *The English Gentleman* (London, 1630), 28–9.

24 "William Latymer's Cronickille of Anne Bulleyne", ed. Maria Dowling, in *Camden Miscellany* (London: Offices of the Royal Historical Society, 1990), 62–3.

25 In *Drama of the English Renaissance*, v. 2, eds. Russell A. Fraser and Norman Rabkin (New York: Macmillan, 1976), 1.3.14, 16, 18.

26 There is plenty of evidence from this period that women were reading other genres of texts, including romances and plays. However, the content of women's reading does appear to have been more strictly regulated than that of men. In her *Meditations*, for example, Grace Mildmay provides a list of the books to which she says she was restricted: Wolfgang Musculus, *Common Places of Christian Religion*, trans. J. Man (London, 1566), *Commentary or Exposition . . . upon the li. Psalme* (London, 1566), John Foxe, *Acts and Monuments* (London, 1563), *De Imitatione Christi*, and various translations by W. Atkinson (1504), R. Whitford (1531), E. Hake (1567), and T. Rogers (1581) (cited in Randall Martin, "The Autobiography of Grace, Lady Mildmay," *Renaissance and Reformation / Renaissance et Réforme* 18.1 [1994], 78).

27 *The Instruction of a Christian Woman*, sig. B7v.

28 *The Necessary, Fit and Convenient Education of a Young Gentlewoman* (London), sigs. G4v, G6r.

29 *The Instruction of a Christian Woman*, sig. L4r.

30 *The Office and Duty of an Husband*, sig. P3r.

31 Ibid., sig. E1r, *The Education of a Young Gentlewoman*, sigs. B6v, B8r.

32 *The Education of a Young Gentlewoman*, sigs. D4v–D6r.

33 *The Mirror of Modesty* (London), sig. B3r.

34 *The Monument of Matrons*, sig. B2r.

35 As cited in Lucas, *Writing for Women*, 41.

36 *The English Gentlewoman*, 30.

37 Caroline Lucas observes that "Greene creates a series of multiple projections;

when he holds up the mirror of his virtuous heroine for his female readers to look into, they see a 'perfected' image of womanhood which, in its complete self-sacrifice and martyrdom, they themselves are unable to attain. The heroine is conscious of her role as mirror, as exemplum; she watches herself being watched, and moulds herself completely into that object role" (*Writing for Women*, 78).

38 *The English Gentlewoman*, 40.
39 *Timber*, ed. Walker, 87.
40 *Monument of Matrons*, sigs. B7v, B8r.
41 Ibid., sig. B1v.
42 Bridget Lyons points out that two contradictory accounts of the Flora legend were in circulation in the Renaissance. According to the Ovidian version, the nymph Chloris was raped and then married by the west wind Zephyrus; she then became Flora and was given dominion over all the world's flowers. According to a second version of the story, one referred to by Plutarch and elaborated by Boccaccio in his *De Claris mulieribus*, Flora Meretrix was a Roman prostitute whom Hercules won for a night in a wager with the keeper of his temple. To reward her, Hercules promises that Flora will be allowed to marry the first man she meets after leaving the temple. Plutarch and Boccaccio differ as to whether the man was young or old, but both describe him as rich. After his death, Flora inherited his fortune, and she, in turn, bequeathed it to the Roman people to sponsor public games on the occasion of her birthday. To hide the fact that a prostitute had contributed the funds, the Roman Senate invented the myth of Flora, the flower goddess. In Renaissance art, Flora is represented as a nature goddess, an urban courtesan, and, in some cases, as an ambiguous combination of the two ("The Iconography of Ophelia," *ELH* 44.1 [1977]: 60–74).
43 Ibid., 61.
44 David Leverenz, "The Woman in Hamlet: An Interpersonal View," in *Representing Shakespeare: New Psychoanalytic Essays*, eds. Murray M. Schwartz and Coppélia Kahn (Baltimore: The Johns Hopkins University Press, 1980), 110–28.
45 *Actes de la recherche en sciences sociales* 84 (1990), 2–31.
46 "Gender and Symbolic Violence: Female Oppression in the Light of Pierre Bourdieu's Theory of Social Practice," in *Bourdieu: Critical Perspectives*, eds. Craig Calhoun, Edward LiPuma, and Moishe Postone (Chicago: University of Chicago Press, 1993), 171.
47 *Essays*, trans. John Florio (rpt. New York: Dutton, 1980), v. 1, 10.
48 *Hamlet*, the Arden edition, ed. Harold Jenkins, 489.
49 *Institutio*, col. 564, as cited in Crane, *Framing Authority*, 74.
50 *Timber*, ed. Walker, 87.
51 *Renaissance Self-Fashioning: From More to Shakespeare* (Chicago: University of Chicago Press, 1980), 85.
52 *Love's Labour's Lost*, 5.2.569–70, 74.
53 *Suffocating Mothers: Fantasies of Maternal Origin in Shakespeare's Plays, Hamlet to the Tempest* (New York: Routledge, 1992), 13.
54 "'His semblable is his mirror:' *Hamlet* and the Imitation of Revenge," in *Critical Essays on Shakespeare's Hamlet* (New York: G. K. Hall & Co., 1995), 206.

55 David Scott Kastan and I each came to this observation independently
    (Kastan, "'His semblable is his mirror'," 198–209, and Sanders, "Enter
    Hamlet Reading on a Book: Gender and Reading in Early Modern England,"
    Studies in Medieval and Renaissance History 15 [1995], 57–92).
56 In *Critical Theory Since Plato*, ed. Hazard Adams (San Diego: Harcourt
    Brace Jovanovich, 1971), 166.
57 *The Aeneid*, trans. Robert Fitzgerald (New York: Random House, 1981), 109.
58 "*Hamlet*: Letters and Spirits," in *Shakespeare and the Question of Theory*, eds.
    Patricia Parker and Geoffrey Hartman (New York: Methuen, 1985), 295.
59 This is an observation that Janet Adelman makes in *Suffocating Mothers*:
    "Hamlet had promised the ghost to remember him in effect by becoming him,
    letting his father's commandment live all alone within his brain; but the
    intensity of Hamlet's need to idealize in the face of his mother's failure makes
    his father inaccessible to him as a model, hence disrupts the identification
    from which he could accomplish his vengeance" (13).
60 *Holinshed's Chronicles* (1587; rpt. New York: AMS Press, 1976), 197.
61 *Essais*, ed. Maurice Rat (Paris: Garnier Frères, 1962), v. 2, 303.
62 *The Complete Woman* (London, 1639), sigs. E3v, E4r–E4v.
63 *Shakespearean Tragedy: Lectures on Hamlet, Othello, King Lear and Macbeth*.
    (London: Macmillan, 1956), 117.
64 *The Practice of Everyday Life* (Berkeley: University of California Press, 1984),
    48.

3 SHE READS AND SMILES

1 William Rowley, *The Birth of Merlin* (1608), sig. B2v.
2 William Davenant, *Albovine, King of the Lombards* (1628), sig. F2v.
3 John Fletcher, *Demetrius and Enanthe* (1619) (The Malone Society Reprints
   1950–51 [Oxford: Oxford University Press, 1963], lines 2596–8).
4 John Webster, *The White Devil* (1612), sig. L2v.
5 Thomas Dekker, *Sir Thomas Wyatt* (1604), sig. A4r.
6 Anthony Munday, *The Death of Robert, Earl of Huntingdon* (1598), sig. D4r.
7 John Marston, *The Wonder of Women, or Sophonisba* (1605), sig. D3r.
8 William Davenant, *The Fair Favourite* (1638), sig. 4N3v.
9 Nathaniel Richards, *Messalina, The Roman Empress* (1635), sig. C1r.
10 William Rider, *The Twins* (1635), sig. F2v.
11 Henry Chettle, *Hoffman, or A Revenge for a Father* (1602), sig. H1v.
12 Thomas Drue, *The Life of the Duchess of Suffolk* (1624), sig. A3r.
13 Cited in Alice Luce, *The Countess of Pembroke's Antonie* (Weimar: Verlag
    von Emil Felber, 1987), 8.
14 *Delia and Rosamond Augmented. Cleopatra*. London, (1594), sig. H6r.
15 Following Philip Sidney, who paid tribute to his sister as his first and primary
    reader in the title of his romance fiction, Abraham Fraunce published four
    similarly titled works: *The Countess of Pembrokes Emmanuel* (1591), *The
    Countess of Pembrokes Ivychurch* (1591), *The Second Part of the Countess of
    Pembrokes Ivychurch* (1591), and *The Third Part of the Countess of Pembrokes
    Ivychurch* (1592). Numerous other writers contributed to Sidney's renown as a
    reader by appealing for her approval in laudatory dedications published with

their works: Gervase Babington, Barnabe Barnes, Nathaniel Baxter, Nicholas Breton, Samuel Daniel, John Davies of Hereford, Abraham Fraunce, Thomas Howell, Aemilia Lanyer, Henry Lok, Thomas Moffett, Thomas Morley, Robert Newton, Edmund Spenser, John Taylor, and Thomas Watson (Mary Ellen Lamb, *Gender and Authorship in the Sidney Circle* [Madison: University of Wisconsin Press, 1990], 29).

16 *The Countess of Pembroke's Arcadia* (London), sig. ¶4r, ¶4v.

17 Cited in Wendy Wall, *The Imprint of Gender: Authorship and Publication in the English Renaissance* (Ithaca: Cornell University Press, 1993), 337.

18 See the collection of essays edited by Margaret P. Hannay, *Silent But for the Word: Tudor Women as Patrons, Translators, and Writers of Religious Works* (Kent, Ohio: Kent State University Press, 1985).

19 *The English Gentlewoman* (London, 1631), 40.

20 *Certain Tragical Discourses of Brandello* (rpt. London: David Nutt, 1898), v. 1, 4.

21 Lamb observes that in Juan Luis Vives' *Instruction of a Christian Woman*, Baldassare Castiglione's *The Courtier*, and Thomas Salter's *Mirror of Modesty*, female virtue is defined by stories in which women prefer death, usually by suicide, to sexual dishonor. In Vives' estimate, the women he mentions represent only a small portion of those "infinite in number, that had leaver be killed, headed, strangled, drowned, or have their throtes cut, then loose [sic] their chastity" (cited by Lamb, *Gender and Authorship in the Sidney Circle*, 120).

22 Cited by Margaret P. Hannay, *Philip's Phoenix: Mary Sidney, Countess of Pembroke* (New York: Oxford University Press, 1990), 25. This chapter is indebted throughout to Hannay's fine biography.

23 *Nobilis, or A View of the Life and Death of a Sidney and Lessus Lugubris*, trans. Virgil B. Heltzel and Hoyt H. Hudson (San Marino, California: The Huntington Library, 1949), 67.

24 *Philip's Phoenix*, 211.

25 "I do call to mind a pretty secret," Carleton wrote, "that the lady of Pembroke hath written to her son Philip and charged him of all her blessings to employ his own credit and his friends and all he can do for Raleigh's pardon; and though she does little good, yet she is to be commended for doing her best in showing *veteris vestigia flammae*." As Hannay points out, the Latin tag is a quotation of words spoken by Dido about Aeneas: "[I recognize] the traces of my old passion" (*Philip's Phoenix*, 123). Chamberlain and Carleton also gossip about Sidney's flirtation, following the death of her husband, with Sir Matthew Lister (Margaret P. Hannay, "'O Daughter Heare': Reconstructing the Lives of Aristocratic English Women," in *Attending to Women in Early Modern England*, eds. Betty S. Travitsky and Adele F. Seeff [Newark: The University of Delaware Press, 1994], 45).

26 The letter accompanied a transcription of three psalms translated by Sidney, Harrington says that he included some meditations of his own to fill up the empty paper: these piece "both of meaner matter, and lighter manner . . . maie serve to waite as a wanton page is admitted to beare a torche to a chaste matrone" (cited by Hannay, *Philip's Phoenix*, 107). Lamb points out that Nicholas Breton and, to a more extreme degree, John Aubrey, charge Mary

Sidney with sexual misconduct. The female speaker of Breton's *The Countess of Penbrooke's Passion* deplores her previous sins. As Lamb suggests, Breton's representation of his "countess's chaste repentance sexualizes her past by implying, somewhat incautiously, her previous improprieties." In his *Brief Lives*, John Aubrey engages in prurient speculation about Mary Sidney's sexual propensities which, he says, included an incestuous relation with her brother (Lamb, *Gender and Authorship in the Sidney Circle*, 31, 52). These charges, however, as Margaret Hannay reminds us, surfaced only sixty years after Sidney's death in the context of Royalist satire; the attacks were meant to sully Philip Herbert, Sidney's son, who had been perceived as a less than fully committed supporter of the king (" 'O Daughter Heare'," 45).

27 *Two Tragedies: Hippolyte and Marc Antoine*, eds. Christine M. Hill and Mary G. Morrison (London: The Athlone Press, 1975), 2.281–2. Subsequent references to this edition will appear in the text. The modern translation of passages that appears in brackets here and below is mine.

28 The play was Etienne Jodelle's *Didon se sacrifiant*. Garnier transfers another of Dido's speeches to Cléopâtre in a scene in which she implores Venus for help and reminds her that Antoine is a blood descendant of Aeneas, her son. In a nearly exact paraphrase, Cléopâtre rehearses Dido's proud last words:

> J'ay vescu jusqu'ici, j'ay la course empennee
> De mes ans accomply selon la destinee:
> J'ai flory, j'ai regné, j'ay la vengence pris
> De mon frere ennemy, qui m'avoit à mepris:
> Heureuse et trop heureuse, helas! si ce rivage
> Seulement n'eust receu le Romain navigage.   (5.1952–7)

> [I have lived this long, run the winged course
> Of my years as destiny willed:
> I flourished, I reigned, I revenged myself
> On the enemy brother who held me in contempt:
> Happy and, alas, all too happy! If only this shore
> Never had welcomed in the Roman fleet.]   (5. 1975–80)

At the end of Book 4 of *The Aeneid*, Virgil transforms the images of fire associated with the destruction of Troy and the queen's passion into the flames of Dido's cremation. After making this speech in Virgil's epic (and in Etienne Jodelle's theatrical adaptation of the story), Dido kills herself on a funeral pyre whose flames shadow Aeneas on his voyage. In Garnier's play, the speech is also followed by images of fire. Mourning Antoine, Cléopâtre weeps and tears her hair; her eyes will be the fires of memorial ceremonies "car d'eux sortit la flamme / Qui t'embrasa le coeur amoureux de ta Dame" [for from these came the flame / That ignited your heart with love for your lady] (5.1980–1). In these lines, the flame that leapt from Cléopâtre's eyes to set fire to Antoine's heart now ignites burning coals inside her, turning her chest to a furnace and evaporating her tears. Cléopâtre performs Dido's enraged self-immolation as a sorrowful burial rite for a loyal lover. The incendiary deathbed prepared by Dido was meant to darken Aeneas' spirits and his name, to publicize his betrayal and strike foreboding in his followers. The fire evoked by Cléopâtre burns in honor of Antoine.

29 *The Aeneid*, trans. Robert Fitzgerald (New York: Random House, 1981), 6.617–621, 629.

30 Maurice Gras suggests that Garnier transformed Cléopâtre from a monster to a wife and mother so that she would be better suited to lament Antoine's passing: "Elle ne correspond plus du tout au monstre qu'en a fait Plutarque et elle ne peut pas lui ressembler si la tragédie doit se terminer sur la mort d'Antoine. Il faut que quelqu'un se lamente et ait des raisons de se lamenter sur cette mort, et Cléopâtre est tout indiquée pour ce rôle. Elle est donc devenue dans *Marc Antoine* une amante fidèle et éplorée et une mère toute dévouée à ses enfants" (*Robert Garnier: Son art et sa méthode* [Geneva: Libraire Droz, 1965], 30).

31 Cassius Dio Cocceianus, *Dio's Annals of Rome*, trans. Herbert Baldwin Foster, v. 3 (Troy, New York: Pafraets Book Company, 1905–6), 323–4. For an account of the use of Cleopatra in Augustan propaganda, see Marilyn L. Williamson, *Infinite Variety: Antony and Cleopatra in Renaissance Drama and Earlier Tradition* (Mystic, Connecticut: Lawrence Verry, Inc., 1974), 17–45.

32 *The Book of the Courtier*, trans. Thomas Hoby (London, 1561; rpt. New York: AMS Press, 1967), 248.

33 *English Gentlewoman*, 29.

34 *Two Tragedies*, 106.

35 *On Copia of Words and Ideas*, eds. and trans. Donald B. King and H. David Rix (Milwaukee: Marquette University Press, 1963), 71.

36 Michel de Montaigne, *Essays*, trans. John Florio (London, 1603), sig. A2r.

37 H. S. Bennett, *English Books and Readers: 1558–1603* (Cambridge: Cambridge University Press, 1965), 104.

38 Suzanne Hull, *Chaste, Silent and Obedient* (San Marino, California The Huntington Library, 1982), 1.

39 Susan Groag Bell, "Medieval Women Book Owners: Arbiters of Lay Piety and Ambassadors of Culture," in *Women and Power in the Middle Ages*, eds. Mary Erler and Maryanne Kowaleski [Athens, Georgia: University of Georgia Press, 1988], 167. Recent work on specific regions of late medieval England confirms, with some caveats because of her emphasis on the nobility, Bell's general hypothesis that book ownership rose among women in the period. Historians have analyzed statistical samplings of wills to argue, as John Friedman does for the north of England, that reading-literacy was higher among women than has been supposed. Out of 942 Yorkshire wills examined by Friedman because they mention books, 74 feature book bequests on the part of women and 13 others stipulate the repair or purchase of a book as part of a legacy (*Northern English Books, Owners, and Makers in the Late Middle Ages* [Syracuse University Press, 1995], 11–12).

40 Josephine Koster Tarvers, " 'Thys ys my mystrys boke': English Women as Readers and Writers in Late Medieval England," in *The Uses of Manuscripts in Literary Studies: Essays in Memory of Judson Boyce Allen*, eds. Charlotte Cook Morse, Penelope Reed Doob, and Marjorie Curry Woods (Kalamazoo, Michigan: Medieval Institute Publications, 1992), 309.

41 Mary Ellen Lamb, "The Cooke Sisters: Attitudes towards Learned Women in the Renaissance," in *Silent But for the Word*, ed. Hannay, 112.

42 Margaret Tyler (1578; rpt. London, 1580), A4v.

43 *The Funeral Sermon of Margaret Countess of Richmond and Derby* (London, 1708), 22.

44 Cited in Jennifer R. Goodman, "'That Wommen Holde in Ful Greet Reverence': Mothers and Daughters Reading Chivalric Romances," in *Women, The Book and the Worldly: Selected Proceedings of the St. Hilda's Conference*, eds. Lesley Smith and Jane H. M. Taylor, 2 (1993), 27.

45 *The Mirror of Princely Deedes and Knighthood.* sig. A4r.

46 Cited by Hannay, *Philip's Phoenix*, 141; Luce, *The Countess of Pembroke's Antonie*, 47.

47 *The Influence of Robert Garnier on Elizabethan Drama* (New Haven: Yale University Press), 98.

48 *Ibid.*, 86.

49 According to Plutarch, Antony went to Syria first when Gabinius Proconsul gave Antonius charge of his horsemen and took him along on a military expedition. There, Antony quashed a rebellion of the Jews led by one Aristobulus and conquered Pelusium at Ptolemy's request. Years later, after defeating Brutus and Cassius in Macedon, Antony returned to Asia. It was then that he met Cleopatra. With a new campaign against the Parthians looming, he summoned her to appear at Cilicia to answer charges of having aided Brutus and Cassius. Though Fulvia was stirring up trouble at the time with Octavius Caesar, Antony was so ravished with love of Cleopatra that he returned to Alexandria with her where they spent their time in gourmandizing and other frivolous pastimes. Then Antony learned that his brother and wife had broken out into open war against Octavius Caesar. In Italy, the triumviri reconciled and Antony married Octavia, though it required a special dispensation of the senate since her husband had not been dead ten months as the law usually required. Antony had consistently bad luck in the company of Octavius Caesar and finally left for Greece with Octavia. Tension erupted between Antony and Octavius Caesar, but Octavia managed to smooth things over. As part of the settlement they reached, Antony received two additional legions to lead against the Parthians. It was then, on his return voyage to Syria, that he began to feel his love for Cleopatra rekindle. He sent for Cleopatra to join him in Syria (Geoffrey Bullough, ed., *Narrative and Dramatic Sources* [New York: Columbia University Press, 1977], v.5, 254–321).

50 *Antonius*, in William Shakespeare, *A New Variorum Edition of Shakespeare: Antony and Cleopatra*, ed. Marvin Spevack (New York: The Modern Language Association of America, 1990), "The Argument," 480. All references to *Antonius* are to the 1592 text reprinted in this edition.

51 "The Style of the Countess of Pembroke's Translation of Philippe de Mornay's *Discours de la vie et de la mort*," in *Silent but for the Word*, ed. Hannay, 132.

52 "Mary Sidney," in *Women Writers of the Renaissance and Reformation*, ed. Katharina M. Wilson (Athens: The University of Georgia Press, 1987), 489.

53 "Mary Sidney's Psalms: Education and Wisdom," in *Silent But for the Word*, ed. Hannay, 179. Fisken also cites moving passages from Psalm 58 and Psalm

139 in which Sidney describes a still-birth and a developing fetus in its mother's womb (177–8).

54 Anne Lake Prescott, "The Pearl of the Valois and Elizabeth I: Marguerite de Navarre's *Miroir* and Tudor England," in *Silent But for the Word*, ed. Hannay, 69–70.

55 As a writer in Catholic France, Garnier was untroubled about depicting Cléopâtre's physical form, her face and breast marked by wounds to signify her grief, in detail. Images of female martyrs suffering bodily torments were still part of the general frame of reference in this country. For an author writing in Protestant England, however, such a move was far more bold. As Frances Dolan suggests in her analysis of confessions and martyrologies, the female body was a vexed subject of representation in English texts. She notes that writers largely evade the corporeal reality of women's deaths in describing the executions of female martyrs or condemned criminals. In *The Book of Martyrs*, one of the most widely read books of this period, John Foxe "suppresses the grisly process of bodily death in deference to a decorum that shapes representations of the executions of wrongfully accused or martyred women, whose virtue is registered by means of their disembodiment" ("'Gentlemen, I Have One Thing More to Say': Women on Scaffolds in England, 1563–1680," *Modern Philology* 92.2 [1994], 162).

56 Lamb, *Gender and Authorship in the Sidney Circle*, 132.

57 The text of the dedicatory verse is cited from the 1594 volume titled *Delia and Rosamond Augmented. Cleopatra* (London, sig. H5r–v). Subsequent references to the text of the play are to the edition in *A New Variorum Edition of Shakespeare: Antony and Cleopatra*, ed. Marvin Spevack (New York: Modern Language Association of America: 1990), 532–79.

58 Daniel's tragedy has been termed "A sequel" (Lamb, *Gender and Authorship in the Sidney Circle*, 132) and as a "companion-piece" to Sidney's *Antonius* (Joan Rees, *Samuel Daniel: A Critical and Biographical Study* [Liverpool: Liverpool University Press, 1964], 50); the same view is taken by Michael Brennan in *Literary Patronage in the English Renaissance: The Pembroke Family* (New York: Routledge, 1988), 79, and by Tina Krontiris, *Oppositional Voices: Women as Writers and Translators of Literature in the English Renaissance* (London: Routledge, 1992), 67.

59 In his narration of her pious death, Phillip Stubbes ascribes the same notion of death as liberation to his wife: "Hee is come, my good Jayler is come to let my soule out of prison. Oh sweete death thou art welcome, welcome sweet death . . . welcome, I say, and thrise welcome, my good Jayler, do thy office quickly, and set my soule at libertie" (*A Crystal Glass for Christian Women* [London, 1592], sig. C4r).

60 Lamb, *Gender and Authorship in the Sidney Circle*, 134

61 *The Tragicomedy of the Virtuous Octavia* (London, 1598), D3v. Subsequent references will be made to this text.

62 *The Complete Woman*, sig. C1r.

63 A list of these redundant phrases reproduces the inflexible and angry tone of Brandon's verse:"vertuous Ladie" (sig. A2r), "vertues flame" (A2r), "vertues shine" (A2r), "vertues plaints" (A2r), "vertues doubled," (A2r), "vertues harmonie" (A2v), "vertues lyne" (A3r), "vertuous wife Octavia" (A4r),

"vertues winges" (A6r), "lampe of vertue" (A6r), "naked vertue" (A6r), "vertue" (A6v), "vertue" (A7v), "princelie vertues" (A7v), "vertuous minde" (A8r), "vertue" (B1v), "vertues paradize" (B3v), "vertuous minde" (B3v), "vertuous Empresse" (B4r), "for vertues sake" (B4r), "vertues scorne" (B5r), "your vertues" (B5r), "innate vertue" (B8v), "vertues love" (B8v), "O vertue" (C1r), "pure vertues liuing flame" (C1r), "O vertue" (C1r), "vertue grieves" (C1r), "O sacred vertue" (C1v), "noble vertues" (C1v), "vertue" (C2r), "vertues sacred flame" (C5v), "vertues foe" (C6r), "vertues measure" (C6r), "vertues little beaten wayes" (C6v), "vertue" (C8r), "vertues sacred name" (C8r), "vertuous wife" (C8r), "vertues lawes" (D1v), "the number of the vertuous" (D2r), "a vertuous act" (D2r), "vertue" (D2r), "vertues love" (D3v), "starveling vertue" (D6v), "vertues praise" (D7r), "sacred vertues" (D7r), "vertuous Queene" (D7v), "vertues monarkes beare" (D7v), "vertue" (D7v), "bright lamp of vertue" (E2v), "vertues" (E2v), "perfect vertue" (E3v), "vertues praise" (E4r), "vertues flight" (E4r), "vertues altar" (E5r), "vertuous minds" (E5v), "vertues flame" (E6v), "vertue" (F1r), "vertue" (F3r), "vertues feaste" (F6r), "vertues height" (F6r), "vertue" (F6v).

64 *The Philosophers Satyrs* (London: 1616), 46–7.

65 The 1592 text of *Antonius* concludes by naming the location at which Sidney completed the translation and the date: "At Ramsburie. 26. of November. 1590," 524.

66 As Margaret Hannay documents in *Philip's Phoenix*, Mary Sidney had many connections with the world of contemporary theatre. Her promotion of Garnier, whose work was part of a theatrical avant-garde on the Continent, had a beneficial impact on English drama. By translating Garnier's tragedy, Sidney encouraged the use of historical drama to comment on contemporary politics, "the use of 'times past' to comment on current affairs" (119). Moreover, there was an important tradition of theatrical patronage in Sidney's family. Her uncles Ambrose Dudley, Earl of Warwick, and Robert Dudley, Earl of Leicester sponsored companies of players before her birth in 1561. There are records indicating visits of travelling players performing for the family. Sir Philip later stood as godfather to the son of Richard Tarleton, an actor in Leicester's company. Mary Sidney's husband continued to sponsor companies of players when he became Lord President of the Council of the Marches of Wales. Sidney herself would have been likely to attend theatrical events sponsored by her family. In the 1590s, the period in which Mary Sidney was most active in writing and patronage, there was a series of performances at Ludlow: the Queen's Men (June 1590 and August 1596), Lord Strange's Men (with whom Shakespeare was associated, in August 1593), Worcester's Men (1595 and 1596), and Essex's Men (1596). At Shrewsbury, another of the regular meeting places for the Council, there was a marked increase in the number of dramatic performances; some ten companies performed, a few repeatedly, including Lord Strange's Men (many of whose members left the company in 1594 to form the Chamberlain's Men) and Pembroke's own company: Pembroke's Men. The will of the actor Simon Jewell shows that Mary Sidney had some degree of responsibility for the players. Jewell's final provision is that "my share of such money as shalbe givenn [sic] by my ladie Pembrooke or by her meanes I will shalbe distributed

and paide towardes my buriall and other charges" (cited by Hannay, 124). In 1603, Mary Sidney's son assumed her patronage responsibilities when he became Earl of Pembroke. This extensive evidence discovered by Hannay effectively debunks Witherspoon's notion of an anti-theatrical conspiracy spearheaded by Mary Sidney, a theory which surprisingly still finds currency among critics (see David Bergeron, "Women as Patrons of English Drama," in *Patronage in the Renaissance*, eds. Guy Fitch Lytle and Stephen Orgel [Princeton: Princeton University Press, 1981], 287).

67 Krontiris, *Oppositional Voices* (London: Routledge, 1992), 69.
68 *Two Tragedies*, 17.
69 Jacqueline de Jomaron, ed. *Le théâtre en France du Moyen Age à nos jours* (Paris: Arman Colin, 1992), 130.
70 (4.1.167, 159), in *Drama of the English Renaissance*, eds. Russell A. Fraser and Norman Rabkin (New York: Macmillan Publishing Co., 1976), v. 1, 198.
71 Frederick S. Boas, "University Plays," in *The Cambridge History of Literature*, eds. A. W. Ward and A. R. Waller (Cambridge: Cambridge University Press, 1919), v. 6, 303.
72 Laurence Michel, *The Tragedy of Philotas* (1949; rpt. Archon Books, 1970), 36.
73 *Complete Works*, ed. and trans. Dana F. Suton (New York: Garland Publishing, 1994), v. 2, 15.
74 Of course, plays might also do the reverse. Thomas Heywood's *A Woman Killed With Kindness* makes the adulteress Anne Frankford into a mouthpiece for the playwright who warns female playgoers against committing marital infidelities. Daniel's 1594 *Cleopatra*, as we have seen, performs a similar function, with Mary Sidney in the role of the woman in the audience who needs to be taught a lesson from the example of an adulteress.
75 "'Antony and Cleopatra' and the Countess of Pembroke's 'Antonius'." *Notes and Queries* 3.3 (1956): 154.
76 Schanzer's article, which expands upon Dover Wilson's observations, lists the parallels I cite with the exception of "I can no more" (4.16.61) which is spoken by Cleopatra in Sidney's play (5.1893).
77 Janet Adelman first elaborated the parallels between Virgil's epic and Shakespeare's tragedy in *The Common Liar*: "In the *Aeneid*, the values which must prevail are supremely temporal and spatial . . . In Egypt, the lovers can claim to be free to make their own, ahistorical, time and place: 'Let Rome in Tiber melt'; 'Eternity was in our lips, and eyes.' Instead of Aeneas' firm *Hic amor, haec patria est*, we have Antony's equally firm 'Here is my space.' We do not accept this new set of values absolutely, but they make at least as great a claim upon us as the Virgilian values. And as the Aeneas whom Antony recalls after Actium is revised, so the whole of *Antony and Cleopatra* may be seen as a revision of the scene on Vulcan's shield, in some sense as a revision of the *Aeneid* itself" (73–74).
78 *Certain Small Works* (London 1607), sig. K7r.
79 *The Countesse of Pembrokes Arcadia* (London), sig. ¶4r.
80 The dedication to Blount in Daniel's 1599 *Poetical Essays* seems intended to pertain to the book as a whole, but it is linked with *The Civil Wars*, the first work listed in the table of contents, by its appearance on the page just before.

81 Daniel dated his reliance on Blount for literary advice to 1596–7 when he claimed to have discussed with him his plans to write Philotas (Pierre Spriet, *Samuel Daniel (1563–1619): Sa vie-son œuvre* [Didier, 1968], 112).

82 *The Poetical Essays*, 2.

83 *A Defence of Rhyme*, Sig. G3r.

84 Spriet, *Samuel Daniel*, 157–8. Daniel's position was made even more precarious by the death in 1605 of George Clifford, the Earl of Cumberland, whose wife had employed him as a tutor to her daughter, Anne Clifford. Daniel's portrait, which appears in the left panel of "The Great Picture" commissioned by Anne Clifford, is discussed in chapter five.

85 *The Civil Wars*, sigs. A3v, P6r.

86 *Certain Small Works*, E3r.

87 That contemporary readers responded to the romantic emphasis of the 1607 play, seeing Antony and Cleopatra as worthy lovers and not as disgraced sinners, is suggested by an inscription that appears in a copy of the text owned by the Folger Shakespeare Library. In the margin next to the scene in which Cleopatra offers sacrifices before Antony's tomb are signatures of a woman's name and a man's name: "Anne Branch" and "Robert Besbeck."

88 See Leslie Thomson, "Antony and Cleopatra, Act 4 Scene 16: 'A Heavy Sight'," *Shakespeare Survey* 41 (1989): 88.

89 John Fletcher and Philip Massinger staged a pro-Cleopatra play titled *The False One* in 1620 (the "false one" named in the title refers to Julius Caesar), Thomas May retaliated with an anti-Cleopatra play acted in 1626. Published only in 1639, with Dio's and Plutarch's references to Cleopatra's treachery duly annotated in the margins, *The Tragedy of Cleopatra* hearkened back to the first version of Daniel's play. May's Cleopatra openly betrays Antony and confesses that she lied in having professed to have loved him earlier.

4   WRITES IN HIS TABLES

1 Christopher Marlowe, *The Massacre at Paris* (1593), sig. C5v.

2 John Marston, *Antonio's Revenge* (1600), sig. B2r.

3 Henry Shirley, *The Martyred Soldier* (1618), sig. E2v.

4 Anon., *The Thracian Wonder* (1599), sig. C2r.

5 Richard Brome, *The Sparagus Garden* (1635), sig. I3v.

6 *The Norton Shakespeare*, ed. Stephen Greenblatt (New York: W. W. Norton, 1997), 4.2.73–4. Citations to all other Shakespeare plays discussed in this chapter, with the exception of *Richard III*, are to this edition.

7 "Historical Differences: Misogyny and *Othello*," in *The Matter of Difference*, ed. Valerie Wayne (Ithaca, New York: Cornell University Press, 1991), 169. Other critics who have commented on the man/writer–woman/paper metaphor include Sarah Eaton, "Defacing the Feminine in Renaissance Tragedy," in *The Matter of Difference*, 185; Harold Love, *Scribal Publication in Seventeenth-Century England* (Oxford: Clarendon Press, 1993), 148–53; and Anne Thompson and John Thompson, *Shakespeare: Meaning and Metaphor* (The Harvester Press, 1987), 177. Susan Gubar traces the endurance of the metaphor in nineteenth- and twentieth-century literature and its revision by women writers such as Isak Dinesen ("'The Blank Page' and Female

Creativity," in *Writing and Sexual Difference*, ed. Elizabeth Abel [Chicago: University of Chicago Press, 1982], 73–93).

8 *The Countess of Pembroke's Arcadia*, 242.

9 *The Conspiracy and Tragedy of Byron*, ed. John Margeson (Manchester University Press, 1988), 1.1.170–1.

10 Harold Love explains that writing paper was "more heavily gelatinized: indeed, much printing paper could not be written on without blurring. Finlay quotes advice from a writer of 1594 that before entering marginalia in a printed book one should first rub the surface with a bag containing resin and sandarach [a resin imported from Africa]" (*Scribal Publication*, 103).

11 *The Introduction to the True Understanding of the Whole Art of Expedition in Teaching to Write*, (London, 1638), sig. B1v.

12 *The Book of the Courtier*, trans. Thomas Hoby (1561; rpt. New York: AMS Press, 1967), 65.

13 For an account of Montaigne's composition of the *Essais* and photographs of the Bordeaux copy he annotated, see George Hoffman, "The Montaigne Monopoly: Revising the *Essais* under the French Privilege System," *PMLA* 108.2 (1993), 308–19.

14 Quoted in Angeline Goreau, ed., *The Whole Duty of a Woman: Female Writers in Seventeenth-Century England* (New York: The Dial Press, 1985), 172.

15 *Essays* (London, 1603; rpt. New York: Dutton, 1980), 15.

16 Richard L. Regosin, *The Matter of My Book: Montaigne's Essais as the Book of the Self* (Berkeley: University of California Press, 1977), 3.

17 Katherine M. Wilson, *Shakespeare's Sugared Sonnets* (New York: Barnes and Noble, 1974), 11.

18 *The Institution of a Gentleman* (London, 1660), 43–4. Francis Bacon proposed a different version of the commonplace: "Reading maketh a Full Man; Conference a Ready Man; And Writing an Exact Man," "Of Studies," in *The Essays or Counsels, Civil and Moral*, ed. Michael Kiernan (Cambridge, Massachusetts: Harvard University Press, 1985), 153.

19 *The Training Up of Children*, 33.

20 *The Dead Term* (London, 1608), sig. C3v.

21 Jacques Du Bosq, *The Secretary of Ladies* (London, 1638), sig. A6r–v.

22 Jennifer E. Monaghan, "Literacy Instruction and Gender in Colonial New England," *American Quarterly* 40.1 (1988), 24.

23 "The Meaning of Literacy in Early Modern England," in *The Written Word: Literacy in Transition*, ed. Gerd Baumann (Oxford: Clarendon Press, 1986), 103.

24 "Literacy Instruction and Gender in Colonial New England," 24.

25 See Desiderius Erasmus, *Erasmus on Handwriting: An Extract from the Dialogue of Desiderius Erasmus, De Recta Latini Graecique Sermonis Pronuntiatione*, trans. A. S. Osley (1528; trans. and rpt. Wormley, England: The Glade Press, 1970), 14–15.

26 *Sermons*, eds. George R. Potter and Evelyn M. Simpson (Berkeley: University of California Press, 1955), v. 10, 196.

27 *The Training Up of Children*, 133.

28 As evidence that boys were expected to personalize their use of the Secretary hand, Harold Love cites a letter of 1622 in which William Bagot apologizes to his father for having shown "a barren invention" in his handwriting. "The trouble," Love suggests, "seems to have been that the younger Bagot was incorporating influences from the italic, and that his father saw this as a regrettable abnegation of the proper independence of an English gentleman" (*Scribal Publication*, 110). Hilary Jenkinson notes that handwriting only began to be included in English school curricula in the late-fifteenth and early-sixteenth centuries ("The Teaching and Practice of Handwriting in England," *History* 11.42 [1926], 130–8). On early modern handwriting, see also Alfred Fairbank and Bruce Dickens, *The Italic Hand in Tudor Cambridge* (London: Bowes and Bowes, 1962) and Jean F. Preston and Laetitia Yeandle, *English Handwriting 1400–1650* (Binghamton, New York: Medieval and Renaissance Texts and Studies, 1992).

29 J. G. Nichols, "Inventories of Henry Fitzroy," *Camden Miscellany* 3 (1855), i–c, 1–55.

30 *Writing Matter: From the Hands of the English Renaissance* (Stanford: Stanford University Press, 1990), 118.

31 *Scribal Publication*, 108.

32 Ibid., 155.

33 The question of how social structures are incorporated as mental structures has been raised with particular force by Michel Foucault and by Pierre Bourdieu. Foucault argues that this process occurs by means of an interplay of technologies of discipline and technologies of the self; on the one hand, individuals are constituted through procedures applied to them as the objects of surveillance and study; on the other hand, individuals constitute themselves through modes of self-monitoring (procedures originating historically in the practice of confession) in which they tell the truth of themselves to themselves and to others. For Bourdieu, it is the habitus – a set of schemes for perceiving, evaluating, and appreciating the world acquired through experience – that organizes one's subjectivity and behavior. In this way, mental structures reproduce social structures and vice versa. Both Foucault and Bourdieu indicate the importance of institutions (judicial, medical, educational, etc.) as sites for the application and dissemination of subjectifying practices (Michel Foucault, *Discipline and Punish: The Birth of the Prison* [New York: Vintage Books, 1979] and Pierre Bourdieu, *Outline of a Theory of Practice* [1977; rpt. Cambridge: Cambridge University Press, 1987]).

   This chapter, while indebted to the work of Foucault and Bourdieu, diverges from the positions summarized above in several ways. First, it emphasizes that practices, including those categorized by Foucault as "disciplinary techniques," can be appropriated for purposes other than those for which they were devised. Foucault differentiates between technologies of discipline and technologies of the self on the basis of whether or not a given practice defines the person as an object on which power is exercised or as a subject endowed with a capacity for self-knowing. I agree with Jean Grimshaw in seeing this distinction as untenable because there are no clear grounds for defining certain practices of self-monitoring (those of mental patients, prisoners, workers, students) *a priori* as undermining autonomy and other practices of self-monitoring (those of elite men in Greek culture) as cultivating autonomy ("Practices of Freedom," in *Up Against Foucault: Explorations of Some Tensions Between Foucault and Feminism*, ed. Caroline Ramazanoglu [New York: Routledge, 1993], 66). My understanding is that a practice can be used for multiple and contradictory ends. To take the example with which this chapter is concerned, humanist practices of writing did, as Goldberg shows, construct students as docile bodies by submitting them to a rigorous, standardized physical discipline; at the same time, it gave them scope for articulating their individual relation to models of an autonomous and privileged scribal masculinity.

Second, the chapter highlights moments at which the process of subjectification is somehow disrupted. While the inculcation of social schemas may take place partly at an unconscious level, I contend that the practices through which this process occurs are also resisted and redeployed by the subjects they are aimed at transforming. Goldberg aptly cites the sample of young Elizabeth's handwriting that Roger Ascham, her tutor, included in a letter as proof of the efficacy of his teaching. To Ascham, the likeness between the two italic inscriptions of the word "quaemadmodum," the upper one in his hand and the lower one in Elizabeth's hand, indicates that he has effectively shaped his pupil's interiority in the process of shaping her hand (*Writing Matter*, 122). Ascham's view of the formative power he wields over his royal charge, however, is contradicted by the use to which Elizabeth puts her newly acquired italic writing. "Quaemadmodum" was the first word of the dedicatory letter to Henry VIII that prefaced Elizabeth's translation of Marguerite de Navarre's *Miroir* which, as we have seen, inverts the gendered terminology of the original (Anne Lake Prescott, "The Pearl of the Valois and Elizabeth I," in *Silent But for the Word*, ed. Hannay, 61–76). Writing, in this case, could be said both to undermine and to cultivate autonomy, to reproduce and to challenge simultaneously the social schemas implicit in Elizabeth's duplication of the writing master's hand.

34 The copy of Jean de Beauchesne's manual referred to is part of the Wing Collection at the Newberry Library, Chicago.

35 Armando Petrucci identifies four reasons behind the increased social demand for writing in late-fifteenth and early-sixteenth-century Italy: the growing role of bureaucracy in relations between citizens and the public administrations of cities and states; the increasing importance of written records in all economic activities; the diffusion of books written in the vernacular; and, the fact that, "enfin et surtout, dans les classes moyennes et inférieures de la société, la capacité d'écrire devient un moyen de promotion, un signe de distinction sociale" ("Pouvoir de l'écriture, pouvoir sur l'écriture dans la Renaissance italienne," *Annales* 43.4 [1988], 831–82). While Petrucci suggests that the four factors are parallel, it seems likely that the social distinction associated with writing was largely a function of the first three factors.

36 *The Dead Term*, sig. F1r.

37 Madonne M. Miner, "'Neither mother, wife, nor England's queen': The Roles of Women in *Richard III*," in *The Woman's Part: Feminist Criticism of Shakespeare*, eds. Carolyn Lenz, Gayle Greene, and Carol Neely (Urbana: University of Illinois Press, 1980), 35.

38 *Suffocating Mothers: Fantasies of Maternal Origin in Shakespeare's Plays, Hamlet to The Tempest* (New York: Routledge, 1992), 1.

39 Marjorie Garber comments on "the play's preoccupation with writing," in "Descanting on Deformity: Richard III and the Shape of History," in *The Historical Renaissance: New Essays on Tudor and Stuart Literature and Culture*, eds. Heather Dubrow and Richard Strier (Chicago: University of Chicago Press, 1988), 88.

40 François Furet and Jacques Ozouf, *Reading and Writing: Literacy in France from Calvin to Jules Ferry* (Cambridge: Cambridge University Press, 1982), 308.

41 Shakespeare's primary source appears to have been the 1587 edition of Raphael Holinshed, *The Chronicles of England, Scotland and Ireland*, which was based on Edward Hall, *The Union of the Noble and Illustrious Families of Lancaster and York*, which, in turn, was based on Thomas More, *The History of King Richard III* (first written in Latin, then translated into English and published in 1557; a version of this text published by another historian, Richard Grafton, is cited nearly verbatim by Hall until the narrative ends abruptly and Hall turns to Polydore Vergil, *Historia Angliae*, for the rest of the story) (Geoffrey Bullough, ed., *Earlier English History Plays: Henry VI, Richard III, Richard II*, v. 3 of *Narrative and Dramatic Sources of Shakespeare* [New York: Columbia University Press, 1960], 222–8, and William Shakespeare, *Richard III*, the Arden edition, ed. Antony Hammond [1981; rpt. New York: Routledge, 1992], 73–97).

42 *Richard III*, the Arden edition, ed. Hammond, 3.5.24–8. Subsequent references to this edition will appear in the text.

43 Bullough, *Earlier English History Plays*, 265.

44 "Rase" has the same denotation in sonnet 25: "The painful warrior famoused for fight, / After a thousand victories once foil'd, / Is from the book of honor razed quite" (the spelling is "rased" in the 1609 quarto). According to the Oxford English Dictionary, this usage goes back to the fourteenth century but was particularly widespread in the sixteenth and seventeenth centuries. Among the examples cited is a phrase from John Gower's *Confessio Amantis* (1390): "Lich to the bok in which is rased / The lettre, and mai nothing be rad."

45 Love, *Scribal Publication*, 159.

46 The sequestering of the play's women from writing appears even more deliberate given that female characters in other plays of Shakespeare do read scribal texts and sometimes write them; Julia, Jessica, Maria, Helena, Imogen, Cordelia, Goneril, Regan, and Cleopatra write letters, Phebe and Dionyza write poems as Beatrice also is reported to have done, Lady Macbeth writes on a slip of paper in her sleep, and Lavinia writes the names of her rapists in the sand; numerous female characters from Rosalind and Portia to Mistresses Page and Ford read handwritten texts on stage without any apparent

difficulty. Writing is not merely a plot device in these plays. Often its use by a female character raises questions about her conformity to models of the virtuous woman. In the case of Lavinia, as I will argue in the next chapter, her attempt to guide a stick inserted in her mouth with the amputated stumps of her arms disturbingly connects female writing with sex and violence.

47 *Writing Matter*, 120.

48 The irony, of course, is that "G" stands for Richard's title, the Duke of Gloucester, as well as for "George," the first name of his brother, the Duke of Clarence.

49 *Erasmus on Handwriting*, 1–3.

50 Béatrice Fraenkel observes that the centrality of the signature in early modern Europe was linked to a new preoccupation with the individuality of the subject: "C'est la singularité de l'être qui est visée, la part du soi irréductible aux autres. L'individu est pensé alors en termes de 'traits', traits de plume, traits du visage, traits de caractère" (*La Signature: Genèse d'un signe* [Paris: Gallimard, 1992], 11). Use of the signature to authenticate documents became widespread only in the early modern period. In twelfth- and thirteenth-century England, the ability to sign one's name was important but not associated with school or writing. Only the signatures or sign manuals of Jews were considered binding; Christians had to sign with a cross, signifying that they were making a promise before Christ crucified (though more often they affixed seals to documents) (M. T. Clanchy, *From Memory to Written Record: England, 1066–1307* [Cambridge, Massachusetts: Harvard University Press, 1979]), 184.

51 Bullough, ed., *Earlier English History Plays*, 264.

52 Raphael Holinshed, *The Chronicles of England* (London, 1587), 740, 753, 757.

53 *Richard III*, ed. Hammond (1981; rpt. New York: Routledge, 1992), 328–9.

54 If Shakespeare had wanted Richmond to give a rousing address, something on the order of Henry V's moving St. Crispian speech, he could have drawn on the chronicle version of events. Hall records Richmond as appealing to his men in vivid, passionate terms: "This one thyng I assure you, that in so juste and good a cause, and so notable a quarell, you shall fynde me this daye, rather a dead carion upon the coold grounde, then a fre prisoner on a carpet in a ladyes chamber. Let us therfore fight like invincible gyantes, & set on our enemies like untimerous Tigers . . . And now avaunce forward trew men against traytors, pitifull persones against murtherers, trew inheritors against usurpers, the skorges of God against tirauntes" (Bullough, ed., *Earlier English History Plays*, 295–6).

55 Hammond, ed., *Richard III*, 329.

56 Ibid., *Richard III*, 340. The first quarto was published in 1597, the second quarto in 1598.

57 Bullough, ed., *Earlier English History Plays*, 300.

5 SHE WRITES

1 Robert Wilson, *The Three Ladies of London* (1581), sig. B4v.

2 John Fletcher, *The Humorous Lieutenant* (1619), F 1647, sig. 3Q3v.

3 John Day, *Law Tricks* (1604), sig. I2v.
4 Thomas Dekker and Thomas Middleton, *The Honest Whore, part 1* (1605), sig. F2v.
5 Gabriel Harvey, *Works*, ed. A. B. Grosart (London: Printed for Private Circulation Only, 1884–5), 81–2. Subsequent references to this text will appear below. The young nobleman was Philip Howard, the son of Thomas Howard, the Earl of Surrey who had been executed in 1572 for his alleged collusion with Mary Stuart. After learning of the scandal involving the sister of his great rival, Thomas Nashe wrote of Harvey's "baudy sister" that she was "as good a fellow as ever turnd belly to belly" (cited in Charles Nicholl, *A Cup of News: The Life of Thomas Nashe* [London: Routledge and Kegan Paul, 1984], 16). In addition to the letters between Mercy Harvey and Philip Howard, the commonplace book contains letters sent and received by Harvey during his years at Cambridge, drafts of his poems, and his correspondence with Edmund Spenser. For discussions of the notebook, see Edward Harman, *Gabriel Harvey and Thomas Nashe* (London: J. M. Ouseley and Son, 1923), 17–35 and Virginia Stern, *Gabriel Harvey* (Oxford: Clarendon Press, 1979), 36–7. I wish to thank Alan Nelson for bringing these letters to my attention.
6 Angel Day, the author of *The English Secretary, Or, Methods of Writing Epistles and Letters*, offers insight into the curt tone of class consciousness audible in the nobleman's letters to Mercy in spite of his courtship of her. In instructing his readers about the importance of suiting one's mode of address to the station of one's correspondent, Day cites the case of a well-born man who wrote a love letter to a woman of "verie meane reckoning." The man signed his epistle with the respectful words, "Thus craving your lawfull benevolence, in not mee rejecting, your answere comfortable and not intolerable." This, Day argues, was a fatal mistake, for "the woman not accustomed to such hote intertainment, and rather bluntlie before time pursued, then daintilie intreated, beganne hereupon (forsooth) to ware coy, and to intende great matter of her self, and vaunting her favour at a higher rate then he belike seemed afterwarde willing to become a purchaser of" ([London, 1599], 5).
7 This copy is part of the Wing Collection at the Newberry Library.
8 Cited in Keith Thomas, "The Meaning of Literacy in Early Modern England," in *The Written Word: Literacy in Transition*, ed. Gerd Baumann, (Oxford: Clarendon Press, 1986), 117.
9 Desiderius Erasmus, *Erasmus on Handwriting*, 10.
10 "On Sanazar's being honoured," *Poems*, ed. C. H. Wilkinson (Oxford: Clarendon Press, 1953), 200.
11 Thomas, "The Meaning of Literacy," 116–17.
12 Merry E. Wiesner, *Women and Gender in Early Modern Europe*, 123.
13 Richard Mulcaster describes reading-only literacy as prevalent among the female population: "To learne to read is very common, where convenientnes doth serve, & writing is not refused, where oportunitie wil yield it" (*The Training Up of Children* [Amsterdam: Da Capo Press, 1971], 177). The implication is that reading is encouraged for girls while writing is only tacitly

tolerated in cases of special "oportunitie." The establishment of reading-only instruction for girls also is documented in contemporary curricula. At the Red Maids' School in Bristol, founded in 1627, girls were indentured for seven years to a schoolmistress who taught them reading and sewing and sold the goods they made for her own profit (Gardiner, *English Girlhood at School*, 278). In a parish school in Hampshire founded in 1791, boys were taught reading, writing, and arithmetic, girls reading, sewing, and knitting (Michael Van Cleave Alexander, *The Growth of Education 1348–1648: A Social and Cultural History* [University Park: Pennsylvania State University Press, 1990], 217).

14 Monaghan, "Literacy Instruction and Gender in Colonial New England," *American Quarterly* 40.1 (1988), 27.

15 Walter, "Apprenticeship Education and Family Structure in Seventeenth Century Massachusetts Bay," M.A. thesis, Bryn Mawr, 1971, 33–4, 42–3.

16 *Reading and Writing: Literacy in France from Calvin to Jules Ferry* (Cambridge: Cambridge University Press, 1982), 179. While detailed comparative analysis of educational curricula for boys and girls in different European countries remains to be undertaken, there is evidence that reading-only literacy was instituted as a specifically female form of competency in schools on the Continent as well as in England. Furet and Ozouf comment that in France limiting literacy to reading was the norm in some institutions; "many documents even hint that in certain places this was what was wanted, not a limitation imposed by poverty, at least where the education of girls was concerned" (167). In fact, as Margaret Ferguson observes, Counter-Reformation synodal regulations and episcopal ordinances in France state clearly that girls, in contrast with boys, should be instructed in reading and sewing but not in writing ("A Room Not Their Own: Renaissance Women as Readers and Writers," in *The Comparative Perspective on Literature: Approaches to Theory and Practice*, eds. Clayton Koelb and Susan Noakes [Ithaca, New York: Cornell University Press, 1988], 115). This was also the case in Italy, where the influence of humanist reform took hold a century earlier. Paul Grendler cites the example of a school for girls in late-sixteenth-century Mantua: "In it two women teachers taught the catechism, reading (but not writing), and sewing to girls aged 7 to 12 who presented certificates of poverty from their parish priests" (*Schooling in Renaissance Italy: Literacy and Learning, 1300–1600* [1989; rpt. Baltimore: The Johns Hopkins University Press, 1991], 101).

17 "Nineteenth-century evidence," Margaret Spufford notes, "shows that as many as three-quarters of the women making marks could read, since writing was frequently omitted from the school curricula for girls from the sixteenth to the nineteenth centuries" (*Small Books and Pleasant Histories: Popular Fiction and Its Readership in Seventeenth Century England* [London, Methuen: 1981], 22). Barry Reay comes to a similar conclusion in his study of the Kentish countryside: "The decline of the so-called 'illiteracy' of laboring women in the rural areas of nineteenth century England may merely reflect the acquisition of an additional skill, that of writing, rather than any spectacular leap from illiterate to literate." Indeed, the reading competency of

rural women, which was said to be more advanced than that of the men, was viewed by authorities as the cause of a millenarian uprising in the area in 1838 ("The Context and Meaning of Popular Literacy: Some Evidence from Nineteenth Century Rural England,"*Past and Present* 131 [1991], 128, 114).

18 Cited in Furet and Ozouf, *Reading and Writing*, 178.

19 Giovanni Bruto, *The Necessary, Fit and Convenient Education of a Young Gentlewoman* (London), trans. W.P., sigs. F8v–G2r.

20 Daniel Tuvill, *Asylum Veneris, Or a Sanctuary for Ladies* (London), 88. The author of the book takes exception to this practice and points out that parents who interdict their daughters' use of the pen should "likewise barre them the use of their needle"; since Philomela used embroidery to relate the story of her rape, "why then may not others expresse their loves, and their affections in the like forme?" (88).

21 *The School of Abuse* (1579; rpt. in Arthur F. Kinney, *Markets of Bawdrie: The Dramatic Criticism of Stephen Gosson* [Salzburg: Institut für Englische Sprache und Literatur, 1974]), 80.

22 *Poems*, 200.

23 *Instruction of a Christian Woman* (London), sig. E2r.

24 *The Pen's Excellency* (London), sig. B4v.

25 Nathaniel Parkhurst, *The Faithful and Diligent Christian Described and Exemplified* (London, 1684), 48–9.

26 A remarkable example of a woman who used the transcription of devotional texts for other than disciplinary purposes is that of Esther Inglis. The daughter of Huguenots who escaped to England from France and later settled in Scotland, Inglis used her expert knowledge of calligraphy on behalf of the Protestant cause. She inscribed texts such as the Psalms and Proverbs in beautiful volumes, of which some fifty-five are extant, and presented them to political figures including Queen Elizabeth, Prince Maurice of Nassau, the Earl of Essex, the Earl of Mar, and Prince Henry. Inglis included self-portraits, often depictions of herself with pen and ink, in at least twenty-two volumes. As Georgianna Ziegler notes, Inglis inscribed her "self" into the texts she transcribed "through her choice of text (how much and what to use); her choice of design: title page, introductory matter, page layout, styles of handwriting, choice of decoration; her selection of patrons; her dedicatory epistles and poems . . . and most literally, by the insertion of her self in author portraits" ("'More Than Feminine Boldness': The Gift Books of Esther Inglis," paper presented at The Folger Shakespeare Library, 14 April 1995).

27 "The Influence of Humanism on the Education of Girls and Boys in Tudor England," *History of Education Quarterly* 25.1–2 (1985), 65.

28 Love, *Scribal Publication in Seventeenth-Century England* (Oxford: Clarendon Press, 1993), 108.

29 *The Writing Schoolmaster* (London, 1631), sig. A1v.

30 *The Pen's Excellency*, sig. C2v. For an example of a lady's typical italic hand, see Jean F. Preston and Laetitia Yeandle, *English Handwriting 1400–1650* (Binghamton, New York: Medieval and Renaissance Texts and Studies), 56–7.

31 Dominique Merllié demonstrates that handwriting is still seen as reflective of one's gender today. In experiments that she supervised, subjects were asked to identify the gender of individuals who had contributed samples of their handwriting. The judges cited the criteria upon which they based their evaluations as neatness, quality of presentation, legibility, regularity, esthetic qualities, roundness of letters, and size of letters. Some said that they would classify a colored ink as feminine and black as masculine and a text written with a fountain pen as feminine and one written with a ballpoint pen as masculine. (In reality, blue and black inks were shared equally between the sexes; more women than men used ballpoint pens.) The classifications at which the judges arrived did bear a clearly positive relation to reality. A majority of the texts were assigned to the correct sex by a majority of judges. However, what was most striking in this study was the degree of consensus among the judges about the criteria upon which they based their classifications. The only text that was unanimously classified was classified "incorrectly" (a male text judged feminine). Three feminine and three masculine texts were classified incorrectly by a strong majority (more than 83 percent). As Merllié observes, "Ce qui pourrait varier le plus, ce n'est pas tant l'aptitude à reconnaître le sexe à travers l'écriture que celle des scripteurs à se laisser reconnaître, c'est à dire leur conformité aux traits de l'écriture majoritaire de leur sexe" ("Le sexe de l'écriture: Note sur la perception sociale de la fémininité," *Actes de la recherche en sciences sociales* 83 [1990], 50). Merllié points out that differences between the forms of handwriting that are normative for each sex (regularity and roundness in female scripts) can probably be attributed partly to the greater compliance of girls vis-à-vis scholastic models of writing learned in school.

32 "Femme qui compose en sait plus qu'il ne faut" (1.1.94). In *L'Ecole des Femmes*, ed. Roger Duchêne (Paris: Le Livre de Poche, 1986). The English translation is mine; the original French text of the passages cited appears in the notes below.

33 "*Les maximes du mariage, ou les devoirs de la femme mariée avec son exercice journalier*"; "Dans ses meubles, dût-elle en avoir de l'ennui, / Il ne faut écritoire, encre, papier ni plumes. / Le mari doit, dans les bonnes coutumes, / Ecrire tout ce qui s'écrit chez lui" (3.2.780–4).

34 1.4.244–8; "Voilà, friponne, à quoi l'écriture te sert, / Et contre mon dessein, l'art t'en fut découvert" (3.4.946–7).

35 Eds. Russell A. Fraser and Norman Rabkin, in *Drama of the English Renaissance* (New York: Macmillan, 1976), v. 2, 5.1.87, 96, 102, 124–6, 134, 146–50, 167–9.

36 "Ravishment and Rememberance: Responses to Female Authority in Spenser and Shakespeare," Ph.D. dissertation, University of California at Berkeley, 1991, 2.

37 *The Whore of Babylon: A Critical Edition*, ed. Marianne Gateson Riely (New York: Garland Publishing, 1980), *Lectori*, 1–7, 101. Subsequent references to this edition will appear in the text.

38 *The Dead Term* (London, 1608), sig. C3r.

39 Ibid., sigs. C3r–C3v.

40 Ibid., sigs. F1r–F2v.

41 *The Stage and Social Struggle in Early Modern England* (New York: Routledge, 1994), 53.

42 Leah S. Marcus, *Puzzling Shakespeare: Local Reading and Its Discontents* (Berkeley: University of California Press, 1988), 70–1.

43 In *Drama of the English Renaissance*, v. 2, eds. Russell Fraser and Norman Rabkin (New York: Macmillan, 1976), 5.4.21.

44 The ambassador to the French king Henri IV gave an unflattering description of Elizabeth's aged appearance in 1597: "As for her face, it is and appears to be very aged. It is long and thin, and her teeth are very yellow and unequal . . . many of them are missing so that one cannot understand her easily when she speaks" (André Hurault, *Journal*, eds. G. B. Harrison and R. A. Jones [Bloomsbury, 1931]), 25–6.

45 *Holinshed's Chronicles* (1587; rpt. New York: AMS Press, 1976), v. 4, 914–15, 917.

46 *The Dead Term*, sig. F1v.

47 As part of their training in writing, students learned to use knives from instructions such as these: "Now to make a Pen, take the first, second, or third Quill in the Wing of a Goose or Raven (Some will if their Quills are too hard, steep them a while in Water; or if too soft, lay them a short space in hot Embers) and having with the back of your Pen-knife, prepared it by Scraping, cut off about a quarter of an Inch or fingers breadth of the end; after that you must enter the edge of your knife just at the end of its back-side, where you have cut, then put in the loose end of your quill, and holding the Thumb of your left hand on the back thereof, you may by twitching up the end of your quill make a slit, long or short, according to your minde; however, that being done, and the quill made smooth by scraping, and not too thin or soft, then cutting each side alike, you may designe the slit to be of such a length as may best fit your hand, and placing it upon your Thumb, hold your knife a little sloping, and cut the end of the nib, but before it be quite cut through, turn your knife downright and cut it off; you may fashion it as you please, leaving it broader or narrower, according to the Size of the letter which you intend to writing. Now presupposing that you are appointed with a good Pen, it followes that you know how to hold, and manage it like a Pen-Man" (Edward Cocker, *Arts Glory. Or The Pen-man's Treasury* [London, 1657], A3r).

48 Folger MS.V.b.198, fol. 59r, 68r.

49 *"My Name Was Martha": A Renaissance Woman's Autobiographical Poem*, eds. Robert C. Evans and Barbara Wiedemann (West Cornwall, Connecticut: 1993), 4, 8.

50 Among the names in the book are those of Lady Elizabeth Drury, Lady Elizabeth Clinton, Lady Douglas Sheffield, and Lady Mary Scudamore. Bowden also finds a high level of writing-literacy among the women whose letters are preserved in two volumes of correspondence addressed to Sir Julius Caesar (1579–1619). Seventy-three letters were sent by forty-three female correspondents, most of whom were of noble birth. Of these, thirty signed their names, six appended a greeting as well as a signature, an additional six wrote the entire letter, while one wrote only her initials ("Women as Intermediaries: An Example of the Use of Literacy in the Late-Sixteenth and Early-Seventeenth Centuries," *History of Education* 22.3 [1993], 223).

51 Randall Martin, "The Autobiography of Grace, Lady Mildmay," *Renaissance and Reformation / Renaissance et Réforme* 18.1 (1994), 38.

52 Ibid., 63. Subsequent references to this text will appear below.

53 Anne Clifford authored a broad range of autobiographical manuscripts and editions. In my analysis of these writings, I have relied on Katherine O. Acheson, ed., *The Diary of Anne Clifford, 1616–19: A Critical Edition* (New York: Garland, 1995) for the text of Clifford's diary for 1616, 1617, and 1619; on D. J. H. Clifford, ed., *The Diaries of Anne Clifford* (Wolfeboro Falls, New Hampshire: Alan Sutton, 1991), for the text of Clifford's 1676 diary and that of her memoir summarizing events from 1603 and 1650–75; on J. P. Gilson, ed., *Lives of Lady Anne Clifford Countess of Dorset, Pembroke and Montgomery (1590–1676) and of Her Parents* (London: Roxburghe Club, 1916) for the text of her autobiography, "The Life of Me the Lady Anne Clifford" and for those of the biographies she wrote of her parents and relatives; and, lastly, on a later modern manuscript copy of Clifford's *Summary of the Lives of the Veteriponts and Cliffords* owned by the Carlisle Library in Carlisle, U.K. (stock number A166 in the Jackson collection) for an extended narrative of the Clifford genealogy going back to the thirteenth century. See also Acheson's discussion of the editorial state of affairs concerning Clifford's writings (*Diary*, 14–31).

54 Graham Parry, "The Great Picture of Lady Anne Clifford," in *Art and Patronage in the Caroline Courts*, ed. David Howarth (Cambridge: Cambridge University Press, 1993), 204.

55 The only lands to which she did not seek title were those belonging to the Cumberland earldom. For accounts of Clifford's life, see Acheson, *Diary*, 1–14, Barbara Kiefer Lewalski, *Writing Women in Jacobean England* (Cambridge, Massachusetts: Harvard University Press, 1993), 125–51; the introduction to *The Diary of the Lady Anne Clifford*, ed. V. Sackville-West (London: William Heineman Ltd., 1923), ix–lxvi; Richard T. Spence, *Lady Anne Clifford Countess of Pembroke, Dorset and Montgomery* (Thrupp: Sutton Publishing, 1997); and George C. Williamson, *Lady Anne Clifford Countess of Dorset, Pembroke and Montgomery 1590–1676: Her Life, Letters and Work* (1922; rpt. S. R. Publishers Ltd, 1967).

56 *The Diary*, ed. Acheson, 45.

57 Ibid., 45.

58 *The Diaries*, ed. Clifford, 239.

59 *Lives*, ed. Gilson, 52.

60 *Diary*, ed. Acheson, 79–80.

61 Williamson, *Lady Anne Clifford*, 193–4.

62 *Diaries*, ed. Clifford, 100.

63 Ibid., 101.

64 Williamson, *Lady Anne Clifford*, 207.

65 *The Diaries*, ed. Clifford, 144.

66 *A Summary of the Lives of the Veteriponts and Cliffords*, 19.

67 *Lives*, ed. Gilson, 6.

68 For a complete list of the books featured in the triptych, see Williamson, *Lady Anne Clifford*, 499–500.

69 Edward Rainbow, *A Sermon Preached at the Funeral of the Right Honorable Anne Countess of Pembroke, Dorset, and Montgomery* (London: 1667), 6.

70 *Diary*, ed. Acheson, 32; *Lives*, ed. Gilson, 35. Clifford elaborates on this point in a vivid, if immodest, self-portrait: "The color of mine eyes were black like my father, and the form and aspect of them was quick and lively like my mother's; the hair of my head was brown and very thick, and so long that it reached to the calf of my legs when I stood upright, with a peak of hair on my forehead, and a dimple in my chin, like my father, full cheeks and round face like my mother, and an exquisite shape of body resembling my father" (*Lives*, 35).

71 Parry, "The Great Picture of Lady Anne Clifford," 214.

72 Rainbow, *A Sermon*, 53.

73 Mary Ellen Lamb, "The Agency of the Split Subject: Lady Anne Clifford and the Uses of Reading," *English Literary Renaissance* 22.3 (1992), 362.

74 Cited in Williamson, *Lady Anne Clifford*, 492.

75 *Lives*, ed. Gilson, 24–5.

76 Ibid., 26.

77 *A Summary of the Lives of the Veteriponts and Cliffords*, 34.

78 Cited in Williamson, *Lady Anne Clifford*, 516.

79 Ibid., 331–2.

80 *Lives*, ed. Gilson, 33.

81 *Diary*, ed. Acheson, 104.

82 On the antiquarian research of Clifford and her mother, see Spence, *Lady Anne Clifford*, 8, 40–58.

83 *Lives*, ed. Gilson, 23.

Bibliography

Primary sources

Anton, Robert. *The Philosophers Satyrs*. London, 1616.

Ascham, Roger. *The Scholemaster*. London, 1570.

Austin, William. *Hæc Homo, Wherein the Excellency of the Creation of Woman is Described*. London, 1637.

Beauchesne, Jean de. *A Booke containing Divers sortes of Hands, as well the English as French Secretarie with the Italian, Roman, Chancelry & Court Hands*. London, 1571.

La clef de l'escriture laquelle ouvre le chemin a la jeunesse, pour bien apprendre a escrire la vraye lettre francoyse & italique. London, 1595.

Le tresor d'escriture, auquel est contenu tout ce qui est requis & necessaire à tous amateurs dudict art. Lyon, 1580.

Becon, Thomas. *Works*. V. 3. Cambridge: Cambridge University Press, 1844.

Bentley, Thomas. *The Monument of Matrones*. London, 1582.

Billingsley, Martin. *The Pen's Excellencie, or, the Secretaries delight*. London, 1618.

Blundeville, Thomas. *The True Order and Methode of Writyng and Reading Hystories*. London, 1574.

Boccaccio, Giovanni. *Concerning Famous Women*. Trans. Guido A. Guarino. New Brunswick, New Jersey: Rutgers University Press, 1963.

Brandon, Samuel. *The Tragicæmedie of the Virtuous Octavia*. London, 1598.

Brathwait, Richard. *The English Gentleman*. London, 1630.

The English Gentlewoman. London, 1631.

Brinsley, John. *A Consolation for Our Grammar Schooles*. 1622. Rpt. Ed. Thomas Clark Pollock. New York: Scholars' Facsimiles & Reprints, 1943.

A Looking-Glasse for Good Women. London, 1645.

Ludus Literarius: Or, The Grammar Schoole. 1612. Rpt. Menston, England: The Scolar Press Limited, 1968.

Brown, David. *The Introduction to the True Understanding of the Whole Arte of Expedition in Teaching to Write*. London, 1638.

The New Invention, Intituled Calligraphia. Saint Andrews, 1622.

Bruto, Giovanni Michele. *The Necessarie, Fit and Convenient Education of a Young Gentlewoman*. Trans. W.P. London, 1598.

Cary, Elizabeth. *The Tragedy of Mariam: The Fair Queen of Jewry, With The Lady Falkland: Her Life By One of Her Daughters*. Eds. Barry Weller and Margaret W. Ferguson. Berkeley: University of California Press, 1994.

Cassius Dio Cocceianus. *Dio's Annals of Rome*. Trans. Herbert Baldwin Foster.
   V. 3. Troy, New York: Pafraets Book Company, 1905–6.
Castiglione, Baldassare. *The Book of the Courtier*. 1561. Trans. Thomas Hoby.
   Rpt. New York: AMS Press, 1967.
Chapman, George. *Bussy D'Ambois*. Eds. Russell A. Fraser and Norman Rabkin.
   In *Drama of the English Renaissance*. V. 2. New York: Macmillan, 1976.
   The Conspiracy and Tragedy of Byron. Ed. John Margeson. Manchester:
   Manchester University Press, 1988.
Church of England. *Sermons or Homilies Appointed to be Read in Churches in the
   Time of Queen Elizabeth of Famous Memory*. Liverpool: The Caxton Press
   by Nuttall, Fisher and Dixon, 1812.
Cleland, James. *The Institution of a Young Noble Man*. London, 1607. Facsimile;
   New York: Scholar's Facsimiles and Reprints, 1948.
Clifford, Anne. *The Diaries of Lady Anne Clifford*. Ed. D.J.H. Clifford. Wolfe-
   boro Falls, New Hampshire: Alan Sutton, 1991.
   The Diary of Anne Clifford, 1616–1619. Ed. Katherine O. Acheson. New York:
   Garland Publishing, 1995.
   The Diary of the Lady Anne Clifford. Ed. Victoria Sackeville-West. London:
   William Heineman, 1923.
   *Lives of Lady Anne Clifford Countess of Dorset, Pembroke and Montgomery
   (1590–1676) and of Her Parents Summarized by Herself Printed from the
   Harley MS. 6177*. Ed. J. P. Gilson. London: Roxburghe Club, 1916.
   A Summary of the Lives of the Veteriponts and Cliffords. Modern manuscript
   copy owned by the Carlisle Library in Carlisle, U.K. The Jackson Collection,
   stock number A166.
Cocker, Edward. *Arts Glory, Or, The Pen-man's treasurie*. London, 1657.
   The Pen's Transcendency, 1660.
   Plumae triumphus. London, 1660.
   *The Youth's Direction: To Write without a Teacher All the usefull Hands of
   England*. London, 1652.
Comenius, John Amos. *The Great Didactic of John Amos Comenius*. Trans. and
   ed. M. W. Keatinge. London: Adam and Charles Black, 1910.
Daniel, Samuel. *Certaine Small Workes*. London, 1607.
   The Civile Wares. London, 1609.
   The Complete Works in Verse and Prose. Ed. Alexander B. Grosart. 5 vols.
   New York: Russell & Russell, 1963.
   A Defence of Rhyme. London, 1603.
   Delia and Rosamund Augmented. Cleopatra. London, 1594.
   The First Fowre Bookes of the Ciuile Wars. London, 1595.
   The Poeticall Essayes. London, 1599.
   The Tragedy of Cleopatra. 1594. Rpt. in *A New Variorum Edition of Shake-
   speare: Antony and Cleopatra*. Ed. Martin Spevack. New York: The Modern
   Language Association of America, 1990. 531–79.
   Works. London, 1602.
Davies, John. *The Writing Scholemaster, or, The Anatomie of Faire Writing*.
   London, 1631.
Day, Angel. *The English Secretary, or, Methodes of Writing of Epistles and
   Letters*. London, 1599.

Dekker, Thomas. *The Dead Tearme, or, Westminsters Complaint for long Vacations and Short Termes.* London, 1608.

The Whore of Babylon: A Critical Edition. Ed. Marianne Gateson Riely. New York: Garland Publishing, 1980.

Donne, John. *Sermons.* V. 10. Eds. George R. Potter and Evelyn M. Simpson. Berkeley: University of California Press, 1962.

Du Bosq, Jacques. *The Complete Woman.* London, 1639.

The Secretary of Ladies. London, 1638.

Elyot, Thomas. *The Defence of Good Women.* London, 1540.

The Boke Named the Governour. 1531. Rpt. London, 1544.

Erasmus, Desiderius. *De Copia.* Trans. Betty I. Knott. In *De Copia/De Ratione Studii.* Ed. Craig R. Thompson. In *Collected Works of Erasmus.* V. 24. Toronto: University of Toronto Press, 1978.

Erasmus on Handwriting: An Extract from the Dialogue of Desiderius Erasmus, De Recta Latini Graecique Sermonis Pronuntiatione. Trans. A. S. Osley. Wormley, England: The Glade Press, 1970.

Fenton, Geoffrey, trans. *Certain Tragical Discourses of Bandello.* 1567. Rpt. London: David Nutt, 1898.

Fisher, John. *The Funeral Sermon of Margaret, Countess of Richmond and Derby.* London, 1708.

Fletcher, John, and Philip Massinger. *The False One.* 1620. Rpt. in *The Dramatic Works in the Beaumont and Fletcher Canon.* Ed. Fredson Bowers. V. 8. Cambridge: Cambridge University Press, 1992. 123–209.

Gager, William. *The Complete Works.* V.2. Ed. and trans. Dana F. Sutton. New York: Garland Publishing, 1994.

Garnier, Robert. *Antonius: A Tragedy.* Trans. Mary Sidney. Ed. Martin Spevack. In *A New Variorum Edition of Shakespeare: Antony and Cleopatra.* New York: The Modern Language Association of America, 1990. 479–524.

Two Tragedies: Hippolyte and Marc Antoine. Eds. Christine M. Hill and Mary G. Morrison. London: Athlone Press, 1975.

Gething, Richard. *Calligraphotechnia.* London, 1619.

Chiro-graphia or A booke of Copies Containing Sundrie Examples. London, 1645.

Gething Redivivus: or The pens master-piece restored. London, 1664.

Gosson, Stephen. *The Schoole of Abuse.* 1579. Rpt. in *Markets of Bawdrie: The Dramatic Criticism of Stephen Gosson.* Ed. Arthur F. Kinney. Salzburg: Institüt für Englische Sprache und Literatur, 1974.

Gouge, William. *Of Domesticall Duties.* London, 1622.

Guazzo, Stefano. *The Civile Conversation of M. Steeven Guazzo.* Trans. George Pettie (vols. 1–3), 1581. Trans. Bartholomew Young (vol. 4), 1586. Rpt. New York: Alfred Knopf, 1925.

Gurnall, William. *The Christians Labour and Reward; Or, a Sermon, Part of which was Preached at the Funeral of the Right Honourable the Lady Mary Vere, Relict of Sir Horace Vere, Baron of Tilbury, on the 10th of February.* London, 1672.

Hall, Edward. *Hall's Chronicle; Containing the History of England during the Reign of Henry the Fourth, and the Succeeding Monarchs.* 1548. Rpt. London: J. Johnson, 1809.

Har, W. *Epicedivm, A Funerall Song, vpon the Vertuous Life, and Godly Death, of . . . Lady Helen Branch*. London, 1594.

Harvey, Gabriel. *Works*. Ed. A. B. Grosart. London: Printed for Private Circulation Only, 1884–5.

Heywood, Thomas. *An Apology for Actors*. 1612. Rpt. Ed. Richard H. Perkinson. Delmar, New York: Scholars' Facsimiles & Reprints, 1978.

A Woman Killed with Kindness. Ed. Brian W. M. Scobie. London, A & C Black Publishers, 1985.

Higford, William. *The Institution of a Gentleman*. London, 1660.

Holinshed, Raphael. *Holinshed's Chronicles*. 1587. Rpt. New York: AMS Press, 1976.

The Chronicles of England. London, 1587.

Hondius, Jodocus. *Hondius on Handwriting*. Trans. A. S. Osley. Wormley, England: The Glade Press, 1970.

Ignatius. *The Spiritual Exercises of St. Ignatius*. 1964. Rpt. Trans. Anthony Mottola. New York: Doubleday, 1989.

Inglis, Esther. *A New Yeeres Guift for Lady Arskene of Dirltoun*. England, 1606.

Jerome. "St. Jerome on Female Education." In *Pamphlets Pertaining to Education. V.3, Education of Girls: Institutions and Suggestions*. California Department of Public Instruction, 1861–96.

Jodelle, Etienne. *Cléopâtre captive*. Ed. Kathleen M. Hall. Exeter: University of Exeter, 1979.

Johnson, John. *The Academy of Love*. London, 1641.

Jonson, Ben. *The Alchemist*. In *Drama of the English Renaissance*. V. 2. Eds. Russell A. Fraser and Norman Rabkin. New York: Macmillan, 1976, 143–90.

Timber, or Discoveries. Ed. Ralph S. Walker. Syracuse, New York: Syracuse University Press, 1953.

Kempe, Margery. *The Book of Margery Kempe*. Trans. B. A. Windeatt. New York: Penguin, 1985.

Kyd, Thomas. *The Spanish Tragedy*. In *Drama of the English Renaissance*. V.1. Eds. Russell A. Fraser and Norman Rabkin. New York: Macmillan Publishing Co., 167–203.

Latymer, William. "William Latymer's Cronickille of Anne Bulleyne." In *Camden Miscellany*. Ed. Maria Dowling. London: Offices of the Royal Historical Society, 1990. 26–65.

The Lay Folks Mass Book. Ed. Thomas Frederick Simmons. 1879. Rpt. London: Oxford University Press, 1968.

Love, Nicholas. *Nicholas Love's Mirror of the Blessed Life of Jesus Christ*. Ed. Michael G. Sargent. New York: Garland Publishing, 1992.

Lovelace, Richard. *Poems*. Ed. C. H. Wilkinson. Oxford: Clarendon Press, 1953.

Makin, Bathusa. *An Essay to Revive the Antient Education of Gentlewomen*. 1673. Rpt. Los Angeles: William Andrews Clark Memorial Library, 1980.

Marguerite, De Navarre. *The Heptameron*. Trans. P. A. Chilton. New York: Penguin Books, 1984.

Les Dernières Poésies de Marguerite de Navarre. Ed. Abel Lefranc. Paris: Armand Colin, 1896.

The Mirror of the Sinful Soul. Trans. Elizabeth I. Ed. Percy W. Ames. London: Asher and Co., 1897.

May, Thomas. *The Tragœdy of Cleopatra.* Ed. Denzell S. Smith. New York: Garland Publishing Inc., 1979.

Meditations on the Life of Christ: An Illustrated Manuscript of the Fourteenth Century. Eds. Isa Ragusa and Rosalie B. Green. Trans. Isa Ragusa. Princeton: Princeton University Press, 1961.

Middleton, Thomas. *A Mad World, My Masters.* Ed. Standish Henning. London: Edward Arnold, 1965.

Moffet, Thomas. *Nobilis or A View of the Life and Death of a Sidney and Lessus Lugubris.* Eds. Virgil B. Heltzel and Hoyt H. Hudson. San Marino: The Huntington Library, 1940.

Molière (Jean-Baptiste Poquelin). *L'Ecole des femmes.* 1662. Rpt. Ed. Roger Duchêne. Paris: Le Livre de Poche, 1986.

Montaigne, Michel de. *The Complete Essays.* 1957; rpt. Trans. Donald M. Frame. Stanford: Stanford University Press, 1989.

Essais. Ed. Maurice Rat. Paris: Garnier Frères, 1962.

Essays. Trans. John Florio. 1603. Rpt. New York: Dutton, 1980.

Moulsworth, Martha. *"My Name Was Martha": A Renaissance Woman's Autobiographical Poem.* Eds. Robert C. Evans and Barbara Wiedemann. West Cornwall, Connecticut: Locust Hill Press, 1993.

Mulcaster, Richard. *The First Part of the Elementary.* 1582. Rpt. Menston, England: The Scolar Press, 1970.

The Training Up of Children. 1581. Rpt. Amsterdam: Da Capo Press, 1971.

A Myrour to Lewde Men and Wymmen. Ed. Venetia Nelson. Heidelberg: Carl Winter, 1981.

The Myroure of oure Ladye. Ed. John Henry Blunt. London: N. Trübner, 1873.

Norwich, Julian of. *Showings.* Eds. Edmund Colledge and James Walsh. New York: Paulist Press, 1978.

Parkhurst, Nathaniel. *The Faithful and Diligent Christian Described and Exemplified.* London, 1684.

Peacham, Henry. *The Complete Gentleman.* 1622. Rpt. Ithaca, New York: Cornell University Press, 1962.

Porete, Marguerite. "Le mirouer des simples ames." In "Il movimento del Libero Spirito." Ed. Romana Guarnieri. *Archivio italiano per la storia della pietà* 4 (1965): 513–635.

The Mirror of Simple Souls. Trans. M. N. Ed. Marilyn Doiron. "Margaret Porete: 'The Mirror of Simple Souls,' A Middle English Translation." *Archivio italiano per la storia della pietà* 5 (1968): 241–355.

Rainbow, Edward. *A Sermon Preached at the Funeral of the Right Honorable Anne Countess of Pembroke, Dorset, and Montgomery.* London, 1667.

Sadoleto, Jacopo. *Sadoleto on Education: A Translation of The De Pueris Recte Instituendis.* Trans. and eds. E. T. Campagnac and K. Forbes. London: Oxford University Press, 1916.

Salter, Frank Reyner. *Some Early Tracts on Poor Relief.* London: Methuen, 1926.

Salter, Thomas. *A Mirrhor Mete for all Mothers, Matrones, and Maidens, Intituled the Mirrhor of Modestie.* London, 1579.

Scalzini, Marcello. *Scalzini On Handwriting. An Essay from Marcello Scalzino's Writing-Book of 1578 Il Secretario, translated from the Italian and Introduced by A. S. Osley.* Wormley, England: The Glade Press, 1971.

Shakespeare, William. *Antony and Cleopatra: A New Variorum Edition of Shakespeare.* Ed. Marvin Spevack. New York: The Modern Language Association of America, 1990.

The First Folio of Shakespeare. Ed. Charlton Hinman. 1968. Rpt. New York: W. W. Norton, 1996.

Hamlet. The Arden Edition. Ed. Harold Jenkins. London: Methuen, 1982.

The Norton Shakespeare. Ed. Stephen Greenblatt. New York: W. W. Norton, 1997.

Richard III. The Arden Edition. 1981. Rpt. Ed. Antony Hammond. New York: Routledge, 1992.

Shakespeare's Plays in Quarto. Eds. Michael J. B. Allen and Kenneth Muir. Berkeley: University of California Press, 1981.

Titus Andronicus. The Arden Edition. 1961. Rpt. Ed. J. C. Maxwell. New York: Routledge, 1991.

Sidney, Philip. *An Apology for Poetry.* Ed. Hazard Adams. In *Critical Theory Since Plato.* San Diego: Harcourt Brace Jovanovich, 1971. 154–77.

The Countesse of Pembrokes Arcadia. London, 1593.

The Countess of Pembroke's Arcadia. New York: Penguin Books, 1977.

Smith, Thomas. *De Republica Anglorum: A Discourse on the Commonwealth of England.* 1583. Rpt. Cambridge: Cambridge University Press, 1906.

Southwell, Anne. *Commonplace Book.* Folger MS.V.b.198.

Spenser, Edmund. *The Faerie Queene.* Ed. Thomas P. Roche. New York: Penguin Books, 1987.

A View of the Present State of Ireland. Ed. W. L. Renwick. London: The Scholartis Press, 1934.

The Statutes of the Realm. V. 2. London, 1816.

The Statutes of the Realm. V. 3. London, 1817.

Stubbes, Philip. *A Christal Glasse for Christian Women Containing a Most Excellent Discourse of the Godly Life and Christian Death of Mistresse Katherine Stubs.* London, 1592.

Tilney, Edmund. *A Brief and Pleasant Discourse of Duties in Mariage, Called the Flower of Friendshippe.* London, 1568.

Tourneur, Cyril. *The Revenger's Tragedy.* Eds. Russell A. Fraser and Norman Rabkin. In *Drama of the English Renaissance.* V. 2. New York: Macmillan Publishing Company, 1976. 21–54.

Tuvill, Daniel. *Asylum Veneris, Or A Sanctuary for Ladies.* London, 1616.

Tyler, Margaret, trans. *The Mirrour of Princely Deedes and Knighthood.* 1578. Rpt. London, 1580.

Virgil. *The Aeneid.* Trans. Robert Fitzgerald. New York: Random House, 1984.

Vives, Juan Luis. *The Instruction of a Christen Woman.* Trans. Richard Hyrd. London, 1529.

The Office and Duetie of an Husband. Trans. T. Paynell. London, 1553.

Whately, William. *A Bride-bush, or A Wedding Sermon.* London, 1617.

Woolf, Virginia. *A Room of One's Own*. 1929. Rpt. New York: Harcourt Brace Jovanovich, 1957.

Wyss, Urban. *Libellus valde doctus . . . multa et varia scribendum litterarum genera complectens*. Zurich, 1549.

Secondary sources

Adamson, J. W. "The Extent of Literacy in England in the Fifteenth and Sixteenth Centuries." *The Library* 10 (1929): 163–93.

Adelman, Janet. *The Common Liar: An Essay on Antony and Cleopatra*. New Haven: Yale University Press, 1973.

———. *Suffocating Mothers: Fantasies of Maternal Origin in Shakespeare's Plays, Hamlet to the Tempest*. New York: Routledge, 1992.

Aers, David. *Culture and History, 1350–1600: Essays on English Communities, Identities and Writing*. Detroit: Wayne State University Press, 1992.

Alexander, Michael Van Cleave. *The Growth of Education 1348–1648: A Social and Cultural History*. University Park: The Pennsylvania State University Press, 1990.

Alexandre-Bidon, Danièle. "La Lettre volée: Apprendre à lire à l'enfant au Moyen Age." *Annales* 44.4 (1989): 953–92.

Althusser, Louis. "Ideology and Ideological State Apparatuses (Notes towards an Investigation)." In *Lenin and Philosophy and Other Essays*. Trans. Ben Brewster. New York: Monthly Review Press, 1971. 127–86.

Anglin, Jay P. "The Expansion of Literacy: Opportunities for the Study of the Three Rs in the London Diocese of Elizabeth I." *Guildhall Studies in London History* 4 (1980): 63–74.

Bartlett, Anne Clark. *Male Authors, Female Readers: Representation and Subjectivity in Middle English Devotional Literature*. Ithaca, New York: Cornell University Press, 1995.

Beal, Peter. "Notions in Garrison: The Seventeenth-Century Commonplace Book." In *New Ways of Looking at Old Texts*. Ed. W. Speed Hill. Binghamton, New York: Medieval and Renaissance Texts and Studies in conjunction with the Renaissance English Text Society, 1993. 131–47.

Bell, Susan Groag. "Medieval Women Book Owners: Arbiters of Lay Piety and Ambassadors of Culture." In *Women and Power in the Middle Ages*. Eds. Mary Erler and Maryanne Kowaleski. Athens, Georgia: University of Georgia Press, 1988. 149–87.

Belsey, Catherine. *The Subject of Tragedy: Identity and Difference in Renaissance Drama*. New York: Methuen, 1985.

Bennett, H. S. *English Books and Readers 1603–1640*. Cambridge: Cambridge University Press, 1970.

———. *English Books and Readers: 1475 to 1557*. Cambridge: Cambridge University Press, 1970.

———. *English Books and Readers: 1558–1603*. Cambridge: Cambridge University Press, 1965.

Bentley, Gerald Eades. *The Profession of Dramatist in Shakespeare's Time, 1590–1642*. Princeton: Princeton University Press, 1971.

Bergeron, David M., ed. *Reading and Writing in Shakespeare*. Newark: University of Delaware Press, 1996.

"Women as Patrons of English Drama." In *Patronage in the Renaissance*. Eds. Guy Fitch Lytle and Stephen Orgel. Princeton: Princeton University Press, 1981. 274–90.

Blair, Ann. "Humanist Methods in Natural Philosophy: The Commonplace Book." *Journal of the History of Ideas* 53.4 (1992): 541–55.

Boas, Frederick S. "University Plays." in *The Cambridge History of Literature*. Eds. A. W. Ward and A. R. Waller. Cambridge: Cambridge University Press, 1919, 293–327.

Boffey, Julia. "Women Authors and Women's Literacy in Fourteenth and Fifteenth-Century England." In *Women and Literature in Britain, 1150–1500*. Ed. Carol M. Meale. Cambridge: Cambridge University Press, 1993. 159–82.

Bornstein, Diane. "The Style of the Countess of Pembroke's Translation of Philippe de Mornay's *Discours de la vie et de la mort*." In *Silent But for the Word: Tudor Women as Patrons, Translators, and Writers of Religious Works*. Ed. Margaret P. Hannay. Kent, Ohio: The Kent State University Press, 1985. 126–34.

Bourdieu, Pierre. *Distinction: A Social Critique of the Judgement of Taste*. Trans. Richard Nice. Cambridge: Cambridge University Press, 1984.

"La domination masculine." *Actes de la recherche en sciences sociales* 84 (1990): 2–31.

Outline of a Theory of Practice. Trans. Richard Nice. 1977. Rpt. Cambridge: Cambridge University Press, 1987.

Bowden, Caroline. "Women as Intermediaries: An Example of the Use of Literacy in the Late Sixteenth and Early Seventeenth Centuries." *History of Education* 22.3 (1993): 215–23.

Bradley, A. C. *Shakespearean Tragedy: Lectures on Hamlet, Othello, King Lear, and Macbeth*. London: Macmillan & Co. Ltd, 1956.

Brennan, Michael. *Literary Patronage in the English Renaissance: The Pembroke Family*. New York: Routledge, 1988.

Brereton, Geoffrey. *French Tragic Drama in the Sixteenth and Seventeenth Centuries*. London: Methuen, 1973.

Brunel, Ghislain, and Elisabeth Lalou, eds. *Sources d'histoire médiévale: IXe-milieu du XIVe siècle*. Paris: Larousse, 1992.

Bullough, Geoffrey, ed. *Narrative and Dramatic Sources of Shakespeare*. V. 3. *Earlier English History Plays: Henry VI, Richard III, Richard II*. New York: Columbia University Press, 1960.

ed. *Narrative and Dramatic Sources of Shakespeare*. V. 5. *The Roman Plays: Julius Caesar, Antony and Cleopatra, Coriolanus*. New York: Columbia University Press, 1977.

Burckhardt, Jacob. *The Civilization of the Renaissance in Italy*. London: Phaidon Press, 1960.

Butler, Judith. *Gender Trouble: Feminism and the Subversion of Identity*. New York: Routledge, 1990.

Bynum, Caroline Walker. *Jesus as Mother: Studies in the Spirituality of the High Middle Ages*. Berkeley: University of California Press, 1982.

Holy Feast and Holy Fast: The Religious Significance of Food to Medieval Women. Berkeley: University of California Press, 1987.

Charlton, Kenneth. "Mothers as Educative Agents in Pre-Industrial England." *History of Education* 23.2 (1994): 129–56.

" 'Not publike onely but also private and domesticall': Mothers and Familial Education in Pre-Industrial England." *History of Education* 17.1 (1988): 1–20.

Chartier, Roger. *Cultural History: Between Practices and Representations.* Trans. Lydia G. Cochrane. Ithaca, New York: Cornell University Press, 1988.

"The Practical Impact of Writing." In *A History of Private Life.* Eds. Phillipe Ariès and Georges Duby. V. 3. *Passions of the Renaissance.* Ed. Roger Chartier. Trans. Arthur Goldhammer. Cambridge, Massachusetts: Harvard University Press, 1989. 111–59.

ed. *Pratiques de la lecture.* 1985. Rpt. Paris: Editions Payot et Rivages, 1993.

Cipolla, Carlo M. *Literacy and Development in the West.* Harmondsworth, Middlesex: Penguin, 1969.

Clanchy, M. T. *From Memory to Written Record: England, 1066–1307.* Cambridge, Massachusetts: Harvard University Press, 1979.

Colledge, Edmund, and Romana Guarnieri. "The Glosses by 'M. N.' and Richard Methley to *The Mirror of Simple Souls.*" *Archivio italiano per la storia della pietà* 5 (1968): 357–82.

Cook, Carol. " 'The Sign and Semblance of Her Honor': Reading Gender Difference in *Much Ado About Nothing.*" *PMLA* 101 (1986): 186–202.

Crane, Mary Thomas. *Framing Authority: Sayings, Self, and Society in Sixteenth Century England.* Princeton: Princeton University Press, 1993.

Cressy, David. *Literacy and the Social Order: Reading and Writing in Tudor and Stuart England.* Cambridge: Cambridge University Press, 1980.

Curtin, Michael. "A Question of Manners: Status and Gender in Etiquette and Courtesy." *Journal of Modern History* 57 (1985): 395–423.

Dagens, Jean. "Le 'miroir des simples âmes' et Marguerite de Navarre." In *La Mystique Rhénane.* Paris: Presses Universitaires de France, 1963. 281–9.

Davies, W. J. Frank. *Teaching Reading in Early England.* 1973. Rpt. New York: Pitman, 1974.

Davis, John. "Joan of Kent, Lollardy and the English Reformation." *Journal of Ecclesiastical History* 33.2 (1982): 225–33.

De Certeau, Michel. *The Practice of Everyday Life.* Trans. Steven Rendall. Berkeley: University of California Press, 1984.

De Grazia, Margreta, and Peter Stallybrass. "The Materiality of the Shakespearean Text." *Shakespeare Quarterly* 44.3 (1993): 255–83.

Dodds, Madeline Hope, and Ruth Dodds. *The Pilgrimage of Grace 1536–1537 and the Exeter Conspiracy 1538.* Cambridge: Cambridge University Press, 1915.

Dolan, Frances E. " 'Gentlemen, I Have One Thing More to Say': Women on Scaffolds in England, 1563–1680." *Modern Philology* 92.2 (1994): 157–78.

Dronke, Peter. *Women Writers of the Middle Ages.* Cambridge: Cambridge University Press, 1984.

Eaton, Sarah. "Defacing the Feminine in Renaissance Tragedy." In *The Matter of Difference.* Ed. Valerie Wayne. Ithaca, New York: Cornell University Press, 1991. 181–98.

Eggert, Katherine. "Ravishment and Rememberance: Responses to Female

Authority in Spenser and Shakespeare." Ph.D. dissertation, University of California at Berkeley, 1991.

Eisenstein, Elizabeth L. *The Printing Press as an Agent of Change: Communications and Cultural Transformations in Early Modern Europe.* Cambridge: Cambridge University Press, 1979.

Elias, Norbert. *The History of Manners.* Trans. Edmund Jephcott. 1939. Rpt. New York: Pantheon Books, 1978.

Power and Civility. Trans. Edmund Jephcott. 1939. Rpt. New York: Pantheon Books, 1982.

The Society of Individuals. Trans. Edmund Jephcott. Ed. Michael Schröter. Cambridge, Massachusetts: Basil Blackwell, 1991.

Emerson, Kathy Lynn. *Wives and Daughters: The Women of Sixteenth Century England.* New York: The Whitston Publishing Company, 1984.

Fairbank, Alfred, and Bruce Dickens. *The Italic Hand in Tudor Cambridge.* London: Bowes and Bowes, 1962.

Ferguson, Margaret. "*Hamlet*: Letters and Spirits." In *Shakespeare and the Question of Theory.* Eds. Patricia Parker and Geoffrey Hartman. New York: Methuen, 1985. 292–309.

"Moderation and its Discontents: Recent Work on Renaissance Women." *Feminist Studies* 20.2 (1994): 349–66.

"Response: Attending to Literacy." In *Attending to Women in Early Modern England.* Eds. Betty S. Travitsky and Adele F. Seeff. Newark: University of Delaware Press, 1994. 265–79.

"A Room Not Their Own: Renaissance Women as Readers and Writers." In *The Comparative Perspective on Literature: Approaches to Theory and Practice.* Eds. Clayton Koelb and Susan Noakes. Ithaca, New York: Cornell University Press, 1988. 93–116.

Fisken, Beth Wynne. "Mary Sidney's Psalms: Education and Wisdom." In *Silent But for the Word: Tudor Women as Patrons, Translators, and Writers of Religious Works.* Ed. Margaret P. Hannay. Kent, Ohio: The Kent State University Press, 1985.

Foucault, Michel. *Discipline and Punish: The Birth of the Prison.* Trans. Alan Sheridan. New York: Vintage Books, 1979.

The History of Sexuality. 1978. Rpt. Trans. Robert Hurley. New York: Vintage Books, 1990.

"Technologies of the Self." In *Technologies of the Self: A Seminar with Michel Foucault.* Eds. Luther H. Martin, Huck Gutman, and Patrick H. Hutton. Amherst: University of Massachusetts Press, 1988. 16–49.

Fraenkel, Béatrice. *La signature: Genèse d'un signe.* Paris: Gallimard, 1992.

Freer, Coburn. "Mary Sidney." In *Women Writers of the Renaissance and Reformation.* Ed. Katharina M. Wilson. Athens, Georgia: The University of Georgia Press, 1987. 481–90.

Friedman, Alice T. "The Influence of Humanism on the Education of Girls and Boys in Tudor England." *History of Education Quarterly* 25.1–2 (1985): 57–70.

Furet, François, and Jacques Ozouf. *Reading and Writing: Literacy in France from Calvin to Jules Ferry.* Cambridge: Cambridge University Press, 1982.

Gallagher, Catherine. "Embracing the Absolute: The Politics of the Female Subject in Seventeenth-Century England." *Genders* 1 (1988): 24–39.

Garber, Marjorie. "Descanting on Deformity: Richard III and the Shape of History." In *The Historical Renaissance: New Essays on Tudor and Stuart Literature and Culture*. Eds. Heather Dubrow and Richard Strier. Chicago: University of Chicago Press, 1988. 79–103.

Gardiner, Dorothy. *English Girlhood at School: A Study of Women's Education through Twelve Centuries*. London: Oxford University Press, 1929.

Gehl, Paul F. *A Moral Art: Grammar, Society, and Culture in Trecento Florence*. Ithaca, New York: Cornell University Press, 1993.

Gelley, Alexander, ed. *Unruly Examples: On the Rhetoric of Exemplarity*. Stanford: Stanford University Press, 1995.

Gellrich, Jesse. "Orality, Literacy, and Crisis in the Later Middle Ages." *Philological Quarterly* 67.4 (1988): 461–73.

Gilbert, Sandra M., and Susan Gubar, eds. *The Norton Anthology of Literature by Women: The Tradition in English*. New York: W. W. Norton, 1985.

Goldberg, Jonathan. *Writing Matter: From the Hands of the English Renaissance*. Stanford: Stanford University Press, 1990.

Goodman, Jennifer R. " 'That Wommen Holde in Ful Greet Reverence': Mothers and Daughters Reading Chivalric Romances." In *Women, The Book and the Worldly: Selected Proceedings of the St. Hilda's Conference*, eds. Lesley Smith and Jane H. M. Taylor, v.2 (1993): 25–30.

Goody, Jack. *The Logic of Writing and the Organization of Society*. Cambridge: Cambridge University Press, 1986.

Goreau, Angeline, ed. *The Whole Duty of a Woman: Female Writers in Seventeenth-Century England*. New York: The Dial Press, 1985.

Grafton, Anthony, and Lisa Jardine. *From Humanism to the Humanities: Education and the Liberal Arts in Fifteenth and Sixteenth-Century Europe*. Cambridge, Massachusetts: Harvard University Press, 1986.

Gras, Maurice. *Robert Garnier: Son art et sa méthode*. Geneva: Librairie Droz, 1965.

Greenblatt, Stephen. *Renaissance Self-Fashioning: From More to Shakespeare*. Chicago: University of Chicago Press, 1980.

   Shakespearean Negotiations: The Circulation of Social Energy in Renaissance England. Berkeley: University of California Press, 1988.

Greene, Gayle, and Coppélia Kahn. "Feminist Scholarship and the Social Construction of Woman." In *Making a Difference: Feminist Literary Criticism*. Eds. Gayle Greene and Coppélia Kahn. London: Methuen, 1985. 1–36.

Greg, W. W. *A Bibliography of the English Printed Drama to the Restoration*. London: Oxford University Press, 1939.

Grendler, Paul. *Schooling in Renaissance Italy: Literacy and Learning, 1300–1600*. 1989; rpt. Baltimore: The Johns Hopkins University Press, 1991.

Grimshaw, Jean. "Practices of Freedom." In *Up Against Foucault: Explorations of Some Tensions Between Foucault and Feminism*. Ed. Caroline Ramazanoglu. New York: Routledge, 1993. 51–72.

Grundy, Isobel. "Women's History? Writings by English Nuns." In *Women, Writing, History: 1640–1740*. Eds. Isobel Grundy and Susan Wiseman. Athens, Georgia: The University of Georgia Press, 1992. 126–38.

Guarnieri, Romana. "Il movimento del Libero Spirito dalle origini al seccolo XVI." *Archivio della storia della pietà* 4 (1965), 353–499.

Gubar, Susan. " 'The Blank Page' and Female Creativity." In *Writing and*

Sexual Difference. Ed. Elizabeth Abel. University of Chicago Press, 1982. 73–93.

Gurr, Andrew. *Playgoing in Shakespeare's London.* 1987. Rpt. Cambridge: Cambridge University Press, 1988.

Hageman, Elizabeth, and Sara Jayne Steen. "From the Editors." In *Teaching Judith Shakespeare [Special Issue].* Shakespeare Quarterly 47.4. (1996), v–viii.

Hamer, Mary. *Signs of Cleopatra: History, Politics, Representation.* New York: Routledge, 1993.

Hampton, Timothy. *Writing from History: The Rhetoric of Exemplarity in Renaissance Literature.* Ithaca, New York: Cornell University Press, 1990.

Hannay, Margaret P. " 'O Daugher Heare:' Reconstructing the Lives of Aristocratic Englishwomen." In *Attending to Women in Early Modern England.* Eds. Betty S. Travitsky and Adele F. Seeff. Newark: University of Deleware Press, 1994.

Philip's Phoenix: Mary Sidney, Countess of Pembroke. New York: Oxford University Press, 1990.

" 'Princes you as men must dy': Genevan Advice to Monarchs in the *Psalmes* of Mary Sidney." *English Literary Renaissance* 19.1 (1989): 22–41.

ed. *Silent But for the Word: Tudor Women as Patrons, Translators, and Writers of Religious Works.* Kent, Ohio: The Kent State University Press, 1985.

Harbarge, Alfred. *Annals of English Drama, 975–1700.* Revised by S. Schoenbaum. Philadelphia: University of Pennsylvania Press, 1964.

Harman, Edward. *Gabriel Harvey and Thomas Nashe.* London: J. M. Ouseley and Son, 1923.

Herrup, Cynthia B. *The Common Peace: Participation and the Criminal Law in Seventeenth-Century England.* Cambridge: Cambridge University Press, 1987.

Hoffman, George. "The Montaigne Monopoly: Revising the *Essais* under the French Privilege System." *PMLA* 108.2 (1993): 308–19.

Houston, R. A. *Literacy in Early Modern England: Culture and Education 1500–1800.* London: Longman, 1988.

Howard, Jean E. *The Stage and Social Struggle in Early Modern England.* New York: Routledge, 1994.

Hull, Suzanne W. *Chaste, Silent and Obedient.* San Marino, California: The Huntington Library, 1982.

Hurault, André. *Journal.* Eds. G. B. Harrison & R. A. Jones. Bloomsbury, 1931.

Jenkinson, Hilary. "The Teaching and Practice of Handwriting in England." *History* 11.42 (1926): 130–8.

Jomaron, Jacqueline de, ed. *Le théâtre en France du Moyen Age à nos jours.* Paris: Arman Colin, 1992.

Jondorf, Gillian. *French Renaissance Tragedy: The Dramatic Word.* Cambridge: Cambridge University Press, 1990.

Jones, Ann Rosalind. "Nets and Bridles: Early Modern Conduct Books and Sixteenth-Century Women's Lyrics." In *The Ideology of Conduct: Essays on Literature and the History of Sexuality.* Eds. Nancy Armstrong and Leonard Tennenhouse. London: Methuen, 1987. 39–72.

Julia, Dominique. "L'apprentissage de la lecture dans la France d'Ancien Régime." In *Espaces de la Lecture.* Ed. Anne-Marie Christin. Paris: Editions Retz, 1988.

Justice, Steven. *Writing and Rebellion: England in 1381*. Berkeley: University of California Press, 1994.

Kastan, David Scott. " 'His semblable is his mirror': *Hamlet* and the Imitation of Revenge." In *Critical Essays on Shakespeare's Hamlet*. Ed. David Scott Kastan. New York: G. K. Hall & Co., 1995. 198–209.

and Peter Stallybrass, eds. *Staging the Renaissance: Reinterpretations of Elizabethan and Jacobean Drama*. New York: Routledge, 1991.

Kelly, Joan. "Did Women Have a Renaissance?" In *Women, History, and Theory: The Essays of Joan Kelly*. Chicago: University of Chicago Press, 1984.

Kelso, Ruth. *Doctrine for the Lady of the Renaissance*. Urbana: University of Illinois Press, 1956.

"The Doctrine of the English Gentleman in the Sixteenth Century." *University of Illinois Studies in Language and Literature* 14 (1929): 1–288.

Kiefer, Frederick. " 'Written Troubles of the Brain': Lady Macbeth's Conscience." In *Reading and Writing in Shakespeare*. Ed. David M. Bergeron. Newark: The University of Delaware Press, 1996. 64–81.

Klapisch-Zuber, Christiane. "Le Chiavi fiorentine di Barbablu: L'Apprendimento della lettura a Firenze nel XV secolo." *Quaderni Storici* 19.3 (1984): 765–92.

Klene, Jean. "Recreating the Letters of Lady Anne Southwell." In *New Ways of Looking at Old Texts*. Ed. W. Speed Hill. Binghamton, New York: Medieval and Renaissance Texts and Studies in conjunction with Renaissance English Text Society, 1993. 239–52.

Knapp, Robert S. " 'There's Letters from My Mother; What th'Import Is, I Know Not Yet'." In *Reading and Writing in Shakespeare*. Ed. David M. Bergeron. Newark: University of Delaware Press, 1996. 271–84.

Krais, Beate. "Gender and Symbolic Violence: Female Oppression in the Light of Pierre Bourdieu's Theory of Social Practice." In *Bourdieu: Critical Perspectives*. Eds. Craig Calhoun, Edward LiPuma and Moishe Postone. Chicago: University of Chicago Press, 1993. 156–77.

Krontiris, Tina. *Oppositional Voices: Women as Writers and Translators of Literature in the English Renaissance*. London: Routledge, 1992.

Lamb, Mary Ellen. "The Agency of the Split Subject: Lady Anne Clifford and the Uses of Reading." *English Literary Renaissance* 22.3 (1992): 347–68.

Gender and Authorship in the Sidney Circle. Madison: The University of Wisconsin Press, 1990.

Larrington, Carolyne. *Women and Writing in Medieval Europe: A Sourcebook*. London: Routledge, 1995.

Leavenworth, Russell E. *Daniel's Cleopatra: A Critical Study*. Ed. James Hogg. In *Salzburg Studies in English Literature*. Salzburg: Institüt für Englische Sprache und Literatur, 1974.

Leverenz, David. "The Woman in Hamlet: An Interpersonal View." In *Representing Shakespeare: New Psychoanalytic Essays*. Eds. Murray M. Schwartz and Coppélia Kahn. Baltimore: The Johns Hopkins University Press, 1980. 110–28.

Levin, Richard. "Women in the Renaissance Theatre Audience." *Shakespeare Quarterly* 40 (1989): 165–74.

Lewalski, Barbara Kiefer. *Writing Women in Jacobean England*. Cambridge, Massachusetts: Harvard University Press, 1993.

Love, Harold. *Scribal Publication in Seventeenth-Century England.* Oxford: Clarendon Press, 1993.

Lucas, Caroline. *Writing for Women: The Example of Woman as Reader in Elizabethan Romance.* Philadelphia: Open University Press, 1989.

Luce, Alice, ed. *The Countess of Pembroke's Antonie.* Weimar: Verlag von Emil Felber, 1897.

Lyons, Bridget. "The Iconography of Ophelia." *ELH* 44.1 (1977): 60–74.

Main, Gloria L. "An Inquiry into When and Why Women Learned to Write in Colonial New England." *Journal of Social History* 24.3 (1991): 579–89.

Marcus, Leah S. *Puzzling Shakespeare: Local Reading and Its Discontents.* Berkeley: University of California Press, 1988.

Marotti, Arthur F. *Manuscript, Print, and the English Renaissance Lyric.* Ithaca: Cornell University Press, 1995.

Mason, John E. *Gentlefolk in the Making: Studies in the History of English Courtesy Literature and Related Topics from 1531 to 1774.* Philadelphia: University of Pennsylvania Press, 1935.

Maus, Katharine Eiseman. "Transfer of Title in *Love's Labour's Lost*: Language, Individualism, Gender." In *Shakespeare Left and Right.* Ed. Ivo Kamps. New York: Routledge, 1991.

McDonnell, Ernest W. *The Beguines and Beghards in Medieval Culture.* New Brunswick, New Jersey: Rutgers University Press, 1954.

McLuskie, Kathleen. *Renaissance Dramatists.* Atlantic Highlands, New Jersey: Humanities Press International, 1989.

McMullen, Norma. "The Education of English Gentlewomen 1540–1640." *History of Education* 6 (1977): 87–101.

McNamer, Elizabeth Mary. *The Education of Heloise: Methods, Content, and Purpose of Learning in the Twelfth Century.* Lewiston: The Edwin Mellen Press, 1991.

McSheffrey, Shannon. *Gender and Heresy: Women and Men in Lollard Communities, 1420–1530.* Philadelphia: University of Pennsylvania Press, 1995.

Martin, Randall. "The Autobiography of Grace, Lady Mildmay." *Renaissance and Reformation / Renaissance et Réforme* 18.1 (1994): 33–81.

Merllié, Dominique. "Le sexe de l'écriture: Note sur la perception sociale de la fémininité." *Actes de la recherche en sciences sociales* 83 (1990): 40–51.

Michel, Laurence. *The Tragedy of Philotas.* 1949. Rpt. Archon Books, 1970.

Miner, Madonne M. " 'Neither mother, wife, nor England's queen': The Roles of Women in *Richard III.*" In *The Woman's Part: Feminist Criticism of Shakespeare.* Eds. Carolyn Lenz, Gayle Greene, and Carol Neely. Urbana: University of Illinois Press, 1980. 35–55.

Mohl, Ruth. *John Milton and his Commonplace Book.* New York: Frederick Ungar, 1969.

Monaghan, Jennifer E. "Literacy Instruction and Gender in Colonial New England." *American Quarterly* 40.1 (1988): 18–41.

Montrose, Louis. "New Historicisms." In *Redrawing the Boundaries: The Transformation of English and American Literary Studies.* Eds. Stephen Greenblatt and Giles Gunn. New York: The Modern Language Association of America, 1992. 392–418.

"The Purpose of Playing: Reflections on a Shakespearean Anthropology."
Helios 7.2 (1980): 51–74.

Morgan, Paul. "Frances Wolfreston and 'hor bouks': A Seventeenth-Century Woman Book-Collector." *The Library* 11.3 (1989): 197–219.

Moss, Ann. "Commonplace-Rhetoric and Thought-Patterns in Early Modern Culture." In *The Recovery of Rhetoric: Persuasive Discourse and Disciplinarity in the Human Sciences.* Eds. R. H. Roberts and J. M. M Good. Charlottesville: University Press of Virginia, 1993.

Neely, Carol Thomas. "Constructing the Subject: Feminist Practice and the New Renaissance Discourses." *English Literary Renaissance* 18.1 (1988): 5–18.

Nicholl, Charles. *A Cup of News: The Life of Thomas Nashe.* London: Routledge and Kegan Paul, 1984.

Nichols, John Gough. "Inventories of Henry Fitzroy." *Camden Miscellany* 3 (1855): i–c, 1–55.

Nielson, James. "Reading between the Lines: Manuscript Personality and Gabriel Harvey's Drafts." *Studies in English Literature* 33.1 (1993): 43–82.

O'Day, Rosemary. *Education and Society 1500–1800: The Social Foundations of Education in Early Modern Britain.* London: Longman, 1982.

Ong, Walter. *Orality and Literacy.* London: Methuen, 1982.

Orme, Nicholas. *Education and Society in Medieval and Renaissance England.* London: The Hambledon Press, 1989.

Orth, Myra D. " 'Madame Sainte Anne': The Holy Kinship, the Royal Trinity, and Louise of Savoy." In *Interpreting Cultural Symbols: Saint Anne in Late Medieval Society.* Eds. Pamela Sheingorn and Kathleen Ashley. Athens, Georgia: University of Georgia Press, 1990. 199–227.

Ozment, Steven. *The Age of Reform 1250–1550.* New Haven: Yale University Press, 1980.

Palmer, Daryl W. "Histories of Violence and the Writer's Hand: Foxe's *Actes and Monuments* and Shakespeare's *Titus Andronicus.*" In *Reading and Writing in Shakespeare.* Ed. David Bergeron. Newark: University of Delaware Press, 1996. 82–115.

Parker, Patricia. "On the Tongue: Cross Gendering, Effeminacy, and the Art of Words." *Style* 23 (1989): 445–65.

Parry, Graham. "The Great Picture of Lady Anne Clifford." In *Art and Patronage in the Caroline Courts.* Ed. David Howarth. Cambridge: Cambridge University Press, 1993.

Patterson, Lee. "Ambiguity and Interpretation: A Fifteenth-Century Reading of *Troilus and Criseyde.*" *Speculum* 54 (1979): 279–330.

Petroff, Elizabeth Avilda, ed. *Medieval Women's Visionary Literature.* Oxford: Oxford University Press, 1986.

Petrucci, Armando. "Pouvoirs de l'écriture, pouvoir sur l'écriture dans la Renaissance italienne." *Annales* 43.4 (1988): 823–47.

Pollard, Graham. *Graham Pollard's Catalogue of Writing Books, 1522–1825.* London: Birrell & Garnett, 1934.

Pollock, Linda. *With Faith and Physic: The Life of a Tudor Gentlewoman Lady Grace Mildmay, 1552–1620.* London: Collins and Brown, 1993.

Power, Eileen. *Medieval English Nunneries c. 1275–1535.* Cambridge: Cambridge University Press, 1922.

Medieval Women. Cambridge: Cambridge University Press, 1975.

Prescott, Anne Lake. "The Pearl of the Valois and Elizabeth I: Marguerite de Navarre's *Miroir* and Tudor England." In *Silent But for the Word: Tudor Women as Patrons, Translators, and Writers of Religious Works*. Ed. Margaret P. Hannay. Kent, Ohio: The Kent State University Press, 1985. 61–76.

Preston, Jean F., and Laetitia Yeandle. *English Handwriting 1400–1650*. Binghamton, New York: Medieval and Renaissance Texts and Studies, 1992.

Prior, Mary, ed. *Women in English Society 1500–1800*. London: Methuen, 1986.

Reay, Barry. "The Context and Meaning of Popular Literacy: Some Evidence from Nineteenth-Century Rural England." *Past and Present* 131 (1991): 89–129.

Rees, Joan. *Samuel Daniel: A Critical and Biographical Study*. Liverpool: Liverpool University Press, 1964.

Regosin, Richard L. *The Matter of My Book: Montaigne's Essais as the Book of the Self*. Berkeley: University of California Press, 1977.

Riché, Pierre. *Ecoles et enseignement dans le Haut Moyen Age: Fin du Ve siècle – milieu du XIe siècle*. 1979. Rpt. Paris: Picard Editeur, 1989.

Robertson, Elizabeth. *Early English Devotional Prose and the Female Audience*. Knoxville: The University of Tennessee Press, 1990.

Sargent, Michael G. "The Transmission by the English Carthusians of some Late Medieval Spiritual Writings." *Journal of Ecclesiastical History* 27.3 (1976): 225–40.

Scarisbrick, J. J. *The Reformation and the English People*. Oxford: Basil Blackwell, 1984.

Schanzer, Ernest. "'Anthony and Cleopatra' and the Countess of Pembroke's 'Antonius'." *Notes and Queries* 3.3 (1956): 152–4.

Schibanoff, Susan. "Taking the Gold Out of Egypt: The Art of Reading as a Woman." In *Gender and Reading: Essays on Readers, Texts, and Contexts*. Baltimore: The Johns Hopkins University Press, 1986. 83–106.

Schofield, R. S. "The Measurement of Literacy in Pre-Industrial England." In *Literacy in Traditional Societies*. Ed. Jack Goody. Cambridge: Cambridge University Press, 1968.

Scott, Joan Wallach. *Gender and the Politics of History*. New York: Columbia University Press, 1988.

Seronsy, Cecil. *Samuel Daniel*. New York: Twayne Publishers, 1967.

Sheingorn, Pamela. "Appropriating the Holy Kinship: Gender and Family History." In *Interpreting Cultural Symbols: Saint Anne in Late Medieval Society*. Eds. Pamela Sheingorn and Kathleen Ashley. Athens, Georgia: University of Georgia Press, 1990. 169–98.

Simon, Joan. *Education and Society in Tudor England*. Cambridge: Cambridge University Press, 1966.

Smith, Hilda L. *Reason's Disciples: Seventeenth-Century English Feminists*. Urbana: University of Illinois Press, 1982.

Smith, Toulmin. *English Gilds: The Original Ordinances of More Than One Hundred Early English Gilds*. 1870. Rpt. Ed. Lucy Toulmin Smith. London: Oxford University Press, 1963.

Sonnet, Martine. "Une fille à éduquer." In *Histoire des femmes en Occident*. V. 3, *XVIe–XVIIIe siècles*. Eds. Natalie Zemon Davis and Arlette Farge. Paris: Plon, 1991. 111–39.

Spence, Richard T. *Lady Anne Clifford Countess of Pembroke, Dorset and Montgomery (1590–1676).* Thrupp: Sutton Publishing, 1997.

Spriet, Pierre. *Samuel Daniel (1563–1619): Sa vie-son œuvre.* N. p.: Didier, 1968.

Spufford, Margaret. "First Steps in Literacy: The Reading and Writing Experiences of the Humblest Seventeenth-Century Autobiographers." *Social History* 4.3 (1979): 407–35.

Small Books and Pleasant Histories: Popular Fiction and Its Readership in Seventeenth-Century England. Athens, Georgia: University of Georgia Press, 1982.

Stallybrass, Peter. "Patriarchal Territories: The Body Enclosed." In *Rewriting the Renaissance: Discourses of Sexual Difference in Early Modern Europe.* Eds. Margaret W. Ferguson, Maureen Quilligan, and Nancy Vickers. Chicago: University of Chicago Press, 1986. 123–42.

and Allon White. *The Politics and Poetics of Transgression.* London: Methuen, 1986.

Stephen, J. F. *A History of the Criminal Law of England.* London: Macmillan, 1883.

Stephens, W. B. "Literacy in England, Scotland and Wales, 1500–1900." *History of Education Quarterly* 30.4 (1990): 545–71.

Stern, Virginia. *Gabriel Harvey: His Life, Marginalia and Library.* Oxford: Clarendon Press, 1979.

Stock, Brian. *The Implications of Literacy: Written Language and Models of Interpretation in the Eleventh and Twelfth Centuries.* Princeton: Princeton University Press, 1983.

Straznicky, Marta. "'Profane Stoical Paradoxes': The Tragedie of Mariam and Sidnean Closet Drama." *English Literary Renaissance* 24.1 (1994): 104–34.

Street, Brian. *Literacy in Theory and Practice.* 1984. Rpt. Cambridge: Cambridge University Press, 1993.

Summit, Jennifer. "William Caxton, Margaret Beaufort and the Romance of Female Patronage." In *Women, the Book, and the Worldly.* Eds. Lesley Smith and Jane H. M. Taylor. Rochester, New York: D. S. Brewer, 1995. V. 2, 151–65.

Tarvers, Josephine Koster. "'Thys ys my mystrys boke': English Women as Readers and Writers in Late Medieval England." In *The Uses of Manuscripts in Literary Studies: Essays in Memory of Judson Boyce Allen.* Eds. Charlotte Cook Morse, Penelope Reed Doob, and Marjorie Curry Woods. Kalamazoo, Michigan: Medieval Institute Publications, 1992. 305–35.

Thomas, Keith. "The Meaning of Literacy in Early Modern England." In *The Written Word: Literacy in Transition.* Ed. Gerd Baumann. Oxford: Clarendon Press, 1986.

Thomas, Max W. "Reading and Writing the Renaissance Commonplace Book: A Question of Authorship?" In *The Construction of Authorship: Textual Appropriations in Law and Literature.* Eds. Martha Woodmansee and Peter Jasz. Durham, North Carolina: Duke University Press, 1994. 401–15.

Thompson, Anne, and John Thompson. *Shakespeare: Meaning and Metaphor.* The Harvester Press, 1987.

Thomson, Leslie. "*Antony and Cleopatra*, Act 4 Scene 16: 'A Heavy Sight'." *Shakespeare Survey* 41 (1989): 77–90.

Travitsky, Betty S., and Adele F. Seeff, eds. *Attending to Women in Early Modern England*. Newark: University of Delaware Press, 1994.

Tudor, Phillipa. "Religious Instruction for Children and Adolescents in the Early English Reformation." *Journal of Ecclesiastical History* 35.3 (1984): 391–413.

Walby, Sylvia. *Patriarchy at Work*. Minneapolis: University of Minnesota Press, 1986.

Wall, Wendy. *The Imprint of Gender: Authorship and Publication in the English Renaissance*. Ithaca, New York: Cornell University Press, 1993.

Walter, Judith. "Apprenticeship Education and Family Structure in Seventeenth Century Massachusetts Bay." M.A. thesis, Bryn Mawr, 1971.

Watson, Foster. *The English Grammar Schools to 1660: Their Curriculum and Practice*. Cambridge: Cambridge University Press, 1908.

Luis Vives: El Gran Valenciano (1492–1540). Oxford: Oxford University Press, 1922.

Vives and the Renascence Education of Women. New York: Longmans, Green & Co., 1912.

Vives: On Education: A Translation of the De Tradendis Disciplinis of Juan Luis Vives. Cambridge: Cambridge University Press, 1913.

Watt, Tessa. *Cheap Print and Popular Piety, 1550–1640*. 1991. Rpt. Cambridge: Cambridge University Press, 1994.

Wayne, Valerie. "Historical Differences: Misogyny and *Othello*." In *The Matter of Difference: Materialist Feminist Criticism of Shakespeare*. Ed. Valerie Wayne. Ithaca, New York: Cornell University Press, 1991. 153–79.

ed. *The Matter of Difference: Materialist Feminist Criticism of Shakespeare*. Ithaca: Cornell University Press, 1991.

Whigham, Frank. *Ambition and Privilege: The Social Tropes of Elizabethan Courtesy Literature*. Berkeley: University of California Press, 1984.

Wiesner, Merry E. *Women and Gender in Early Modern Europe*. Cambridge: Cambridge University Press, 1993.

Williamson, George C. *Lady Anne Clifford Countess of Dorset, Pembroke and Montgomery 1590–1676: Her Life, Letters and Work*. 1922. Rpt.: S. R. Publishers Ltd, 1967.

Williamson, Marilyn L. *Infinite Variety: Antony and Cleopatra in Renaissance Drama and Earlier Tradition*. 1922. Rpt. Mystic, Connecticut: Lawrence Verry, Inc., 1974.

Wilson, Katharina M., ed. *Medieval Women Writers*. Athens, Georgia: The University of Georgia Press, 1984.

Shakespeare's Sugared Sonnets. New York: Barnes & Noble, 1974.

ed. *Women Writers of the Renaissance and Reformation*. Athens, Georgia: The University of Georgia Press, 1987.

Winn, Colette H. "La Femme écrivaine au XVIe siècle: Écriture et transgression." *Poétique* 84 (1990): 435–52.

Wiseman, Susan. "Gender and Status in Dramatic Discourse: Margaret Cavendish, Duchess of Newcastle." In *Women, Writing and History 1640–1740*. Eds. Isobel Grundy and Susan Wiseman. Athens, Georgia: The University of Georgia Press, 1992. 159–177.

Witherspoon, Alexander Maclaren. *The Influence of Robert Garnier on Elizabethan Drama*. New Haven: Yale University Press, 1924.

Wood, Norman. *The Reformation and English Education*. London: Routledge, 1931.

Woodbridge, Linda. *Women and the English Renaissance: Literature and the Nature of Womankind, 1540–1620*. Urbana: University of Illinois Press, 1986.

Woodhouse, John. "Some Developments in the Courtesy Manual after Castiglione." *Journal of Anglo-Italian Studies* 1 (1991): 1–15.

Wright, Louis B. "Handbook Learning of the Renaissance Middle Class." *Studies in Philology* 28 (1931): 58–86.

"The Reading of Renaissance Women." *Studies in Philology* 28.4 (1931): 139–56.

Wrightson, Keith. *English Society 1580–1680*. New Brunswick, New Jersey: Rutgers University Press, 1982.

Youings, Joyce. *Sixteenth-Century England*. 1984; rpt. New York: Penguin Books, 1991.

Ziegler, Georgianna. "'More Than Feminine Boldness': The Gift Books of Esther Inglis." Paper presented at the Folger Shakespeare Library, 14 April 1995.

Zwicker, Steven. "The Politics of Reading *c.* 1649." Paper presented at the Folger Shakespeare Library, 21 April 1995.

Index

Cambridge Studies in Renaissance Literature and Culture

General editor
STEPHEN ORGEL
Jackson Eli Reynolds Professor of Humanities, Stanford University